Foreign Exchange Handbook

Managing Risk and Opportunity in Global Currency Markets

Paul Bishop
Associate Professor of Finance
School of Business
University of Western Ontario

Don Dixon
Senior Manager
Treasury Group
Bank of Montreal

McGraw-Hill, Inc.

New York   St. Louis   San Francisco   Auckland   Bogotá
Caracas   Lisbon   London   Madrid
Mexico   Milan   Montreal   New Delhi   Paris
San Juan   São Paulo   Singapore
Sydney   Tokyo   Toronto

Library of Congress Cataloging-in-Publication Data

Bishop, Paul (Paul M.)
    Foreign exchange handbook / Paul Bishop, Don Dixon
       p.   cm.
    Includes index.
    ISBN 0-07-005474-6
    1. Foreign exchange futures   2. Dixon, Don (Donald)   II. Title.
HG3853.B57 1992
332.4'5 – dc20   91-26927
                                                    CIP

1 2 3 4 5 6 7 8 9 0 DOC/DOC 9 7 6 5 4 3 2 1

ISBN   0-07-005474-6

The sponsoring editor for this book was Caroline Carney, the editing supervisor
was Caroline Levine, and the production supervisor was Donald F. Schmidt. It
was set in Baskerville by McGraw-Hill's Professional Book Group composition
unit.

Printed and bound by R. R. Donnelley & Sons Company.

To my wife Carolyn, and to our children,
Paul, Nicole, Suzanne, and Kyle,
for all their support, understanding, and
inspiration

And to my parents, Lila and Ivan,
for all their ongoing encouragement and
support

Don Dixon

Contents

Part 2. Foreign Currency Products, How to Price and Trade Them

7. The Forward Market   153

8. Currency Options   187

Part 3. Corporate Foreign Currency Exposure and Management

Preface

Our increasingly global business environment is presenting new problems and opportunities for many organizations. Effective management in these situations frequently involves new skills and knowledge. In most organizations, such management requires a fundamental knowledge of foreign exchange exposure, markets, and products at many levels throughout the organization.

This book is for managers whose success is affected by foreign currency exchange rate movements. You do not have to be the CEO of a multinational corporation to be affected by currency price movements, although certainly all of them are. Your job may involve actual trading or dealing in foreign currencies, which of course means you already know the impact currency pricing can have. If you are involved in a corporate planning, accounting, credit, or audit function, your involvement with foreign exchange may be less direct. However, remember that the ultimate success of what you and your employer do depends in many cases on currency prices. Consider, for example, importing or exporting goods and services, trading commodities, sourcing or investing funds abroad, or being involved in a wholly domestic operation which is in competition with foreign-currency-based organizations. This book was written to help managers faced with such issues to work effectively in a much smaller world.

Foreign exchange is frequently considered to be far more complicated and mysterious than it really is. We, as authors, assume no background in foreign exchange on the part of our readers, and yet the book is able to deal with a very wide range of practical foreign currency management problems and opportunities. The material builds from the basic ideas and foundations of currency value, through straightforward cashflow hedge or cover applications, and on to more sophisticated topics such as corporate economic exposure and the pricing of currency options and cross-rate forwards.

The book is designed to meet a wide range of interests in foreign exchange. For example, chapters are provided to explore and explain basic ideas and procedures specifically for persons at an introductory level. More experienced practitioners, such as treasury staff, will benefit from several chapters in which the markets, market pricing mechanisms, and trading practices are described and explained in some detail. For senior management, topics such as economic exposure and the development of an overall corporate hedging policy are included. Readers can pursue a wide variety of issues, or pick and choose what they want.

The book is organized in three parts. Part 1 deals with the factors affecting currency value and the forecasting of future currency prices. This section is devoted to understanding the fundamental forces driving the market. Part 2 describes foreign exchange products, markets, and participants. Here we discuss what you need to know to make the market work *for* you. Finally, Part 3 examines foreign currency exposure from a corporate point of view. For the organization as a whole, what is the nature and extent of the current exposure, what are the risks and rewards for accepting this exposure, and how should management respond?

The book is written from the point of view of the manager or practitioner. The emphasis is on clarity and usefulness. Readers who wish a more theoretical treatment of the material are directed to the excellent references listed in the Bibliography.

The authors are grateful to the numerous friends, colleagues, business associates, and students who have all been very generous with their time, support, and effort. In particular, Alan Boyle, Alice Daniel, Tim Dorey, Michael Dwyer, Mieke Findlay, Fiona Jones, Ray Kohanik, Kim MacNeil, Al Magrath, June Melsted, Marilyn Menzies, Richard Nason, Branca Pachowski, Brian Palfreyman, Dan Rissin, David Rogers, Rick Robertson, Michele Stratton, Alasdair Turnbull, Ron Wirick, Rob Wittmann, and John Wleugel have all provided invaluable material, feedback, and suggestions. These people have a diverse background in foreign exchange trading, accounting, communications, marketing, finance, and general management. Their collective contributions have greatly added to the value of the book. Any remaining errors or omissions are, of course, the sole responsibility of the authors.

The authors would like to acknowledge with thanks the highly competent and very patient work of the McGraw-Hill editing and production staff, and particularly that of Caroline Carney and Caroline Levine, with whom we had direct contact.

Finally, financial support from the Plan for Excellence at the School of Business Administration, University of Western Ontario, is gratefully acknowledged.

Comments and suggestions from readers are welcomed.

Paul Bishop   *Don Dixon*

PART 1

Understanding Foreign Currency Price Movements, Past and Future

1

Introduction and Outline of the Book

Executive Summary

This short chapter introduces the concept of currency exposure. It continues with a summary of the colorful history of currency markets and concludes with a survey of the structure and content of the book.

Introduction

This book is about foreign currency markets, trading, and, in particular, foreign exchange exposure for corporations. Foreign exchange exposure for corporations typically arises when they do business in any currency other than their own or when the competition is foreign-currency-based. The exposure can be obvious, as in future foreign-currency-denominated cashflows. It can also be more subtle, such as a gradual erosion of competitive position caused by currency exchange-rate adjustments.

Examples of foreign exchange losses are plentiful. Laker Airways, a British airline, lost heavily on its unhedged U.S. dollar debt as the dollar strengthened against sterling in 1982. These losses contributed to the airline's subsequent bankruptcy. Eastman-Kodak estimates that pretax earnings were reduced by US$3.5 billion over the 1980–1985 period due to the strong dollar. Perhaps of more consequence, Kodak's share of important offshore markets also fell substantially. Caterpillar lost profits and market share to Komatsu during the same period. Canon, the Japanese camera firm, reported a 69 percent reduction in pretax profit in 1986, due to the strengthening yen. Allied-Lyons PLC, a British food and drinks group, reported a loss of US$260 million in fiscal 1991 on foreign exchange trading. Smaller firms have similar exposures and undoubtedly suffer equally serious, but less widely reported, losses.

The significance of each exposure varies with the speed and extent of the currency adjustment. Management's capacity to handle the problem depends in part on its understanding of currency price movements and markets. This chapter begins with a brief introduction to the evolution of these currency markets. It closes with an outline of the remaining chapters, which describe and explain the operation of the markets and the attendant problems and opportunities.

A Brief History of Foreign Exchange Markets

Early Origins

Trading of goods and services has evolved over thousands of years. Initially, barter functioned as the method of payment, and primitive as it was, it helped achieve the basic objective of allowing exchange of goods and services among the countries of the world.

Some 4000 years ago, considerable progress was made through the development and use of coins bearing the stamp of a banker, merchant, temple, sultan, or king. The use of monetary metal gradually became commonplace in international trade. Initially, value was determined according to the value of the metal in the coins themselves. However, as the number of coins in circulation increased and confidence in their value as a medium of exchange grew, professional money changers in the ancient Middle East were able to exchange certain coins on the basis of the coins themselves. With this development, a crude form of foreign exchange trading had begun.

After the collapse of the Roman Empire and throughout the Dark Ages, the frequency of foreign exchange transactions declined because of unstable financial and political conditions and a widespread reduction in foreign trade. By the eleventh century, however, money changing was back in vogue. As international trade and capital flows increased, physical exchange of coins became less and less practical.

To meet the needs of the increase in international commerce, a form of international merchant banking evolved. The merchant banks opened branches and developed formal relationships with correspondent banks in other trading countries. Bills of exchange, which are unconditional orders in writing directing the addressee to pay a third party a specific sum, became transferable. When the payee of the bill of exchange could transfer value to a third party, a new form of currency was created. This development gave the market enhanced flexibility and led to sizable increases in foreign exchange dealings. As travel became easier and faster, increased use of bank transfers further encouraged development of the markets. The market had now moved from a pure cash system to a combination of cash and credit.

In general, the growth of the foreign exchange markets during the second millennium had many problems to overcome in addition to slow and difficult communications and travel. For instance, the church for many years frowned on such activities; and governments, in some cases, considered dealing in foreign exchange not only unethical, but illegal. In the late 1800s, a cable was laid across the Atlantic, providing a great improvement in communications between Europe and North America, and marking perhaps the beginning of the global financial markets as we know them today.

First World War and the Great Depression

During the twentieth century, the two world wars disrupted the development of the market. Countries stopped dealing with the enemy, and markets became fragmented and smaller. In the initial years after World War I, the foreign exchange markets were extremely volatile and subject to large-scale speculative interest. Commercial transactions requiring the purchase or sale of foreign currency involved considerable risk, and hedging using forward contracts became the norm. In fact, this practice was so widespread and accepted in some areas that the act of forward hedging was regarded as a basic component of doing business. However, many banks, politicians, and policymakers in other jurisdictions believed that forward contracts were speculative in nature, and did not support the development of the market. In spite of such resistance, commercial needs prevailed and the market grew.

The suspension of the gold standard in 1931 combined with bank failures and problems of settlement with some currencies gave the foreign exchange markets a significant setback. It was very difficult to deal foreign exchange in the early 1930s, but as with other markets, conditions returned more or less to normal by the middle of the decade. London became the largest center of foreign exchange dealings in the period between the two world wars, but other centers such as Paris, Zurich, Amsterdam, and New York also developed prominent roles.

Post-World War II

Britain lost much of its financial prominence during World War II. Following the war, the U.S. dollar became the dominant currency. Sterling still continued to play a key role, nevertheless, because of a frequent scarcity of dollars and the leading role of London as a financial center. Government involvement in markets occurred fairly often in the 1930s, became more prevalent in the early post-World War II era, and has, in fact, continued ever since. Unlike the post-World War I period, which witnessed wild fluctuations in currency markets, the 25 years following World War II were characterized by stability and tight controls on currency values, with most currencies pegged within a narrow trading range.

The starting point for the post-World War II era actually began before the end of the war, with a United Nations Conference held at Bretton Woods, New Hampshire. Memories of the Great Depression and of the financial aftermath of World War I remained clear in the delegates' minds. At the conference, the intent was to develop a framework that would create stability, generate confidence, and, thereby, foster worldwide growth and prosperity.

The Bretton Woods Agreement in 1944 did bring the desired stability and order to the foreign exchange markets. Exchange rates for the major trading currencies were pegged to the U.S. dollar, which, in turn, was pegged to gold at the rate of $35 per ounce. The pegs for individual currencies were adjusted from time to time in response to market pressures. The U.S. dollar became the reserve currency of choice for many central banks because, for central banks, the United States guaranteed convertibility of dollars to gold, on demand, at the pegged rate.

The pegged-exchange-rate system broke down in 1971, largely due to payments imbalances among countries and to the sharply increasing foreign holdings of U.S. dollars. After an attempt to reinstate the system in 1973, a period of primarily floating exchange rates began, which is still in effect. The major trading currencies float under the watchful eye of their respective central banks. The banks intervene in the open market from time to time to foster more orderly trading in the currency or to try to nudge the rate in the direction considered desirable at that time. Currencies of smaller countries are frequently pegged to one of the major currencies, usually the U.S. dollar or the currency of the country with the closest trading ties. The floating-rate system clearly makes future spot rates more difficult to anticipate, but it is much better equipped than its predecessor to handle the pressures and shocks experienced by the foreign exchange markets in the last 20 years.

Recent Market Turbulence

The 1970s and 1980s witnessed a trend to increasing volatility and unpredictability in foreign exchange markets. One reason for this development was a dramatic increase in the number of market participants trying to take advantage of exchange-rate moves. In addition, the technological resources available to these traders, financial managers, and corporate hedgers had improved substantially.

In the early 1990s, bank and investment dealers continue to be major players in the markets, but their terms of reference tend to restrict their activities primarily to trading. Corporations are frequently active in foreign exchange risk management and often utilize selective hedging and/or trading programs. Their trading decisions can have significant impact on currency markets in both the short and long term and are sometimes underestimated as a factor in the marketplace. Individuals can also be major factors as they access the market through different mechanisms, including the futures markets and purchases of foreign currency stocks and bonds.

It should be recognized that traders, whether a corporation, a funds manager, a banker, or an individual, need volatility to make money. These agents usually do not care which direction a currency move takes. The key is that the exchange rate moves and thus provides profit opportunities.

A second reason for market turbulence is the increasing payments imbalances among countries. Capital now flows relatively freely among the major currencies in response to trade and service account deficits and surpluses, and the large increases in pension and other investment funds provide ready sources of funding. In addition, public and private borrowers also tap various foreign currency markets, and as this capital moves from currency to currency, significant pressures on exchange rates often result.

While both pools of capital and financing requirements were growing, global markets experienced volatile interest rates, which also increased the size and frequency of major capital flows. Excessive inflationary pressures arose in the 1970s, caused by price increases in oil and other commodities, excessive wage demands, rapid growth in credit and money supply, differing attitudes to inflation by central banks, and inflationary expectations. Capital will often flow to currencies with attractive interest rates, and, at times, major strengthening moves in currencies have been aided or even caused by interest-rate differentials. However, when those interest rates were no longer attractive, the capital would move out, and the currencies often weakened dramatically.

A related factor compounding the volatility in the markets has been the increase in U.S.-dollar-denominated assets owned by foreigners. The U.S. dollar is the world's dominant currency, and major moves in it affect almost every other currency. While foreign holdings of dollars increase global market liquidity, they also increase the size of international capital flows that occur from changes in interest-rate differentials and payments imbalances. For example, if the market turns bearish, or negative, on the dollar, there are a large number of market participants who can and do aggressively sell dollar assets.

Outline of This Book

This chapter has served as an introduction to the concept of currency exposure and has provided a brief history of currency markets. The remainder of the book is divided into three parts. Part 1 explores the basic determinants of currency value and explains how to anticipate changes in this value in the future. Chapter 2 traces the development of the international payments system to our current floating-exchange-rate regime, and reviews recent rate adjustments in several major trading currencies. It also explains from a macroeconomic viewpoint how payments imbalances among countries and other pressures give rise to these adjustments. Chapter 3 provides an overview of the money markets in the United States and Canada, and explains the key role played by interest rates in the foreign exchange markets. Chapter 4 reviews our ability to anticipate or forecast future change in currency values. While Chapter 2 relates country economics and competitive position to longer-term currency value, Chapter 4 examines both the fundamental analysis and the technical analysis of currency price movements as predictors of future price levels.

Part 2 introduces the actual foreign currency products and contracts and the market participants who deal and trade them. Chapter 5 identifies these participants, with insights regarding their objectives and motivation. Chapter 6 is a beginner's guide to buying and selling foreign exchange, explaining the spot market, currency codes, and the key pricing and dealing conventions. Chapter 7 introduces the forward market and shows how it is priced off the spot market to reflect interest differentials. Chapter 8 covers the burgeoning currency options market. The chapter includes an explanation of the mechanics of the option contract, the option pricing process, and examples of option payoff charts. Chapter 9 deals with foreign currency and interest-rate swaps: how they work and why they are so useful in both cash-management and risk-management activities. To close Part 2, Chapter 10 assumes the view of the foreign exchange market maker and looks at contract pricing, trading, and risk management from an interbank dealing perspective; here is really why the market operates the way it does.

Part 3 examines the problems and opportunities posed for corporations by foreign exchange price movements; this part explores how the markets allow these players to manage the problems and capitalize on the opportunities. Chapters 11 through 14 deal with the identification, measurement, and management of corporate foreign currency exposure. The exposure is broken into three categories: transaction, accounting or translation, and economic. The point of view is that of a corporate manager defining, measuring, and controlling currency exposure. A separate chapter is included on exposure resulting from commodity transactions. Chapter 15 reviews the various forms of credit risk borne by market participants and offers suggestions for the management of this risk. Finally, Chapter 16 explores guidelines for establishing and monitoring a corporate currency hedging policy.

2
Why Foreign Exchange Spot Rates Move

Executive Summary

This chapter reviews the nature of foreign-exchange-rate movements and explores the reasons for these rate adjustments. First, the distinction between a nominal and a real (inflation-adjusted) currency price change is established. To illustrate the degree of actual price volatility, nominal and real price changes for five major currencies are charted. The evolution of the international payments system is then traced as a means of explaining our current, largely floating, exchange-rate regime. Finally, the chapter reviews in some detail the current sources of pressure for currency price adjustment, including the cause and effect of country payments imbalances and the influence of government policy on currency pricing.

Introduction

If foreign exchange rates were always the same, a large amount of valuable management time would be saved, and, in fact, this book would be unnecessary. However, rates do move, and sometimes with dramatic and disconcerting rapidity. Even the best known and most widely used currency in the world, the U.S. dollar (USD), has experienced major rate adjustments in the last decade. For example, the dollar traded at 195 yen in December 1978, increased 36 percent in value against the yen to 265 yen in September 1982, and then fell 53 percent to 124 yen in December 1987. By mid-1990 it was trading in the 160-yen range and fell again to about 135 yen in early 1991. The purpose of this chapter is to explore why these and other exchange-rate adjustments occur. Subsequent chapters will look at what these changes mean to corporations, and what managers can do to protect their firms in the face of such rate changes and to capitalize on opportunities thus presented.

How Foreign Exchange Rates Have Moved in the Past

There are several important foreign exchange rates in addition to the Japanese yen/USD rate mentioned above. Before we consider why they move, it is useful to look briefly at how they have moved in the recent past. First, however, we must define two types of exchange-rate moves, a nominal one and a real one.

Nominal- and Real-Exchange-Rate Adjustments

A *nominal-exchange-rate move* is simply the total observed movement in the exchange rate. It is not adjusted for inflation or for any other factor. A *real-exchange-rate move* is the nominal-rate movement adjusted for the differential in inflation.

For example, if British inflation has been 10 percent over the past year, while German inflation has been 0 percent, and the pound sterling devalues against the mark by 10 percent in the same time period, the nominal-rate move would be 10 percent, but the real adjustment is zero. We would say that nothing has happened. It takes 10 percent more pounds to buy a mark and, therefore, 10 percent more pounds to buy a loaf of bread in Germany. However, it also takes 10 percent more pounds to buy a loaf of bread in England because of the 10 percent inflation there. In other words, German bread still costs the same as English bread; the basic exchange rate between English and German goods has not changed. There has been no change in the real exchange rate, for either goods or money.

An adjustment in the real currency exchange rate is, therefore, one that represents an adjustment in the exchange rate for real goods and services. If the rate of inflation is the same in each country and the exchange rate moves, a real-rate move has occurred. If a bushel of British wheat costs 1 pound, and 1 pound buys 1 mark, and 1 mark buys 1 pair of German shoes, then the bushel of wheat is worth a pair of shoes and can be exchanged for those shoes by selling the wheat for a pound, exchanging the pound for a mark, and using the mark to buy the shoes. Now, if there is no inflation anywhere, there is no change in either the pound price of wheat or the mark price of shoes. However, over time, a currency-rate move, to 2 marks per pound for example, will alter this relationship. The wheat can still be sold for a pound, but the pound will now buy 2 marks, which will buy not 1 pair, but 2 pairs, of shoes. Because the exchange rate for real goods (wheat for shoes) has been altered, a real-currency-rate move has occurred.

As illustrated by the preceding example, the distinction between a real- and a nominal-currency-rate change is important. It matters to managers because nominal-rate changes do not necessarily alter corporate competitive positions, but real ones do. In addition, the distinction is important to government economic policy and tactics. As we shall see, for example, it is not clear whether governments can cause lasting real-exchange-rate movement by forcing changes in the nominal rate. A nominal-rate change, by definition, is offset by the inflation differential between the currencies and, therefore, will not do much to help with a trade deficit. We will look at these issues shortly. First, though, we will look at what actually happened to exchange rates in the period 1974–1990, both real and nominal, for some of our more widely traded currencies, as shown in Exhibits 2.1 to 2.5. In all cases, the consumer

Exhibit 2.1. Canadian/U.S. Dollar Exchange Rate

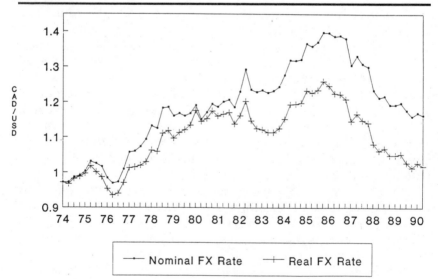

Exhibit 2.2. Japanese Yen/U.S. Dollar Exchange Rate

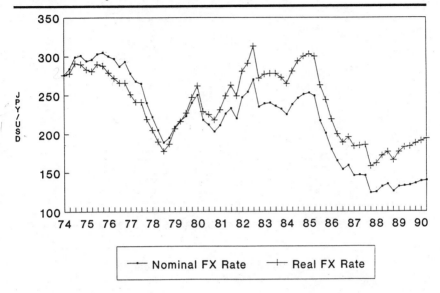

Exhibit 2.3. Swiss Franc/U.S. Dollar Exchange Rate

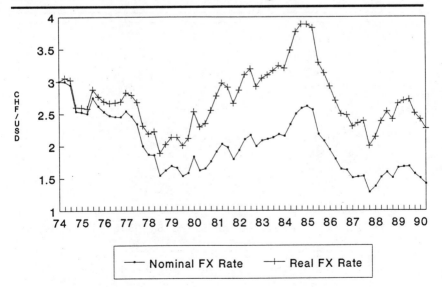

Exhibit 2.4. U.S. Dollar/Sterling Exchange Rate

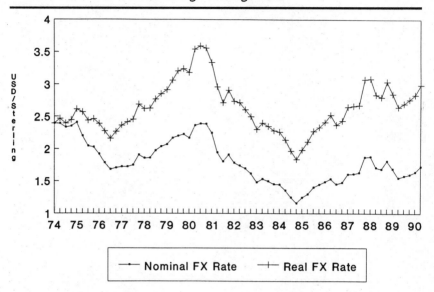

Exhibit 2.5. Deutsche Mark/U.S. Dollar Exhange Rate

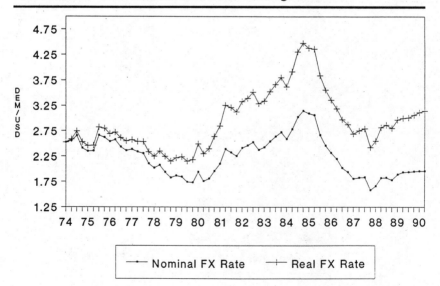

price index was the measure of inflation used to calculate the real exchange rate from the nominal one.

All the rates in Exhibits 2.1 through 2.5 are quoted against the USD. Real exchange rates are the nominal rates adjusted for inflation since our arbitrary starting point in 1974. For example, in early 1974 it took less than .98 Canadian dollar (CAD) to buy one U.S. dollar. Ten years later, the nominal rate had moved to 1.28 CAD/USD. However, cumulative inflation in the decade was 140 percent in Canada, but only 116 percent in the United States. Adjusting the nominal 1984 exchange rate for this inflation differential produces a real 1984 rate (relative to the .98 CAD/USD rate in 1974) of 1.15 CAD/USD, as follows:

$$1.28 \times (2.16/2.40) = 1.15$$

There was, therefore, a real-exchange-rate adjustment in the period of about 17 percent:

$$(1.15 - .98)/.98 = .174$$

It took 17 percent more Canadian goods to buy the same quantity of U.S. goods in 1984 compared with 1974. The terms of trade (the price of foreign goods in terms of domestic goods) changed, together with the relative competitiveness of Canadian and American firms (abstracting from productivity changes), as well as the relative wealth of Canadians and Americans. Note that the change in the nominal exchange rate was much greater than 17 percent. It was actually 31 percent [(1.28 - .98)/.98], but almost half of this nominal move was offset by the higher rate of inflation in Canada.

In summary, the real foreign exchange line in Exhibits 2.1 to 2.5 shows what has happened to the purchasing power of each of the currencies relative to that of the U.S. dollar since 1974. For example, in real terms the Canadian dollar had weakened by more than 25 percent by 1986 (CAD/USD .98 to 1.25). That is, 25 percent more Canadian goods were required to buy a comparable basket of American goods in 1986 compared with 1974. The recovery from early 1986 to mid-1989 was even more dramatic (CAD/USD 1.25 to 1.05). By the end of the overall period, the cumulative real-exchange-rate move was a devaluation of only 7 percent for the Canadian dollar,

$$(1.05 - .98)/.98 = .0714$$

even though the nominal adjustment was 22 percent.

$$(1.20 - .98)/.98 = .224$$

calculation: If the nominal rate at the end of the period had
~~~ather than 1.20, there would have been no net adjustment at all
~~~ exchange rate in the period. This is because the cumulative Ca-
~~~ iflation in the period was 198 percent (prices were almost three
times as high), while the American inflation was 162 percent:

$$.98 \times (298/262) = 1.11$$

The preceding exhibits show considerable movement in the nominal
rates and somewhat less in real rates. At this point, it would be helpful
to know what gives rise to these adjustments. Understanding the forces
that have produced these observed changes should give us some help in
anticipating similar changes in the future. The basic explanation for
rate changes is a supply-and-demand argument for currencies in the
marketplace, based on the idea that the foreign exchange rate is simply
the price that clears the market. To understand this price and its movements, it is necessary to understand factors that determine the relative
supply-and-demand situation for a currency.

The supply-and-demand balance for a currency is determined when
a country settles its international accounts. This settlement is accomplished in what is called the *international payments system*, which is really an international market for currencies. The evolution of the system
is an interesting story in its own right, and knowledge of this evolution
helps to understand how the system works today. Appendix 2.1, at the
end of this chapter, traces the development of the system from the gold
standard, through the gold exchange standard, to the postwar pegged-
exchange-rate system, and, finally, to the current floating-rate system,
which has been in place since the early 1970s.

Floating Exchange Rates

The floating-exchange-rate regime for major currencies, which began in
1973, has two important modifications. The European Economic Community (EEC) has developed its own internal pegged-exchange-rate system.
The initiative began in 1972, with a joint floating arrangement that limited
the movement of EEC-member currencies with respect both to themselves
and also, collectively, to the dollar. This European Joint Float Agreement
was only a few months old when the United Kingdom withdrew in response to market pressures, followed by Denmark and Italy. The agreement has been replaced by the more successful European Monetary System (EMS), established in March 1979.

The EMS created a new official currency, the European currency unit
(ECU), which acts as a reserve currency and is used by members to settle
accounts with one another. Initially, the EMS faced some difficulty, with

the first three years producing upward valuations of the deutsche mark and the guilder and devaluations of the French, Danish, and Italian currencies. Britain initially declined to join. However, the remarkable economic integration of Europe now planned for 1992 can perhaps trace some of its origins to these early attempts to stabilize and control currency fluctuations that are disruptive to international trade.

2. The second major modification of our current system of freely floating currencies is the tendency of currencies to float in blocks. These blocks are now formed around four major currencies: the dollar, the pound, the deutsche mark, and the yen. In addition, the currencies of some smaller countries are pegged to other currencies. In other cases, the peg is much looser, but for trade or other reasons, these countries tend to stabilize the movement of their exchange rates against a single currency or a group of currencies. Exhibit 2.6 shows the formal stabilization relationships as of June 30, 1990. These official arrangements may be unofficially modified by the blocking tendencies mentioned above. For example, the Canadian dollar is officially listed as "independently floating." However, that float is, in fact, substantially constrained by its relation to the U.S. dollar.

The evolution of the international payments system, from the gold standard, through the system of pegged exchange rates administered under the Bretton Woods Agreement, to our current system of floating rates, has taken almost 80 years. The trend throughout the period, except for minor interruptions, has been toward increasing flexibility in exchange-rate determination. This, in turn, allows more freedom and latitude, as well as less urgency, in the process of restoring external equilibrium on the part of individual countries.

How Well the Payments Systems Have Worked

Countries, like people, must eventually pay their bills. The only question is when. A good payments system is one which:

1. Encourages individual countries to stay more or less in equilibrium in international transactions

2. Provides a means for countries to move back toward equilibrium when necessary without extremely painful internal adjustments

3. Encourages the growth of international trade.[1]

Pegged Systems

Under the gold system, payment was required and made immediately. If the external trade account was not in balance, payment was de-

Exhibit 2.6. Exchange Rate Arrangements
(As of June 30, 1990)[1]

		Currency pegged to		
U.S. dollar	French franc	Other currency	SDR	Other composite[2]
Afghanistan	Benin	Bhutan	Burundi	Algeria
Angola	Burkina Faso	(Indian rupee)	Iran, I.R. of	Austria
Antigua & Barbuda	Cameroon	Kiribati	Libya	Bangladesh
Bahamas, The	C. African Rep.	(Australian dollar)	Myanmar	Botswana
Barbados	Chad	Lesotho	Rwanda	Cape Verde
Belize	Comoros	(South African rand)	Seychelles	Cyprus
Djibouti	Congo	Swaziland	Zambia	Fiji
Dominica	Cote d'Ivoire	(South African rand)		Finland
Dominican Rep.	Equatorial Guinea	Tonga		Hungary
Ethiopia	Gabon	(Australian dollar)		Iceland
Granada	Mali			Israel
Guyana	Niger			Jordan
Haiti	Senegal			Kenya
Iraq	Togo			Kuwait
Jamaica				Malawi
Liberia				Malaysia
Nicaragua				Malta
Oman				Mauritius
Panama				Morocco
Peru				Mozambique
St. Kitts & Nevis				Nepal
St. Lucia				Norway
St. Vincent				Papua New Guinea
Sudan				Poland
Suriname				Romania
Syrian Arab Rep.				Sao Tome & Principe
Trinidad and Tobago				Solomon Islands
Yemen, Republic of				Somalia
				Sweden
				Tanzania
				Thailand
				Uganda
				Vanuatu
				Western Samoa
				Zimbabwe

SOURCE: International Financial Statistics, November 1989.

[1]Excluding the currency of Democratic Kampuchea, for which no current information is available. For members with dual or multiple exchange markets, the arrangement shown is that in the major market.

[2]Comprises currencies which are pegged to various "baskets" of currencies of the members' own choice, as distinct from the SDR basket.

manded, usually in gold. This outflow of money caused price and income effects in the domestic economy, which tended to push the trade balance back to equilibrium.

Under the pegged-exchange-rate system, exchange-rate adjustment was not yet freely available to provide a buffer and, perhaps, delay the required domestic adjustments. Exchange-rate moves were possible, but not encouraged. However, the practice of central bank borrowing to support the currency was widely accepted. Price and income adjust-

Exhibit 2.6. Exchange Rate Arrangements (Continued)
(As of June 30, 1990)

Flexibility limited in terms of a single currency or group of currencies		More flexible		
Single currency[3]	Cooperative arrangements[4]	Adjusted according to a set of indicators[5]	Other managed floating	Independently floating
Bahrain	Belgium	Chile	China, P.R.	Argentina
Qatar	Denmark	Columbia	Costa Rica	Australia
Saudi Arabia	France	Madagascar	Ecuador	Bolivia
United Arab	Germany	Portugal	Egypt	Brazil
Emirates	Ireland		Greece	Canada
	Italy		Guinea	El Salvador
	Luxembourg		Guinea-Bissau	Gambia, The
	Netherlands		Honduras	Ghana
	Spain		India	Guatemala
			Indonesia	Japan
			Korea	Lebanon
			Lao P.D. Rep.	Maldives
			Mauritania	New Zealand
			Mexico	Nigeria
			Pakistan	Paraguay
			Singapore	Philippines
			Sri Lanka	Sierra Leone
			Tunisia	South Africa
			Turkey	United Kingdom
			Viet Nam	United States
			Yugoslavia	Uruguay
				Venezuela
				Zaire

SOURCE: International Financial Statistics, November 1989.
[3]Exchange rates of all currencies have shown limited flexibility in terms of the U.S. dollar.
[4]Refers to the cooperative arrangement maintained under the European Monetary System.
[5]Includes exchange arrangements under which the exchange rate is adjusted at relatively frequent intervals, on the basis of indicators determined by the respective member countries.

ments could be postponed, sometimes for a long time. Countries could run a deficit on trade or other international accounts for as long as the international community was prepared to finance them. In practice, private borrowing sources tended to become inaccessible as soon as the imbalance appeared to be serious or structural, causing borrowers to turn to the prime public lending source, the International Monetary Fund (IMF). When this occurred, conditions changed, as the IMF has a history of imposing increasingly severe constraints and conditions on the loans unless the underlying problems are addressed.

Floating Systems

The floating-rate system adds one more degree of freedom in the management of national economies. Private and public loans are still available to delay adjustment. In addition, it is now possible to use the exchange rate more freely as part of the adjustment process. For the currencies without an official peg, central bank intervention could be used to moderate the rate fluctuations that would otherwise occur, and perhaps to nudge the rate in the direction considered appropriate for the national interest. Whether it is possible to effect any long-term change in the real exchange rate, and hence the terms of trade, by this process is not clear. However, under a floating-exchange-rate system, external equilibrium can be at least partially (if temporarily) restored by allowing the exchange rate to adjust. This adjustment may have less unpleasant consequences for the domestic population than would an attempt at equilibrium restoration through direct price and income adjustment.

One result of the increasing latitude in the external balance adjustment process has been the increasing ability of countries to go into debt. The day for paying the bills can be postponed. Eventually, of course, residents of a country can consume only as much as they produce, where production is broadly defined to include the returns of capital loaned or invested as well as real goods and services produced. In the short run, consumption can be maintained when production falters as long as others will lend, or as long as there are assets available that others wish to purchase. While significant borrowing and lending activity did take place from time to time under the gold system, the current degree of freedom to do so represents a truly substantial change from conditions in that earlier era.

The extent to which consumption can exceed production can be illustrated by observing the speed and magnitude of the change in status of the United States from the world's largest creditor (as recently as 1980) to the world's largest debtor today. This reversal provides an excellent example of the flexibility afforded, in part, by the floating-exchange-rate system, but it does overstate the case. In the first place, the size of the net creditor or debtor position is usually measured in absolute dollars, and as such, it does appear to be a massive swing. However, the positions should be scaled relative to the size of the United States economy. When viewed in this way, the change is much less significant. Second, some would argue that the capital inflows resulted from investor decisions based on worldwide market conditions and that these inflows produced an overvalued U.S. dollar. This, in turn, discouraged domestic production in favor of imports. In any event, Exhibit 2.7 shows the recent change in the net investment position of the United States and includes comparable data for Japan and Canada.

The swing for the United States in dollar terms was, in fact, nearly $500 billion, from creditor to debtor, in seven years. This is, at least, a rough measure of the extent to which consumption exceeded domestic production in the period, and the gap was made possible by borrowing, by selling assets, and by allowing, when necessary, the dollar exchange rate to adjust.

Exhibit 2.7. Net Investment Position at Year End, for United States, Japan, and Canada

	1980	1981	1982	1983	1984	1985	1986	1987	1988	1989	1990*
United States											
US$ billions†	106	141	137	90	3.6	(112)	(269)	(378)	(532)	(642)	(800)
% of GNP‡	3.8	4.6	4.3	2.6		2.8	6.3	8.3	10.9	12.3	14.1
Japan											
US$ billions§	21	25	32	53	88	137	223	310	390	447	504
% of GNP‡	1.8	2.2	2.8	4.4	7.4	8.6	10.6	11.1	13.3	16.4	16.0
Canada											
CAN$ billions¶	(106)	(131)	(134)	(143)	(154)	(166)	(194)	(218)	(228)	(242)	(258)
% of GNP‡	35	38	37	36	36	36	40	41	39	39	38

*Estimated.

†Data through 1988 are from the 1988 and 1989 *Economic Report of the President;* 1989–1990 estimates are based on current account forecasts in the IMF *World Economic Outlook,* April 1989. (Based on book values of assets and liabilities. Use of market values would improve the net position but not change the trend.)

‡Authors' calculation.

§Japan's cumulative current account balances from 1970 were used as a proxy for net investment position. The data through 1987 are from IMF *I.F.S. Yearbook, 1986/87* and for 1988–1990 from IMF, *World Economic Outlook,* May 1990.

¶Data through 1988 are from Statistics Canada, *Canada's International Investment Position, 1981–1984,* 67-202, 1984, and from *Quarterly Estimates of Canada's Balance of International Payments,* 67-001, 1988. Data for 1989–1990 are based on current account balances from IMF, *International Financial Statistics.*

Currency Values in a Floating System

As indicated, Exhibits 2.1 to 2.5 show the extent of the nominal- and real-exchange-rate adjustments which have occurred, in the period 1974–1990, for several of the main trading currencies. This period covers the time since the current floating-rate system was established. Some of the nominal-rate changes observed have no doubt resulted from intervention by the central banks of the countries concerned. In the floating-rate system the same external imbalances provide pressure for rate adjustments as under the pegged system, except that the adjustments are supposed to happen more quickly and uniformly.

One of the key factors in an external imbalance, and the resulting pressure for exchange-rate adjustment, is the relative demand for a country's goods and services abroad. This offshore demand, of course, depends on external prices, and these, in turn, depend on the exchange rate. However, inflation differentials between the trading partners can also alter the relative prices and thus affect demand and trade flows, creating an imbalance and pressure on exchange rates. The relationship between inflation differentials and exchange rates is described in purchasing-power parity theory; we will outline this relationship later in the chapter.

In addition to trade flows, three other major factors may alter the supply-and-demand balance of a currency. These factors can, at least in the short run, substantially modify the rate adjustments that might otherwise occur in response to a trade imbalance:

1. The current investment value of the currency and the resulting short- and long-term capital flows for investment purposes

2. The country's net investment position and the capital flows resulting from prior international loans and investments

3. The government's interest in exchange-rate control and the use of central bank operations for rate adjustments

Before exploring each of these factors, however, we need to consider the measurement and interpretation of a basic external payments imbalance.

The Balance of Payments Statement

The primary method of measuring the degree of external balance and of interpreting the effect of this balance, or lack thereof, on the currency value is the *balance of payments* account. This account summarizes all transactions between residents of a country and the rest of the

world, and groups the transactions in categories to aid interpretation.
The net result is a summary statement of the demand-and-supply pressures on a currency during the time period covered by the account.

A traditional balance of payments statement follows the format
shown in Exhibit 2.8.

Each of the four "balances" includes the prior ones; they are cumulative. The change in the reserves will always equal the official balance
because the system is based on double-entry bookkeeping. The debits
will always equal the credits. The trick in interpreting the statement is to
know in which accounts it is best to have debits and in which accounts
credit balances are preferred.

A credit transaction increases purchasing power and creates a demand for domestic currency on the foreign exchange markets. Thus a
credit can be, for example:

1. Export of goods or services

2. Receipt of a gift from abroad (a unilateral transfer)

3. Receipt of cash flows from prior investments (interest and dividend
   receipts credited to the service account)

4. Borrowing abroad in any of its many forms (credits to the short- or
   long-term capital accounts)

5. Receipt of foreign direct investment (a long-term capital account
   credit)

All these transactions increase the purchasing power of the residents
of the country, whereas a debit is defined as a transaction that results in
decreased international purchasing power for the residents of the coun-

Exhibit 2.8. Traditional Balance of Payments Format

Exports	A
Imports	B
Trade balance	C = A − B
Service	D
Unilateral transfers	E
Current account balance	F = C + D + E
Foreign direct investment	G
Other long-term capital	H
Basic balance	I = F + G + H
Short-term capital	J
Official balance	K = I + J
Change in reserves	L = K

try. It adds to the supply of the domestic currency on the foreign exchange markets. Typical debit transactions would include:

1. Imports of goods or services
2. Gifts made to residents of foreign countries
3. Payments made on capital that was originally sourced abroad
4. Loans abroad
5. Foreign direct investments in other countries

Interpreting the Balance of Payments Statement

The key question in analyzing a balance of payments statement is whether the country's financial position has improved or deteriorated in the period covered by the statement. An improvement is an increase in purchasing power or in the ability to acquire the goods and services of other nations. A deterioration is a reduction in purchasing power.

Interpreting the statement involves classifying transactions into autonomous and compensating groupings. Autonomous transactions are those that occur because of economic conditions or opportunities, while compensating transactions are those that occur as a result of the autonomous ones. For example, an export would be the autonomous transaction and the payment for the export would be the compensating one.

Conventional wisdom suggests that a "strong" balance of payments is one with credits for the autonomous transactions and debits for the compensating ones. This, in turn, suggests positive or credit trade and current balances, and negative or debit capital account balances. Such a country earns its way in the world on the strength of its exports of goods and services and uses the purchasing power so acquired to invest abroad. These investments, if well chosen, should provide an even stronger statement later, when the dividend and interest receipts show up in the services account.

A second and more basic interpretation of the balance of payments statement stems from the fact that it must always balance. The net balance is always zero. Summarizing all transactions in five groups, we have

$$\text{Exports} - \text{imports} + \text{capital inflows} - \text{capital outflows}$$

$$\pm \text{ change in official reserves} = \text{zero}$$

Under a pegged-exchange-rate system, any net imbalance on the first four accounts must be absorbed by the official reserves. If these reserves are not equal to the task and no other action is taken to relieve the imbalance, the exchange rate must break with the peg and move. Under a floating system, the rate is theoretically free to move and thus protect the reserve position. Under both systems, exports and capital inflows are credits, while imports and capital outflows are debits. More credits than debits, excluding the official reserve account, will either increase reserves or cause an upward valuation of the currency or both, and an excess of debits will, of course, do the opposite.

An obvious, but important, point is that the particular source of the debits or credits does not matter. The net effect is the same pressure for an exchange-rate adjustment. It is, therefore, possible for a country to run a large and persistent deficit (debit) on its current account and still have a strong and buoyant currency, if capital inflows far exceed capital outflows. According to the earlier interpretation, based on the distinction between autonomous and compensating transactions, this situation should signal a weakening currency. The reconciliation of these interpretations lies in the planning horizon assumed. Currency strength based on capital inflows (possibly excluding direct investment) tends to be short-lived. Unless the proceeds are used for productive investments, loans and portfolio investments will produce a later drag on the currency from principal, interest, and dividend payments. Long-run currency strength usually requires international competitiveness at the trade or current account level, which the autonomous/compensating distinction attempts to recognize.

Exhibit 2.9 shows the United States balance of payments accounts for the years 1980–1988, in a condensed format. The trade and current accounts become steadily more negative in the period, offset by net capital inflows. The currency value rises strongly during the first half of the period and falls sharply in the last three years shown. While generalization from a sample of one is dangerous, this experience is consistent with the interpretive approaches discussed above. That is, on the autonomous/compensating transaction measure, the U.S. payments statement showed weakness from 1980 onward, with a negative trade account followed by a negative current balance. However, these outflows were more than offset in the early part of the decade by large capital inflows, resulting in upward pressure on the exchange rate. One could argue that, when these capital inflows faltered in mid-decade, the exchange rate began to reflect the weakness signaled earlier by the trade and current account balances.

One caveat should be observed concerning the preceding very basic interpretation. The external transactions of the United States are a relatively small part of its overall economy. On account of the relative wealth and unused borrowing capacity involved, foreigners have been and still are willing to hold increasing amounts of U.S. dollars and

Exhibit 2.9. Selected United States Balance of Payments Accounts
(USD Billions)

	1980	1981	1982	1983	1984	1985	1986	1987	1988	1989
Exports	224.3	237.1	211.2	201.8	219.9	215.9	224.0	249.6	320.1	360.5
Imports	-249.8	-265.1	-247.7	-268.9	-332.4	-338.1	-368.5	-409.9	-446.4	-475.3
Trade balance	-25.5	-28.0	-36.5	-67.1	-112.5	-122.2	-144.5	-160.3	-126.3	-114.9
Service	34.9	42.4	36.7	30.3	17.5	22.0	20.9	21.2	5.2	11.8
Unilateral transfers	-7.6	-7.5	-8.9	-9.5	-12.1	-15.0	-15.3	-13.4	-13.6	-14.8
Current balance	1.8	6.9	-8.6	-46.3	-107.1	-115.2	-138.9	-152.5	-134.7	-110.0
Foreign direct Investment	0.6	18.3	15.3	16.3	51.3	65.4	77.9	33.7	81.1	40.5
Other long-term capital	-9.0	-19.0	-22.7	-18.0	-12.8	7.9	-5.2	-0.6	12.8	44.8
Short-term capital	-27.4	-27.4	-18.1	32.7	42.6	29.9	16.9	54.1	7.4	14.6
Errors and omissions	25.0	20.0	36.1	11.2	26.7	17.8	15.6	8.4	-2.8	22.6
Official balance	-8.4	-2.1	0.9	-5.7	-1.4	10.2	-28.5	-50.3	-38.3	-16.8
Change in reserves	-7.6	-3.2	-3.9	0.5	-1.0	-8.2	-5.1	2.6	-1.8	-26.8

SOURCE: IMF, *International Financial Statistics*, various issues.

dollar-denominated financial assets. As a result, the expected linkage between the nature of the U.S. balance of payments and the dollar exchange rate is much less direct than for smaller or less wealthy economies.

Exhibit 2.10 shows the balance of payments on current account balances for several countries. If the current account is positive, the offsetting position will be an increase in official reserves (which would be unsustainable in the long run), a negative capital account, or a combination of the two. Following the autonomous/compensating transaction distinctions made earlier, these current account data should be, at least in the long run, a rough guide to currency strength; that is, current account surpluses (mostly autonomous transactions) should be associated with stronger currencies. Interested readers can compare the current account performances of individual countries from Exhibit 2.10 with the relative strengths of their currencies as shown in Exhibits 2.1 to 2.5.

Problems with the Balance of Payments Data

Pressure for exchange-rate adjustment as suggested by balance of payments data is usually not well correlated with actual exchange-rate movements, for several reasons.

1. Reported capital flows do not include the activities of the world's underground economy. Large amounts of cash can be moved from country to country outside of normal channels. These "hidden" transactions show up as "errors and omissions" on the balance of payments account. For some countries, this item can be significant.

2. Forward contracts are not included in the balance of payments account. Consider the impact of hedged versus unhedged foreign currency borrowings. In unhedged debt, the foreign currency is borrowed and converted to local currency. This transaction creates demand for the local currency and causes the local currency, all things being equal, to strengthen. Repayment of the interest and principal will result in selling of the local currency in the future. When these sales occur, the local currency will tend to weaken. On the other hand, fully hedged debt involves the simultaneous execution of all the above transactions. The result is a net sale of the local currency in the amount of the total interest payments. The local currency would thus tend to weaken now, in spite of the foreign currency borrowing, which, according to theory, should cause the currency to strengthen. The balance of payments account will show only the borrowing activity (currency support), and not the forward sales.

Exhibit 2.10. Balance of Payments on Current Account, 1981–1989
(In Billions of U.S. Dollars and as a Percentage of GNP)

	1981	1982	1983	1984	1985	1986	1987	1988	1989	1990*
United States	6.9	-7.0	-44.3	-104.2	-112.7	-133.3	-143.7	-126.5	-106.0	-113.3
% of GNP	0.2	-0.2	-1.3	-2.8	-2.8	-3.1	-3.2	-2.6	-2.0	-2.0
Canada	-5.1	2.3	2.5	2.1	-1.4	-7.6	-7.1	-8.4	-16.6	-20.2
% of GNP	-1.7	0.8	0.8	0.6	-0.4	-2.1	-1.7	-1.7	-3.0	-3.5
Japan	4.8	6.9	20.8	35.0	49.2	85.8	87.0	79.5	57.2	57.4
% of GNP	0.4	0.7	1.7	2.8	3.6	4.3	3.6	2.8	2.0	2.1
Germany	-3.6	5.1	5.3	9.9	16.6	39.3	45.0	48.5	52.8	62.3
% of GNP	-0.5	0.8	0.8	1.6	2.6	4.4	4.0	4.0	4.4	4.4
United Kingdom	14.1	8.0	5.7	2.5	4.2	-0.2	-6.1	-26.2	-34.2	-25.7
% of GNP	2.7	1.6	1.2	0.6	0.9		-0.9	-3.2	-4.1	-2.9

SOURCE: International Monetary Fund, *World Economic Outlook*, April 1989 and May 1990.
*Estimated.

It can, therefore, give an incorrect signal in the case of fully hedged debt.

3. The trade account does not reflect long-dated forwards dealt to hedge commercial transactions. If an exporter has a sale calling for shipment and payment in years 1 through 5, it may hedge its exposure by selling the foreign currency revenue stream via use of forward contracts. The impact on the spot exchange market of these transactions occurs when the forward contracts are initially dealt, long before the goods were shipped and the export shows up in the balance of payments data.

In summary, the balance of payments account suffers from unreported transactions and from timing problems with some of the transactions that are reported. There is also a substantial time lag required for the collection and reporting of the data. However, it remains one of the most useful, publicly available sources of information on the relative economic performance of individual countries, and, therefore, on the supply-and-demand prospects for their currencies.

Financing the Current Account Deficit

For many governments, achieving external balance means managing a substantial current account deficit. As indicated earlier, this does not necessarily mean short-run pressure on the currency. There are several major factors to consider.

Current Investment Value of the Currency.   Capital markets today in most major currencies are easily accessible and very liquid. A modest difference in real (inflation-adjusted) return on bank deposits and on fixed-income securities, both long and short term, will attract considerable funds. A speculative element may also be a factor in the flow of cross-border investment funds. If investors believe a currency will strengthen, their collective actions may make it happen. Finally, political and economic instability in many parts of the world may make some currencies more attractive than they otherwise would be and, consequently, give rise to capital flows. For these reasons, in the near term at least, the short- and long-term capital accounts can provide a perhaps temporary, but effective, cushion for a current account imbalance.

In the economic management of a country, large-scale capital flows can be both a help and a hindrance. Certainly, as indicated, opportunities are available to finance a current account deficit, perhaps for some time, by raising domestic interest rates to attract capital inflows. Moreover, if higher interest rates are part of a strategy to reduce domestic inflation, the capital inflows will tend to put upward pressure on the currency, which will indeed help to reduce inflation. However, if the strategy is to reduce inflation as well as to help the external trade account, the stronger currency may actually cause the trade picture to deteriorate, not improve.

Speculator or investor interest involves both short-term investment opportunities and long-term financial assets as portfolio investments. The long-term capital account also includes foreign direct investment (FDI), usually defined as private-sector investment, where an element of management control exists over the investment. FDI can create a significant demand for a currency, so much so that many governments encourage it as a means of financing a current account deficit. In the right circumstances, FDI can be a source of new technology and employment. If carried too far, however, it can result in allegations of loss of control of the economy or domination of the private-sector decision-making process by nonresidents.

In summary, a currency supply-and-demand situation based on the trade or current account balance can be offset, at least in the short run, by capital account transactions. In this sense, these capital account transactions could be considered autonomous, and the offsetting current account transactions occur to permit them to happen. For example, if a country produces inadequate savings to finance needed private-sector investment, a trade deficit will allow the required importation of capital without the accumulation of reserves or upward pressure on the currency.

Country Net Investment Position.   Before we leave this basic interpretation of a balance of payments statement using current and capital account balances, it is useful to look briefly within the current account at the trade and service account balances. For some countries, the net investment position is such that the current account balance is strongly affected.

Exhibit 2.7, presented earlier, shows the net investment position of three countries, the United States, Japan, and Canada. For the United States and Japan, the net investment positions are changing over time but are relatively small as a percentage of GNP. For Canada, the position has been stable over time relative to GNP, but it has been much larger relative to the size of the economy. The Canadian net position is negative; that is, Canadian residents owe much more than they own abroad. As a result, the Canadian service account has a large negative balance, so much so that recently it has more than offset the trade account, as the figures in Exhibit 2.11 show.

Exhibit 2.11. Canadian Current Account Balance
(Selected Years, CAD Billions)

	Trade account	Service account		Current account balance
		Net investment income	Other service	
1981	7.3	−11.3	−2.1	−6.1
1983	17.5	−11.6	−2.8	3.1
1985	16.4	−14.3	−4.1	−2.0
1987	11.3	−16.5	−4.1	−9.3
1989	4.7	−22.4	−1.9	−19.6
1990*	9.6	−25.5	−0.7	−16.2

*Estimated.

The net result is potential downward pressure on the exchange rate. In Canada's case, this pressure was offset in this period by strong capital inflows, in part in response to high Canadian interest rates. However, analysis of the Canadian balance of payments must include recognition of the high and rising net investment income outflow relative to the trade balance, and the slim prospect of trade surpluses sufficient to offset it, at least at the exchange rates prevailing at the end of the decade. In addition, the current capital inflows seem likely to contribute to future investment income deficits. One could conclude, therefore, that the Canadian dollar should make some downward adjustment in the 1990s relative to the currencies of Canada's trading partners.

As a final observation on net investment position, there are countries for which the investment position is even more important to their balance of payments than is the case for Canada. These countries include many of the developing countries of the world. In some cases, external debt is so high that policies fostering currency stabilization and domestic growth must be subordinated to debt service requirements. In these cases, consideration of the net investment position and the resultant investment income/payments situation can be the dominant issue in balance of payments analysis.

Government Control; Central Bank Operations. For pegged currencies, government intervention through central bank open-market operations is almost mandatory, from time to time, to keep the currency within its agreed trading range. In the case of floating currencies, intervention is more discretionary in nature. In both cases, within the limits of the available foreign exchange reserves plus borrowing capacity, the central bank can buy and sell its currency in an attempt to stabilize the currency value. To do this, central banks would buy their own currency when it weakened and sell it when it became too strong.

Central bank activity in this area has been increasing, at least as measured by the amount of funds maintained to do the job. For example, total reserve holdings, excluding gold, of the G-7 countries increased from US$60 billion in 1973 to more than US$310 billion in 1988.

With finite resources, central bank intervention by itself will clearly not alter the long-run supply-and-demand relationship of a currency, but it can have some impact in the short run. Because it is generally conceded that governments and their central banks can cause changes in the long-run nominal foreign exchange rate through the exercise of domestic fiscal and monetary policy, the signaling effect of central bank intervention is important. Open-market operations may be used to signal the wishes of the central bank and thus change the behavior of other participants in the market.

As indicated, governments can attempt to adjust currency values more directly, if they wish, by several methods, including the following:

1. Domestic monetary and fiscal policy

2. Wage and price controls

3. Direct controls, such as duties and tariffs, trade quotas, and, ultimately, foreign exchange controls

All these methods may have substantial penalties for domestic economic growth and employment. However, the formidable range of options available suggests that discussing currency price movements without considering government policy or the central bank may not be productive. In fact, rather than enjoying the freedom in domestic economic management afforded by an unpegged exchange rate, many governments may see the foreign exchange rate as just another tool available to accomplish their economic management goals. If this is so, then currency value may not respond as anticipated to economic pressures, and forecasting without knowledge of the government's agenda becomes more difficult.

Of the three policy options listed above, the first is favored by the industrialized countries with floating currencies, while the other two are more frequently found in developing economies with pegged or more tightly managed currencies. Since government intervention at this level does occur, and since such intervention suggests that long-term changes in at least the nominal exchange rate will result, two areas are of interest. What do governments want the exchange rate to be, and how do the measures work to push the rate in that direction?

What Governments Want

We can assume that most governments want maximum long-term economic growth consistent with full employment and price stability. In theory, it should be possible to pursue these objectives, and a floating exchange rate would adjust to accommodate the process. In practice, it does not seem to be that simple. It may be that the optimum domestic economic policy package is politically unacceptable in a democracy. Voters may be too impatient or may prefer unearned consumption now at the expense of possible economic problems later. In any event, management of the foreign exchange rate is sometimes used as a means to achieve short-run economic goals, or to avoid the more unpleasant alternative methods of goal achievement.

In determining the best rate for a currency at any particular time, some trade-offs exist. In general, a stronger currency makes exports more expensive abroad and imports cheaper at home. It depresses the level of economic activity and is deflationary. It also permits residents to have a higher level of consumption through the cheaper imports. Conversely, a weaker exchange rate boosts economic activity, contributes to inflation (more export demand and higher import prices), and reduces import-based consumption. The preferred exchange rate would thus seem to be the highest rate that is consistent with full employment and stable prices.

The temptation to meddle with exchange rates arises when a change in relative factor costs, or an inadequate productivity gain, leaves the country less competitive in international trade. In this case, the rate should weaken. An overcorrection, producing an artificially low foreign exchange rate, can increase competitiveness in export markets and suppress consumption (encourage savings) at home, both of which support growth. If such a policy is pursued in conjunction with factor cost or productivity advantages, it can become the engine for truly impressive economic growth.

How Governments Influence the Exchange Rate

1. Monetary and Fiscal Policy. Monetary and fiscal policy can affect the trade balance and, therefore, the supply-and-demand balance for a currency through both a price and an income effect. Increases in domestic money supply will raise prices, making imports more attractive. Fiscal surpluses will reduce economic activity and incomes, reducing demand for imports and freeing up resources to produce for the export market. The effectiveness of these policies depends on the price and income elasticities of demand for the traded goods. High price elasticity of demand means that the volume of a good traded is sensitive to a change in price; high income elasticity means that volume demanded is sensitive to income levels.

It is interesting to observe that, under the gold system, the price and income effects were usually triggered by a decline in the money supply caused by a trade deficit. The exchange rate was inflexible. Under our current floating-rate regime, the exchange rate is available to act as a shock absorber. It will, at least partially, insulate the domestic economy from pressures caused by an external imbalance. If a government chooses to force the exchange rate from its equilibrium position, for whatever reason, it can resort to the same domestic price and income changes that would have been forced on it by an imbalance under the gold standard.

A country can have almost any exchange rate it chooses, as long as the residents will accept the consequences of getting there. For example, a strong trade balance certainly contributes to a strong currency, and lower consumption/higher savings through lower incomes/higher taxes will help make the trade balance strong. These measures also support the currency through a reduction in inflation. The only problem is that people may not want to live that way.

In addition to the trade balance, monetary and fiscal policy may affect the exchange rate through the capital account. As indicated earlier, high real interest rates attract investment funds, and evidence of fiscal responsibility does encourage investor confidence. Net capital inflows supply direct support for the exchange rate.

Before we leave this discussion of governments and their exchange rates, it is interesting to consider whether monetary policy alone can really accomplish anything in the management of exchange rates. So far we have assumed that it can, but we need to present the alternative argument.

For monetary policy to affect the exchange rate through the trade balance, it must change the terms of trade. To do this, a change in the real, not the nominal, foreign exchange rate is required. When a government seeks to lower the exchange rate through monetary policy, the money supply will be increased, a strategy that usually lowers interest rates and increases economic activity. Lower rates contribute to capital outflow, and higher growth leads to a deficit on trade balance. If all else is equal, the result is a lower nominal exchange rate, but the increase in money supply is also inflationary. If the resulting inflation differential matches the exchange-rate move, the real exchange rate will be constant, and there will be no change in the terms of trade, or in the competitiveness of the country's goods and services. In this view, relative prices affect exchange rates, not vice versa. According to this argument, there is no simple relationship between the nominal exchange rate and the competitiveness or employment levels of a country, nor does the nominal-exchange-rate movement directly affect the trade balance.

A more conventional argument suggests a sluggish adjustment process. That is, it is possible to lower the foreign exchange rate by increasing the money supply, and there will be a useful time period in which exports are more competitive, before higher domestic inflation wipes out the relative price advantage. In other words, a trade deficit can be handled by weakening the currency. Observation suggests that this latter view has many supporters. Both the United States and Canada have had declining, or negative, trade balances in the 1980s, and there certainly has been much talk about overvalued dollars on both sides of the border.

2. Wage and Price Controls; Purchasing-Power Parity. Governments influence domestic price stability through regulation of the money supply and, in more extreme cases, with wage and price controls. These measures also affect the exchange rate through the linkage between inflation and the currency value. This linkage, called *purchasing-power parity*, deserves inspection.

In a world free from all impediments to trade, including information flows and transport costs, a given article would cost the same everywhere. Absolute purchasing-power parity requires that the exchange rate equal the ratio between domestic and foreign price levels. If a barrel of oil costs 20 USD in the United States and 40 DEM in Germany, then the exchange rate must be 2.0 DEM/USD, and the oil will cost the same in both countries. The purchasing-power parity view would be that the dollar will buy the same amount of oil in both countries; that is, its purchasing power is the same everywhere.

Because of market imperfections, transport costs, and various barriers to trade, absolute purchasing power is rarely found in practice. However, relative purchasing-power parity is more easily demonstrated. Relative purchasing power holds that, even though the purchasing power of a currency is not the same everywhere, relative price changes between countries will be matched by corresponding exchange-rate adjustments so that the purchasing-power relationship remains unchanged. In other words, the inflation differential will be offset by an exchange-rate adjustment. If country A has zero inflation and country B experiences 10 percent inflation, country B's currency must devalue by 10 percent relative to that of country A. The exchange-rate adjustment will maintain the ratio of the country's prices as it was before the inflation.

If relative purchasing power worked immediately and exactly, then monetary policy would not help in correcting a trade imbalance. Any change in relative price levels achieved by a money-supply change would be immediately offset by an exchange-rate move. In practice, relative purchasing power does influence rate adjustments, but with delay and with a great amount of noise in the system. The tendency is there, but many factors can distort the relationship in the short run. Purchasing-power parity theory says the real exchange rate never moves as a result of differential inflation, and is, therefore, relatively independent from and stable compared with the nominal rate. We know this is not true. Exhibits 2.1 to 2.5 show considerable real-rate movement in all the selected currencies, as well as a real rate correlated with the nominal. As a result, relative inflation can be a major factor in real-exchange-rate adjustments, and wage and price controls or other measures that influence the rate of inflation, even if only in the short run, are important in exchange-rate management.

3. Exchange Controls, Tariffs, and Quotas.   Finally, when more subtle approaches fail, governments can attempt to manage the supply-and-demand balance of their currencies by direct controls. Currency control usually means restrictions in freedom to use foreign currency at home or abroad. For example, domestic agents earning foreign exchange may be required to exchange it for domestic currency immediately at the central bank at a stipulated price. Access to foreign currency is tightly controlled, and it is released only for authorized purposes.

Tariffs and nontariff barriers to trade attempt to reduce demand for imports and thus reduce the supply of a currency on world markets. Overt trade barriers invite retaliation and are generally dysfunctional to the world economy, so much so that a great deal of effort has gone into negotiating treaties worldwide (or among particular groups of trading partners) to control the practice.

Summary: Why Foreign Exchange Rates Move

Currency exchange rates respond to the balance of supply-and-demand pressures in the marketplace. These pressures, which result from a wide variety of international transactions, are measured on a historical basis in the balance of payments statement. The marketplace is really the international payments system, which, in the last 80 years, has steadily evolved in the direction of more latitude and flexibility in exchange-rate adjustment.

Governments can modify currency supply-and-demand pressures through a variety of means, and they frequently do. In the case of floating currencies, they will act to moderate rate fluctuations or even try to push the rate in the direction considered desirable. To understand observed foreign-exchange-rate adjustments over time, one might start with a country's balance of payments statement for a historical perspective and then consider what changes in the supply-and-demand balance are likely to occur as a result of economic developments, what the governments involved would like to see, and how willing and able these governments are to get what they want.

Appendix 2.1
Evolution of the International Payments System

As suggested in Chapter 1, currencies and exchange rates originated as a means of facilitating trade in real goods and services. Domestic trade became much easier when currency was used in place of barter, and currency exchange rates were necessary to settle foreign trade accounts. In fact, our elaborate and sophisticated international payments system has evolved to allow countries to settle their international accounts.

The Gold System

Before 1914, payments between countries were made under what was known as the *gold system*. It was very simple compared with what we have today. Countries guaranteed to redeem their currencies on demand, for gold, at a specified and constant price. Thus, exchange rates between currencies were also frozen, based on this gold exchange standard. Given confidence in the ability and willingness of governments to exchange paper for gold at a fixed rate, individuals were content to hold and use gold certificates rather than the real thing.

The amount of gold required to back the paper money was actually quite small. England was able to maintain confidence in the pound sterling with less than 5 percent of the value of the paper money in circulation actually held as reserve in gold. At that time, sterling was by far the most important currency in world trade, and the economic strength of England was unquestioned. In addition, however, the very modest

38

reserves worked because the interest rate on sterling was adjusted to offset the demand for gold. When the bank experienced an outflow of reserves, it would raise the rediscount rate on commercial paper, which, in turn, attracted new deposits. Paper investments were thus made more attractive than gold, and the reserves were protected.

As a means of maintaining international equilibrium among countries, the gold standard was an iron disciplinarian. If you could not pay, you did not buy. Because each country was required to redeem its currency for gold, purchasing power depended entirely on gold supplies. Typically, if a country overbought, an outflow of gold would result. The gold outflow would cause a reduction in the domestic money supply, which would produce a reduction in the level of economic activity, with falling prices and incomes. Since the foreign exchange rate was fixed, a reduction in domestic prices would mean a real-exchange-rate move (decline) had occurred. This, in turn, would make exports cheaper and imports more expensive, producing a more positive trade balance. In addition to the price effect, the income effect also helped restore equilibrium. With falling domestic incomes the demand for imports would fall, and more resources would be available to supply the export markets.

The gold standard did have several problems which eventually caused it to break down. First, it was too inflexible. There was virtually no opportunity to shield a domestic economy from the pressures imposed on it from abroad. For example, one of the important mandates of most governments is to achieve full employment. Under the gold standard, however, there was little opportunity to avoid pressure for a recession. If the overall external balance was negative for any reason, even a temporary or self-correcting one, an economic slowdown was almost inevitable. Second, many governments wanted to be able to finance expenditures in excess of tax receipts by printing money. The gold system did not allow this. A third and more urgent problem concerned the inability of the gold system to handle and absorb large and sudden disequilibrium situations, such as those caused by war.

The Great War, that of 1914–1918, brought an end to the gold standard in its pure form. Following the war, there were several attempts to put it back together again, but Germany's hyperinflation, triggered in part by massive reparation payments, followed by the Depression beginning in 1930–1931, proved too great a burden. As the Depression became more pronounced, the pressure mounted on individual countries to improve employment. In an attempt to increase export demand, sterling was devalued in 1933, followed by a devaluation of the U.S. dollar in 1934. Belgium dropped the gold standard in 1935, and all other European gold standard countries followed suit in 1936.

The Bretton Woods Agreement

The Depression was ended by the Second World War. This war also brought pressures on the international payments system. Immediately following the war's conclusion, the leaders of the Western alliance moved to restore order in an attempt to speed the recovery of world trade and economic growth. In an agreement reached at Bretton Woods, New Hampshire, in 1944, all countries were required to fix or peg the value of their currencies to gold via dollars. However, they were not required to exchange their currencies for gold on demand, as was the case under the pure gold standard. Countries were required to exchange their currencies for dollars, and the dollar was to be convertible to gold at the request of central banks acting for their governments, at the rate of $35 per ounce.

The dollar's official convertibility immediately qualified it as a central bank reserve currency. As long as the United States was prepared to honor its commitments, the dollar was "as good as gold." Other countries held dollars as a reserve for their own currencies, and the presence of these dollar reserves provided confidence in the value of the individual currencies. These currencies, although pegged to the dollar, were initially not privately convertible either to gold or to dollars. As the economies recovered from the war, the currencies were eventually made convertible to dollars on demand. Pegged dollar exchange rates were maintained by central banks, and the banks were assisted in this process by the IMF, a lender to central banks created as part of the Bretton Woods Agreement. Countries provided resources to the IMF based roughly on their proportion of world trade, and the IMF made loans to central banks to support their currencies as required. Individual countries agreed not to engage in competitive devaluations. However, a country could devalue by up to 10 percent on its own initiative to correct a persistent trade balance problem. Countries, in general, followed IMF guidelines and were largely policed by their desire to stay on good terms with the IMF and with other members of the agreement.

The Bretton Woods Agreement provided much more latitude in the management of an individual country's economy. Countries were obliged to maintain their exchange rates relative to the dollar, but, in the short run at least, there were ways to do this without sacrificing domestic growth. IMF loans could be arranged, and even before that, it was usually possible to negotiate a loan from other central banks or even from the private sector. The loan proceeds would, of course, be used to buy back that country's currency in the open market and thus support the exchange rate. Meanwhile, it was not necessary to use domestic price and income adjustments to correct the external balance problem, and the domestic economy could proceed unimpeded.

All the major trading nations achieved full convertibility to dollars, not gold, by 1959. Because of this convertibility, countries could hold other major currencies such as sterling, Swiss francs, or deutsche marks as part of their official reserves, in addition to dollars. However, the system still worked on the basis of confidence in the dollar. The availability of dollars to boost reserves and support increases in the world money supply played a major part in the growth of world trade and in the general economic prosperity experienced in the decade before 1970.

As indicated, pegged exchange rates without the automatic adjustment system of the gold standard depend largely on confidence to hold their levels. Such a system invites speculators to take a position on what appears to be an undervalued or overvalued currency. If the currency can be forced to adjust, the speculators win. If not, the speculators liquidate their positions, paying only minor transaction costs. Sterling went through such speculative attacks as the decade drew to a close. In addition, and of more importance, the United States began to develop some payments problems of its own. Persistent trade deficits were exacerbated by the war in Vietnam. The offshore float of dollars became so large, relative to the gold held in reserve, that it strained the credulity of even America's friends. As it became increasingly obvious that the dollar was no longer worth one thirty-fifth of an ounce of gold, central banks and others holding dollars felt substantial exposure to the risk of devaluation. In August 1971, President Nixon bowed to the inevitable and suspended official purchases and sales of gold by the U.S. Treasury. In addition, a variety of constraints and controls were put in place to provide support for the dollar.

The Smithsonian Agreement

Suspension of official convertibility of the U.S. dollar to gold marked the end of the gold exchange system. The dollar could still be used as a reserve currency, but at the holder's risk. In the fall of 1971, most major trading currencies floated relative to the dollar. In December 1971, an attempt was made to re-establish the system with the Smithsonian Agreement. The dollar would be devalued from $35 to $38 per ounce of gold, and other major trading currencies would be revalued upward relative to the dollar by specific amounts. No attempt was made to make the dollar officially convertible to gold again, but currencies were once again pegged to the dollar, with a trading band of plus or minus 2.25 percent, rather than the 1 percent band used earlier.

The Smithsonian Agreement lasted less than a year. Market pressures were too great for the pegged-exchange-rate system to survive. The pound sterling floated in June 1972, the Swiss franc floated in January 1973, and the dollar devalued by 10 percent to $42.22 per ounce of gold in February 1973. Speculative interest in several of the major currencies continued to mount, and by the end of March 1973, all the major currencies were floating. The float was officially sanctioned at an IMF meeting in Jamaica in January 1976. IMF member quotas were increased to provide more lending power with which members could seek to smooth fluctuations in their exchange rates, and gold was demonetized as a reserve asset; that is, members were allowed to sell their gold reserves at market prices rather than at some officially prescribed par value. This floating-exchange-rate regime is still in effect today.

References

1. These criteria are originally attributed to Sir Maurice Parsons, "Stabilizing the Present International Payments System," *The International Adjustment Mechanism*, Federal Reserve Bank of Boston, Boston, 1970, p. 41.

3

The Money Markets

Executive Summary

Chapter 3 provides an overview of the North American money markets. The evolution of the markets and the key instruments are briefly reviewed. Market mechanics, including pricing, compound and effective interest, splits and safekeeping, and the yield curve, are examined. The chapter concludes with a brief discussion of the measurement of money-market returns, including cash versus accrual accounting and book losses.

Introduction

No free market is totally independent of all other markets. Foreign exchange markets principally affect and are affected by the stock markets, commodity markets, and bond and money markets. For the foreign exchange market, the money market is the most important.

Forward points (the spread between the spot and the forward exchange rate) perhaps best demonstrate the close relationship between the two markets. As explained in Chapter 7, forward points are really interest-rate differentials. Chapter 9 shows that a swap transaction, which is a simultaneous foreign currency purchase and sale but for different maturity dates, is really an interest-rate transaction priced and executed through the foreign exchange market.

This chapter briefly reviews some of the basic aspects of the money market that are helpful in understanding the foreign exchange market.

Overview of the Money Market

The U.S. money market is a wholesale market for short-term, high-quality debt instruments. Original maturities are one year or less, much of the trading is in very short maturities, and there is usually a very active secondary market. There is no central exchange. Trading is carried out on an over-the-counter basis in the trading rooms of investment dealers and banks, working with electronic communication rather than communicating face-to-face. The dollar size of individual trades is large; $100 million is not uncommon. The total market volume runs to hundreds of billions of dollars each day.

Before the formation of the Federal Reserve System in 1914, the money market was based on commercial paper, as well as call and time loans to securities dealers. With the Federal Reserve in operation, the federal (fed) funds market developed quickly, as a market in which Federal Reserve member banks borrow (buy) needed or lend (sell) surplus deposits to meet their reserve requirements with the Federal Reserve. The fed funds market is both active and large because member bank deposit levels at their district Federal Reserve banks fluctuate with the reserve system check-clearing activity. In addition, because no interest is paid on these deposits with the Federal Reserve Bank (the Fed), member banks are encouraged to keep the deposits to the minimum required by the reserve system.

The money market now serves two primary purposes. First, it provides the means by which the Fed can implement monetary policy as developed by the Federal Reserve Board. The open-market operations of the Fed involve the purchase or sale of government securities, which, in turn, control commercial bank reserves, credit expansion, and the money supply. For example, if the Fed buys securities from the commercial banks, payment will be credited to the banks' accounts at the Fed. (The actual transactions may be through brokers or dealers, but the effect is the same.) These additional reserves allow commercial banks to increase loans, therefore adding to the money supply and encouraging an easing of interest rates in the short term.

The second function of the money market is that of any capital market, to move resources from sectors with surplus funds to those in a deficit position. In the economy in general, the traditionally surplus sector is made up of individuals (households), while the deficit sector contains corporations. Governments are expected to be neutral. In the 1980s, however, governments in North America tended to become deficit sectors and joined corporations as net users of funds. Because the money market is a wholesale market, households tend to supply the savings through intermediation by financial institutions, although some individuals purchase money-market paper directly. On the demand side, corporations and governments issue paper to meet their funding needs, sometimes with terms and maturities to appeal to particular groups of investors. In the money market, however, many of the transactions reflect a need by economic sectors to manage their short-term cash flows, as opposed to the long-term transfer of funds.

There are about three dozen government security dealers in the United States, some of which are bank subsidiaries, and perhaps another two dozen banks that trade actively in the market. In addition, a number of brokers trade without positioning; that is, they never buy government paper to be held in inventory. They simply broker deals between two counterparties, which may be banks or dealers. There is no secondary market in fed funds, and there is only a limited one in banker's acceptances. The secondary market in treasury bills, commercial paper, and federal government agency paper is very active.

Money-Market Instruments

The principal instruments in the U.S. money market include fed funds, treasury bills and government agency notes, Eurodollars, certificates of deposit, commercial paper, banker's acceptances, and repurchase agreements. Each is briefly discussed in the next few pages.

Fed Funds

As previously indicated, the fed funds market is used by commercial banks to manage their reserve requirements efficiently. Because it permits the banks to hold only the minimum reserves, it makes the banking system more responsive to the monetary policy initiatives of the Federal Reserve Bank. Of the principal instruments, fed funds are the most liquid, interest-bearing, near-cash asset. Borrowers and lenders are well known to each other; credit risk is short-term, relatively small, and easily assessed. Due to the volatility of reserve levels, most loans are overnight, although fed funds are dealt for several months. An element of capital transfer may also exist in the market, such as when larger money center banks have loan opportunities that exceed their deposits and seek longer-term funding from smaller or regional banks.

The interest rate on fed funds is the base rate for the money market. Other instruments tend to be priced off fed funds, depending on relative liquidity and default risk. Before October 1979, the Fed used the fed funds rate as its primary instrument to implement monetary policy. For much of the 1980s, the emphasis has been on controlling the money supply, not the interest rate. As a result, the market has experienced sharply increased interest-rate volatility in the last decade, which certainly has had a destabilizing effect on markets in general. A second problem with management of the money supply is that of actually defining money and measuring the amount in circulation. As a result, the Fed is once again focusing on interest-rate management. The fed funds rate is perhaps the most important single rate in the U.S. money market.

Treasury Bills

The U.S. Treasury issues a variety of securities to finance government spending requirements. Instruments with an original maturity of one year or less are called *bills, notes* have maturities from one to ten years, and *bonds* are securities with a maturity of ten years or more. The district Federal Reserve Banks act as agents and will sell the securities without fees. "Governments" may also be purchased on a fee basis from dealers and brokers, for both primary and secondary distribution. Only a few issues, like savings bonds, are not negotiable. Bills are issued in three-, six-, and twelve-month maturities, with primary distribution by auction. Noncompetitive bidding, up to $1 million per bidder per auction, is available for buyers who want a guaranteed fill and are willing to accept the average auction price, whatever it turns out to be.

Banks, insurance companies, pension funds, and corporations are all large investors in treasury bills. Foreign central banks and institutions are also buyers, as are individuals, particularly when rates are high. Treasury bills offer virtual freedom from default risk, very good liquidity by virtue of the active secondary market, and freedom from taxation at the state level.

Eurodollars

The term *Eurodollar* is commonly used to refer to U.S. dollar balances held by foreign nationals. The prefix *Euro-* is derived from the evolution of the market, a market which originated in London. For many years, banks outside the United States had accepted deposits in U.S. dollars. However, during the 1950s tension between the Soviet Union and the United States began to change the nature of the market. Balances held by Eastern bloc countries in New York City banks were slowly transferred to banks in the United Kingdom. Concerns over the liquidity and safety of dollar deposits held on behalf of Warsaw Pact countries motivated the shift in funds. As the size of the market grew, so did interest in borrowing and lending offshore dollars free from U.S. government interference. Thus the market in Europe (i.e., the Eurodollar market) was born. Several other factors contributed to the growth and development of the Eurodollar market, most notably U.S. legislation that effectively taxed foreign issuers of U.S. dollar debt (the *interest equalization tax*), and Regulation Q, a law that effectively prevented banks from financing dollar loans in the United States.

Eventually these legislative barriers were removed (1974) in an attempt to regain market share and dollar-denominated business.

Today, the Eurodollar market is viewed as an extension of the domestic money market. The two markets are obviously closely related. In fact, Fed funds and overnight (o/n) Eurodeposits move in tandem with a spread of 1/16 between the two rates on average. The Euromarket is very active, with terms regularly quoted from overnight to one year. Each day a group of banks in London is asked to quote fixed-date (i.e., term) Euro rates, the average of which is used to price many corporate loan-and-swap agreements. The rates quoted are referred to as the 11:00 a.m. Libor fixing. The quotes in the Euromarket are typically 1/8 percent wide (bid-ask spread) with LIBID, LIMEAN, and LIBOR referring to the bid, mid-market, and offered side of the market, respectively.

Certificates of Deposit

In the late 1950s, commercial banks did not pay interest on corporate demand deposits. As corporate treasurers became more aggressive in the use of treasury bills and commercial paper as investment vehicles for short-term surplus funds, the banks countered with the negotiable certificate of deposit (CD). A CD is an unsecured bank liability in denominations of $100,000 and more. Original maturities range from two weeks to five years or more, and interest is paid on the face amount.

CD interest rates for prime banks average about 100 basis points higher than treasury bills, and regional banks may pay an additional 10 to 40 basis points. These differences reflect differences in liquidity and default risk. CD rates also increase in times of high loan demand when banks seek extra funding. As demand for the investor's money increases, the price of the money, i.e., interest rates, will also increase. The primary investors are mostly institutions and corporations that are usually seeking short-term, liquid, low-risk investments.

Longer-term CDs are sometimes issued on a variable-rate basis, with interest rates reset on three- or six-month intervals. There are no reserve requirements on CDs with a term of more than 18 months. Consequently, banks will sometimes issue long-term, fixed-rate CDs and swap them into floating-rate paper, and thereby achieve a useful reduction in floating-rate funding costs.

Commercial Paper

Commercial paper is the corporations' counterpart to the banks' CDs. Large and well-known corporations can issue their own paper, bypassing the intermediation of the banks. Finance companies typically issue directly to the investor, while most nonfinancial corporations distribute their commercial paper primarily through investment dealers; commercial banks are not authorized to distribute commercial paper on a primary basis.

Commercial paper (CP) has a fixed maturity, usually 30 days or less. Almost all paper is less than 270 days in original term; longer terms would have to be registered with the Securities and Exchange Commission (SEC). Most commercial paper is issued under SEC 3A3 exemption, which allows an issuer to issue without SEC registration and filing if the paper is under 270 days, is sold to sophisticated investors (not retail), and its use is current. Commercial paper is really an unsecured promissory note. Many investors purchase it with the expectation of holding it to maturity.

Many issuers expect to realize more or less permanent funding with this instrument by replacing or rolling the paper on maturity. This is usually possible, except in unusual and difficult market conditions. To guard against a liquidity problem, many issuers, for a small fee, back their outstanding paper with standby lines of credit at a bank.

The major buyers of commercial paper are banks, mutual funds, pension funds, and other corporations. Issuers will sometimes tailor the issue to the investor's needs. In the United States, fewer than 100 companies place paper directly, supplying more than half the market. Perhaps 1000 other issuers use dealers, who charge approximately 10 basis points on primary distribution. The paper is sold at a discount like treasury bills, and rates depend on the maturity, the amount, and the credit rating of the issuer. Rates are higher than treasury bill rates, reflecting more default risk and less liquidity.

Banker's Acceptance

A banker's acceptance (BA) is an unconditional order in writing to pay a specific sum to the bearer or designated party at a particular time. The paper has been "accepted" by a bank, which means the bank has guaranteed payment. The quality of the paper is as good as the credit of the bank giving the guarantee. Once accepted, the BA is a negotiable instrument.

In the United States, the primary role of the BA is to provide financing for international trade, and BAs are now used to some extent for domestic trade as well. For example, if an exporter wishes to extend credit to an importer, the exporter may issue a time draft, specifying payment at some time in the future. The importer accepts this draft, gaining possession of the goods, and returns the paper to the exporter. The exporter can hold this draft to maturity and collect at that time, or, as is almost always the case, the exporter can discount the draft; that is, sell it at a discount from face value to a bank. If the goods were shipped under a letter of credit, the draft already carries the guarantee of the importer's bank. For a small fee, the exporter's bank will add its acceptance to the paper. Historically speaking, there has been a very low default risk due to the underlying trade transaction supporting the BA and the guarantee provided by the bank(s). Consequently, BAs generate a low discount rate and thereby offer a relatively low-cost source of trade finance.

The accepting bank may hold the paper to maturity, or it can sell the paper in the market. Most original BA maturities are 30 to 180 days. The rate tends to be slightly lower than that for commercial paper, which bears only the guarantee of the issuing corporation. BAs, on the other hand, are actually a "two-name" debt instrument. Consequently, BAs are high-quality, highly liquid instruments. Securities dealers, money-market funds, central banks, corporations, and institutional investors all buy them. Individual denominations of $1 million and higher are common, and payment is usually made in federal funds.

Repurchase Agreements

Repurchase agreements (repos) are short-term collateralized loans used by securities dealers and other market participants as a source of low-cost financing for a securities inventory. Dealers often inventory securities far in excess of their equity. If rates are expected to decline, a dealer may wish to establish a substantial long position in debt instruments. Such positions can be financed with bank loans. The banks fund these loans with fed funds, adding a markup of 10 or 15 basis points. A less expensive form of financing for the dealer may be to sell some of the securities, usually federal government or agency paper, on an overnight basis with an agreement to buy them back the next day. Transfer of the securities is made by the Commissioner of Public Debt wire transfer system operated by the Federal Reserve. Longer-term sale and repurchase arrangements are also possible if a dealer wants longer-term financing.

Rates in the repo market are typically below federal funds rates. Fed funds trade on the credit of the borrowing bank with no additional collateral given to support the loan. The repo market, on the other hand, gives the investor possession of very high quality collateral. Corporations, money-market funds, and institutions with money to place overnight are the most active buyers of repos. The minimum amount is usually $5 million. The Fed is active in this market, using repos and reverse repos with government security dealers to make adjustments in bank reserves.

Dealers may also want to *short* the market if they believe rates will rise. To do this, they sell securities they do not own, expecting to buy them back at lower prices later. In order to deliver the securities, they may borrow them on the repo market. This transaction is called a *reverse repo*, or simply a *reverse*, because the initiative comes from the investor, not the borrower. In this case, the dealer is offering money for securities.

The Canadian Market

The Canadian market has developed more slowly than the U.S. money market, and there are a few differences.

In order for a money market to develop, borrowers and lenders willing to exchange large amounts of money for short periods of time are necessary, and suitable negotiable instruments must also be developed. These conditions were absent in Canada until the 1930s. Conditions began to change with the issuance of the first Government of Canada treasury bills in 1934. A central bank, the Bank of Canada, was formed the following year, and the chartered bank reserve adjustment operations were repatriated from London and New York to Canada. A small amount of outstanding treasury bills and a central bank do not, however, make a money market. Initially, only the commercial banks bought the bills, and there was little trading done.

In 1953, the Bank of Canada made lines of credit available to selected investment dealers, providing them with financing should their traditional lines with the chartered banks dry up. In turn, the banks began to make day-to-day loans available to the dealers, and agreed to make these loans and treasury bills part of their most-liquid assets, held as reserves with the central bank. The market now had well-financed dealers and at least one negotiable instrument, treasury bills.

The next step was taken by corporate borrowers, led by sales finance companies, who found they could fund part of their needs more cheaply by bypassing the banks and issuing their own paper directly. The business of many of these borrowers was highly seasonal, as was their need for funds. As a result, they were potentially both lenders and borrowers in the market. As investors, they could earn slightly higher returns than those available on bank deposits. Dealers developed the buy-back, or repurchase, market to accommodate both themselves and their customers. The banks, aided by the removal of the 6 percent rate ceiling on deposits by the Bank Act of 1967, developed new fixed-term deposit instruments, including notes in bearer form, and foreign currency swapped deposits.

Two other environmental factors helped shape the development of the Canadian money market. Because branch banking on a national basis was permitted, the Canadian banks were few in number, but they were large and sophisticated relative to the size of the economy. Many nonfinancial corporations, on the other hand, had close ties with U.S. parents or affiliates, and through them, had access to or knowledge of the burgeoning U.S. money market. These factors permitted much faster development of the market than would otherwise have been the case. In addition, Canada is much more of a trading nation, in relation to the size of its economy, than is the United States. As a result, the need for trade finance was high, and instruments, such as banker's acceptances, came into wide use very quickly.

Today the Canadian money market is similar to that in the United States, although obviously much smaller and less liquid. The Investment Dealers Association reports total money-market trading in 1988 on the order of $1.2 trillion, with almost half the market in treasury bills, followed by commercial paper and BAs. Canada does not have a direct counterpart to the U.S. fed funds market; Canadian chartered banks do not yet swap deposits at the Bank of Canada to manage reserve requirements, as do their American counterparts. However, in many other respects, the markets are similar.

Pricing and Dealing the Markets

We have looked at the markets and the types of instruments traded in these markets. Now we will briefly consider the actual dealing practices in the markets and the way the instruments themselves are priced.

Standard Dates

Like foreign exchange markets, money markets have standard dealing dates. Overnight, one-, two-, three-, six-, and twelve-month dates are standard. However, some markets view one month as 30 days beyond the current date, while others treat one month as 30 days beyond the current spot date, which is two business days from the current date. Individual issuers may deal to a range of standard and nonstandard dates depending on their views or maturity requirements.

Discount Pricing

Money-market instruments can be issued on either a discount or an interest-bearing basis. Most wholesale instruments in the United States and Canada are on a discount basis. However, the term *discount* tends to have different meanings in the two markets. In both cases, discount instruments specify the amount to be received at maturity, usually a round number such as $5 million. The investor will pay the issuer a lesser amount. The difference in the two amounts represents the interest, or discount, on the transaction.

In the U.S. T-bill market, a rate or price quoted to an investor is the amount of money that the investor would need to pay for every $100 of face value that is purchased. For instance, if the rate on one-year T-bills was 10 percent, the price of the bills would be $90.00. An amount equal to $900,000 would need to be paid to purchase $1 million worth of bills. Interest earned would be $100,000, which indeed represents an annual yield of 10 percent, on the face value amount. However, the investor actually earned the $100,000 on an initial cash outlay of only $900,000. The true return, or effective yield, on this investment is 11.11 percent:

$$\frac{(\text{Interest} \times \text{rate basis/term})}{\text{principal}} = \text{effective interest rate}$$

$$\frac{\$100,000 \times 360/360}{\$900,000} = 11.11\%$$

For some money-market products in the United States and for all money-market products in Canada, the rates that are quoted reflect the rate that is earned on the actual cash proceeds initially invested. It represents a true yield earned on the funds and is referred to as a *money-market yield*. The initial purchase price of a money-market-yielding instrument can be determined in different ways. Conceptually, an investment at maturity consists of the original principal plus interest. When this amount at maturity is divided by the initial principal, a compounding factor is determined, as shown in Exhibit 3.1.

If an investment is for $1 million for 90 days at 10 percent, the compounding factor would be as follows:

$$1 + \frac{.10 \times 90}{360} = 1.0250$$

Exhibit 3.1. Calculation of Compound Factor

$$\frac{\text{Principal} + \text{interest}}{\text{Principal}} = \text{compounding factor}$$

If the principal is 1, the compounding factor can be determined by the following formula:

$$\frac{1 + \left(\frac{\text{rate}}{100} \times \frac{\text{term}}{\text{rate basis}}\right)}{1}$$

In other words, for every one USD invested today for 90 days at 10 percent, the maturing principal and interest will be 1.0250 times as much.

Conversely, if we know the maturing amount, we can similarly calculate the amount to invest by dividing the maturing amount by the compounding factor of 1.0250. If the maturing amount is $1 million, the amount to invest today that will earn 10 percent for 90 days is $975,609.75.

$$\$1,000,000/1.0250 = \$975,609.75$$

The amount invested can be thought of as the price for the maturing $1 million note. In this case, the price before rounding is .97560975 per dollar. In practice, some instruments are not rounded and the price reflects all decimal points. Prices on other instruments are rounded to, perhaps, five decimal places (.97561) or are expressed as a price per $100 and rounded to three decimal places (97.561). For the sake of illustration, rounding is used in the examples that follow.

It should be noted that the rounding on price causes a slight increase or decrease in the cashflows; this results in a slight change in the interest paid and received. Consequently, the true interest rate is slightly different from that quoted. One should also recognize that the same price can be generated for different yields, a characteristic especially prevalent for short-dated product. For instance, yields of 9.96 through 10 percent on a seven-day product generate the same price and, consequently, are identical from a cashflow standpoint. As the term increases, this phenomenon is less pronounced, as outlined in Exhibit 3.2.

The concept of price is common in money-market transactions and is determined by simply taking the reciprocal of the compounding factor determined above.

$$1/\text{compounding factor} = \text{price}$$

Exhibit 3.2. Calculation of Price for Various Terms

Term, days	Yield, %	Price
7	9.96	99.809
7	10.00	99.809
270	9.96	93.138
270	10.00	93.112

A shortcut to determining price is to combine the two formulas:

$$\text{Price} = \frac{1}{1 + [(\text{rate}/100) \times (\text{term}/\text{rate basis})]}$$

When issuing CAD money-market products such as banker's acceptances, the borrower receives less than the face value. Because of this shortfall, a perception frequently occurs that the interest is paid up front, as opposed to in arrears, which is the norm. The key to resolving this issue is to determine if the interest paid is on the net cash proceeds exchanged on day 1 or on the actual face value. If the interest is calculated based on the face value, such as on U.S. treasury bills, and this interest is then subtracted from the face value, then one could indeed say the interest is paid up front:

Face value	$1,000,000	
Interest	100,000	$\left(\frac{1,000,000 \times 360}{360} \times .10\right)$
Net proceeds	$ 900,000	

While this methodology is more straightforward to calculate, it does have the inherent weakness of not accurately reflecting the true rate that was earned. In this case, the investor earns an effective yield of 11.11 percent, and not 10 percent.

$$100,000 / \frac{(900,000 \times 360)}{360} = 11.11\%$$

If the interest is calculated on the net proceeds received, the interest cannot be said to be paid up front, nor does the formula need any adjustments. The borrower receives cash on day 1 and then repays that principal plus the interest on that principal at maturity.

To verify this, consider an example where a borrower wants to issue

Exhibit 3.3. Verification That Interest Is Paid in Arrears on Money-Market Notes

Price: $1/\left[1 + \dfrac{.12 \times 90}{365}\right] = \quad 97.126$

Principal: $\dfrac{\$10,000,000 \times 97.126}{100} = \$\ 9,712,600$

Interest: $\dfrac{9,712,600 \times .12 \times 90}{365} = \quad 287,400$

Principal + Interest $\qquad \$10,000,000$

$10 million in CAD BAs for 90 days at 12 percent. The price and proceeds are determined in Exhibit 3.3.

One of the major reasons for dealing on a discount or money-market basis is to facilitate trading in the secondary market. Borrowers or issuers of such notes usually sell the notes to banks and investment dealers. These intermediaries then sell the notes to the end investor. Some investors hold money-market assets until maturity, but many will sell the notes before maturity. A particular note may thus wind its way through several hands during its economic life. In addition, an issue of notes by one borrower may be sold in smaller amounts to many different investors.

Consider the scenario in Exhibit 3.4, where a dealer has $40 million in inventory of Company XYZ negotiable interest-bearing notes, all of which mature in 90 days. Moreover, the paper was issued anywhere

Exhibit 3.4. Sample Inventory of Interest-Bearing Notes

Date of issue	Face amount issued, MM CAD	Original term, days	Re-maining term, days	Interest rate, %	Initial proceeds	Amount at maturity
Day 1	10	270	90	10	$10,000,000	$10,739,726
Day 91	10	180	90	15	10,000,000	10,739,726
Day 121	1	150	90	13	10,000,000	10,534,247
Day 181	10	90	90	12	10,000,000	10,295,890
Total	40				$40,000,000	$42,309,589

Exhibit 3.5. Sample Inventory of Money-Market Notes

Date of issue	Face amount issued, MM CAD	Original term, days	Re-maining term, days	Interest rate, %	Initial proceeds	Amount at maturity
Day 1	10	270	90	10	$ 9,311,200	$10,000,000
Day 91	10	180	90	15	9,311,200	10,000,000
Day 121	1	150	90	13	9,492,800	10,000,000
Day 181	10	90	90	12	9,712,600	10,000,000
Total	40				$37,827,800	$40,000,000

from 1 to 180 days previous. The interest rates at time of issue also varied, from 10 to 15 percent.

If a dealer wanted to sell some Company XYZ paper from inventory, the dealer would have to specify the particular notes being sold, as the maturity amounts differ from issue to issue. In Exhibit 3.4, the information is available and would not seem to pose much of a problem. However, dealers can have hundreds of different pieces of inventory; and if the available denominations required the dealer to take some notes from several different issues, the dealer would have to calculate the appropriate discounted amount for each grouping of notes and then determine the total proceeds required from the investor. This task, though straightforward as it seems, is time-consuming and inefficient.

If the notes were traded on a discount basis, the dealer would have an inventory that looks like the one shown in Exhibit 3.5.

Selling product from this inventory is much easier than from the interest-bearing inventory because the maturing notes all have a round number for a maturity value. A $1 million note has a maturity value of $1 million regardless of when it was issued or at what rate. This homogeneity of product at maturity facilitates trading because notes for a particular guarantor with the same maturity can all be lumped together.

Rate Basis

Interest rates are the price of money. The investor or lender earns the interest rate; the borrower pays the interest rate. The amount of interest paid or earned on a transaction is a function of four items:

	Transaction A	Transaction B
1. Principal	$1,000,000	$1,000,000
2. Term	360 days	90 days
3. Interest rate	10%	10%
4. Rate basis	360 days	360 days

The formula for calculating interest is

$$\frac{\text{Principal} \times \text{interest rate}}{100} \times \frac{\text{term}}{\text{rate basis}}$$

The interest rate quoted in money markets reflects an annualized rate. In some currencies, the normal annualized rate quoted reflects a term of 360 days. For others, most of which are in the British Commonwealth, the annualized term or rate basis is 365 days. A listing of various countries' rate bases is given in Exhibit 3.6.

If the transaction term matches the rate basis, as in transaction A, the interest would be the full rate quoted (i.e., 10 percent) of the principal. If the transaction term and rate basis differ, such as in transaction B, which has a term of only 90 days, the interest is adjusted by the ratio of the term divided by the rate basis.

$$90/360 = 25\% \text{ of annual interest}$$

The difference between a 360- and 365-day rate basis can be quite significant. Consider a 90-day investment of $10 million at 10 percent:

Exhibit 3.6. Summary of Rate Basis for Various Countries

360 days	365 days
Australia	Belgium
France	Canada
Germany	Hong Kong
Italy	Singapore
Japan	South Africa
Netherlands	United Kingdom
Switzerland	
United States	

$$\frac{\$10,000,000 \times .10 \times 90}{365} = \$246,575.34$$

$$\frac{\$10,000,000 \times .10 \times 90}{360} = \$250,000.00$$

The difference of $3,424.66 is due entirely to the rate basis and effectively works out to 13.9 basis points when rates are at 10 percent. In other words, 10.139 percent on a 365-day basis is basically equal to 10 percent on a 360-day basis.

$$\frac{\$10,000,000 \times .10139 \times 90}{365} = \$250,002.73$$

To determine the rate differential for other levels of interest rates, simply follow these guidelines:

1. To convert rates quoted on a 360-day basis to their 365-day equivalent, first multiply the rate by 365 and then divide by 360.
2. To convert rates quoted on a 365-day basis to their 360-day equivalent, divide the rate by 365 and then multiply by 360.

Other interest-rate transactions may use a different basis. Credit cards may use terms such as 2 percent per month. The 2 percent sounds low until one recognizes that the adjustment to an annualized basis involves multiplying it by 12. When compounding of interest is considered, the next issue addressed, the effective interest rate is considerably higher than 24 percent (2 × 12).

Compound Interest

Consider two investments of $10 million at 10 percent for 360 days. The rate basis is 360 days.

Investment A has the interest paid once, at maturity. Total principal and interest at maturity is $11 million.

Principal		$10,000,000
Interest	$\dfrac{(10,000,000 \times .1 \times 360)}{360}$	1,000,000
Principal and interest		$11,000,000

Investment B has interest paid semiannually. If the initial interest paid in 180 days is not reinvested, the final principal and interest is also $11 million.

Principal		$10,000,000
Interest: Day 180	$\left(\dfrac{10,000,000 \times .1 \times 180}{360}\right)$	500,000
Day 360	$\left(\dfrac{10,000,000 \times .1 \times 180}{360}\right)$	500,000
Principal and interest		$11,000,000

However, the investor would assuredly reinvest the interest received on day 180 and thus further enhance the earnings on the investment. Assume the reinvestment rate of the interest was again at 10 percent.

Compound interest	$\left(\dfrac{500,000 \times .10 \times 180}{360}\right)$	25,000
Total principal and interest		$11,025,000

The effect of compounding interest is significant and must be watched from both a personal and a business standpoint. Consider Exhibit 3.7, the credit card example in which the rate was 2 percent per month.

A rate of 2 percent per month before compounding is equivalent to 24 percent annual interest (2 × 12). On $1000, the interest would be $240. However, because of compounding, $240 interest was reached before the end of November, and the total interest is $268.23. The effective rate is, therefore, 26.82 percent.

Exhibit 3.7. Compound Interest Calculations at 2% per Month

Month	Beginning principal, $	Interest at 2%, $	Ending principal and interest, $
January	1,000	20	1,020
February	1,020	20.40	1,040.40
March	1,040.40	20.81	1,061.21
April	1,061.21	21.22	1,082.43
May	1,082.43	21.65	1,104.08
June	1,104.08	22.08	1,126.16
July	1,126.16	22.52	1,148.68
August	1,148.68	22.97	1,171.65
September	1,171.65	23.43	1,195.08
October	1,195.08	23.90	1,218.98
November	1,218.98	24.38	1,243.36
December	1,243.36	24.87	1,268.23

Exhibit 3.8. Time Required for Money to Double, Annual Compounding

Interest rate, %	Number of years for money to double
2	35
4	18
6	12
8	9
10	7.3
12	6.1
14	5.3
16	4.7
18	4.2
20	3.8

Another example of the significance of compounding is the time it takes for money to double in value. A summary is given in Exhibit 3.8.

Effective Interest Rates

One result of compound interest is that the stated yield may not reflect the true or effective interest rate. The effect of compounding as shown above is one example. Another is found in some forms of discount pricing, such as on U.S. treasury bills, where we saw that a quoted yield of 10 percent represents a true yield of 11.11 percent.

In any investing or borrowing transaction, a key step in calculating the true interest rate is to determine the actual interest paid or earned. Let us use the $10 million investment example in the previous section on rate basis to illustrate a simple way of determining dollar interest:

1.	Total cashflow at maturity (i.e., principal plus interest)	$11,025,000
2.	Less cashflow at inception (i.e., the principal)	10,000,000
3.	Equals interest	$ 1,025,000

To calculate the effective interest rate, the following formula is used:

$$\left(\text{Interest} \times \frac{\text{rate basis}}{\text{term}} \right) / \text{principal}$$

$$\left(\$1,025,000 \times \frac{360}{360} \right) / 10,000,000 = 10.25\%$$

One first annualizes the interest by multiplying the interest ($1,025,000) by the ratio of rate basis (numerator of 360) divided by the term (denominator of 360). Finally, one determines what percentage the annualized interest is of the principal. The result is the effective interest rate.

As another example, recall the credit card charge of 2 percent per month. Assume the interest rate was 2 percent per 30-day period, not 2 percent per month. Annualizing the interest of $268.23 to 365 days, we find the effective interest rate on the credit card is 27.20 percent, again considerably higher than the implied 24 percent.

$$\left(268.23 \times \frac{365}{360}\right)/1000 = 27.20\%$$

Bid and Offer

Similar to foreign exchange markets, money markets trade on a two-way, or bid-and-offer basis. Consider the following 30-day T-bill rates:

USD Eurodollar deposits	8.23–25%
CAD banker's acceptances	10.23–20%

The 8.23 percent bid on the USD Eurodollar deposits represents the market maker's willingness to buy cash in exchange for a bank deposit receipt at 8.23 percent.

The 10.23 percent bid on the CAD banker's acceptance represents the market maker's willingness to buy BAs in exchange for cash at 10.23 percent.

Knowing whether the bid is a bid for cash or a bid for paper is made easier by recalling the axioms:

1. Market makers will buy low and sell high

or

2. The bid-and-offer spread works in favor of the market maker.

In the money markets, buying low and selling high is obvious when dealing in prices. When it comes to dealing in yields, the market maker wants to earn the highest yield and pay the lower yield. Thus, the higher rate in a two-way market reflects the rate at which the market maker will give up cash (i.e., invests or lends) and take paper. The lower rate reflects the rate at which the market maker will take cash (i.e., borrow) and give up paper.

Money-Market Points

Consider the following market yields and prices for CAD banker's acceptances:

	30-day term		60-day term	
	Bid	Offer	Bid	Offer
Yields	10.23 %	10.20 %	10.23 %	10.20 %
Prices	99.166	99.169	98.346	98.351

If a market maker buys and sells $10 million at the same time, the cash profits would be as follows:

	30-day term	60-day term
Price paid	$ 9,916,900	$ 9,835,100
Price given	(9,916,600)	(9,834,600)
Trading gain	300	500
Transaction costs	(100)	(100)
Net gain	$ 200	$ 400

In both cases, the market maker made three basis points on trading. The cash profits vary significantly, however, because of the impact of term and the transaction costs. Also note that while the 60-day term is double the term of the 30-day term, the trading gain profit is not double. There are three main reasons for this:

1. The price on the transaction is truncated at three decimal places, which can skew the margins one way or the other.
2. The spread of three points is calculated on the initial principal that is dealt up front. The 60-day product involves less principal.
3. The actual interest is earned over the life of the investment and received at maturity. In this case where the product was bought and sold, the profit of three points is discounted and received in today's dollars. On the 60-day term, the three points for the initial 30 days is more profitable than the three points on the second 30-day period. A reverse form of interest compounding comes into play.

In contrast, in foreign exchange markets, a point profit is essentially a point profit. A bid-and-offer of three points would yield $3000 on a $10 million deal (10,000,000 × .0003). The term of the transaction does not have this same effect, although on forward markets, the cash profit is often not realized in terms of cashflow until the actual forward contracts settle. Consequently, the time value of money will come into play and reduce the current value of the profit. However, in nominal terms, a point profit remains a point profit.

From a dealing standpoint, it is usually harder to make money trading money markets than it is trading foreign exchange. There are several reasons:

1. The bulk of money-market transactions are 90 days or less, which causes any "point" revenues to be smaller because of the impact of the term. On the other hand, transaction costs are essentially the same whether a deal is for 2 weeks or 1 year.

2. Competitive pressures are often as high on money markets as they are on foreign exchange, which tends to keep the bid-and-offer spreads narrow.

3. It is just as easy to go short a currency as it is to go long. In the money markets, it is typically harder to go short because of the risk of not being able to buy the product shorted, or at least not being able to buy the product back at a reasonable price. A dealer caught in a short position, on, say, commercial paper, can get squeezed by the longs and have to pay a premium in order to get covered. Moreover, while futures, forward rate agreements, and when-issued markets exist, all of which facilitate taking both long and short positions, they only exist on a few key products in a limited number of currencies.

   Consequently, money-market dealers tend to make most of their money on commissions for distribution of commercial paper, on margins taken on smaller deals, and from profits from trading their portfolios. Trading profits are generated on the bid-and-offer spreads as well as positioning of the portfolios to take advantage of market swings. When interest rates are expected to decline (i.e., prices go up), dealers will try to own large amounts of inventory. When rates go up (and prices decline), dealers try to reduce inventories and minimize losses.

4. Holding foreign exchange positions does not usually involve utilizing many assets. Leverage is very high. Buying money-market assets essentially involves a dollar of cash for every dollar of product held. Leverage is basically nonexistent in most money-market dealings.

5. Arbitrage transactions in the money market can involve the creation of additional assets. If return on assets is a concern, which it is in banking, many transactions that would generate profits are not executed because they do not make enough of a spread to meet the required rates of return. Moreover, such activities increase the credit risk faced by the organization (will the borrowers repay?) and may also use up some of its sources for funding ongoing activities.

6. Holding of product requires the dealer to finance the inventory. Frequently, dealers finance money-market inventories by raising short-term cash, often on an overnight basis. Overnight financing involves daily compounding of interest, which can make it a very expensive proposition, especially if the yield curve is inverted. In such an environment, for example, 90-day paper yielding 13 percent could be financed by overnight money that costs 14 percent.

Yield Curve

An interest rate is the price for the use of money for a given period of time. For each future date, there is a specific interest rate for each specific instrument. When all the dates are put together, a line connecting all the rates can be drawn. This line is called the *yield curve*.

We saw before that interest rates vary according to the creditworthiness of the guarantor of the paper. Federal government paper is the starting point for interest rates and is usually the paper on which yield curves are determined. However, a yield curve can be constructed for any kind of investment-grade paper. In fact, it is a recommended exercise to do when actively involved in the various money-market products.

Interest rates generally vary along a yield curve. The variation can occur for several reasons, three of which are as follows:

1. *Compounding of interest.* All else being equal, shorter-term interest rates are lower than longer-term rates due to compounding. A single deal for 1 year has no compounding. A series of 30-day rollovers does. Consequently, for the two to be equivalent, the longer-term rate needs to be higher than the 30-day rate.

2. *Price risk.* The price of a negotiable money-market instrument is affected by term and rate. The longer the term, the greater the change in price for a given change in yield. There is also a greater risk of shifts in the yield curve. Consequently, this risk of price movement will tend to cause investors to command a higher rate for longer terms.

3. *Credit risk.* The farther into the future one goes, the more possible that the credit status of any guarantor can deteriorate.

4. *Expectations.* The expectations of changes in short-term rates will affect the slope of the yield curve. Long-term rates are, in some sense, an average of expected future short-term rates.

It should also be noted that different groupings of borrowers will pay higher interest rates because of the perceived higher credit risk. Consequently, at any point in time there are actually a number of yield curves.

Chapter 7 discusses forward points and demonstrates that they are a

Exhibit 3.9. Positive and Inverted Yield Curves

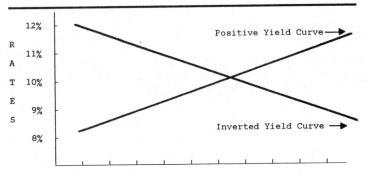

result of interest differentials and are not a market forecast of future spot exchange rates. The yield curve, on the other hand, is a consensus forecast of future interest rates. The factors mentioned above all indicate that interest rates should increase with term. A positive, or upward-sloping, yield curve should result. As a general rule, this is the case. However, longer-term rates can be less than shorter-term rates when the market believes that interest rates are going to decline. This expected decline can be due to a number of reasons, such as market expectations of a slowdown in the economy or a decline in inflation. This scenario is called an *inverted yield curve.*

The interest rate for any particular term can be viewed as an average of the expected rates for the interim periods, compounding included. If rates are expected to decline and then increase again, the yield curve could include a series of positive and inverted yield curves (see Exhibits 3.9 and 3.10).

Rates can also change due to abnormal market or technical conditions.

Fears of major defaults typically will send investors on a "flight to quality," where they want to hold short-term, high-quality credit paper,

Exhibit 3.10. Positive and Inverted Yield Curves

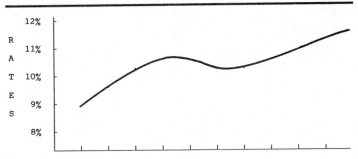

such as U.S. government T-bills. The demand for this paper causes their prices to rise (and yields to fall), which will usually cause the short end of the yield curve for T-bills to decline. Alternatively, the demand for lesser-quality credit paper declines so that the respective yields for it rise (and prices fall), especially in the longer term. In all terms, the spread between government and lower-quality paper will widen.Both would be more positive than they were before. The key difference is that the change on the T-bill is due to a decline in the short end, while the change in slope for the commercial paper yield curve is due to a larger increase in the longer end than in the short end.

Another factor that can cause rates to shift significantly is a shortage of paper for a particular term for which there is strong demand. This will cause prices to rise and yields to fall. Alternatively, a surplus of paper can cause prices to fall and yields to rise.

Real and Nominal Interest Rates

Chapter 2 explained real and nominal exchange-rate movements. A nominal exchange-rate move is one that is completely offset by inflation. A real exchange-rate move occurs when a nominal move is only partially offset by inflation, or is in the opposite direction to what would normally be expected, given inflation differentials.

Interest rates have an inflationary and real component as well. Fixed-income investors want to earn a return on their investments in financial instruments that at least exceeds the base inflation rate. If not, they tend to seek other investment alternatives that provide a hedge against inflation. The degree to which the nominal interest rate exceeds the inflation rate is called the *real rate of return*. This relationship is typically viewed as follows:

$$\text{Real rate} = \text{nominal rate} - \text{inflation rate}$$

$$5\% = 10\% - 5\%$$

Although many practitioners view real rates in this way, the actual relationship is as follows:

$$1 + \text{real rate} = \frac{1 + \text{nominal rate}}{1 + \text{inflation rate}}$$

$$1.047619 = \frac{1 + 10}{1 + .05}$$

and the real rate of return is only about 4.76 percent, not 5 percent as shown in the approximation. The reason is because the inflation reduces the purchasing power of the interest earned as well as that of the principal.

The real interest rate can also be calculated on a current time basis as well, as the current nominal interest rate less the current inflation rate. The expression *real interest rate* has many interpretations. For example, the term of interest rate, the use of historical as opposed to expected inflation, the actual means by which inflation is measured, and the impact of tax on investors and borrowers can all produce variation in the calculated result. However, a simple, but useful, way to calculate the real interest rate is as follows:

Current 90-day federal government interest rate
minus
The change in the consumer price index for the last 12 months
equals
The corresponding real interest rate

Real rates and real-rate movements are important for several reasons:

1. The higher the real rates of return, the more likely that foreign investors will invest in the currency on an unhedged basis. Foreign borrowers will also tend to shy away from unhedged borrowings in that currency. The more buying and less selling of a currency, the stronger the currency will be.
2. The higher the real interest rate, the greater the likelihood of a stronger currency, with the following types of pressure on the domestic economy:
   a. Higher interest rates will reduce domestic demand, slowing the economy.
   b. A stronger currency will tend to increase imports and decrease exports, both of which will also tend to slow the economy.
   c. Higher interest rates add to inflation because of extra financing costs that producers have to recoup. However, more significant deflationary pressures arise from the reduction in economic growth caused by the higher interest rates. In addition, lower import prices also tend to reduce inflation.
   d. Lower economic growth tends to reduce government revenues and increase government expenditures. If a country is running fiscal surpluses (a rare event these days), the surplus will be smaller. The more likely result is a higher deficit, which adds further upward pressure on interest rates because of the government's increased demand for funds.

Splits

Money-market instruments can be issued in various denominations. Some discount instruments are issued in denominations small enough for the average retail investor to buy. Other instruments are issued in larger denominations and are geared to wholesale investors.

For example, a commercial paper issuer, Comm Pap Inc., which wants to raise $10 million in 30-day paper at 10 percent (price = 99.185), may be asked to issue the notes as outlined in Exhibit 3.11.

To meet this request, 17 notes will be required. One note would be preferable from an administrative-cost point of view, but this is usually not feasible because issuers, such as Comm Pap Inc., must ultimately respect the desires of the investor(s).

If a single note was issued and bought by a dealer, the investor group to which the note can subsequently be sold is a small portion of the total investor base:

1. Only investors with $10 million to spend are candidates.

2. Not all investors with the $10 million to spend will want to invest for the maturity date on the note.

3. Investors should have limits on how much of a single issuer's paper they will own. The $10 million may exceed many limits.

4. Some investors are active traders and want to be able to easily resell the paper they buy. If there is a restricted market for the block, they may be reluctant to buy it.

The market for the issue is thus reduced. However, if the splits are issued as requested, there is considerably more flexibility in putting together different combinations to meet various investors' needs. Exhibit 3.12 provides an illustration.

It should be noted that on instruments such as commercial paper, where the issuer is clearly identifiable, a dealer in possession of notes can often exchange them in return for notes with smaller splits.

On the other hand, interest-bearing items such as bank deposits,

Exhibit 3.11. Example Splits on Issuance of Commercial Paper

Note amount	Number of notes	Total face value	Net proceeds
$5,000,000	1	$ 5,000,000	$4,959,250
1,000,000	2	2,000,000	1,983,700
500,000	4	2,000,000	1,983,700
100,000	10	1,000,000	991,850
Total	17	$10,000,000	$9,918,500

Exhibit 3.12. Example of Splits Required for Investor Base

	Splits needed for investor				Total investment
	100,000	500,000	1,000,000	5,000,000	
Open inventory	10	4	2	1	$10,000,000
Investor A		3	2		3,500,000
Investor B	3				300,000
Investor C	3	1		1	5,800,000
Total	6	4	2	1	$ 9,600,000
End inventory	4	0	0	0	$ 400,000

which are nonnegotiable, are issued in the one note. Moreover, because an even amount is not required at maturity or at inception to aid secondary trading, these notes can be issued for any amount, for example, $358,123.45. This flexibility, made available by the direct relationship between the issuer and the investor, allows investors to invest every single penny they have on hand, to the exact desired date.

Negotiable and Nonnegotiable Instruments

Bank term deposits typically represent the funding of loan activities. On many deposits, the name of the buyer is put on the actual note, and the note is not allowed to be sold or transferred to another buyer. The note is thereby registered. It usually cannot be redeemed before maturity, and if early redemption is allowed, a significant interest penalty is charged. Such instruments are termed *nonnegotiable* because they cannot be readily traded or exchanged for cash. If the physical note is stolen, the true owner is protected because the registered note is only of value to the investor whose name is on the note.

Other instruments, such as treasury bills, are negotiable. The owner can sell them at any time. The note is a general promissory note, payable to the bearer on demand. Bearer form simply means that the note is not registered to a specific owner. Therefore, it is deemed to be the property of the person or corporation that submits it for sale or redemption (i.e, the bearer). The physical safety of the note is critical because whoever holds the note can present it for payment.

Safekeeping and Issuance

A money-market transaction involves the investor lending money to the borrower for a specified period of time. At maturity, the borrower pays back the original principal and interest.

In the case of a bank deposit, the bank knows the investor, and the entire transaction can be very simple. The bank can debit the customer's account at inception and credit it on maturity. A term deposit receipt would be issued confirming the details.

Other transactions are not so simple. Comm Pap Inc., which issued $10 million in commercial paper, as shown in Exhibit 3.11, will issue the notes in exchange for cash. At maturity, however, Comm Pap Inc. may have no idea who owns the notes. If the original buyer was a dealer, the notes could have been sold to one or several investors. Moreover, these investors may, in turn, sell some or all of the paper themselves before maturity. The original $10 million could conceivably be owned by seventeen different investors, each owning one note. In addition, the investors could be located throughout the world.

To facilitate payment and control, money markets have centralized payment and delivery locations. Borrowers appoint a financial institution to look after the issuance and redemption of the notes. At the time of issuance, this issuing and paying agent specifies, in accordance with the instructions of the issuer, the total amount to issue, the splits, the name of the buyer(s), the price, and the amount of cash that the notes are to be sold for. On presentation of payment, usually a certified check, wire transfer, or equivalent form of guaranteed payment, the notes are exchanged. The name of the agent is listed on the actual notes so that investors know where to present the notes at maturity for repayment.

Investors may have a financial institution that does similar work for them. This safekeeping organization will hold the notes for the investor and exchange them for payment as notes are sold or matured.

Book-Based Money Market

In the case of U.S. government treasury bills, no physical note is actually issued. Rather, bills are bought and sold via a book-based computer system, which keeps track of the owners of the bills. On the basis of the U.S. Treasury's having $500 billion in bills outstanding with an average term of 90 days, $2 trillion worth of bills would need to be sold each year.

$$(\$500 \text{ billion} \times 360)/90 = \$2000 \text{ billion}$$

If the average size of an individual bill were even $1 million, 2 million T-bills would need to be printed and handled, if the market worked on a paper issuance basis. The administration of a paper system would be slow and expensive. The book-based system is much more efficient and will no doubt be extended to more products in more countries in the future.

Interest-Rate-Driven Transactions Using the Foreign Exchange Market

Chapter 9 outlines several kinds of swap transactions that involve both the foreign exchange and money markets:

1. Investment swaps

2. Financing swaps

3. Cash-management swaps

4. Money-market hedge

In the context of the banking industry, major banks will typically have a deposit base with funds to invest in a variety of currencies for a variety of terms. Seldom, it seems, do the currencies and terms requested by the depositors match the borrowers' needs.

For instance, Bank A may receive a deposit in Swiss francs for a one-month term from Client B. Client C wants to borrow one-month USD. This currency mismatch is handled by simply doing a swap to sell Swiss francs spot against USD and buy them back forward. The swap generates USD for the bank which it uses to fund the USD loan.

As opposed to the swap, Bank A could have tried to acquire USD deposits to fund the loan and could have invested the Swiss francs in a deposit. However, this is often not the best action for the following reasons:

1. If Bank A did not receive funds on a deposit basis, but had to "buy" the funds on the street, it would pay the offer side of the market and would forgo a market bid-and-offer spread gained through the swap.

2. The additional funding and investment activity increases the balance sheet of the bank. As banks use *return on assets* (ROA) as one measure of performance, the ROA results will decline due to the increase in assets without any incremental return.

3. The swap transaction can give benefits to the foreign exchange trading operation. Not utilizing the swap eliminates this possible profit opportunity.

The preceding transaction may seem too simple to happen, but it does. Banks have large deposit bases and loan portfolios. Because they have mismatches in currencies and terms, they do various swap transactions on an internal basis to adjust their funding to meet their lending opportunities. They are doing cash management in the same spirit as would a corporation. Perhaps the major difference is that a bank tends to have more ways to manage its cash effectively and will also have more people in cash management, who should have more expertise. However, the people do work in different bank profit centers; if teamwork does not exist, the synergy of the group may not be fully realized.

Foreign Exchange Intervention and Interest-Rate Management

Chapter 5 reviews central banks' activities in the foreign exchange market. Direct intervention to hold down a currency, for example, the Australian dollar (AUD), would involve the Australian Central Bank's selling the AUD and buying the USD. In so doing, the Australian Central Bank is adding AUD to the Australian domestic economy. The increased supply of money can lead to some softening in interest rates, which would further help to weaken the AUD.

However, the increase in the money supply can be inflationary, which may be of concern. The Australian Central Bank may want to offset this inflationary pressure, and to do so it could sell T-bills in the market, thus transferring funds from commercial bank reserves to the central bank's account. Alternatively, it may do cash-management swaps in the foreign exchange market. Doing either tightens the money supply by reducing bank reserves, and "sterilizes" the money supply from the effect of foreign exchange intervention.

Related Markets

Several other markets and products are also part of the money market. Consider the following:

1. There are futures markets on some money-market products. The largest and most significant of these are for U.S. T-bills.

2. Forward rate agreements (FRAs) are a variation of the financial futures market. In an over-the-counter market, FRAs are used to trade or hedge short-term interest rates up to two years forward.

3. When issued (WI) markets exist on USD and CAD federal government T-bills. Auctions for U.S. T-bills are held every Monday for de-

livery the following Thursday. The amounts to be issued the following week are announced each Tuesday. In Canada, auctions on federal government T-bills are held every Thursday, with delivery on Fridays. Once the weekly auction results are announced, the WI market starts trading for the next week. It is a form of short-dated futures market that operates administratively like the forward market.

4. Interest-rate-options markets exist, both on a futures exchange and on an over-the-counter basis. While fundamentally similar to foreign exchange options, interest-rate options do have their own nuances which need to be properly understood.

5. Interest-rate swaps can involve both the money market and the bond market. These transactions are used primarily to switch from financing on short-term rates to longer-term rates, or vice versa, and from one currency to another. They do not actually provide the cash for the financing, but rather permit borrowers to pay interest on a different basis.

Accounting—Accrued Interest and Book Loss

As indicated, a close relationship exists between foreign exchange and money markets. Because of this relationship, there are some basic accounting issues arising from the money markets that foreign exchange practitioners may find useful. A key issue is the treatment of book losses, but in order to appreciate fully that issue, a brief discussion of how entities measure interest income is warranted.

Accrued Interest

Interest expense, or revenue, is generated each day that money is used. The interest itself, however, is not received or paid daily, but rather it is paid at maturity or at specific intermittent points in time.

Consider an investor who places $10 million on May 31 for one day to mature June 1. May 31 is the month end for the investor who wants to calculate all the revenues and expenses for the month of May. On this particular investment, there is one-day revenue. The question is, Does it belong to May's or June's revenues?

The answer should be May, because the investor gave up use and value of the money on May 31 to the borrower and, for that loss of usage, expects to be compensated. On June 1, the investor has the cash again, which can be used for another purpose. The actual cash interest is received at maturity on June 1, but the income was generated on May 31.

Interest that is earned, but not yet received, is not recorded on financial statements if a cash basis accounting system is used. Consequently, under a cash basis, the above interest would be reported for June. Most individuals, for instance, report their interest income on their tax returns on the basis of how much cash interest was received.

Alternatively, the income or expense item can be included if accrual accounting methods are used. Entries to financial records for accrued interest can vary from organization to organization, but a common system is to use journal entries. Such entries are made in the financial records every month end and are reversed in the following month.

Calculations of accrued interest are similar to regular interest calculations. Consider a CAD banker's acceptance investment for $10 million face value at 11.25 percent for value May 31 and maturing July 15, a term of 45 days.

Price	$\dfrac{1}{[1 + (.1125 \times 45)/365]}$	= $	98.632
Cash invested	$\dfrac{10,000,000 \times 98.632}{100}$	=	$9,863,200
Interest	$10,000,000 - 9,862,300$	= $	136,800

The interest income for each month would be a pro rata share of the total interest based on the number of days that the investment was outstanding during the month. Exhibit 3.13 summarizes the results for the BA investment for the three months.

In Exhibit 3.13, the interest was calculated in the normal way [i.e., (principal × rate × term)/rate basis]. In doing so, the total interest would not equal $136,800 because of the rounding of the price. As a

Exhibit 3.13. Calculation of Monthly Accrued Interest—Method A

Month	Calculations		Interest
May	($9,862,300 × .1125 × 1)/365	=	$ 3,039.75
June	($9,862,300 × .1125 × 30)/365	=	91,192.50
July	($9,862,300 × .1125 × 14)/365	=	42,556.50
Grand total—unadjusted			$136,788.75

Exhibit 3.14. Calculation of Monthly Accrued Interest—Method B

			Month	Cumulative
May	($136,800 × 1)/45	=	$ 3,040.00	$ 3,040.00
June	($136,800 × 30)/45	=	91,200.00	94,240.00
July	($136,800 × 14)/45	=	42,560.00	$136,800.00
Grand total			$136,800.00	

result, an adjustment is usually made in the last month to balance the cashflows and the income statement.

Many entities will take an alternative approach by determining the total interest and then allocating it to the accounting periods according to the formula:

$$\text{Total interest} \times \frac{\text{Number of days in month}}{\text{Total number of days invested}}$$

The interest income by month is then as per Exhibit 3.14.

The accounting entries on the above interest items would be as outlined in Exhibit 3.15.

The net balance sheet and income statement accounting entries would be as per Exhibit 3.16.

Exhibit 3.15. Accounting Entries for Accrued Interest

	Accrued interest		Interest income	
May 31:				
Journal entries	DR	3,040.00	CR	3,040.00
June 30:				
Reversals	CR	3,040.00	DR	3,040.00
Journal entries	DR	94,240.00	CR	94,240.00
Net entries	DR	91,200.00	CR	91,200.00
July 31:				
Reversals	CR	94,240.00	DR	94,240.00
Interest received			CR	136,800.00
Net entries			CR	42,560.00

Exhibit 3.16. Period Balance Sheet and Income Statement Entries

	Cash		Investments		Accrued interest		Interest income	
May	CR	9,863,200	DR	9,863,200	DR	3,040	CR	3,040
June					DR	91,200	CR	91,200
July	DR	10,000,000	CR	9,863,200	CR	94,240	CR	42,560

Accounting for Book Losses

Consider an investment in XYZ's commercial paper at 10 percent for 90 days. A few minutes after the CP was bought, another dealer showed the investor a deal in which the dealer would buy back the XYZ paper at 10.10 percent in exchange for ABC paper with the same credit rating but at a yield of 10.15 percent. To do this second trade, referred to as a "switch," the investor picks up .05 percent, or 5 cents. The yield on the portfolio is enhanced from 10 percent to 10.05 percent. The cashflows arising from these trades would be as shown in Exhibit 3.17.

The sale of XYZ paper creates a book loss of $2400. The sale of the product is at a lower price (higher yield) than the price at which it was originally purchased. Many organizations are prevented from taking this kind of book loss, even though the overall economics favor doing the transaction. The main reason, in many cases, is that financial statements may be the only means that investors have to analyze a company's performance. Sizable book losses may reduce the perceived corporate performance and are thus avoided. The interest according to the accrual methodology allows the company to report a fairly even revenue stream, all else being equal, which is indeed desirable.

Exhibit 3.17. Benefits of Incurring Book Loss for Economic Gain

	Price	Cashflow, in/(out)
Original purchase of XYZ paper	97.561	(9,756,100)
Switch:		
Sale of XYZ paper	97.537	9,753,700
Net		(2,400)
Purchase of ABC paper	97.525	(9,752,500)
Net investment		(9,754,900)

Book losses can be undesirable, as they can cause revenue statements to fluctuate significantly from one period to the next. However, the question should also be asked about whether or not the market value of the portfolio should be determined at every period end. Any professional trader has regular mark-to-market analysis in order to determine performance. Interest income is only one dimension, and the price changes on a portfolio must also be taken into account. The same argument could also apply to many corporate and government entities. If this were done, a book loss (or gain) would materialize, whether a trade were closed out or simply marked to market. Therefore, there would be no reason why a valid trade should not be undertaken.

Note Material for sections of this chapter was drawn from Marcia Stigum, *The Money Market*, 3d. ed., Dow Jones-Irwin, Homewood, Ill., 1990.

4

Forecasting Foreign Exchange Rates

Executive Summary

Forecasting future movements of the foreign exchange market may be more of an art than a science. We certainly have discovered no magic formulas to guarantee success. This chapter first introduces efficient market theory—and its argument that successful forecasting should be difficult, if not impossible. The chapter then describes how fundamental factors are used to predict market movements, and continues with a review of technically based market forecasting. Charting, moving averages, trend lines, and other popular technical tools are discussed. Finally, the chapter concludes with a brief discussion of market advisory services and a summary of market quirks and forecasting guidelines.

Introduction

All market players would like to know what future foreign exchange rates will be. Firms with currency exposure would like to know whether a hedge is desirable, and currency traders would like to know which positions will be profitable. The demand for accurate forecasts is high.

For a trader, the combination of forecasting and trading skill is deemed to be successful when he or she can earn consistent profits above those required to justify the risk in the activity. If a company can earn 10 percent on money invested in treasury bills, a currency trader must be expected to generate significantly more than a 10 percent return on the capital required to support the trading function. Similarly, a portfolio manager should earn consistently more than 10 percent on a foreign currency portfolio.

For a hedger, successful forecasting is harder to define. Preventing a loss on a currency exposure is clearly successful, but suppose the hedge prevents a profit that would have otherwise resulted from that exposure. According to one yardstick, loss prevention at reasonable cost should be seen as successful. A more demanding criterion would be to hedge those exposures that would otherwise generate a loss, and to not hedge those that would turn a profit if left unhedged. This framework requires selective hedging and, if the forecasting is good enough, should be possible to accomplish.

At first glance, it certainly looks as if forecasting should be possible. There is very good information about how exchange rates have moved in the past. There is also a wealth of information about factors that are, or seem to be, associated with these currency moves. If one could take this past experience and directly apply it to the current market, forecasting should be feasible. Unfortunately, forecasting is not that simple.

Real-world evidence that forecasting can work is presented by the large number of market players who proactively take market risks with the objective of making trading profits. Their continued presence in the markets would suggest that they, to a degree at least, are able to make or acquire useful market forecasts. Clearly, accurate forecasts are critical to the success of selective hedgers and profit-oriented market participants. This chapter will review both fundamental and technical forecasting methods and procedures.

Efficient Markets

Forecasting will not work if the markets are efficient. An efficient market is one in which *all available* information is already reflected in the current price. Such a market is characterized by the random arrival of new information relevant to pricing in that market, and by a widespread group of participants with roughly equal access to the new information, each of whom will trade on that information and thus adjust the price. This description would appear to characterize the foreign exchange markets. The challenge in this kind of market is to gain a disproportionate share of the new information, or find a way to use the available information more efficiently, or both.

Giddy and Dufey, in their article "The Random Behaviour of Flexible

Exchange Rates," suggest that there are four ways to forecast future rates successfully.[1] They are:

1. Develop and use a better forecasting model.
2. Consistently access relevant information before other forecasters.
3. Take advantage of small temporary deviations from equilibrium.
4. Successfully predict government intervention in the foreign exchange market.

The first method tends to be self-defeating. Because there is such wide demand for successful forecasting and because so many players attempt to do it, successful forecasting models or processes will soon be copied. Secrets that make a lot of money are hard to keep.

The second method may offer some opportunity for particular groups of market participants. A useful input for short-term forecasting is knowledge of the actual foreign exchange flows in the market. The major market makers, such as large banks and investment dealers, are continually making prices to other market participants. This activity gives them an excellent vantage point to observe the market flows and assess whether the buying or selling interest is dominant. Such a perspective provides an ongoing competitive advantage in forecasting short-term movements. Other participants may, for a short time, have better information than the market in general. For instance, market participants that are executing a large transaction have demand-and-supply information not available to other players. Their forecasting should, as a result, be more accurate. However, once the transaction is completed, the comparative advantage from an information point of view is gone.

The third alternative may work for those willing to be very fast off the mark, but the profit potential is limited. It is this activity that keeps the markets efficient in the first place. The fourth alternative offers possibilities, but it is really a subset of the second approach.

We should take the efficient markets hypothesis a step further, both because some people do believe it and also because, if true, it does suggest what traders and hedgers should do.

In foreign exchange, if the market is theoretically efficient, or in equilibrium, the following conditions will be met:

1. Spot exchange rates will adjust to reflect differences in inflation between the two currencies. If this were not true, the effective price of goods would vary between the two countries with different rates of

inflation, and trade flows would occur. The trade flows should, in turn, put the required pressure on the exchange rates.

2. Real interest rates will be the same in all currencies. Real rates are what is left after inflation is subtracted from the nominal rates. Therefore, differences in nominal rates between currencies reflect differences in inflation, assuming no or equal default and maturity risk premiums.

3. Spot exchange rates adjust to reflect differences in nominal interest rates. In other words, you cannot earn higher returns by investing in high-interest-rate currencies; the currency you bought will devalue enough to offset the higher interest.

4. The premium or discount of the forward price relative to the spot is equal to the interest differential between the currencies. If this were not true, traders could arbitrage between the spot and forward markets by buying a currency spot, investing for a period of time, and selling forward.

These ideas are certainly not new. The first point is called *purchasing-power parity*; the second and third points are the *Fisher effect* and the *international Fisher effect,* respectively; and the last reflects the effect of covered interest arbitrage. These conditions are most likely to be found where exchange rates float freely without government intervention and where money markets and foreign exchange markets are well developed and widely accessible. We know all these conditions do not happen, or at least not very often. However, no one suggests that the above conditions hold perfectly. The question is, Are they sufficiently accurate descriptions of reality to be useful?

If these conditions did exist, they would tell us a great deal about future spot rates. The first condition says the future spot price must offset differential inflation. The second condition says interest rates also reflect the same differential inflation. The fourth condition says the forward price compared with the spot must reflect the interest differentials, which, in turn, reflect the differential inflation. So both the future spot rate and the forward price are driven by the same inflation differential. Therefore, they must be the same, at least on an expected-value basis. This is a powerful conclusion. If you want to know what the future spot will be, simply look at the current forward price. The question then becomes, Who needs forecasters?

This set of relationships and the above conclusion should be easy to test empirically. One simply has to write down the current forward price, wait the required length of time, and compare it with the (future) spot. Because the relationships sound plausible, and because the result would be so useful if true, empirical tests of this nature have been undertaken many times.

Unfortunately, the results are, at best, inconclusive. The forward rate and the future spot rate are rarely the same, or even very close. The question then becomes whether the errors would average out over a period of time, with many repetitions. If this were so, the forward price would be at least an unbiased expectation or forecast of the future spot. In other words, the future spot would be above the forward rate as often as below. If this were the case, the forward rate would still be useful as a forecast, particularly to managers with many individual exposures to hedge. However, even this relationship does not hold up well when tested in the market. Examples of such tests include work by Giddy and Dufey[1] and Logue, Sweeney, and Willett.[2]

To illustrate the difficulty in interpreting the test results, a small and very simple test was undertaken by the authors. Six-month forward rates for four different currencies, all priced against the U.S. dollar, were compared with the actual spot six months later. The currencies selected were the Canadian dollar, the deutsche mark, the British pound, and the yen. The time period was from January 1982 to January 1989. Using nonoverlapping six-month periods, this provides 15 observations per currency, or a total of 60 comparisons.

The results are typical of those of much more sophisticated studies. On average, the future spot differed from the forward price by 7.85 percent. This result was calculated using the following formula for each of the 60 observations, and then averaging the 60 numbers regardless of whether they were positive or negative.

$$\frac{\text{Forward} - \text{future spot}}{\text{future spot}}$$

The forward price, in this sample, did not even do well in anticipating the direction of the future-spot-rate adjustment. To be correct in this test, both the forward and the future spot should be on the same side of the current spot. For example, if the forward price was above spot, the future spot should be stronger as well. In our 60 observations, the forward price forecast the direction of the spot-rate movement correctly on 27 occasions. It was incorrect 33 times. For six-month holding periods, at least, the forward price does not seem to present a lot of money-making opportunities.

Our sample is small enough to permit the reader to usefully look at the entire data base. For this reason, all the data are shown in Exhibit 4.1. The data were taken from the *Wall Street Journal,* on the first trading day of the month. On the basis of this small sample, most persons would conclude that the forward price is not a good forecast of the future spot, regardless of the efficient market rationale cited above. Most market practitioners would agree with that conclusion.

The forward price, based on the preceding arguments, is priced off the spot rate using the interest-rate differential. The interest-rate differential should, in turn, depend on the inflation differential. Therefore, efficient market forecasting, using the forward price, really uses only inflation or inflation expectations. Differential inflation will provide pressure for rate adjustment, at least in the long run. While the forward rate may not be a reliable forecast for rate movements in the short term, it may possibly serve as a guide to movements in the longer term.

If the forward price does not accurately forecast the future spot rate, what does? Many factors other than inflation impact a market in both the short and long term. If these factors can be identified and correctly incorporated in a forecasting model or decision-making process, it should be possible to improve substantially upon the forecasting ability of the forward price.

Remember, however, that just because the forward price does not seem to accurately forecast the future spot, we cannot conclude that another procedure is sure to be more successful. Logic suggests that successful forecasting should be difficult, simply because many people are trying to do it; and the market decisions of the more successful ones tend to move prices, so that there is less opportunity for those who follow.

The remainder of the chapter will examine conventional forecasting methodology, focusing on two basic approaches: fundamental analysis and technical analysis.

Forecasting Based on Fundamental Models

Fundamental analysis is based on a detailed examination of macroeconomic variables. The assumption is that the exchange rate is related to the performance of the underlying economy, relative to other countries. In addition, measurable changes in specific macroeconomic variables are assumed to lead or precede the changes in the exchange rate.

For instance, analysis of the balance of payments and national accounts leads to a family of flow account models. These models assume, for example, that if the economy is growing and incomes are rising, the demand for imports will increase. The resultant trade deficit may produce selling pressure on the currency. Higher levels of economic activ-

Exhibit 4.1. Forward Rate as a Forecasting Tool
Forward Rates vs. U.S. Dollar
Jan. 1982–Jan. 1989

| | 1982 | | 1983 | | 1984 | | 1985 | | 1986 | | 1987 | | 1988 | | 1989 |
	Jan.	July	Jan.	July	Jan.	July	Jan.	July	Jan.	July	Jan.	July	Jan.	July	Jan.
Canadian dollar															
Spot	0.8429	0.7725	0.8098	0.8147	0.8038	0.7580	0.7576	0.7359	0.7153	0.7216	0.7241	0.7515	0.7695	0.8245	0.8382
6-mo. forward	0.8365	0.7673	0.8055	0.8152	0.8049	0.7573	0.7534	0.7307	0.7112	0.7152	0.7166	0.7468	0.7649	0.8183	0.8313
Actual 6-mo. spot	0.7725	0.8098	0.8147	0.8038	0.7580	0.7576	0.7359	0.7153	0.7216	0.7241	0.7515	0.7695	0.8245	0.8382	0.8357
Difference	0.0640	-0.0425	-0.0092	0.0114	0.0469	-0.0003	0.0175	0.0154	-0.0104	-0.0089	-0.0349	-0.0227	-0.0596	-0.0199	-0.0044
% difference	8.28	-5.25	-1.13	1.42	6.19	-0.04	2.38	2.15	-1.44	-1.23	-4.64	-2.95	-7.23	-2.37	-0.53
Trend 5/15 right	Y	N	N	N	N	Y	Y	Y	N	N	N	Y	N	N	Y
German DM															
Spot	0.4459	0.4060	0.4199	0.3931	0.3676	0.3596	0.3175	0.3299	0.4090	0.4558	0.5203	0.5480	0.6371	0.5518	0.5638
6-mo. forward	0.4540	0.4198	0.4270	0.4018	0.3747	0.3720	0.3231	0.3340	0.4155	0.4609	0.5239	0.5578	0.6499	0.5613	0.5745
Actual 6-mo. spot	0.4060	0.4199	0.3931	0.3676	0.3596	0.3175	0.3299	0.4090	0.4558	0.5203	0.5480	0.6371	0.5518	0.5638	0.5126
Difference	0.0480	-0.0001	0.0339	0.0342	0.0151	0.0545	-0.0068	-0.0750	-0.0403	-0.0594	-0.0241	-0.0793	-0.0981	-0.0025	-0.0619
% difference	11.82	-0.02	8.62	9.30	4.20	17.17	-2.06	-18.34	-8.84	-11.42	-4.40	-12.45	-17.78	-0.44	12.08
Trend 8/15 right	N	Y	N	N	N	N	Y	Y	Y	Y	Y	Y	N	Y	N

British pound														
Spot	1.9820	1.7340	1.6200	1.5275	1.4525	1.3570	1.1592	1.3095	1.4452	1.5400	1.4830	1.6175	1.8870	1.7120	1.8085
6-mo. forward	1.9173	1.7603	1.6140	1.5289	1.4574	1.3759	1.1547	1.2835	1.4200	1.5189	1.4499	1.6039	1.8743	1.6957	1.7782
Actual 6-mo. spot	1.7340	1.6200	1.5275	1.4525	1.3570	1.1592	1.3095	1.4452	1.5400	1.4830	1.6175	1.8870	1.7120	1.8085	1.5530
Difference	0.1833	0.1403	0.0865	0.0764	0.1004	0.2167	-0.1548	-0.1617	-0.1200	0.0359	-0.1676	-0.2831	0.1623	-0.1128	0.2252
% difference	10.57	8.66	5.66	5.26	7.40	18.69	-11.82	-11.19	-7.79	2.42	-10.36	-15.00	9.48	-6.24	14.50
Trend 5/15 right	Y	N	Y	N	N	N	N	N	N	Y	N	N	Y	N	Y

Japanese yen (×100)														
Spot	0.4580	0.3900	0.4271	0.4170	0.4320	0.4213	0.3978	0.4027	0.4896	0.6121	0.6329	0.6812	0.8264	0.7513	0.8001
6-mo. forward	0.4742	0.4070	0.4325	0.4240	0.4398	0.4344	0.4037	0.4062	0.5031	0.6192	0.6390	0.6869	0.8399	0.7642	0.8190
Actual 6-mo. spot	0.3900	0.4271	0.4170	0.4320	0.4213	0.3978	0.4027	0.4896	0.6121	0.6329	0.6812	0.8264	0.7513	0.8001	0.6961
Difference	0.0042	-0.0201	0.0155	-0.0080	0.0185	0.0366	0.0010	-0.0834	-0.0090	-0.0137	-0.0422	-0.1395	0.0886	-0.0359	0.1229
% difference	21.59	-4.71	3.72	-1.85	4.39	9.20	0.25	-17.03	-17.81	-2.16	-6.19	-16.88	11.79	-4.49	17.66
Trend 9/15 right	N	Y	N	Y	N	N	Y	Y	Y	Y	Y	Y	N	Y	N

Trend is right 27/60
Average absolute % difference = 7.85

ity may also add to inflationary pressures as demand outstrips capacity. Higher inflation will also tend to depress the exchange rate.

Models based on this type of reasoning can be constructed using variables, such as economic growth, inflation, unemployment rates, and so on. At the more sophisticated level, models may use a series of more detailed economic factors to forecast aggregate variables, such as economic growth and inflation. Inflation may be forecast, for instance, using data on unemployment rates, changes in taxation policy, industrial capacity utilization, prior exchange-rate movements, and changes in wage rates. These are flow account or econometric models. These models usually involve regression analysis, and the skill is in choosing the independent or explanatory variables to include and the transformations required.

For example, if the trade deficit is to be included, should it be this quarter's, last quarter's, or some previous quarter's, and should it be measured in dollars, or in percentage of exports, or in some other way? There is a great deal of choice. The traditional test is to see whether the model as specified, and using historical data, will explain subsequent historical rate movements. The sensitivity of the exchange rate to each of the independent variables (regression coefficients) can be assessed at this time. More recent values for the explanatory variables are then used, and an exchange-rate forecast is produced.

A major assumption underlying the approach is that what worked in the past will work now. That is, the basic conditions have not changed. If this assumption is true, and the model is good enough, it may fulfill the first forecasting-success criterion listed above and work for a while, or at least until others discover the model and exploit the opportunities thus presented.

An alternative approach, still based on fundamental analysis, views a currency as an investment vehicle or a store of value. These are asset-market models, and they suggest that currency strength, not weakness, is associated with higher rates of economic growth. The argument suggests that high-growth economies have good investment opportunities. Capital is scarce, and *real* interest rates are high. As a result, foreign investors want to invest in that economy and purchase the currency to do so, providing the upward price pressure. If the investment attributes of a currency are dominant, as they may well be in the short run, then other explanatory variables may be required in the regression model.

Fundamental analysis using econometric modeling is widely practiced. As indicated, the actual models used can become very complex. Economic theory usually guides their initial development, with possibly an element of pragmatism as the development proceeds; if it works, use it. The success rate is harder to measure because the model outputs are usually sold and not as readily available for testing as is the forward price, which was examined earlier. Nevertheless, since market practitioners do pay for forecasting services based on these approaches, the suggestion is that the results are useful.

Fundamental analysis also can be done at a much more basic level, without the use of mathematical models. In fact, this is probably its most frequent method of application. It is what people think or sense will happen based on what they see around them. The processing of the data may be almost intuitive; certainly, it is based on experience rather than formal analysis. For instance, one can simply make a list of the key bullish and bearish factors that could be important in the market for a particular currency for the chosen time horizon. One then decides which of the factors are likely to dominate the market, and observes what the factors are doing. For instance, a list could be constructed as follows:

Bearish	Bullish
Declining interest rates	Increasing trade surplus
Heavy intervention by the central bank	Safe-haven capital flows
Seasonal current account drain:	Large corporate deals
Quarterly dividend outflows	
Month-end tax payments	
Trading market is long (i.e., traders are likely to take profits near current levels by selling their long positions)	

Each factor could prove dominant at a particular time, depending on the overall environment. Large corporate transactions, for instance, could dominate a currency market in the short run and move it in the direction opposite to what it "should" move.

These short-run, largely random, effects are difficult to capture in any fundamental modeling procedure, either intuitive or mathematical. As a result, they lead to errors in the forecasts. Lack of accuracy using fundamental approaches has contributed to increased interest in technical market forecasting.

Forecasting Based on Technical Analysis

Technical analysis has two branches: charting and trend analysis. The first, *charting*, involves examining the history of price and volume movements in an attempt to discover patterns of movement that will be repeated in the future. *Trend analysis* is the mathematical analysis of the historical price and volume data, in an attempt to determine the underlying trends, which may be hidden by more superficial price volatility.

The primary assumption behind the technical analysis approach is that all the relevant information about future price movements is already in the price, and so nothing but the price and volume movements need be considered. However, using the historical pattern of price movements to forecast future price changes directly contradicts efficient market theory. If there were exploitable information in historical price movements (data which are there for all to see), the market would have already exploited it.

As a result, technical analysis has its very strong proponents and its very strong opponents. To be fair, the same argument supporting fundamental analysis can also be invoked in support of technical analysis; there may be useful and unexploited information in past price movements simply because no one, or very few, has yet tried hard enough to discover what it is and how to use it.

In any event, for the interested reader, the balance of the chapter is a fairly detailed outline of the basics of technical analysis. We include this material because many market participants believe in it, or at least pay for it; and to many it seems much more mysterious than the fundamental analysis. It should also be rather interesting reading for a newcomer to the area.

As indicated, technical analysis does not deal with the actual causes of market movements. Rather, it views the market as a big melting pot into which the various market factors flow. The melting pot digests all the factors and produces the price, which is the market's collective assessment of the value of the currency. The price is viewed as all-knowing, as it already incorporates all the fundamental factors in the market. Consequently, focusing on the price, as opposed to the various fundamental factors, is the best means of predicting future market direction.

Technical analysis is, therefore, based on three fundamental premises:

1. All relevant factors are reflected in one number, the price. No one can know all things affecting a market at a given time. The collective impact of all factors is known, however, via the price mechanism.

2. Prices move in one of three trends: upward, downward, or sideways.

Technical analysis tries to determine the trend, so that one can join the trend and profit from it.

3. History repeats itself time and time again. Efficient markets and random-walk theory suggest that there is no correlation between the past and the present. Believers in technical analysis think otherwise.

Technical analysis initially involves documenting historical price movements. These movements are then analyzed to determine what patterns have consistently repeated themselves over time. Once such patterns are identified, they are compared with current price movements to determine if the patterns are once again forming. If so, the trader can forecast future price movements and trade the markets profitably.

Whether one believes in technical analysis is actually quite immaterial. The reality is that many market participants use it and most major participants try to be aware of what the technicians are saying.

It should be noted that much of the literature on technical analysis is based on commodity and stock markets. Much of the material is concerned with uptrending and downtrending markets and the differences between the two. These markets trade on the basis of a stock or commodity measured against a financial price, such as the U.S. dollar. The stock or commodity itself, e.g., wheat, is viewed as strengthening or weakening against the financial measure, e.g., the U.S. dollar. However, one does not think of the U.S. dollar as strengthening or weakening against wheat. Foreign exchange markets differ in that they work both ways. One can view the U.S. dollar as weakening against the British pound or the British pound strengthening against the U.S. dollar. It is important to keep this distinction between currency markets and other markets, such as commodities or equities, in mind.

Technical analysis keys on three pieces of market information: volume, open interest, and price or price movements. Of the three, price is the most important, and the bulk of our discussion will focus on price. First, however, let us look at volume and open interest.

Volume

Volume is used to determine the underlying strength of the related movement in prices. Actually measuring the volume dealt on major currencies on a particular day is essentially impossible. Volume on futures markets is reported, but this is a fraction of global foreign exchange volumes. However, remember two points:

1. Technical analysis is an art, not a science.

2. Everything is relative.

Consequently, the key to volume is to determine if the volume was high, average, or low. The best source of this information is usually ongoing discussions with market contacts.

An upward-trending market will typically see more volume during price advances than on declines. The higher volume on advances shows the market has good demand to perpetuate the move. If prices weaken and volume is light, it shows some profit taking and a limited amount of new selling. However, the light volume sell-off shows the market still is geared to continuing the general uptrend.

Similarly, a downward-moving market should see its heaviest volumes during declines as additional selling hits the market. Volume should be light on corrective rallies, reflecting limited buying interest, even at these lower levels. If the volumes are light on the declines, however, the market could be running out of steam. Sellers are declining, and buyers could well be many.

As a general rule, high volume when the market is moving in the direction of the long-term trend indicates the trend will be sustained. Extremely high volume, however, should be viewed with caution. Some market participants may have bad positions (i.e., they are losing money) and have decided to unwind. Other participants, who waited for clear evidence of a move, have now seen the move and may have joined the bandwagon and established positions. This rationale for dealing does not reflect a belief in the market. Rather, the pain of losing, or not participating in the move, has forced these participants to get in.

When almost everybody thinks the market is going up, sell. The main reason for this is that when people express this opinion, they are likely to have already bought most, if not all, of what they want to buy. There is little or no buying interest left to continue the uptrend. Instead, everybody is really waiting to sell, once the market goes up. When it does not rise, the selling begins. Those in the retail sector are infamous for getting into a market at about the time they should be getting out. The market movement influenced them to get into the market. However, by the time they get in, the price will have largely, or perhaps completely, incorporated the factors leading to the price increase.

Open Interest

Open interest is another statistic of which traders should be aware. The term is usually associated with futures markets because these markets make up the one significant marketplace that reports such information. Open interest is also of importance in markets where it is the focal price-making mechanism. Open interest is the total amount of open contracts. Any purchase necessarily has an offsetting sale. For example, in the futures markets, if a participant buys 100 contracts of wheat for

March delivery and then sells 75 contracts later in the day, a net long position of 25 contracts is held with the futures exchange. The other 75 contracts are liquidated. Open interest, all else being equal, would be increased by 25 contracts.

At first glance, open interest may seem meaningless, as every long position is offset by a short position. As with volume, however, the key is the change in open interest. Consider the following:

1. If open interest increases, net new long and short positions are established. An increase can have different meanings.

In a stable market, it can signify growing disagreement between buyers and sellers about future price direction. Both expect a movement; they simply disagree on the direction.

In an upward market, buyers are buying more on the belief that the trend will continue. Conversely, sellers continue to think prices are too high and sell even more. The key is that the buying interest, which has generated the trend, is receiving additional impetus, and the trend should continue until the buying interest stops. When positions start to get unwound, open interest declines and the market retreats.

2. If open interest on the nearest futures month is rolled or swapped to later futures months, it maintains the total level of open interest. It also shows that traders want to stay with their open position, as they expect prices to continue to move in their favor. If they do not swap their position, it shows a decision to unwind it.

When analyzing open interest on foreign exchange futures, it is important to recognize that distortions can occur.

1. Consider arbitrage activities. Trader ABC simultaneously buys in the interbank market and sells in the futures market. The result is a risk-free profit. The futures will show an increase in volume and open interest, and yet the deals have nothing to do with market sentiment or position taking.

2. Futures traders may also use over-the-counter markets, especially when the futures markets are closed. A purchase on the futures market during the day may be offset, at least from a risk standpoint, by an over-the-counter deal. If the futures seller also covered on the over-the-counter market, the futures market reflects open interest which does not really exist from an overall risk standpoint.

In the over-the-counter or interbank market, open interest is basically impossible, if not impractical, to try to measure. Imagine trying to determine, on a global scale, currency by currency, some of the following:

1. Actual, but unhedged, trade and service account exposures
2. Hedges placed on anticipated futures exposures
3. Unhedged foreign currency investments or borrowings
4. Open trading positions held by banks, dealers, corporations, and individuals

If all parties, at a particular time, were to forward this and other relevant information to a centralized body, a crude estimate of the global open interest could possibly be generated. However, by the time the data were summarized, significant changes would in all likelihood have already been made, and the number would be irrelevant. Moreover, what would one compare the results with? Open interest in the over-the-counter market is not a practical statistic to pursue. Instead, what market participants try to do is gain a sense of what traders, corporate hedgers, funds managers, and other players are thinking and planning to do in the markets.

Price and Price Movements

At any time, the price of a commodity or a currency reflects what the marketplace has determined the fair value to be. Market participants will not individually agree, but the overall consensus of the market is that the price is the fair value for the commodity or currency. If it were not, the market would buy if it were too low or sell if it were too high. The price, according to technical analysis, represents everything one has to know about the market, all rolled into one number. Consequently, technical analysis looks to price as the foundation for determining market direction.

Technical analysis is done in a variety of ways. Many techniques use graphs to portray prices, volumes, and open interest as well as other calculated statistics. The most common graphical technique used is bar graphs.

Bar Graphs

The bar graph plots time on the horizontal axis against price on the vertical axis. The graph involves plotting for each day the high and low for a currency, which are joined by a vertical line. The closing level is indicated by a dash to the right of the vertical line. Some bar graphs may also show the opening level by placing a dash to the left of the line.

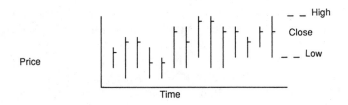

Market movements are never completely in one direction for very long. A currency may strengthen, then weaken, then strengthen and weaken again. This zigzag price action is very common and is an integral part of technical analysis. A key challenge in technical analysis is determining the levels to which a currency will zig up and run into selling pressure (resistance levels) and the levels to which a currency will zag down and run into buying interest (support levels).

Support and Resistance

Support levels are prices below current market levels at which sufficient buying interest will surface and lead to a rebound in prices. There may be one or more key support points at any time. In a bar chart, the support point(s) can be found by drawing straight lines that touch successive lows.

The line joining the support points in an upward-trending market is highly significant because it identifies the direction, or trend, of the move. It is called a *trend line*. Breaking below the support points in an upward-trending market is significant, as it could signal the end of the market move.

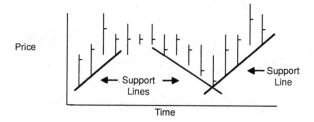

In a downward-trending market, the support points are less significant. Breaking them indicates that the downward move will continue, and possibly at a faster pace.

Resistance levels are prices above current market levels. They are found by drawing lines that join the peak points of market movements.

In an upward-moving market, resistance levels represent a pause in the trend. Some profit taking may be done by players with long positions, while participants with short positions may increase their short positions. Selling interest is expected to be stronger than buying interest, and advances beyond these points will run into resistance. When resistance points are broken, it indicates that a steeper increase in prices may well occur. Failure to reach the points may indicate the market is toppish.

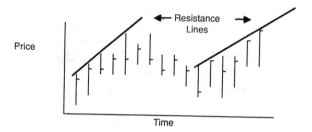

In a downward-moving market, the line connecting the resistance points defines the downward trend and is considered the *trend line*.

Breaking of the resistance points in a downward-trending market is significant, as it could signal a reversal in the market.

A line joining two points indicates minor support or resistance. A line joining three points represents considerably stronger support or resistance, as the third point confirms that the trend line is valid. Moreover, the strength of the support or resistance increases in two ways:

1. The greater the number of times it has been tested

2. The longer the time frame covered by the trend line

If prices move sideways within a relatively small range, the support and resistance points can remain essentially the same for several days or weeks, conceivably even months. However, when the market trend is up or down, support and resistance points change with the passage of time. Determining the various support and resistance points is, consequently, an ongoing task.

Trend Lines

In an upward-trending market, each successive support and resistance level needs to be higher than the previous level in order for the trend to continue. A resistance level one day will not be a resistance level the next day simply because of the overall upward trend that is moving all points higher each day. It should be recognized that the market does not move continuously up or down. There will be retracements or consolidations of the upward move. However, after a consolidation, which can be days, weeks, or months, the next time the market starts to go upward, its target is the next resistance point that is higher than the previous point.

When the market resumes its upward trend, it should move past the previous resistance point. If it does not, it is a sign that the market may be topping out. Similarly, if the market corrects all the way back to the previous support point, it can also be a signal that the upward trend may be changing to either a sideways or a downward trend.

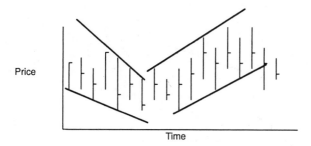

If the lines joining the support and resistance points are basically parallel, they create a channel that usually indicates the market is in either a major upward or downward move. As a guideline, a trend line connecting three points is considered to be a major support or resistance line. Similarly, if a channel is formed with three or more points on both sides, the channel is viewed as having both strong support and resistance.

Failure of the market to reach one side of the channel suggests that the market is changing and that it may break out the other side. If a breakout occurs, the market is likely to continue to move in the new direction shown.

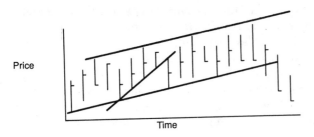

If the market trades through a major support line but comes back up through it, the support of that trend line is even stronger. Lack of enough activity to sustain the break gives the original direction fresh fuel on which to move upward. However, if the market penetrates below the support line in an upward-trending market by a noticeable degree, then the trend line no longer acts as a support line, *but as a resistance line*. Whereas this area previously indicated buying interest, the market movements below the line now indicate that buying interest is no longer dominant. No longer is it a cheap buying opportunity. Instead, the market is turning, and that level represents a good selling opportunity for longs to liquidate or shorts to add to their positions.

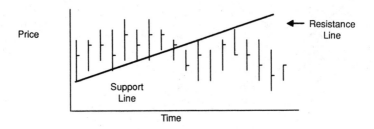

Charting is an art that involves a great deal of subjectivity. Different people looking at the same graphs may come to different conclusions. Judgment also is involved when specifying support and resistance points. While raw data can be the same, interpretations can and do vary. Consider the following:

1. One can draw a series of different support and resistance lines by connecting different points.
2. Any time frame can be covered. The more time covered, the more information available. The chartist has to determine what time frame to analyze and what lines are the key ones. Many practitioners maintain charts of different time frames; for example:
   a. Daily price activity for the past year
   b. Weekly price activity for the past 5 years
   c. Monthly price activity for the past 20 years
   Broken support lines become resistance lines, in days, weeks, months, and even years later. Maintaining the various graphs will help identify these longstanding lines, if you pay attention to them.

3. There can be a series of trend lines in place during a particular move. Determining the lines on which to focus is not always obvious.

Identifying a support or resistance level is often easy. Specifying whether the support price is exactly 1.2499 or 1.2500 is not easy. Nor does it matter that much, especially as the time frame lengthens. Round numbers are easily identifiable and easy to remember. Consequently, one often finds that quoted support and resistance numbers, especially of a longer-term nature, are round numbers such as 1.25 as opposed to 1.2499.

Trend lines highlight key support and resistance levels. The slope of the line itself can also be of great value. If the trend line has a small slope to it, it may indicate that the move does not have a lot of steam behind it and could fizzle. Alternatively, if a trend line is too steep, it is unlikely to be sustained for long, and a correction is in order. W. D. Gann's work, for instance, indicates that a 45° line drawn from a prominent bottom or top is an ideal trend line, as it keeps price and time in balance.[3] Trend lines significantly above 45° cannot be sustained; lines significantly below 45° should be viewed with suspicion. To the newcomer, one could say that by adjusting the scale of price and/or time, any graph can be constructed to yield a 45° angle. This is indeed true. However, Gann's work is highly complex, and adjusting the scale would only serve to defeat the purpose of the analysis at hand. The slope of a trend line is an important factor and, regardless of the scales used, should be considered relative to the trend lines of earlier months and years.

As mentioned previously, a long-term market move need not maintain its direction consistently. There will likely be a series of interim movements that deviate from the long-term major trend line. Moreover, these moves, which can be a few weeks or months in length, can be broken by shorter-term moves, of hours, days, or weeks. Consequently, trend lines need to be drawn and viewed in the context of the underlying long-term trend line, the intermediate trend lines that test the long-term line, and the short-term trend lines, which represent short-term swings in supply-and-demand pressures.

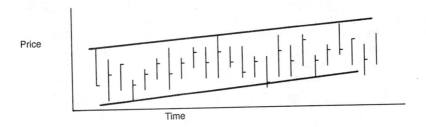

Price

Time

Continuation Patterns

Identifying trends and then going with them is a great way to trade a market profitably. Finding graphical patterns that the market will continue to follow in its current long-term trend is important. Such patterns are called *continuation patterns*.

Flags.   As indicated earlier, markets do not go in the same direction forever. Corrections, even though temporary, will occur. A flag formation is one such correction pattern. After a quick and significant market move, the market corrects in the opposite direction and forms a small channel that looks like a flag. Once formed, and the move has been consolidated, the original price movement resumes. The flag is believed by many to mark the midpoint of a major move's price objective.

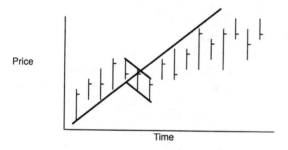

A pennant is similar to the flag except that its shape is more of a symmetrical triangle, whereas the flag is rectangular.

Gaps.   Consecutive transactions can be dealt at significantly different prices. Price gaps that occur within a day's trading do not show up on a bar graph because the graph will show the range for the day. However, if the closing high on one day is below the low of the next day (or one day's low is above the next day's high), a gap actually shows on the bar graph.

There are four basic kinds of gap. One, the runaway gap, reflects a continuation of the move. A runaway gap appears after a significant move has already occurred. It indicates that the move has received a second wind and is ready to go higher with relative ease. The runaway gap frequently occurs approximately halfway along a major move.

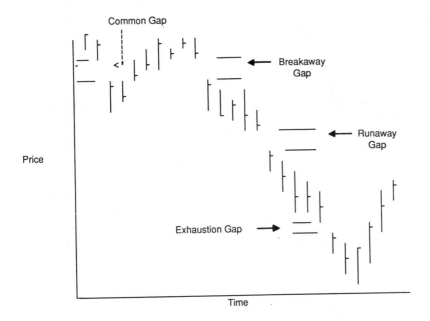

Two of the other three kinds of gap, the common gap and the breakaway gap, are important in terms of market reversals. The common gap materializes on one day but subsequently gets filled in. It often is nothing more than the result of thin markets. It is viewed by most practitioners as a false signal, although it can be an indication that the market is leaning to break out in the direction of the gap.

The breakaway gap frequently occurs at the end of a consolidation phase, at the end of a key price pattern, or after a major support or resistance line has been broken. It usually represents the beginning of a fairly major move. A breakaway gap is often sharp because those with wrong positions not only will get out of the bad position they are in, but will also establish positions in line with the market move. A breakaway gap may get partially filled in, but not totally.

The fourth kind of gap, an exhaustion gap, occurs near the end of the market move. The market tries to jump forward, but there is little support for the move, and the market quickly retraces. When prices come back through the gap, it is a fairly reliable barometer that the move is over. The exhaustion gap often correlates to the period when small players enter the market. When that happens, it is another signal to be a contrarian and to expect the market to reverse.

Triangles

After a period of high volatility, markets may trade quietly for a time. This reduction of volatility can create a triangularly shaped pattern, which can be used to help determine when and in what direction the markets will move.

An *ascending triangle* would normally indicate a breakout on the upside. The top line reflects the selling interest, which is flat. The lower line reflects the buying interest which is dominant at successively higher levels. Consequently, the ascending triangle is bullish.

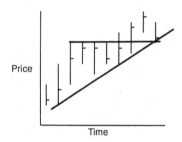

A *symmetrical triangle* indicates a breakout is likely, one way or the other. The top, or seller's, line is declining, while the buyer's line is increasing. Most often, the symmetrical triangle will be followed by a continuation of the previous trend.

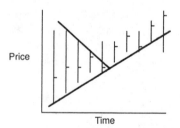

A *descending triangle* would normally indicate a breakout on the downside. The top line is declining, which reflects dominant selling interest at successively lower levels. The bottom line is flat, which reflects limited buying interest.

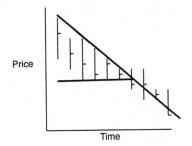

Market Reversal Patterns

A market move does not last forever. Determining the end of a rising or falling market is critical so that positions can be liquidated or reversed to benefit from the subsequent moves in the opposite direction. The sooner one detects that the market has peaked or bottomed, the sooner one can establish these positions. Once again, there are distinct patterns which experience suggests will indicate a turn in the market.

Gaps. The breakaway and exhaustion gaps described above are both good barometers for forecasting future market reversals. The breakaway gap represents the beginning of a major move, while the exhaustion represents the end of one.

Triangles. An ascending triangle in a downtrending market would indicate that an upward move in the market may follow. Similarly, a descending triangle in an upward-trending market is also reason to believe that the market may turn down. Consequently, triangles can be both continuation and market reversal patterns. It just depends on the triangle and the trend.

Fan Principle. A market move that is ending does not necessarily end abruptly. Instead, it may gradually change direction. This gradual change can lead to the development of a series of trend lines that become less and less steep. These trend lines constitute a fan. If the third fan, or trend line, is broken, the market move is usually over and prices will reverse.

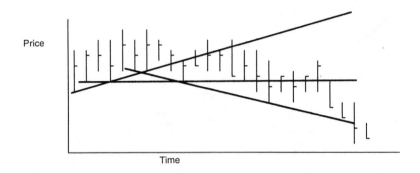

Head and Shoulders. The head-and-shoulders formation is one of the most well-recognized patterns. In an upward market, the left shoulder represents a typical resistance point. The head represents new highs, but often falls short of the corresponding resistance points. The steam of the move is starting to weaken. If the price movements after the head formation reach below the top of the left shoulder, the uptrend may be in jeopardy and the development of a head-and-shoulders formation becomes quite likely.

For the formation to occur, the rebound to the right shoulder should see prices top out in the general area of the left shoulder. Generally, the left shoulder is slightly lower. A subsequent weakening from the right shoulder through the neckline is reason to believe that the trend has indeed broken and one should trade the other way.

Volume is heaviest on the left shoulder, is lighter on the head, and is significantly lighter on the right shoulder.

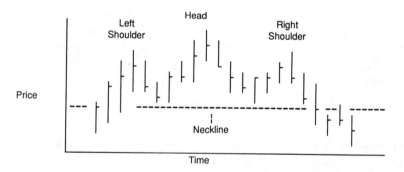

Once the neckline has been broken, it serves as a very strong resistance point. However, if the market closes above the neckline, the signal of a reversal was wrong and the market will likely continue to move upward.

The head-and-shoulders formation in a falling market is referred to as an inverted head and shoulders or a head-and-shoulders bottom. The same principles apply.

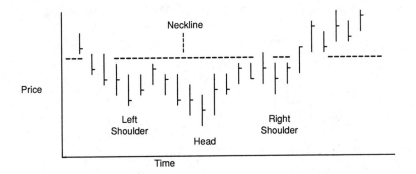

Triple Tops and Bottoms. A close cousin of the head and shoulders is the triple tops and bottoms. The key difference is that there are three peaks or troughs at the same basic level. The basic interpretation is the same.

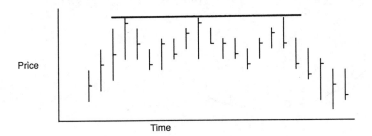

Double Tops and Bottoms. Double tops and bottoms are more common than, but not as significant as, triple tops and bottoms. A double top is referred to as an M, while a double bottom is termed a W.

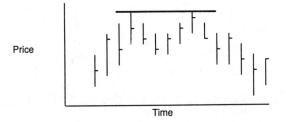

Spikes. The market can sometimes move too far, too fast. It gets carried away; and not only is it unlikely to sustain its speed of movement, but it is unlikely to retain the movement already made. When the market recognizes this occurrence, the retraction can be equally as quick and far-reaching. After the fact, the graph shows a big spike.

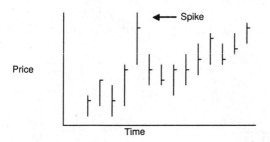

Saucers. The above formations tend to reflect fairly distinct changes in market direction. However, some market changes are gradual, and the resulting patterns look like saucers or bowls. The corresponding volume statistics also take on a bowl shape as they decline during the construction of the left half of the saucer and then increase as the right half forms.

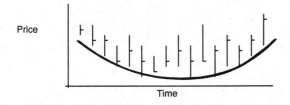

Reversal Days. The head-and-shoulders formation, triple tops and bottoms, double tops and bottoms, and the exhaustion gap are all good indicators of a change. The reversal day is popular as a complement to these formations in signaling a market turn.

A reversal day in an upward-trending market is marked by a market that, on that day:

1. Sets a new high for the move
2. Trades lower than the previous day's low
3. Closes lower than the previous day's close

A reversal day in a downward-trending market is identified when the market on that day:

1. Sets a new low for the move
2. Trades higher than the previous day's high
3. Closes higher than the previous day's close

Also apparent on reversal days are an increase in volume and a decrease in open interest. Consider a downtrending market. If open interest is declining, both long and short positions are being liquidated. Long positions are being liquidated to cut the losses, while short positions are being covered to take profits. Selling is not coming from new sellers who have a conviction that the market is going lower; rather, it is coming from the longs who are getting rid of their pain. Once this distress selling is complete, there is no other selling pressure. Consequently, prices rise quickly into new territory.

The reversal day may turn out to be nothing, or it may turn out to be the beginning of a major market reversal. In the latter case, the reversal day is referred to, in hindsight, as a *key* reversal day. A reversal day is not a strong indicator of a market change, but it is one indicator that should be recognized and taken into account along with all the other factors.

In addition to the reversal day, there are also two-day, weekly, and monthly reversals which the reader may want to explore.

Moving Averages

Bar charts are a useful forecasting tool, but their value can be further improved if used in conjunction with other technical tools, such as moving averages. A *moving average* is an average of rates for a period of time. A simple three-day moving average on day 3 would be the average closing rate for day 1, day 2, and day 3. On day 4, the moving average would be the average closing rate for day 2, day 3, and day 4.

Day	Closing rate	Simple 3-day moving average
1	1.00	
2	2.00	
3	3.00	2.00 [(1.00+2.00 + 3.00)/3 = 2.00]
4	3.00	2.67 [(2.00+3.00 + 3.00)/3 = 2.67]

Some participants believe that the most recent close is more important than the previous closes. One way to incorporate this opinion is to use weightings. For instance, in the first three days of the example above, one could weight the most recent day with a factor of 3. The previous day will have a factor of 2, and the first day in the average will have a weighting of 1.

Day	Closing rate	Weighting factor	Weighted 3-day moving average
1	1.00	1	1.00
2	2.00	2	4.00
3	3.00	3	9.00
		6	14.00

Weighted 3-day moving average: 14.00/6.00 = 2.33

Rather than simple weighted averages, some practitioners use other, more sophisticated, approaches such as exponential weighting factors. Such approaches tend to give more weight to the recent trading days and incorporate a longer period of time. When used in the futures markets, the exponential approach often includes every day in the life of the futures contract.

A single moving average can be calculated and transposed onto the bar graph. If the closing prices remain above the moving-average price, the market is still in an upward trend. If it closes underneath the moving average, the trend could be reversing. As per the following graph, a 3-day moving average tracks daily price movements very closely. Many buy and sell signals can be generated. On the other hand, a 15-day moving average responds more slowly and generates fewer buy or sell signals, as illustrated in Exhibit 4.2.

Since false signals are common, the trader has to determine if this is a false or true signal of a change. To minimize the risk of acting on a wrong signal, traders may impose some test rules such as the following:

1. If the next day also closes below the moving average, the upward trend is more than likely reversed.

2. If the market moved y points or x percent through the moving average, the signal is valid.

3. The move must be verified by another pattern.

4. The actual trade will not be made until one or more days later.

Moving averages can be calculated for any term. Historical analysis will help to determine the best single or combination of moving averages to use for a particular currency. The best combination can change,

Exhibit 4.2. Canadian Dollar Daily Bar Graph and
Moving Averages

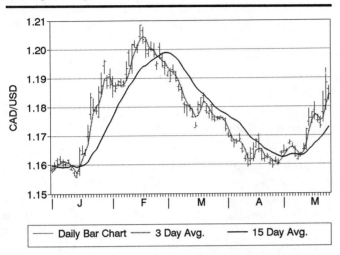

however, and periodic review is probably in order (in one's spare time,
of course).

Many traders will use two or more different moving averages. For instance, one may use a 3-day, 9-day, and 15-day moving average and plot
them on the bar graph as well. (See Exhibit 4.3.) The longer-term av-

Exhibit 4.3. Canadian Dollar Summary of Moving
Averages

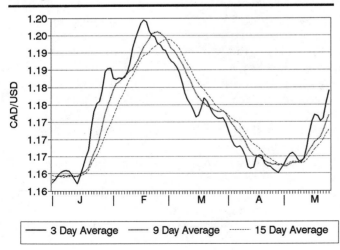

erage is used to reflect the basic trend of the market. The shorter-term averages reflect when the trend may be turning and give guidance on when positions should be reversed or assumed. Some sample guidelines using the three moving-average lines in a downward-trending market are as follows:

1. If the 3-day average crosses above the 9-day line, the trader should be on the alert to buy.

2. If the 3-day average crosses above the 15-day line, the trader might establish a small long position. If the 9-day also crosses the 15-day average, the trader should definitely buy.

3. If the trader has a long position and the 3-day average crosses back under the 9-day average, the trader should be on the lookout to liquidate part of the long position. If the 3-day average crosses under the 15-day average, the trader should liquidate the position. A small short position could even be established. If the 9-day average crosses under the 15-day average, the trader should establish a short position.

Moving averages reflect past movements only and are geared to demonstrate the trend. Unlike bar charts, they do not indicate how far a move may go. Moreover, they usually are used as a long-term trading tool. They ensure that a position is established relatively early in a long-term move and will maintain that position for the duration. Premature closing is usually avoided. If such closing does happen, however, the averages will soon get the trader back into the position.

Signals given by moving averages are relatively few, except when the market is trading within a narrow range. In these market conditions, numerous false signals can be generated. Following such signals can be frustrating and expensive. If the market is moving in a narrow range, the timing of the signal to buy may well be the time when one should instead be selling. The painful experience of being whipsawed in range trading markets is commonplace; accordingly, traders will try to ignore longer-term moving averages if they are in a range trading market. They know, however, that they must be quick to move if the market shifts a certain amount outside the range.

Some traders will use variations of the moving average, described above, to assist them in short-term trading. Averages can be calculated on a minute and hourly basis to determine intraday trading levels. The bar graph may show the basic channel, but it may not be helpful in anticipating key support and resistance levels that are likely to come into play on that particular day.

The concept of moving averages is a simple mathematical analysis of historical price movements. It is a trend-following tool. Extremely detailed analysis has been done on various markets, and elaborate computer models have been built to help traders deal. Computer-based trading is a major factor in the markets, and, obviously, some of these models must work since they continue to be used.

The bar charts and moving averages discussed above were based on daily records of price movements. While daily records are logical, a day is, nonetheless, an arbitrary period of time.

Predicting Lengths of Moves

Moving averages help to predict the direction, but not the length, of the move. Formations on bar charts can, however, be used as a guide in determining duration. A few rules of thumb are as follows:

1. Markets will retrace anywhere from one-third to two-thirds of a move. A 50 percent retracement is a commonly targeted move.

2. Runaway gaps, pennants, and flags occur about the midpoint of a move.

3. On a head-and-shoulders formation, the amount of the breakout below the neckline is at least the distance between the neckline and the top of the head.

4. On a double top or bottom, the market will move the other way at least by the distance from the peak of the top or bottom to its base.

Momentum Lines

Momentum lines measure the rate of changes in prices. Shifts in the rate of price changes can help detect when trends are ending.

Day	Exchange rate	Day	Exchange rate	Change from 10 days ago
1	1.21	11	1.25	+.04
2	1.22	12	1.25	+.03
3	1.23	13	1.255	+.025
4	1.235	14	1.250	+.015
5	1.24	15	1.245	+.005
6	1.24	16	1.235	−.005
7	1.245	17	1.230	−.015
8	1.25	18	1.225	−.025
9	1.245	19	1.23	−.015
10	1.25	20	1.22	−.03

Exhibit 4.4. Momentum Lines

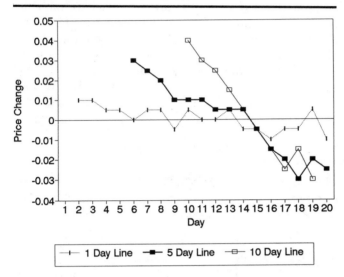

If the rate of price change is plotted graphically, the 1-, 5-, and 10-day momentum lines are created, as shown in Exhibit 4.4.

Using the 10-day momentum line in this example, the price advances in days 11 through 14 were not as large as the price increases in the 10 days prior. Consequently, the momentum increases became smaller, indicating that a topping out in the market could be developing, an event that indeed happened.

This example is a simplification of market action, but it does demonstrate the frequent ability of momentum lines to detect the change in the trend before the trend actually occurs. In trading, the crossing of the zero line represents a signal to buy or sell. However, doing so on this one signal is not a common or suggested practice. An example of momentum lines for the CAD/USD for a longer period of time is shown in Exhibit 4.5.

Oscillators

Markets do not move continuously in one direction until the end of the move, and then make a distinct about-face and move continuously in exactly the opposite direction. A downward-moving market, for instance, will run into support, whether it is from a lack of new sellers, profit taking, hedgers with buying interest, or traders taking long positions. The support and consolidation of market movements are key fac-

Exhibit 4.5. CAD/USD Momentum Lines

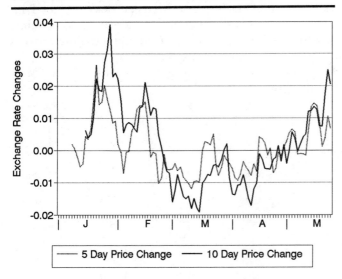

tors in forecasting the markets. It is critical to determine if a retrace-ment is simply a consolidation or is actually a reversal. Making the wrong call can be expensive.

Markets do get carried away and become overbought or oversold. An overbought market is one where the price has risen too much, too fast. The price increases cannot be maintained, let alone sustained. An over-sold market is one where the price has fallen too much, too fast. The price declines are excessive, given the time they took to occur.

A market is likely to be overbought or oversold when:

1. The market has few corrections.

2. The corrections are small in relation to the advances.

Determining whether a market is overbought or oversold is impor-tant. The only question is how to do it!

Oscillators represent a mathematical analysis of market movements that is geared to identifying overbought or oversold markets. One sim-ple analysis is to compare the number of days the market moved up with the number of days it moved down in the preceding specified time period.

$$\frac{\text{No. of days up}}{\text{No. of days down}} = \frac{18}{12} = 150\%$$

This statistic shows that the market increased more often than it declined. However, if the total declines were larger than the total increases, the result would be a net decline, not an increase, and certainly it would not reflect an overbought position. Consequently, the analysis must look at the actual price changes as well.

Consider the following market results over a 20-day time frame. Market rates are the daily close.

Day	Exchange rate	Daily change	Day	Exchange rate	Daily change
0	1.225				
1	1.23	+.005	11	1.235	+.005
2	1.235	+.005	12	1.24	+.005
3	1.23	−.005	13	1.255	+.015
4	1.235	+.005	14	1.260	+.005
5	1.24	+.005	15	1.265	+.005
6	1.235	−.005	16	1.275	+.010
7	1.23	−.005	17	1.270	−.005
8	1.24	+.010	18	1.275	+.005
9	1.235	−.005	19	1.280	+.005
10	1.23	−.005	20	1.285	+.005

The above market action shows 14 up days when the market moved 900 points. The market declined 300 points over 6 days. The market seems overbought, especially over the last 10 days. Some market movements, however, may not be so obvious, and thus a mathematical analysis of the results can be quite helpful.

The relative strength index (RSI) developed by J. Welles Wilder, Jr., is one oscillator measure that is widely used.[4] The first step, using Wilder's approach, is to calculate the relative strength (RS), which is

$$RS = \frac{\text{average of days up closes}}{\text{average of days down closes}} = \frac{.0900/20}{.0300/20} = \frac{.0045}{.0015} = 3$$

The relative strength is then used to determine the relative strength index.

$$RSI = 100 - \left[\frac{100}{1 + RS}\right]$$

$$RSI = 100 - \left[\frac{100}{1 + 3.0}\right] = 100 - \left[\frac{100}{4.0}\right] = 100 - 25 = 75$$

As a guideline, if the RSI is above 70 for the 20-day time frame, the market is viewed as overbought. Conversely, if the RSI is below 30, the market is oversold.

If a shorter time frame, such as 9 days, is used, more extreme RSIs, such as 80 and 20, are used in classifying a market as overbought or oversold. The higher cutoffs are used because the calculations can be more easily affected by one or two sharp movements. In the above case for the period from day 12 to day 20, the RSI is 92, which again indicates an overbought market.

$$RS = \frac{.055/9}{.005/9} = \frac{.0061}{.00056} = 11$$

$$RSI = 100 - \left[\frac{100}{1 + 11}\right] = 100 - \left[\frac{100}{12}\right] = 100 - 8 = 92$$

One should recognize that a market can stay overbought or oversold for an extended period of time. The sole fact that it is overbought or oversold is not a reason to expect a market turn. However, when such a divergence exists, market participants should be on the lookout for a reversal in trend. It is, at the very least, another indicator to induce wariness. Moreover, the longer a market remains in an overbought or oversold position, the more likely the retracement, and the larger and more rapid the retracement will probably be.

Stochastics

Upward-trending markets tend to see prices closing in the upper end of the price range. Similarly, downward-trending markets tend to have prices closing in the lower end of the price range.

The stochastics process, developed by George Lane, defines in percentage terms the case where the closing price is relative to the price range for a given period of time.[5] This relationship is calculated each day using the following formula:

$$\frac{\text{Latest close} - \text{low of range}}{\text{High of range} - \text{low of range}}$$

The points are then connected to form what Lane termed the K line. Using the following example market scenario, the five-day K-line results are as follows:

Day	High	Low	Close	K line
1	1.22	1.21	1.2175	
2	1.23	1.22	1.225	
3	1.24	1.225	1.2375	
4	1.24	1.23	1.2325	
5	1.24	1.2325	1.2375	92%
6	1.235	1.225	1.23	50%
7	1.23	1.22	1.2275	38%

The K-line stochastic of this market for day 5 using a five-day period for the range is as follows:

$$\frac{\text{Day 5 close} - \text{low of range}}{\text{High of range} - \text{low of range}} = \frac{1.2375 - 1.21}{1.24 - 1.21} = \frac{.0275}{.0300} = 92\%$$

To help smooth out fluctuations, a second line, called the D line, is also calculated. The D line is a three-day rolling average calculated as follows:

$$\text{D line} = \frac{\text{sum (numerators for last 3 days' K-line calculations)}}{\text{sum (denominators for last 3 days' K-line calculations)}}$$

For day 7, the D line would be 64 percent, calculated as follows:

$$\frac{.0275 + .0100 + .0075}{.0300 + .0200 + .00200} = \frac{.0450}{.0700} = 64\%$$

The K and D lines obviously move between values of 0 and 100 percent. Using the stochastic results is similar to the principles discussed in the section on the relative strength index. For instance, a D-line stochastic over 70 percent is a high extreme, while below 30 percent it is a low extreme. If a stochastic is over 70 percent, and the market prices continue to go up, the market is increasingly likely to turn down. This likelihood is increased if the formation of the D line makes a bearish pattern, such as a double top. Moreover, if the K line crosses the D line after the double top is formed, a very strong sell signal is generated.

Significance of Threes

Technical analysis is based on repetition. John J. Murphy noted that, in many ways, the number three seems to have a special status.[6] Consider the following:

1. The fan principle uses three lines.
2. There are three kinds of gaps.
3. Major market movements have three primary phases.
4. Several key patterns have three key peaks or bottoms.
5. There are three classifications of trends: minor, secondary, and major.
6. There are three key directions of trend lines: up, stable, and down.
7. There are three key triangles for continuation patterns.

8. There are three key pieces of information: price, volume, and open interest.
9. Moving averages frequently uses three different lines.
10. Support and resistance points are significantly stronger if the line touches three points.
11. There are three main kinds of graphs: bar, line and point, and figure.

Dealing in the markets will also produce one of three results: profits, losses, or breakeven.

Other Technical Tools

Considerable literature exists on such topics as market cycles, waves, point and figure charts, and line charts. The student of technical research should explore these areas to obtain a well-rounded approach. Their exclusion from this book is not because they do not have value. Rather, it is because this chapter is intended to give a broad overview of some of the simpler and more widespread practices. Space, unfortunately, does not permit a review of all areas.

Forecasting Using Fundamental and Technical Analysis: A Summary

Market movements result from a complex web of facts, emotion, and money. Facts speak. Emotions speak. Money speaks. The key is to determine how to get one's arms around all these factors, which are no longer of a local, but a global, nature.

Forecasting using only fundamental analysis has weaknesses. For instance, it does not consider the psychology of the marketplace, which cannot be readily quantified, but which is an important element in markets.

Another weakness of fundamentals is that they are difficult to use in forecasting either the timing or the duration of market moves. While fundamentals sooner or later will affect the market, participants could quickly go broke dealing on the basis of "what the markets should be doing according to the fundamentals."

It should also be remembered that fundamental factors can influence a market in different ways at different times. Consider the following:

1. As indicated earlier, in the distinction between flow account and asset-market models, higher inflation should weaken a currency because of the effect of purchasing-power parity. However, higher inflation can lead to higher interest rates, which can attract foreign capital to a country's financial markets. The result is a stronger, not a weaker, currency.

2. A larger trade surplus, by itself, results in net purchases of a currency. The currency should strengthen. However, if the surplus is due to declining imports, reflecting a slowing economy, then interest rates could fall, leading to an outflow of capital and a weaker currency.

Finally, fundamentals can be temporarily overwhelmed by short-term market conditions. Large amounts of capital can quickly flow internationally from one market to another. Competition to gain better returns on financial assets is intense. Movement from one currency to another is often a means for achieving these superior returns. Diversifying a portfolio is done not only on the basis of term, liquidity, and credit risk, but also on the basis of currency. In addition, money will sometimes seek political security rather than maximum economic returns. Currency trading volumes are on the order of several hundred billion dollars per day. Traditional fundamental factors can be overwhelmed by short-term capital flows; and while the fundamentals will eventually prevail, it may take some time.

Technical analysis has dimensions that complement the weaknesses of fundamental analysis. In particular, it attempts to capture market sentiment, mood, and expectations. In the short run, expectations, if widely held, may be self-fulfilling prophecies. If enough participants expect the market to move, the positions they then assume will cause the expected market action. As a result, technical analysis, and the influence on the markets by those who follow it, cannot be ignored.

On the other hand, the underlying premise that history will repeat itself is not always true. Circumstances change, and what has worked in the past will not always work in the future. Therefore, technicians should not ignore the fundamental factors. By using both approaches, the confidence in a forecast is greatly enhanced, particularly if the fundamental and the technical analysis results are in agreement.

Forecasting Suggestions

For anyone active in the markets, market contacts and dialogue are necessary to have a good read on the market. Through dialogue, one gains a sense of what others are thinking and are likely to do. This, in turn, helps form one's own opinion about what is important and what is likely to occur. Advisory services can play a role in this regard.

Newcomers to forecasting first need to determine what basic framework of forecasting is required. A spot foreign exchange trader needs information on a minute-to-minute basis, while corporate planners typically work on a much longer time frame. Some guidelines that may be of help when forecasting market movements beyond the minute-by-minute trading are given below. They are not universal, nor applicable to everyone.

1. Establish outside market contacts who have a good track record and who share their rationale behind the forecast, not just the forecast. Moreover, brainstorm with both internal and external contacts.

2. Read different market documents to gain a broader perspective. Do not try to read everything that comes across your desk. You will probably forget most of it, and you will never get anything else done.

3. Identify the key bullish and bearish fundamental factors.

4. If time permits, undertake your own technical analysis to see for yourself the key points and patterns as they form. If time does not permit, review technical charts completed by someone else.

5. Write a concise forecast, especially when new to the markets. This time-consuming exercise forces one to focus on the most important factors and helps crystallize one's thoughts. With practice, it becomes much easier and, ironically, less needed.

Anyone attempting to forecast the market should also trade the market at some time. If the individual does not have the authority to trade a small position, paper trading will suffice. Paper trading involves specifying the trades without actually executing them. To put some credibility in the exercise, advise an associate of all trades the minute that they are done. Losses will sometimes be generated, which is a humbling experience to most people, and should provide a few important lessons. Some of these lessons might include the following observations:

1. The markets are not easy to beat on a consistent basis.

2. Markets do not always behave rationally.

3. There are always market factors at work of which one is unaware. Sometimes they help; sometimes they do not.

4. Second-guessing someone else's market decision is of little value, unless one is actually taking charge and assumes responsibility for the decision.

Checklist of Factors

The time frame chosen determines which factors are most relevant. A corporation concerned about a receivable due in six months' time is not concerned about the factors affecting a market in the next five minutes. On the other hand, a spot trader is not worried about the factors affecting the currency over the next six months. He or she is worried about the next few minutes or hours.

The interbank spot trader has an extremely short time frame. Keeping abreast of trading flows is probably the most critical aspect, and traders work hard to determine what business is actually happening in the market. Access to information on flows is critical to trading the spot market, and represents one reason why major banks and investment dealers have a competitive advantage in spot and forward dealing compared with corporate and government entities. If such dealers do not see the direct flows themselves, having direct-dealing relationships with others who do see the flows is the next best thing. With such relationships in place, the bank is one of the first to get a call when dealers lay off the positions.

As evidence, consider that the primary market makers in a country's currency are usually the large banks in that country. These same banks may try as hard in other currencies, but they do not have the same access to information as does a domestic bank. Corporations, as a general rule, have the same problem as a "foreign" bank, and thus are not usually minute-to-minute traders. Instead, they are usually better suited for forecasting and trading a market on a longer-term basis.

Forecasting is not a science. As indicated, many approaches can be and are followed. A short list of 10 popular inputs to the process follows:

1. Observed support and resistance levels
2. Relevant economic releases
3. Interest rates and forecasts of future interest rates
4. Pending deals
5. Political events, policies, and results
   a. Elections, budgets, statements
   b. Taxation
   c. Fiscal results
6. Market sentiment
7. Developments in other markets such as bond, commodity, and equity markets
8. Central bank intervention

9. Economic fundamentals
   a. Economic activity
   b. Balance of payments
   c. Inflation
10. Developments elsewhere in the world

In the good old days, the exchange markets were largely driven by domestic considerations. Now, they are driven by both domestic and international events.

Some Market Characteristics and Quirks

Upcoming political events, such as elections and budgets, usually cause a currency to weaken because of the uncertainty involved. On some occasions, the market may be very sure of the outcome, and will trade based on that expected outcome and what it means for the currency.

The gist of published economic data is usually known by the marketplace before publication. Assumptions about the forthcoming release are made and discussed in the market. Trading is done based on these assumptions, and the new information becomes fully discounted, that is, built into the current price. Consequently, when the statistic is actually released, if it is in line with market expectations, no additional movement in rates will occur. If it differs, markets will react accordingly.

The same process is followed in the case of market rumors. Where there is smoke, there often is fire. If a rumor appears credible, the market will respond and the currency will move accordingly. If and when the rumor is substantiated, there may be no impact. The old adage of "Buy the rumor, sell the fact" reflects this process.

Intervention by central banks has become commonplace and must be considered. A little background is perhaps in order.

The exchange rate is a critical price in an economy, and active management of the rate may be considered important, not only for the economy in question, but, in some cases, for the global economy. Central bankers know the economic fundamentals probably better than most market participants. They also know what the relevant technical points are, and they have considerable resources available, especially if they work together.

Markets do get carried away. It is difficult to justify a move of up to 50 percent, in a couple of years, for a major currency on the basis of fundamentals. Good business decisions sometimes become bad ones, simply because of unfavorable currency movements. International economic growth is facilitated by stable prices, which central banks have a responsibility to try to achieve. Pursuing price stability does not suggest that they should control the markets, but rather that they do have legitimate interests and, if possible, market movements should be constrained within some broad boundaries. Central banks may seek only to reduce volatility, or they may attempt to nudge the rate in a particular direction.

If the buying interest for a currency is strong, direct intervention means the central bank sells the currency. If a relatively small amount is sold, the currency may weaken slightly, but in all likelihood it will keep on moving up. The intervention may, in effect, simply allow the buyers to buy the currency at a price lower than they would otherwise have had to pay.

If the intervention is heavy, the market could turn and the currency could weaken. However, if heavy demand remains after the intervention, the market could move up extremely quickly, as the buyers know that the intervention has not slowed the demand and there is little likelihood that the currency will weaken in the short term. Consequently, the currency is bought.

The way in which the intervention is done can determine its impact on the market.

1. Dealing at key support or resistance points adds to the likelihood of the market turn. Limited intervention here can have the same impact as heavy intervention during major price moves.

2. Intervention does not represent "real" market interest. Real transactions are more meaningful in terms of what is going on in the market than are "artificial" transactions. If a central bank deals through particular banks, which are required to keep confidential the source of the activity, the activity may give the market the perception of additional "real" interest and may cause market participants to take more notice than if it were clearly driven by intervention.

3. If the central bank wants its currency to decline in an orderly fashion, it may intervene on both sides. To slow the descent, it may buy the currency at various levels. However, if the currency rebounds too much, the central bank may then sell the currency.

4. Concerted and extended intervention by several central banks at the same time can have a significant impact on prices. If stop-loss orders begin to kick in, the momentum can start the other way, at least for awhile.

5. At times, the market can become worried about possible intervention. The threat of the intervention overhanging the market will slow

the advances or declines, because participants are cautious about establishing positions that may be made less attractive by intervention. Once the intervention occurs, however, the market will often take off. The intervention in this case is less significant than the threat of it.

6. Central banks can also influence exchange rates through interest-rate policy. However, the market will often expect such changes; and the actual rate adjustments, when they happen, will have been discounted and, therefore, will have little or no impact.

In summary, central banks can intervene strictly to maintain orderly markets. They may intervene with the intention of turning the market, or they may be simply testing the waters. They may try to maneuver a currency in a particular direction by working both sides. They will use direct and indirect foreign exchange intervention and interest-rate policy. They will also use moral suasion. Sometimes, they are successful in what they want to do; sometimes, they are not. Central banks as a whole, however, are now sophisticated and very well informed; and, more than ever, their wishes and activities must be viewed as a significant market factor.

Advisory Forecasting Services

A wide variety of external advisory services are available. Some are well into their second decade; we assume there must be many satisfied customers. The reasons for purchasing a forecasting service might include:

1. The advisory company has no vested interest in client dealing, and any recommendations should be objective.

2. Some forecast users cannot justify the expense of an in-house forecasting activity, based on their frequency and volume of trading. Advisory companies, through simple economies of scale, can offer research depth and individual specialists.

3. The advisory service provides another opinion, forecasting methodology, or point of view.

4. The service can often be customized in terms of markets that are covered, periodic summary reports of special topics, or open-ended telephone access to specialists.

5. The advisory service can be used to actually make the decisions and to "take the blame" for any losses that occur.

The type of service offered can be based on either fundamental or technical analysis, or both, and can vary from computer-driven on-line buy/sell recommendations for the trader to long-term forecasts for the corporate treasury officer. Many services offer a periodical mailing service, while others prefer to act as consultants to particular organizations, presumably tailoring the advice to that organization's circumstances and current needs. Some specialize in less well-known currencies; others combine currency with commodity forecasting.

Prices depend on the services required, and run from as low as $1000 per year for a monthly letter, to perhaps $20,000 per year for a standard client package, to $50,000 per year and up for more detailed consultancy relationships, involving not only foreign exchange, but overall financial risk management. Some of the advisory companies also offer money-management services, in which they manage portfolios of foreign currencies for a fee or for a percentage of profit.

References

1. Giddy, Ian H., and Gunter Dufey, "The Random Behaviour of Flexible Exchange Rates," *Journal of International Business Studies*, Spring 1975.

2. Logue, Dennis E., Richard J. Sweeney, and Thomas D. Willett, "The Speculative Behaviour of Foreign Exchange Rates during the Current Float," *Journal of Business Research*, vol. 6, no. 2, 1978.

3. Gann, W. D., *How to Make Profits in Commodities*, Lambert-Gann Publishing Company, Pomeroy, Washington, 1976.

4. Wilder, J. Welles, "New Concepts in Technical Trading Systems," *Trend Research*, 1978.

5. Lane, George, "Lanis Stochastics," *Technical Analysis of Stocks and Commodities*, June 1984.

6. Murphy, John J., *Technical Analysis of the Futures Markets*, New York Institute of Finance, New York, 1986.

PART 2

Foreign Currency Products, How to Price and Trade Them

5

Foreign Exchange Market Participants

Executive Summary

Chapter 5 introduces the various categories of market participants, including primary and secondary price makers, price takers, advisers, brokers, speculators, and central banks. It also briefly describes the function or role of each market sector to give an overview of how the market works. It is quick and easy to read.

Primary Price Makers

Primary price makers, or professional dealers, make prices to each other on a two-way basis. When requested, they will quote a bid-and-offer price and are willing to either buy or sell, in reasonable volumes, at these prices. Primary price makers include major banks, large investment dealers, and some large corporations. Banks have historically been the major players in the price-making role. Banks provide a number of financial services to a broad base of clients. The foreign exchange activity is an inherent part of these financial services, and it was logical for banks to develop a key role in the foreign exchange market. Banks will probably continue to play a leading trading role in the foreign exchange market, but there will continue to be stiff competition in some parts of the world from investment dealers, multinational corporations, and managers of financial assets.

Investment dealers have typically provided specialized services to a more particular sector of the business community. Until a few years ago, most dealers viewed foreign exchange as an add-on type of service and would do their transactions on a back-to-back basis with a bank. However, the significant profits recorded by banks, coupled with the globalization of the financial markets, have provided increased incentive for dealers to become primary price makers.

Very few corporations have assumed the role of primary price maker. The expertise required to run a trading room covers many areas. In addition to the obvious trading skills required, considerable resources are required from a management, control, and operations standpoint. The attitude and decision-making style of a trading room are quite different, in most cases, from those of most businesses and organizations, and these skills are not easily found. In addition to finding the right resources, there is also the matter of paying for the people and their infrastructure of computers, news services, communication equipment, and other related assets.

Some multinational corporations may become more involved in the price maker's role in the future. The financial activities of these organizations often require proactive and aggressive management of cash-flow, interest-rate risk, and foreign exchange risk. The resources for these tasks are, in many cases, in place in these corporations, and the next step to becoming a niche primary price maker may not be that big for some players. Moreover, their financial strength is often superior to many traditional major market makers, and with the capital adequacy constraints facing banks, corporations may often have a competitive advantage over existing primary dealers in some markets. Late entrants to the market will also benefit from the ability to acquire the latest in dealing technology at costs far less than most banks have invested.

In the past, some corporations have attempted to develop relationships with other corporations through which they could offset their foreign exchange exposures with each other. In so doing, the two firms expect to remove the bid-and-offer spread and save money. However, foreign exchange markets are competitive, and the bid-and-offer spread facing corporations is fairly small, if there is one at all. Moreover, simple, but significant, problems arise if the two parties do not agree on the amounts, the delivery dates, or the time when the rates are to be set. The entities are also taking on credit risk with each other which may or may not be a problem. This kind of trading is, therefore, unlikely to become commonplace.

International capital flows constitute a significant part of foreign exchange dealings. Pension and mutual funds frequently search for investments globally. Whether explicitly stated or not, such global investing is to a large extent foreign exchange management, as the foreign exchange gains and losses will frequently dwarf the returns on the underlying assets purchased. In these circumstances, taking the step to formally invest in a foreign exchange trading operation to manage one's own exposures may often be prudent.

As indicated, two-way pricing distinguishes primary price makers. When Bank A asks Bank B for a price, Bank A does not indicate whether it has an interest in buying or selling, only that it would like a price. Bank B responds with both a buying and a selling price, referred to as bid and offer. Bank A then either passes on both prices or will deal at one of the two prices.

Bank B's prices should be good up to certain amounts and represent a professional spread, that is, the difference between the bid and offer should be reasonably small. If Bank B does not give good prices to Bank A, Bank B will be unlikely to receive good prices in return. While primary price makers are competitors, they nonetheless need each other. Their basic survival depends on their ability to operate on a basis of reciprocity under which they can contact each other and expect to receive professional market prices.

Primary price makers play a key role in terms of making market prices; taking the risk from another dealer, corporation, or individual; and then transferring this foreign exchange exposure to other entities that have offsetting foreign exchange exposures. They should be willing to make bids and offers at almost any time during a local market's normal dealing hours. In doing so, they absorb the market risk from any and all market participants into their own positions. They provide a key role to the market, and in return for this risk management, they hope to make money.

As discussed in Chapters 2 and 4, a spot exchange rate is determined by several factors. The combined impact of these factors is felt in the supply and demand for a currency which ultimately determines its exchange rate. The primary market makers are most actively involved in the markets and are usually, apart from the central banks, most aware of the current or expected supply-and-demand pressures on a currency. The sheer size of the foreign exchange markets and the number of market makers in major currencies, however, make it very difficult even for these principal dealers to determine which way the markets will move, when they will move, and to what extent they will move. A more detailed review of how these primary market makers trade is given in Chapter 10.

Secondary Price Makers

Secondary price makers include entities that make foreign exchange prices but do not deal in the market on a two-way reciprocity basis. Examples of these organizations include many service businesses, such as restaurants and hotels, which will typically take a customer's foreign currency as payment for bills. Some companies may also specialize in buying and selling foreign exchange to the retail public. They typically have wide spreads between their buying and selling rates and, as their needs dictate, buy their requirements or sell their surplus positions to a more active market player.

Many banks and financial institutions cannot justify the development of a primary price-making group in foreign exchange. They may, however, need to provide a foreign exchange service to their client base. To do so, they solicit prices on a customer basis from a price maker and then reflect these prices to their own clients.

Futures traders are also a form of secondary market trader. Such traders will show their interests in either buying or selling or both buying and selling; however, they do not have to show a price to their dealing colleagues. Two-way reciprocity does not prevail, although it certainly does occur.

Price Takers

The third tier of market participants consists of entities that take the prices of primary or secondary price makers and deal for their own purposes. They do not reciprocate and make market prices. They are price takers. These entities include corporations, governments, small banks, wealthy individuals, and the retail public at large.

Large banks are also price takers on many occasions, such as when they deal in currencies in which they are not usually active. Such price-taking approaches are practical and are often part of general reciprocity between the dealing groups at two or more banks.

Advisory Services

Technical competence, information, and a good dose of luck are frequently cited as reasons why money is made dealing in foreign exchange. The timing of buying or selling of a currency is critical, and numerous organizations exist in the world for the purpose of advising clients what and when to buy or sell. Other advisory services get very heavily involved in determining strategies and approaches that best suit clients. For their advice, they typically charge fees, although profit-sharing arrangements are fairly common as well.

Advisory services operate in a variety of ways. Some provide running commentary on Reuters, Telerate, or Knight-Ridder. Others send out daily fax or telex summaries. Some send out regular newsletters with market summaries and recommendations, and some will only send out information when they have a strong buy or sell recommendation. The personal touch is also available, perhaps involving a form of ongoing consulting on exposure management, in which a consultant is familiar with the details of the company's exposures and works closely with the client's treasury people.

Most major banks and dealers also provide variations of these services. Most of the time, the service is provided to build a relationship with the client and to earn the right to see and do the actual business of the client. The fee, if it can be called that, is "collected" on this subsequent business, which is expected to generate profits.

Foreign Exchange Brokers

Primary price makers deal in a variety of ways. One common method is to telephone another price maker directly. Another way is to contact price makers directly via telex or electronic dealing systems into which dealers can link. In addition, it is also possible to use foreign exchange brokers. Using a broker allows one to show prices into the market on an anonymous basis. If the prices are as good as or better than the other ones available to the broker, the broker will quote these prices to the market. The process of spreading current price information and ultimately bringing buyers and sellers together earns the broker a commission.

Foreign exchange brokers are not principal traders. That is, they do not buy or sell currencies for their own position. When a trade is done, the broker advises the two parties, usually banks, that they have dealt with each other. As long as there are no restrictions, such as credit, which prevent the two players from dealing, they then write up a trade ticket with each other. The broker does not stand between the two banks on the trade, but simply provides a service to the interbank market. Major brokerage houses are frequently global in nature and service the interbank market 24 hours a day, in much the same way as primary price makers are able to service their client base around the clock.

In the futures trading pit, dealing is done on a face-to-face basis. Some traders are principals in that they trade for their own account, while others are brokers acting on behalf of clients. In addition, in the futures market, each party buys or sells from the exchange. Consider, for example, Trader A who buys dollars from Trader B. The two traders indicate who their counterparty is on their respective trade tickets, but the actual trade position shows the futures exchange as selling dollars to Trader A and buying dollars on identical terms from Trader B. If Trader B is a broker, the trade could be shown for its account (on behalf of a client that is not a member of the exchange), or it could be directed to the name of the broker's client if the client is a member.

Speculators

Speculators in the foreign exchange market consist of many different players. Consider the following situations, which are examples of entities knowingly taking or maintaining foreign exchange risks:

1. Primary price makers actively take positions in the market.

2. Corporations enter into business transactions that incur foreign exchange exposure and delay coverage, or do not cover the exposure until the cashflows materialize.

3. Governments borrow or invest in foreign currencies and delay coverage or do not cover the associated foreign exchange exposure until maturity.

4. Individuals buy foreign currency stocks, bonds, or other assets without covering the foreign exchange risk.

5. Entities take positions in commodities whose inherent value is based on a currency other than the currency dealt in the transaction (see Chapter 13).

Each of these parties could gain or lose depending on foreign exchange movements. The risk is the same, and one could argue that all such transactions are speculative. The dividing line between speculation and prudent business decisions (or diversification of risk or other descriptive phrases) is often difficult to define. The issue is particularly clouded when the foreign exchange position arises as a result of normal (nonfinancial) business transactions. Some would say failure to immediately cover is speculation, while others would reserve the term for exchange positions that are created strictly for the purpose of trading the currency markets. However, risk is risk regardless of how it arises, and the key challenge is to manage the risk properly.

The term *speculation* conjures negative images in many people's minds. Speculators are often blamed for major moves happening in a market. Sometimes the blame is fairly placed. The speculative or trading sector in foreign exchange markets is very large and can cause significant swings in exchange rates, swings that are often detrimental to the global economy. However, the speculative element is needed in the markets to provide the liquidity for handling "nonspeculative" deals. Without this market liquidity, foreign exchange markets would have wider bid-and-offer spreads, slowness in receiving prices, and difficulty in executing large or unique transactions. Consequently, while the speculative element may have some negative implications in the view of some people, it also makes a major, and perhaps unappreciated, contribution to the efficiency with which the markets operate.

Central Banks

The mandate of central banks will vary from country to country. However, a common thread would include the responsibility for managing the country's supply of credit and money, from both a short-term and a long-term perspective. This activity is known as monetary policy. While a detailed discussion of monetary policy is beyond the scope of this book, a brief summary will help to explain the activities of central banks in the money and foreign exchange markets.

The central bank is typically the bank that acts for the government. The government typically maintains bank accounts at the central bank and processes its receipts and disbursements through these accounts. If the government is running a deficit, it will need to raise new money, and it will do so by issuing either short- or long-term debt. The central bank can often play a role in the management of this debt:

1. The central bank can give advice to the government on what debt should be issued and at what rates.

2. The central bank can physically look after the issuance and redemption of the debt.

3. The central bank can do the actual buying and selling of the debt instruments.

The last point is of particular interest. If the government has $100 million in debt maturing on a given day and issues $100 million in new debt, it would seem that there is no real change in the supply of money. This is indeed true some of the time, but not always. Consider the following three situations:

1. If investors own the maturing debt and purchase the new debt, there is no change. It is a simple switch of debt.

2. If investors own the maturing debt, but the central bank buys the new debt, there is an increase in the money supply. The central bank makes a payment to the government which is used by the govern-

ment to repay the maturing debt. Meanwhile, the investors have $100 million in cash to spend elsewhere in the economy. This method of increasing the money supply is called *monetizing the debt.*

3. On the other hand, if the central bank owns the maturing debt, but other investors buy the new debt, there will be an actual contraction of money in the economy.

If debt is monetized, there is more money in the economy competing for scarce resources. Inflation, as a general rule, will increase.

Inflation and economic growth are two of the prime concerns of the central bank. Excessive focus on one can create real problems with the other. Consequently, the central bank is faced with a balancing act when trying to foster economic growth without causing excessive inflation.

Inflation is caused by many factors, one of which, as suggested, is an increase in the money supply. Very briefly, to prevent inflation from getting out of control, the central bank will often restrict the growth of money. Monetizing debt, for instance, will be minor or not done at all. This forces the government debt to compete for investment dollars against all other borrowers in the marketplace. The increase in demand for the investment dollar pushes up the price of money, which is, of course, interest rates. Higher interest rates, in turn, reduce the amount of borrowing and increase the amount of saving by the private sector. This, in turn, by causing economic activity to decline, leads to an easing in inflation.

Foreign Exchange Intervention and Interest Rates

Higher interest rates are used to fight inflation, usually that arising from within the domestic economy. In addition, interest rates can also be used to adjust the value of a currency. Higher rates will tend to support a currency by attracting foreign capital. A stronger currency makes imports cheaper and puts downward pressure on domestic prices. The trade-off, unfortunately, is a slower economic growth.

Interest rates are influenced by the central banks in a number of ways. The key ones are as follows:

1. Monetizing or not monetizing the debt when issued.

2. Open-market operations. Purchases or sales of government debt instruments previously issued represent a contraction or an expansion of the money supply.

3. Withdrawing cash from or adding cash to the bank system. In Canada, for instance, each major bank has an account with the Bank of

Canada. The Bank of Canada can simply withdraw cash from or add cash to the banks' accounts. The banks will then act to either raise cash or spend it by investing or lending.

4. Changing the level of reserves on deposits. Raising the level of reserves, for instance, will reduce the amounts that banks can lend. This reduction, in turn, reduces the money supply. Changing reserve requirements is infrequently done, but nevertheless it remains available for most central banks.

Direct intervention to hold down a currency, such as the CAD, can be done by the Bank of Canada by selling the CAD and buying the USD or another reserve currency, such as the JPY. If done on a spot basis, the bank is immediately adding CAD to the domestic money supply. To offset this increase, the bank could act in a couple of ways. First, it could sell treasury bills in the market, or, second, the bank could execute cash-management swaps (see Chapter 9), wherein it sells USD value spot and buys back the USD on forward basis. In both cases, the bank "sterilizes" the money supply from the effect of the spot foreign exchange intervention. If the intervention is done on a forward instead of spot basis, the impact on the money supply is delayed until the foreign contracts settle. At that time, sterilization activities may again be needed.

Central banks can intervene directly in the foreign exchange markets in a variety of ways:

1. Directly with banks

2. Through brokers

3. Through futures markets

4. Through other central banks dealing on their behalf

Central banks can intervene to maintain orderly markets, or they may intervene with the intention of turning the market. Sometimes they may simply test the waters to gauge the impact of a potential major intervention. They may try to maneuver a currency in a particular direction by working both sides. In addition to direct intervention, they can also use monetary policy or moral suasion.

The actual mechanics for intervening directly in the foreign exchange markets are described in more detail in Chapter 10. The amount of intervention, the timing, the methodology, and the status of the market all will determine the effectiveness of intervention. Continued use of intervention or a particular tool takes away much of the psychological impact, and central banks must be reasonably selective in their activities. In many cases, the threat of intervention is more significant than the actual intervention itself.

6
Foreign Exchange: Some of the Basics

Executive Summary

Chapter 6 is a beginner's guide to buying and selling foreign exchange. The chapter lists the international trading codes for key currencies. It explains the dominant role of the U.S. dollar and how to determine prices when the U.S. dollar is not one of the two currencies traded. It demonstrates how to price transactions using different quotation methods. The chapter also reviews currency codes, bids and offers, points and pips, and value dates. The chapter concludes with the new cross-rate pricing model and some examples of how to use it.

ISO Codes

Foreign exchange markets are global. To work effectively, standardization of certain elements is essential. One such aspect has been the creation of a standard three-letter abbreviation of each currency. These abbreviations were created by the International Organization for Standardization and are appropriately referred to as ISO codes. The ISO codes of some of the more widely traded currencies are shown in Exhibit 6.1.

Hereafter, we will use the ISO codes extensively. You may want to pay particular attention to the currencies denoted with an asterisk (*), since they are the currencies most frequently used in various examples that follow.

Many currencies also have nicknames that are routinely used in the

Exhibit 6.1. ISO Codes for Selected Currencies

Country	Currency	ISO Code
Australia	dollar	AUD*
Canada	dollar	CAD*
Denmark	kroner	DKK
France	franc	FRF
Germany	deutsche mark	DEM*
Great Britain	pound	GBP*
Hong Kong	dollar	HKD
Ireland	punt	IEP
Italy	lire	ITL
Japan	yen	JPY*
Netherlands	guilder	NLG
New Zealand	dollar	NZD
Norway	krone	NOK
Saudi Arabia	riyal	SAR
Singapore	dollar	SGD
Spain	peseta	ESP
Sweden	krona	SEK
Switzerland	franc	CHF
United States	dollar	USD*

marketplace. For instance, sterling is known as *cable*, the New Zealand dollar as *kiwi*, and the French franc as *Paris*.

Benchmark Prices for Currencies

Foreign exchange transactions involve the exchange of one currency for another. There are over 150 countries in the world, about 30 of which have currencies that are actively traded in world markets. With just these 30 currencies, there are 29 different exchange rates for each currency. A total of 435 different exchange rates could be quoted at any time.

It would be difficult to visualize the global foreign exchange markets operating on a basis where every currency was directly valued and traded against every other currency. In such an environment, it would be extremely difficult for most market participants to ensure that all rates properly reflected all changes in all markets.

Such a situation would be similar to a fruit market in a nonmoney economy in which each trader brings his or her produce to exchange. It would be necessary to determine prices on the basis of so many apples per pear, peach, orange, and banana. There would also be prices on pears per peach, orange, and banana, as well as prices on peaches per orange and banana, and, finally, prices on oranges per banana.

This kind of market could work if there were few varieties and consistently stable prices. However, it would be much simpler to price each fruit against a standard unit of account such as the country's currency in which the fruit is being sold. A system of directly valuing and trading each currency against all other currencies could also exist if there were few changes in exchange rates. This, however, would require that all the participating countries experience similar rates of real economic growth and inflation, as well as similar political policy and leadership.

The reality of the situation, however, is that there are often significant differences in economic and political policy as well as economic and financial performance. Major differences exist between developing countries and the developed nations of the world. Among the developed nations, Japan, Germany, Great Britain, France, Canada, Italy, and the United States are referred to as the *G-7*. Even within this group, significant differences exist in terms of inflation, economic growth, government deficits, debt burden, taxation, international trade, and other key variables.

Largely as a result of these differences, substantial volatility occurs in the exchange rates. Markets in which all currencies traded against all other currencies on a direct-value basis would function poorly. For this and other reasons, the markets have evolved so that currencies tend first and foremost to be valued against one currency—the U.S. dollar.

The Kingpin Currency— The U.S. Dollar

The United States is the world's largest economy and is often referred to as the economic locomotive for the rest of the world. By way of comparison, the GNP of the United States was 5.5 trillion USD in 1990, while that of Japan, the second largest economy, was 2.9 trillion USD. The United States is directly involved in about 15 percent of international trade as either an importer or exporter. The United States also plays a major role in international capital flows, a large component of which is the purchase of United States government debt instruments by foreigners. The USD is the most important currency because of the relative size of the United States economy. International developments, such as Europe 1992, could cause the USD to lose its preeminent role. However, for the foreseeable future, the USD will almost surely remain a major currency in global currency markets.

A currency that is to function well in the domestic and international marketplace must be able to perform as a monetary standard. Three main criteria are required of such currencies:

1. There must be confidence in the currency as a store of value.
2. The currency must be able to act as a unit of account in international trade.
3. The currency must be able to serve as a medium of exchange.

In effect, a currency must have a constant source of buyers and sellers. In other words, there must be a ready market for the currency at all times. The USD has met these criteria for most of the twentieth century. The markets, at times, have seen marked reductions in the value of the USD against other currencies, and the question could be asked whether or not the dollar does function as a store of value. However, all major currencies are weak from time to time, and while owning USD or USD assets may not always have produced the best financial return, there is always a ready market for the USD in the exchange markets. Moreover, in times of international tension, when capital is looking for a safe haven, the USD is usually one of the first currencies to be bought.

Additional evidence suggesting that the USD is the dominant currency in the world follows:

1. Central banks around the world hold several currencies in addition to gold in their foreign exchange reserves. However, the main reserve asset held is the USD.
2. Almost all major commodities in the world are valued in terms of the USD.
3. The currency in which most international trade is conducted is the USD.
4. The majority of international debt is denominated in USD.
5. When traveling internationally, one finds the USD is the most universally accepted currency at the retail level.
6. The value of almost all currencies is expressed in terms of the USD.

The last point best reveals the role of the USD in exchange markets. Member countries of the European Economic Community, such as Germany, Switzerland, France, Italy, Spain, and Austria, have their main economic relationships with each other. However, the EEC currencies are not valued in world markets against each other. Instead, the currencies are primarily valued and traded against the USD. A shift to increased cross-trading between such currencies as pounds sterling and Japanese yen and between the German deutsche mark and Swiss franc has materialized. However, the underlying pricing relationship for most currencies still remains primarily with the USD.

Cross Rates

The relative value of two currencies is typically determined by comparing the value of each of the two currencies against the USD.

$$1.0 \text{ GBP} = 2 \text{ USD}$$

and $\quad\quad$ 1.5 DEM = 1 USD $\quad\quad$ (or 3.0 DEM = 2 USD)

Therefore, $\quad$ 3.0 DEM = 1 GBP

This process is shown schematically in Exhibit 6.2.

Exchange rates between two currencies, neither of which is the USD, are termed *cross rates*. In executing cross-rate deals, usually only one price is quoted between the client and the institution making the market price, i.e., the price maker, which is usually a bank. The price maker may also be able to trade the transaction on one price when it tries to cover the transaction. However, while cross-rate deals are developing and becoming a fairly common part of professional trading, they are not the dominant form by which transactions are completed. Instead, most dealing rooms still treat the transaction as two separate deals.

Exhibit 6.2. Cross-Rate Determination

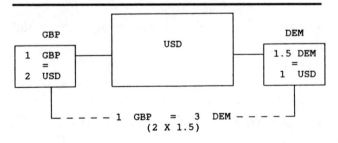

Exhibit 6.3. Summary of Cashflows on a Cross-Rate Transaction

	Company ABC		Market Maker		
	DEM	GBP	DEM	USD	GBP
Company ABC: Buys DEM vs GBP	6,000	(2,000)	(6,000)		2,000
Market-Maker: i. Sells GBP vs USD ii. Buys DEM vs USD			6,000	4,000 (4,000)	(2,000)
NET	6,000	(2,000)	0	0	0

Consider a scenario where Company ABC needs to buy 6 million deutsche marks and wishes to pay for the deutsche marks with pounds sterling.

In a market where 1 GBP = 3 DEM, Company ABC would sell 2 million GBP in order to buy the desired 6 million DEM. The company would see one exchange rate and, on the settlement date, would pay GBP and receive DEM.

From the market maker's standpoint, it sold DEM and bought GBP. To cover its position, it needs to do the opposite. For instance, it could cover its 6 million short DEM position by buying 6 million DEM and selling 4 million USD at the market rate of 1.5 DEM/USD. Similarly, it may sell 2 million GBP and buy 4 million USD at the market rate of 2.0 USD/GBP. A summary of the cashflows is shown in Exhibit 6.3.

Quotation Methods

Foreign exchange rates are frequently quoted in either the direct or indirect method. The *direct* method of quotation expresses the number of units of local or domestic currency in terms of a single unit of a foreign currency. This method is a price quotation showing the price of the foreign currency. For example:

> In Canada,   .5 CAD = 1 DEM
>
> In Germany,   2 DEM = 1 CAD

The *indirect* method is a quotation that expresses the number of units of foreign currency per unit of local currency. This method is commonly viewed as a volume quotation. For example:

In Canada,   2 DEM = 1 CAD

In Germany,   .5 CAD = 1 DEM

A direct quote in Germany on DEM/CAD transactions represents an indirect quote in Canada. Similarly, an indirect quote in Germany would be classified as a direct quote in Canada.

For parties located in another country, such as Australia, a DEM/USD rate is neither a direct nor an indirect quote, as both currencies are foreign to Australia. There is no local currency involved. In practice, the market will often refer to pricing methods as either European terms or North American terms.

European terms imply that the quotation is expressed as the number of units of currency per USD:

2.0 DEM = 1 USD

North American terms imply that the quotation is expressed as the number of units of USD per unit of currency:

.50 USD = 1 DEM

While the direct-indirect and European–North American terms are used quite commonly, the two categories do not cover all situations. For example, consider a DEM/CAD quotation by a Norwegian-based party. None of the above systems applies.

From the viewpoint of market makers, a key element of price quotations is to make them as consistent and simple as possible. In this regard, a rule of thumb that usually holds true is that the exchange rate quoted between two currencies will be greater than 1.0000. In other words, the stronger currency will usually be the unit of account, and the rate will be stated as the number of units of the weaker currency per single unit of the stronger currency. For example, consider the following:

1.1500 CAD = 1 USD	and not	.8696 USD = 1 CAD
1.7500 USD = 1 GBP	and not	.5714 GBP = 1 USD
1.6500 DEM = 1 USD	and not	.6061 USD = 1 DEM
2.8875 DEM = 1 GBP	and not	.3463 GBP = 1 DEM

Another framework for quoting prices is occasionally seen in the market but is not clearly defined. It is similar to North American and European terms, but it is more flexible. This quotation system could be called "American and currency terms" and is the basis for the cross-rate pricing model outlined in Exhibit 6.9. If the rate reflects the number of USD per unit of foreign currency, the rate is said to be in *American terms*. All other quotes would be said to be quoted in *currency terms*. Moreover, within the broad category of currency terms, a quote can be more specific and said to be in terms of a particular currency, such as Canadian terms or German terms.

German terms imply that the quotation is to be made in terms of the number of deutsche marks per unit of the other currency, regardless of the currency. Similarly, *Canadian* terms imply that the quotation is made in terms of the number of Canadian dollars per unit of foreign currency, regardless of the currency.

German Terms	Canadian Terms
2.0 DEM = 1 CAD	.50 CAD = 1 DEM
3.0 DEM = 1 GBP	2.00 CAD = 1 GBP
2.0 DEM = 1 AUD	1.00 CAD = 1 AUD

All currencies at any given time have a certain value, and this value remains unaffected by the method of quotation. For many years, there was no universal norm for foreign exchange quotations, and different methods were used in the various local markets. Foreign exchange markets have now developed to a point where they are global in nature; standard quotation methods are necessary and have indeed evolved for each currency.

Most currencies are traded in currency terms, i.e., the number of units per USD. The notable exceptions are the following countries, whose currencies are quoted in American terms, i.e., the number of USD per currency unit:

Country	Currency
Australia	Dollar
Great Britain	Pounds sterling
Ireland	Punt
New Zealand	Dollar
South Africa	Rand

It should also be noted that within a particular country, most retail and small commercial transactions are made on the basis of the number of units of local currency per unit of foreign currency.

Reciprocal Quotations

As indicated, currencies can be quoted in terms of the number of units of A per unit of B or, alternatively, the number of units of B per unit of A. The two rates represent equal value and are reciprocals of each other. To convert from one method to the other, one simply divides the number 1 by the rate.

$$.5000 \text{ USD/DEM} = \frac{1}{.5000} \text{ DEM/USD}$$

$$= 2 \text{ DEM/USD}$$

When changing from one method to another, the resulting answers will often not be perfectly equal due to rounding. For example:

1. The reciprocal of 1.7265 is not .5792 but .5792064....
2. The reciprocal of .5792 is not 1.7265 but 1.7265193....

Points and Pips

Exchange rates for major currencies, excluding the JPY and ITL, are usually quoted to four decimal places in the wholesale market.

$$1.7505 \text{ DEM} = 1 \text{ USD}$$

$$1.8000 \text{ USD} = 1 \text{ GBP}$$

The fourth decimal place (.0001) is called a *point*. Some quotes involve finer pricing, and so a fifth decimal place is used. The fifth decimal point (.00001) is referred to as a *pip*.

The key factor in determining the number of decimal points that should be used in deals is the monetary significance involved. Exhibit 6.4 demonstrates the change in USD equivalent arising from a single point change in price for four currencies.

Exhibit 6.4. Cashflow Significance per Single-Point Change in Rate

Currency code	Amount	Market rate A	Market rate B	USD Equivalent Rate A	USD Equivalent Rate B	Change per point, $
AUD	1,000,000	.8025	.8026	802,500	802,600	100
GBP	1,000,000	1.7500	1.7501	1,750,000	1,750,100	100
DEM	1,000,000	1.8000	1.8001	555,555	555,525	30
CAD	1,000,000	1.2500	1.2501	800,000	799,936	64

Exhibit 6.5. Significance of Points for JPY and ITL Quoted in Currency Terms

Currency	Amount of currency	Market rate A	Market rate B	USD Equivalent		Change per point, $
				Rate A	Rate B	
JPY	100,000,000	125.00	125.01	800,000	799,936	64
ITL	1,000,000,000	1400.25	1400.26	714,158	714,153	5

Transactions in these currencies all involve 1 million units of currency. A single point (.0001) change in the rate is worth anywhere from $30 to $100. That level of incremental change is significant, yet not unreasonable. If three decimal places were used, the increments would be $300 to $1000, which is excessive. On the other hand, use of five decimal places would not materially change the price and is thus unnecessary for most transactions.

In the case of the JPY and ITL, consider the results as shown in Exhibit 6.5.

These two currencies exchange at hundreds and thousands of units per USD. Rates are only quoted to two decimal places, however, since anything finer has no material impact on the price. A point on these currencies refers to the second decimal place in this method of quotation.

When the price quotations of USD/JPY or USD/ITL are used, a point refers to the sixth decimal place for JPY and the seventh place for ITL. Exhibit 6.6 demonstrates that using the same JPY and ITL volumes as in Exhibit 6.5, the change per point in a four-place decimal system is $10,000 for JPY and $100,000 for ITL. Such value increments are excessive, and consequently, prices showing the number of USD per unit of JPY or ITL are quoted to six and seven decimal places, respectively. In so doing, a point change is now worth $100, which is a reasonable level of increment of change.

As a rule of thumb for the newcomer, the number of decimal places

Exhibit 6.6. Significance of Points for ITL and JPY Quoted in American Terms

Currency	Amount of currency	Market rate A	Market rate B	USD Equivalent		Change per point, $
				Rate A	Rate B	
JPY	100,000,000	.0080	.0079	800,000	790,000	10,000
ITL	1,000,000,000	.0007	.0006	700,000	600,000	100,000

to use in the reciprocal quotes is usually three more than the number of digits before (to the left of) the decimal point in a regular quote. For instance, USD/GBP has one digit before the decimal point in American terms, and so four digits (1 + 3) should follow the decimal point in reciprocal quotes in currency terms. Similarly, JPY has three digits before the decimal point in its regular currency terms quote and should, therefore, have six digits after the decimal point in its reciprocal quotation in American terms.

From a historical perspective, the methods of quotation and the norms in the market have changed considerably. It was only a few decades ago, for instance, that some currencies were quoted in terms of fractions.

$$1 \text{ USD} = 1.01 \ 19/32 \text{ CAD}$$

In today's market, that rate would be quoted as 1.0159, where the 19/32 equals .0059.

Settlement of Foreign Exchange Transactions

Foreign exchange deals involve two currencies. A participant in a deal sells or gives delivery of one currency and buys or takes delivery of another currency.

What constitutes taking or giving delivery of a currency will vary. In retail transactions, such as when an individual buys some cash notes before going on a foreign holiday, the person receives ownership of money in physical form. The legal tender held by the traveler can be presented as payment in the country of destination in the same way one makes payment in local currency.

If the stakes were changed to perhaps $10 million, the most common method of executing settlement would be wire transfers. Wire transfers are the predominant form simply because of their ability to effect payment in developed countries on the same day, or at worst, a day or two later. Wire payments can be made using such systems as CHIPS, SWIFT, FEDWIRE, and telex.

Checks can also be used, but this alternative is often impractical. In Canada, if a Canadian dollar check is deposited at a Canadian bank before the close of business, the depositor will receive same-day value. In other words, if a check is drawn on Bank A and deposited at Bank B, Bank B processes the check through a centralized clearing process and receives value from Bank A. Bank A debits the account of the client issuing the check to make itself whole. Similarly, Bank B is able to credit the depositor's account. However, if a USD check drawn on another Canadian bank is presented within Canada, it normally takes one business day for the USD check to be cleared through the system. If the check is drawn on a U.S. bank, the check could take several days, even weeks, to clear.

It should be noted that countries have varying financial systems, and same-day clearing for the domestic currency, such as Canadian dollars in Canada, is not at all universal. Clearing times may take several days, and cash-management practice must bear these clearing times in mind when transactions are being planned. While each country's practices vary, the basic concept presented in the next few paragraphs tends to hold.

Domestic Clearing Systems: An Example

Collectively, financial organizations process millions of such transactions on a daily basis. In order for this clearing process to function properly, the banks need to cooperate and work in a standardized, uniform fashion. On check clearings, for instance, consider a country known as Moneyland where there are four banks: Bank A, Bank B, Bank C, and Bank D. On a particular day, each bank receives a variety of negotiable items that were deposited by their clients. These banks clear or present their items for reimbursement to Moneyland's central bank, as shown in Exhibit 6.7.

Bank A presents items totaling $900 to the central bank of Moneyland. The total of all items drawn on Bank A and presented to the central bank for reimbursement is $800. As a result, the central bank credits Bank A's account with the central bank for the net amount of $100.

Exhibit 6.7. Example of Clearing Items Presented to Moneyland Central Bank

Presenting bank	Total items drawn on and presented to bank				
	Bank A	Bank B	Bank C	Bank D	Total
Bank A		100	300	500	900
Bank B	200		200	300	700
Bank C	300	400		100	800
Bank D	300	300	300		900
Total	800	800	800	900	3300

Bank B presents $700 and is presented with $800 in items drawn on it by its clients. The central bank debits Bank B's account with the central bank for $100. Banks C and D have offsetting amounts of $800 and $900, respectively, and the central bank thus makes no entry to their accounts.

The individual banks are given the items drawn on them, which they, in turn, handle individually and use to debit the various customer accounts on which they are drawn. For instance, Bank A may debit Client A's account for $100, Client B's account for $300, and Client C's account for $500.

If Client C's account does not have sufficient funds to cover the amount of the check, the bank needs to recoup its money that it effectively paid to Bank D when Bank D presented the check. Bank A may contact the client and ask that the client make a deposit to cover the check. Alternatively, Bank A may return the check to Bank D and seek repayment. Bank D will do so and, in turn, will seek reimbursement from the depositor. The depositor will then go back to the issuer of the check, Client C, for reimbursement. The normal course of events is such that, unless special arrangements are made, checks presented on accounts in which there are insufficient funds will be sent back through the clearing process for reimbursement.

Settling International Transactions: An Example

Let us return to the international arena. If Buyer A in a country such as Canada wanted to make a payment to Supplier B in Australia in Australian dollars, Buyer A would typically purchase Australian dollars via a foreign exchange transaction. Buyer A then would instruct its foreign exchange bank, Canadian Bank 123, to pay the Australian dollars to Supplier B's account at Australian Bank 789.

Buyer A's Canadian bank can effect the payment in several ways. One of the simplest methods occurs where it has an account at Australian Bank 789. In this case, Canadian Bank 123 ensures that there are enough Australian dollars in its account to fund the payment to Supplier B. If Canadian Bank 123 does not have an account with Australian Bank 789, it will use its accounts at another Australian bank to make a payment to Australian Bank 789, which, in turn, is paid to Supplier B.

Canadian Bank 123 is not part of the Australian banking system. It, therefore, uses its relationship with an Australian bank to gain access to that market. These correspondent bank relationships are essential for global commerce. These working relationships have produced some new expressions, two of which are vostro and nostro.

Nostro refers to the accounts that one's own bank has with other banks. Nostro, derived from the Latin word *noster*, represents *our* accounts. *Vostro* refers to accounts that other banks have with our bank. Vostro, derived from the Latin word *voster*, means *your* accounts.

Returning to the previous business example, Buyer A could have paid Supplier B in other ways, such as a draft in Australian dollars. The draft will only clear, or give true good value, when it is presented to the drawee bank in Australia. This can often be a time-consuming process. In many countries, credit issues, foreign exchange controls, turbulent market conditions, or difficulties in converting some foreign currencies will often necessitate foreign currency drafts or equivalents to be sent on collection. While this process can take several weeks for some currencies, it is the only practical means for the foreign exchange settlement to occur.

Value Dates

On a normal business day, global foreign exchange transactions total hundreds of billions of dollars. Each transaction has its own characteristics in terms of amount of currency and countercurrency, rate, and date on which the deal will settle. A foreign exchange deal made on a Monday could result in the exchange of currency on that day or some date in the future.

Standardization and simplicity of dealing are essential for the foreign exchange markets to run effectively. If Bank ABC calls Bank DEF seeking a spot price such as USD/CAD, the conversation may go as follows:

BANK ABC: "Bank ABC calling. Price on funds, please."

BANK XYZ: "Ten fifteen."

BANK ABC: "Five dollars yours at ten."

In Bank ABC's first statement, the bank introduced itself and asked for Bank XYZ's market on the Canadian dollar against the USD. *Funds* is a term used to specify this market.

Bank XYZ's market is really 1.2510/1.2515. However, both entities know the first three digits are 1.25, and thus Bank XYZ is able simply to state the last two digits. Moreover, XYZ's response of "ten fifteen" means that it will buy USD and sell CAD at 10 (1.2510) and will sell USD and buy CAD at 15 (1.2515). Bank ABC likes Bank XYZ's bid and decides to sell 5 million USD to Bank XYZ at 1.2510. In return for the 5 million USD, it will receive 6,255,000 CAD. Both banks know that the prices reflect settlement on the next business day.

Interbank trading goes on throughout the day, and such spot transactions need a standard settlement date for an entire day's trading. The current business day is not workable as a standard settlement date for CAD/USD trading because, beyond a certain point in the day, payments cannot be made to each other for value that date. However, the next business day that both countries are open for business is workable as a standard spot date. Both countries are in the same basic grid of time zones, and adequate time exists for any deal done on one day to be processed and settled on the next common business day.

Transactions involving other currencies may have more difficulty settling on the next common business day because the relevant time zone can be significantly different from that of the United States. Consequently, the standard spot settlement date is two common business days hence for other currencies.

Cross-rated deals between European currencies would involve comparable time zones, and thus a value of two days hence may appear unnecessarily slow. As indicated earlier, though, these currencies are usually traded and valued against the USD, which is the underlying market on which the cross-rated prices are based. Consequently, the norm for spot transactions is for settlement to be made two days hence. However, there are exceptions to everything, and while the standard date may be one or two days hence, transactions are dealt for value before the standard spot date.

Bid and Offer

As we shall see in greater detail in Chapter 10, the foreign exchange markets trade mainly on the basis of two-way markets. That is, market makers will simultaneously show prices at which they will buy (their bid) and at which they will sell (their offer). The example in the previous section used a 1.2510–1.2515 market. The 1.2510 rate represents the market maker's bid for USD, and the 1.2515 represented the market maker's offer for USD.

Because a foreign exchange deal constitutes the sale of one currency and the purchase of another, the bid of 1.2510 for USD is also essentially an offer of CAD at 1.2510. Similarly, the offer of USD at 1.2515 also represents a bid for CAD.

Market practice dictates that the first price given, i.e., the one on the left, is the bid and the price on the right is the offer. Consequently, in the above example, if someone asks for a bid and says nothing else, the inference is that he or she is asking for a bid in order to sell USD.

Cross-Rated Bid and Offer Pricing

Earlier in this chapter, distinctions were made among quotation methods and between deals done against the USD versus cross-rate deals between currencies, neither of which were the USD. The actual mechanics of pricing cross-rate deals require a clear understanding of the quotation methods being used. This is because one cross-rate deal may be priced by dividing one rate by another, while another deal may involve the multiplication of the two rates. Furthermore, a particular deal may involve two bids, two offers, or a bid and an offer. Finally, when the correct rate has been determined, one must also know which currency is the unit of account. In other words, does the rate reflect the number of units of currency A per unit of currency B, or does it reflect the number of units of currency B per unit of currency A?

If the two currencies are quoted the same way, e.g., both in American terms, the rates show the number of USD that equal one currency unit.

$$USD/GBP = 1.8020 \qquad USD/AUD = .7800$$

The two rates reveal a comparative value in that both are quoted in terms of the number of USD per unit of that currency. To determine the exchange rate between GBP and AUD, one can follow through the steps shown in Exhibit 6.8.

Exhibit 6.8. Detailed Steps to Determine AUD/GBP Cross Rate

1.	.7800 USD = 1 AUD
2.	$\dfrac{.7800 \text{ USD}}{.7800} = \dfrac{1 \text{ AUD}}{.7800}$
3.	1 USD = 1.2821 AUD
4.	1 GBP = 1.8020 USD
5.	1 GBP = 1.8020 USD × 1.2821 AUD/USD
6.	1 GBP = 2.3103 AUD

An alternative to this time-consuming process is to simply divide the two rates to determine their comparative value, i.e., their exchange rate. In this case, one could divide 1.8020 by .7800 to determine the rate of 2.3103 AUD/GBP.

It may not be intuitively obvious that the rate reflects a rate of 2.3103 AUD per GBP. It may also not be intuitively obvious that the two rates should have been divided. Moreover, should the bids or offers be used?

Cross-Rate Examples Using a Pricing Model

The markets are fairly consistent throughout the world in most respects, but they are certainly not consistent in the way currencies are quoted. Cross-rate pricing can be quite tricky and confusing to the newcomer. As a result, a standard framework or model is often useful to help newcomers price foreign exchange transactions. Exhibit 6.9 outlines a framework developed by the authors. Three examples of cross-rated pricing are given using this framework and the following example markets:

USD/GBP	1.8020–1.8030
DEM/USD	1.7610–1.7625
CAD/USD	1.2070–1.2075

Example A: Market Maker Buys GBP and Sells CAD

1. GBP is quoted in American terms. Therefore, as the market maker is buying GBP, it will use the bid side of the market, or 1.8020 USD for each GBP.

2. CAD is quoted in currency terms. As the market maker is selling CAD, it will again use the bid side of the market, or 1.2070 CAD per USD.

3. As one rate is in currency terms and the other is in American terms, the two rates should be multiplied. Moreover, as the GBP is the currency quoted in American terms, GBP will be the unit of account, and the final rate will reflect the number of CAD per GBP:

1.8020 USD/GBP × 1.2070 CAD/USD = 2.1750 CAD/GBP

Exhibit 6.9. Authors' Spot Market Cross-Rate Pricing Model
from Perspective of Market Maker

```
                     QUOTATION METHOD FOR CURRENCIES
                     --------------------------------

                     American Terms   Currency Terms
                     --------------   --------------
 Currency Bought:    Bid: _____     Offer: _____

 Currency Sold:      Offer: _____   Bid: _____
```

```
 *    A) Both AMERICAN Terms:  - Divide the two rates;
                                 numerator is unit of account.

 **   B) Both CURRENCY Terms:  - Divide the two rates;
                                 denominator is unit of account

 ***  C) One AMERICAN Term     - Multiply the two rates;
          & one CURRENCY Term    currency quoted in American
                                 terms is unit of account.
```

Currencies Quoted in American Terms		Currencies Quoted in Currency Terms	
Australia	dollar	Austria	schilling
Great Britain	pound	Belgium	franc
Ireland	punt	Canada	dollar
New Zealand	dollar	Denmark	krone
South Africa	rand	France	franc
		Germany	deutsche mark
		Hong Kong	dollar
		Italy	lira
		Japan	yen
		Mexico	peso
		Netherlands	guilder
		Norway	krone
		Portugal	escudo
		Saudi Arabia	riyal
		Singapore	dollar
		Spain	peseta
		Sweden	krona
		Switzerland	franc

```
 * American Terms is number of USD per unit of countercurrency.

 ** Currency Terms is number of units of currency per USD.

 *** Unit of Account is the currency against which the counter
     currency is measured.  For example, the unit of account
     in a quote of .90 CAD/AUD is the AUD.
```

Example B: Market Maker Buys DEM and Sells CAD

1. Deutsche marks are quoted in currency terms. As the market maker is buying DEM, it will use the offer side of the market, or 1.7625 DEM per USD.

2. CAD is quoted in currency terms. As the market maker is selling CAD, it will use the bid side of the market, or 1.2070 CAD per USD.

3. Since both quotes are in currency terms, the two rates will be divided. As the customer wants the price made in terms of number of CAD per DEM (i.e., DEM is the unit of account), the CAD rate is the numerator and the DEM rate is the denominator:

$$\frac{1.2070 \text{ CAD/USD}}{1.7625 \text{ DEM/USD}} = .6848 \text{ CAD/DEM}$$

Example C: Market Maker Sells GBP and Buys DEM

1. GBP is quoted in American terms. Therefore, as the market maker is selling GBP, it will use the offer side of the market, or 1.8030 USD per GBP.

2. DEM is quoted in currency terms. As the market maker is buying DEM, it will again use the offer side of the market, or 1.7625 DEM per USD.

3. One rate is in currency terms and the other is in American terms, and so the two rates should be multiplied. Moreover, as the GBP is the currency quoted in American terms, GBP will be the unit of account, and the final rate will reflect the number of DEM per GBP:

$$1.8030 \text{ USD/GBP} \times 1.7625 \text{ DEM/USD} = 3.1778 \text{ DEM/GBP}$$

If the client wanted the quote with the DEM as the unit of account, the reciprocal of 3.1778 would be determined and reflected.

$$1/3.1778 = .3147 \text{ GBP/DEM}$$

7

The Forward Market

Executive Summary

This chapter is quite technical in many areas. It explains why forward markets reflect interest-rate differentials and why the forward rate is not a reliable forecast of the future spot rate. The chapter examines in considerable detail the factors and steps that are involved in calculating various forms of forward prices. It reviews different products and their pricing, and it compares futures markets with forward markets. Finally, it outlines a basic framework on which the forward market is professionally traded.

Introduction

An exchange rate is the price at which one currency can be bought or sold in exchange for another currency. The settlement date of a foreign exchange deal can be anywhere from the dealing date to several years forward. The single most important settlement date for foreign exchange deals is found in the spot market, which calls for settlement one or two business days hence, depending on the currency. The spot value of a currency reflects what the market has determined to be the appropriate value of the currency.

The exchange rate for deals settling on a day other than the standard spot date has two components. The first component is the spot rate. The second component is the points that reflect the interest-rate adjustment for a different settlement date. Deals done for same-day value are known as *cash deals,* while deals done beyond spot value are termed *forward deals.* A tabular summary of cash, spot, and forward deals is shown in Exhibit 7.1.

Exhibit 7.1. Summary of Value Dates for Cash, Spot, and Forward Transactions

	Trades between USD, CAD, and Mexican peso	Trades between all other currencies (e.g., DEM, JPY, and USD)
Cash	Today	Today, today + 1
Spot	Today + 1	Today + 2
Spot next	Today + 2	Today + 3
Forward	Today + 3 or more days hence	Today + 4 or more days hence

Exactly when a contract is deemed to be a forward contract is a judgment call by individual market players. Some may believe that any contract beyond spot value is a forward contract. However, the day after spot, known as *spot next*, is a key date for professional traders in their management of their forward book. As shown later in this chapter and again in Chapter 10, it would be inappropriate to classify it as a forward date because of double counting of positions and credit exposure.

Forward Points

If the spot rate is 1.2000 CAD/USD and the three-month forward rate is 1.2050, the difference of .0050 is referred to as the *forward points*. A number of factors determine the size of the point spread:

1. Supply relative to demand for the currency on the settlement date in question. If sellers are the majority, the points will differ from a market dominated by buyers, particularly on longer dated forwards.

2. Market expectations about future developments in the interest rate and foreign exchange markets.

3. Interest-rate differentials between the countries.

For freely traded currencies that have an accessible domestic money market, the dominant factor determining forward points is the interest-rate differential. Forward points, therefore, are really interest-rate differentials between two countries, expressed as foreign exchange points.

Consider a company that needs to buy GBP for delivery one month hence to pay for equipment. Either the company can buy the GBP spot and invest the GBP for a month, or it can buy the GBP for delivery one month forward.

If the company buys the GBP spot and invests the GBP, the company earns interest on the GBP and forgoes interest on the USD spent to buy the GBP. As the GBP is typically a higher interest-rate currency than the USD, the company will earn more interest than is forgone. Dealing spot may, therefore, seem advantageous; however, buying GBP forward may require less USD than on a spot basis. If this saving is greater than the interest gained by dealing spot, the forward alternative would be superior. In other words, it may make sense to buy GBP forward even if the GBP carries a higher interest rate, because the forward points, the difference between the spot and forward rates, more than offset the interest-rate differentials.

As a general rule, the two methods will produce the same basic result. If they do not, two things should occur. First, companies will use the most advantageous method, likely causing this method's advantage to disappear. Additional buying will eliminate a cheap source of funding, while selling will eliminate attractive rates of investment return. Second, arbitrage may also take place. Arbitrage occurs when one can simultaneously undertake offsetting transactions so that a risk-free profit can be achieved. Arbitrage will also affect the prices in the market, moving the two alternatives closer together, and thereby reducing the potential for profitable arbitrage.

Arbitrage

The previous section referred to arbitrage as a process that would tend to keep forward points consistent with interest-rate differentials. To illustrate the process of arbitrage, an exaggerated hypothetical example is given in Exhibits 7.2 and 7.3. Numerically, the results of the arbitrage shown in Exhibit 7.2 would be those shown in Exhibit 7.3.

The forward rate in Exhibit 7.3 was the same as the spot rate, and thus there were no forward points. As a result, the arbitrage process would allow one to borrow at 10 percent, invest at 15 percent, and lock up a risk-free gain of 5 percent. In practice, the forward rate would have offset most, if not all, of the interest-rate differential. There will be some discrepancies, and the markets will not be perfectly balanced, but they will be closely aligned. Some "imperfections," for instance, will result from differences in liquidity and risk between the various instruments that are dealt in conjunction with the forward market. However, the forward market for the major currencies is quite efficient and fairly reflects the interest-rate differentials.

Exhibit 7.2. The Steps of Covered Interest-Rate Arbitrage

USD/GBP exchange rates	
Spot	2.00
1-year forward	2.00
1-year interest rates	
GBP	15.0%
USD	10.0%

Arbitrage process

Day 1
STEP 1 ABC borrows USD at 10%.
STEP 2 ABC converts USD to GBP at the spot rate and invests GBP proceeds at 15%.
STEP 3 ABC sells GBP principal and interest forward for USD.

Day 365
STEP 4 ABC matures GBP investment.
STEP 5 ABC delivers GBP on the forward contract and receives USD.
STEP 6 ABC pays back USD loan with the proceeds from the forward contract.
STEP 7 ABC takes the arbitraged profit.

Exhibit 7.3. Numerical Example of Covered Interest-Rate Arbitrage

		ABC Cashflows	
Day 1		GBP, in/(out)	USD, in/(out)
STEP 1	Borrow USD		2000
STEP 2	Convert to GBP and invest	1000	(2000)
		(1000)	
STEP 3	Sell forward GBP P & I		
	Net cashflow	0	0
Day 365			
STEP 4	Mature GBP investment		
	Principal	1000	
	Interest	150	
STEP 5	Deliver on forward contract	(1150)	2300
STEP 6	Repay USD loan		
	Principal		(2000)
	Interest		(200)
	Net cashflow	0	100

In this example, the forward rate that would perfectly offset the interest-rate differentials is 1.9130, calculated as follows:

$$\frac{\text{Principal and interest of USD loan}}{\text{Principal and interest of GBP investment}} = \frac{2200}{1150} = 1.9130$$

Note that if the forward rate in step 5 in Exhibit 7.3 had been 1.9130 (rather than 2.000), the forward contract would have provided 2200 USD, an amount just sufficient to repay the USD loan.

Calculating Theoretical Forward Points

In determining the forward points that should exist according to theory, the market elements that affect the calculations are as follows:

1. *Interest rates.* The relevant rates are those of high-quality, short-maturity instruments. As banks are the dominant players, the forward points tend to reflect the interest rates of bank paper, e.g., Eurodollar deposit rates, CAD banker's acceptances rates. While bank paper is still the key rate source, other instruments such as futures and forward-rate agreements are becoming more frequently used as rate sources for trading the forward market.

2. *Spot exchange rate.* Unless the exchange rate is at par, the absolute number of units of the two currencies involved will differ. This difference in amount provides a larger or smaller base on which interest is "earned" or "forgone" for each currency. For example, an exchange rate of 1.2000 CAD/USD will see interest "earned" on 1.2 CAD for every single USD on which interest is "forgone." The calculations must thus incorporate the current spot rate in order to accommodate the difference in currency units involved.

3. *Term.* The farther the forward is in the future, the larger is the actual amount of net interest created by the interest-rate differentials.

Consider the yield curves shown in Exhibit 7.4, which have varied interest differentials.

Note that the interest rate applicable for a forward price is the interest rate on an instrument maturing on the forward date. Changes in the yield curve in either of the two countries can, therefore, alter the interest-rate differentials significantly. Consequently, forward prices do not always follow a uniform trend line. For instance, the 180-day forward is not automatically twice the 90-day forward. As per Exhibit 7.5, the forward points

Exhibit 7.4. Yield Curve of Two Currencies

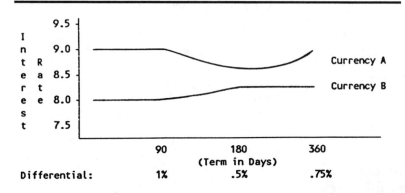

	90	180	360
	(Term in Days)		
Differential:	1%	.5%	.75%

Exhibit 7.5. Impact of Changing Yield Curves on Forward Points

Term	Interest rate, currency A, %	Interest rate, currency B, %	Interest-rate differential, %	Forward points
90	9.0	8.0	1.0	.0033
180	8.75	8.25	.50	.0033
360	9.0	8.25	.75	.0098

are the same for 90 and 180 days because the differential narrows in the 180-day term and offsets the impact of the longer term. Similarly, the 360-day forward is three times the 180-day due to a doubling of term and a 50 percent increase in the interest-rate differential.

Calculating the forward points can be done in different ways. In all cases one has to know the spot exchange rate, the term of the forward, and the relevant interest rates. The calculations shown in Exhibits 7.6 and 7.7 are based on the following example market rates.

Spot exchange rate	1.3000 CAD/USD	
Term (number of days)	90	
	USD	**CAD**
Interest rate	10.50%	12.00%
Rate basis	360 days	365 days
Adjusted rate:		
360	10.50%	11.84%
365	10.65%	12.00%

As described in Chapter 3, interest rates are calculated on a 360-day basis in some countries and a 365-day basis in others. The only real significance is that the 360-day basis yields higher interest than does a 365-day basis.

For example,   ($1,000,000 × 10.50% × 90 days)/360 = $26,250

whereas   ($1,000,000 × 10.50% × 90 days)/365 = $25,890

To convert a 360-day yield, such as 10.50 percent, to a 365-day basis, simply multiply the 10.50 percent by a factor of 365/360. The result is 10.645833 percent, which can be verified as follows:

$$($1,000,000 × 10.645833\% × 90 \text{ days})/365 = $26,250$$

To convert a 365-day yield, such as 12.00 percent, to a 360-day basis, simply multiply the 12.00 percent by a factor of 360/365. The result is 11.835616 percent.

Formulas for Calculating Forward Points

A quick and easy method for *approximating* forward points is to multiply the spot rate by the interest-rate differential and then adjust this annualized result by the actual term of the forward. Exhibit 7.6 calculates 90-day, CAD/USD forward points, where Canadian interest rates are 12 percent, U.S. interest rates are 10.5 percent, and the spot rate is 1.30 CAD/USD.

The primary weakness of the formula in Exhibit 7.6 is that it recog-

Exhibit 7.6. Formula for Approximating Forward Points

$$\frac{(\text{Spot rate} \times \text{interest-rate differential} \times \text{term})}{\text{rate basis}}$$

$$= \frac{1.3000 \times [.1200 - (.1050 \times 365/360)] \times 90}{365}$$

$$= \frac{1.3000 \times (.1200 - .10646) \times 90}{365}$$

$$= .00434 \quad \text{or } 43.4 \text{ forward points}$$

Exhibit 7.7. Detailed Calculation of Forward Points

STEP 1 Calculate the interest for each currency for the term:

$$\text{Interest} = \frac{\text{currency units} \times \text{interest rate} \times \text{term}}{\text{rate basis}}$$

$$\text{USD interest} = \frac{1.0000 \times .1050 \times 90}{360} = .02625$$

$$\text{CAD interest} = \frac{1.3000 \times .1200 \times 90}{360} = .03847$$

STEP 2 Determine the all-in forward exchange rate as follows:

$$\text{Forward rate} = \frac{\text{unit amount currency B} + \text{interest on currency B}}{\text{unit amount currency A} + \text{interest on currency A}}$$

$$= \frac{1.3000 + .03847}{1.0000 + .02625} = 1.30423$$

STEP 3 Calculate the forward points:

Forward rate − spot rate = forward points

$$1.30423 - 1.3000 = .00423 \qquad \text{or 42.3 forward points}$$

nizes the interest differential but does not adjust for the fact that the principal amounts of the two currencies vary. Thus, for every one USD that the 10.5 percent interest rate applies to, the 12 percent interest rate applies to 1.3 CAD.

A second, more time-consuming, but also more accurate, formula is outlined in Exhibit 7.7.

Exhibit 7.6 produced forward points of approximately 43.4. The actual points are 42.3.

Reciprocal Forward Points

The USD was the unit of account in the exhibits just discussed. If the CAD had been the unit of account, the spot exchange rate would have been the reciprocal of 1.3000, or .7692 (1/1.3000). The reciprocal of the forward rate of 1.3042 is .7667 (1/1.3042), which produces forward points of 25 discount (.7667 − .7692). This is shown in Exhibit 7.8.

The two spot and forward prices in Exhibits 7.7 and 7.8 are the reciprocals of each other and generate the same results in transactions. However, two items should be noted.

First, the number of forward points changed significantly simply be-

Exhibit 7.8. Calculation of Reciprocal Forward Points

$$\text{Interest currency A} = \frac{.7692 \times .1050 \times 90}{360} = .020192$$

$$\text{Interest currency B} = \frac{1.0000 \times .1200 \times 90}{365} = .029589$$

$$\text{Forward rate} = \frac{.7692 + .020192}{1.0000 + .029589} = .7667$$

$$\text{Forward points} = .7667 - .7692 = -.0025$$

cause the currency that is the unit of account changed. The USD is the unit of account in the 1.3000 CAD per USD quote, while the CAD is the unit of account in the .7692 USD/CAD quote. In relative terms, the first method has 1.7 times the number of units per unit of account as does the second method (1.3000/.7692 = 1.7). Consequently, the forward points should also be approximately a factor of 1.7, which indeed they are (.00423/.0025 = 1.69). When rounding is considered, the relationship holds.

Second, reciprocal forward points were added to spot when quoted in Canadian terms (1.3000 CAD per USD) and subtracted from spot when quoted in American terms (.7692 USD per CAD). One way to verify that these calculations are correct is to recall that the forward-points adjustment must offset the interest-rate differentials. If USD interest rates are lower than Canadian rates, the USD will be worth more in the forward market than in the spot market. In Canadian terms, it should, therefore, take more CAD per USD in the forward market. In American terms, it should take less USD per CAD in the forward market. If this were not the case, players would arbitrage the market.

Calculating Interest-Rate Differentials from Forward Points

The process of calculating interest-rate differentials from forward points is the reverse of that described above. The interest differentials can be quickly determined using the relationship in Exhibit 7.9.

As already stated, Canadian rates were 12 percent, or 1.35 percent above USD rates of 10.65 percent when adjusted to a 365-day basis. When considering rounding, the relationship holds.

Exhibit 7.9. Calculating Interest-Rate Differentials from Forward Points

$$\begin{aligned}
\frac{\text{Interest-rate}}{\text{differential}} &= \frac{\text{Forward points} \times \text{rate basis} \times 100}{\text{Spot rate} \times \text{term}} \\
&= \frac{.0043 \times 365 \times 100}{1.3000 \times 90} \\
&= 1.34\%
\end{aligned}$$

Bid and Offer

Forward traders incur risk by selling and buying interest-rate differentials. Forward markets trade on a bid-and-offer basis. In addition to the basic feature of having two-way prices in any trading market, one should also recognize that the underlying market behind forward points, i.e., interest rates, is also traded on a bid-and-offer basis. Calculations of the forward rates must necessarily take this into account. If the above interest rates are the midpoint between the bid and offered

Exhibit 7.10. Framework for Calculating Forward Bid-and-Offer Points

Forward Bid   = Spot x $\left[\dfrac{\text{AO x (days/RB) - BB x (days/RB)}}{1 + (\text{BB x days/RB})} \right]$

Forward Offer = Spot x $\left[\dfrac{\text{AB x (days/RB) - BO x (days/RB)}}{1 + (\text{BO x days/RB})} \right]$

Where: AB is the rate at which major bank paper is trading for banks to lend cash in Currency A. It is referred to hereafter as the money market bid.

AO, the money market offer, is the rate at which major bank paper is trading for banks to raise cash in Currency A.

BB is bid side for major bank paper in Currency B.

BO is offer side for major bank paper in Currency B.

Days is number of days from spot date to the forward date;

RB represents the rate basis for the respective currencies

Exhibit 7.11. Numerical Example for Calculating Forward Bid-and-Offer Points

---

$$\text{Forward Bid} = 1.3000 \times \left[\frac{.1195 \times 90/365 - .1055 \times 90/360}{1 + (.1055 \times 90/360)} \right]$$

$$= 1.3000 \times \frac{.0294657 - .026375}{1.026375}$$

$$= .00391 \text{ or } 39.1 \text{ points}$$

$$\text{Forward Offer} = 1.3000 \times \left[\frac{.1200 \times 90/365 - .1050 \times 90/360}{1 + (.1050 \times 90/360)} \right]$$

$$= 1.3000 \times \frac{.0295890 - .026250}{1.026250}$$

$$= .00423 \text{ or } 42.3 \text{ points}$$

---

rates for both currencies, the forward prices calculated previously are midpoint prices as well. One can create a two-way 90-day forward price of 24–26 by creating a single basis-point spread on each side of the midpoint price of .0025.

To directly calculate the bid-and-offer forward points, one would need to use the appropriate bid-and-offer rates in the money markets and calculate each forward bid and offer independently. A framework for this is outlined in Exhibit 7.10.

Chapter 3 suggested that the bid in the Canadian money markets typically represents a bid for paper, while a bid in USD markets usually represents a bid for cash. In the formula given in Exhibit 7.10, all bids and offers are for cash, not paper. Exhibits 7.6 and 7.7 outlined the basic formulas for calculating forward points, without consideration of the bid-and-offer spreads. Using the same basic scenario of a spot rate of 1.30, Canadian 90-day interest rates of 12.00–11.95 percent and U.S. rates of 10.55–10.50 percent, the forward bid-and-offer points would be those shown in Exhibit 7.11.

Premiums and Discounts

The terms *premium* and *discount* can have different implications in different situations. In forward markets, forward points are said to be at a premium when they are to be added to the spot rate. Forward points are said to be at a discount when they are to be subtracted from the spot rate.

Premium does not denote extra value, nor does discount imply cheapness. The CAD/USD quotes in Canadian terms will result in forward points being at a premium, while a quote in reciprocal American terms will show the points at a discount. It is not meaningful or appropriate, therefore, to read value or lack of it into the two terms.

	Canadian terms	American terms
Spot	1.3000	.7692
Forward rate	1.3042	.7667
Forward points		
Premium	.0042	
Discount		.0025

Determining whether to add or subtract the forward points to produce a forward rate can be done using the following two rules:

1. If the forward bid is less than the offer, add the forward points to spot.
2. If the forward bid is larger than the offer, subtract the forward points from spot.

The two rules are simple in themselves, but sometimes they can be forgotten. There are a couple of ways to double-check whether forward points should be added or subtracted. One way is to remember that the currency with the lower interest rate will be worth more in the forward market than in the spot market. In the previous case, USD interest rates are lower than the comparable CAD rates, and thus the forward rate for the USD should be more valuable than the spot rate. To verify that, simply calculate the number of CAD per 1 million USD on both a spot and a forward basis.

$$\text{Spot} \quad 1,000,000 \text{ USD} \times 1.3000 = 1,300,000 \text{ CAD}$$
$$\text{Forward} \quad 1,000,000 \text{ USD} \times 1.3042 = 1,304,200 \text{ CAD}$$

If the forward points of .0042 had been subtracted from spot instead of added, the forward rate would have yielded less than the $1,300,000 generated on the spot market.

$$\$1,000,000 \times 1.2958 = \$1,295,800$$

A second method is to look at the forward quotations on a bid-and-offer basis. A representative market scenario of spot, forward, and the resulting outright rates is as follows:

	Market	Bid-and-offer spread	Outright bid	Outright offer	Total bid-and-offer spread
Spot	1.3000–05	.0005	1.3000	1.3005	.0005
3 months	42–44	.0002	1.3042	1.3049	.0007
6 months	85–88	.0003	1.3085	1.3093	.0008

In the above market, the three-month bid of 42 points is less than the offer of 44 points. Consequently, the forward points should be added to spot. The same holds true for the six-month forward points.

To double-check, one can calculate the all-in three-month forward prices on both the bid (1.3042) and the offer side (1.3049). The spread between the two is .0007, which is composed of the bid-and-offer spread on the spot market of .0005 and the three-month forward market spread of .0002.

If the forward points were subtracted by mistake, the outright forward prices would have been 1.2958 (1.3000 − .0042) and 1.2961 (1.3005 − .0044). The bid-and-offer spread of only 3 points is less than the combined bid-and-offer spreads in the spot and forward markets and indicates an error was made.

Forward Dates

Standardized dealing dates are important for a forward market to deal efficiently. The dates typically shown and routinely dealt in the interbank forward market include one month, two months, three months, six months, and one year. Other terms are, of course, available and routinely dealt, especially between market makers and their clients in the corporate and government sectors.

As discussed in Chapter 6, the USD is the most important currency, and global forward markets are effectively based on the interest-rate differentials between the United States and all the other currencies. However, forwards are also routinely done on a cross-rate basis, and forward points can be calculated in one of two ways:

1. They can be calculated on the basis of their respective interest-rate differentials against the USD.

2. They can be calculated directly using each currency's appropriate interest rates.

The starting point for determining standard forward dates is the spot date. As different currencies can have different spot dates on a given day, they can, therefore, have different standard forward dates.

Similar to the spot market, the standard forward dates for a currency must be on dates that are open for business in both the United States and the country in question (hereafter referred to as the *valid date*). If businesses in the United States are closed for a holiday, all forward dates will be similarly affected. However, if another country, for example, France, has a holiday on what would normally be a standard forward date, only the French franc's forward date will be affected.

The rules for determining forward dates may be summarized as follows:

1. Standard forward dates will be the same calendar date as the spot date.
2. Each subsequent calendar month will have a standard forward date.
3. If the current spot value date is the last spot date for that month, the standard forward dates will also be the last common business date in each month in the United States and the other country.

Some examples that may clarify these rules are as follows:

1. If spot is June 20, forward dates will be on the twentieth of each successive month provided they are valid business days. If the twentieth and twenty-first of July are holidays in one or both countries, then the next common business day, in this case it is July 22, will be the one-month forward date.
2. A standard forward date could be the same for more than one dealing date. For instance, in the previous example, if spot value for the next two days is June 21 and June 22, respectively, the standard one-month forward date will be July 22 for all three spot days.
3. One-month forward rates are *not* a standard 30-day term. Moreover, a standard forward date must occur in each successive month. If spot is January 30, the one-month forward date will be the last common business date in February, which could be anywhere from February 25 to February 29.
4. If spot is February 27 and it is the last spot date for February, all successive standard forward dates will be the last common business

date in each month. The standard forward dates would typically be March 31, April 30, May 30, June 27, and so on.

5. If today is Thursday, February 26, spot CAD/USD is one day hence, or Friday, February 27. Spot DEM/USD is Monday, March 2. The one-month forward date for CAD/USD is March 27, while the one-month forward date for DEM/USD is April 2.

   One day hence, February 27, spot USD/CAD would be March 2, and one month forward would be April 2. Spot DEM/USD will have changed to March 3, and the one-month forward date would be April 3.

It is critical to be aware of forward dates for several reasons:

1. Changes in the forward points from one day to the next, particularly for short-dated forwards, may be significant. However, the changes may have nothing to do with movements in interest rates. The changes may simply be the result of a change in the number of days involved. Overnight swap points, for instance, incorporate one day during the week, but can incorporate up to four days on a long weekend. All else being equal, overnight swap points will, therefore, be three or four times as large on Friday as any other day during the week.

2. Forward points shown in the market refer to specific dates. Dealing for other dates requires adjustments, sometimes highly significant ones. Consider, for instance, bids for USD value spot versus value cash. If spot is 1.2000 CAD/USD and the overnight swap points are .0005, the cash bid is only 1.1995.

3. When dealing cross-rated forwards (two currencies, neither of which is the USD), one forward may require no adjustment, while the other may need adjustments. Do not assume the same adjustments apply to both markets. For example, recall the fifth example on standard dates, wherein one month forward for CAD/USD was March 27 while one month forward for DEM/USD was April 2. A transaction for value March 27 requires no adjustment to the quoted forward points on the CAD/USD price, while it requires five days' adjustment for the DEM/USD price component.

Odd-Dated Forwards

Forward dates that are not the standard forward dates are termed *odd-dated*. Pricing of these forwards can be done by determining the relevant interest rates for the term and calculating the price in the standard

Exhibit 7.12. Market Scenario for Calculating Odd-Dated Forward Points

	Value date	Days past spot	Market
Spot	March 15	0	1.2000–10
One-month forward	April 15	31	18–20
Two-month forward	May 15	61	38–41
Forward date	April 21	37	?

manner. Alternatively, interpolation using the standard dealing dates usually is used. For example, consider the market scenario in Exhibit 7.12 where you want to price an all-in forward contract to April 21 on the bid side of the market.

The forward points to April 21 are determined in two steps. From spot to April 15, the forward points are 18 points premium. From April 15 to the desired date of April 21, six more days are involved. There are 20 points premium between the standard one- and two-month forwards (38 − 18), a span of 30 days from April 15 to May 15. By interpolation, you can calculate that 6 days out of 30 days is worth 4 points [(6/30) × 20]. The forward on the bid side is thus 22 points, which comprise the 18 points for the straight one-month and 4 points for the six days beyond the one-month. The all-in rate is 1.2022.

Spot	1.2000
Forward points (18+4)	.0022
All-in forward rate	1.2022

Interpolation has weaknesses, however, and caution must be taken to use it properly. For instance, there is a significant length of time between the standard six- and twelve-month dates. The yield curve could change significantly within this time frame, and pricing a deal such as a seven-month forward using straight interpolation could be faulty.

One method of gaining comfort is looking at other rates. For instance, interpolating a seven-month forward using six- and twelve-month forward rates can be checked by looking at the five-month forward rate. The points per day between the five- and six-month forwards should be basically the same as between the six- and seven-month forwards.

Cross-Rate Forward Points

Cross-rate forwards are forward contracts between two currencies, neither of which is the USD. The most practical way of calculating the cross-rate forward points when using the forward points already known against the USD involves three steps:

1. Determine the spot rate and the all-in forward rate between each currency and the USD.
2. Calculate the cross-rate prices for spot and forward value.
3. Subtract the spot cross rate from the forward cross rate to determine the forward cross-rate points.

Consider the following exchange rates and price quotations:

	USD/GBP	DEM/USD	CAD/USD
Spot	1.8020–30	1.7610–25	1.2070–75
One-month forward	15–13	14–12	20–22
Three-month forward	50–45	45–40	56–59
Currency bid or offered in quote (i.e., unit of account)	GBP	USD	USD

A market maker's price to buy GBP for CAD for value one month forward would follow the same basic process as that used for spot prices, explained in Chapter 6. For forward prices, the only significant change is the inclusion of the forward points.

1. The bid or buying rates for sterling are a spot of 1.8020 and forward points of 15 points discount. The all-in one-month forward is thus 1.8005. The 1.8020 and 1.8005 reflect the number of USD per GBP.
2. The offer or selling rate for CAD is the bid for USD of 1.2070 spot plus forward points of 20 points premium. The all-in one-month forward is thus 1.2090. The spot and forward prices reflect the number of CAD per USD.
3. The spot rate for buying GBP and selling CAD is 2.1750 (1.8020 × 1.2070). The all-in forward rate is 2.1768 (1.8005 × 1.2090), which reflects 2.1768 CAD per GBP.
4. The forward points are 18 points premium (forward of 2.1768, less the spot of 2.1750).

The spot and forward rates show that GBP is slightly stronger in the one-month forward than it is for spot value. That tells us that GBP interest rates are lower than CAD rates in the one-month term. Checking that out will also help to verify that the pricing was done correctly. Exhibit 7.13 shows a cross-rate pricing model for forward contracts.

Exhibit 7.13. The Authors' Forward Market Cross-Rate Pricing Model from Perspective of Market Maker

PART A: BASE CURRENCY RATES	Currency Bought	Currency Sold		QUOTATION METHOD	
				American Terms	Currency Terms
1. Spot Rate vs USD:	_____	_____			
2. Forward Points vs USD:	_____	_____	Currency Bought:	Bid	Offer
3. All-In Forward Rate vs USD:	_____	_____	Currency Sold:	Offer	Bid

Part B: CALCULATING CROSS RATES		ADDING OR SUBTRACTING FORWARD POINTS
4. Cross Rate Spot:	----------	
5. Cross Rate Forward:	----------	Bid < Offer - Add to Spot Rate
6. Forward Points:	----------	Bid > Offer - Subtract from Spot Rate

Currencies Quoted in American Terms		Currencies Quoted in Currency Terms		MULTIPLY OR DIVIDE BASE CURRENCY RATES
Australia	dollar	Austria	schilling	Both American Terms - Divide the rates; numerator is unit of account.
Great Britain	pound	Belgium	franc	
Ireland	punt	Canada	dollar	Both Currency Terms - Divide the rates; denominator is unit of account.
New Zealand	dollar	Denmark	krone	
South Africa	rand	France	franc	One American & one Currency - Multiply; currency quoted in American terms is the unit of account.
		Germany	deutsche mark	
		Hong Kong	dollar	
		Italy	lira	
		Japan	yen	American Terms is the number of USD per unit of countercurrency.
		Mexico	peso	
		Netherlands	guilder	
		Norway	krone	Currency Terms is the number of units of currency per USD.
		Portugal	escudo	
		Saudi Arabia	riyal	
		Singapore	dollar	Unit of Account is the currency against which the countercurrency is measured. For example, the unit of account in a quote of .9000 CAD/AUD is the AUD.
		Spain	peseta	
		Sweden	krona	
		Switzerland	franc	

Asking for Prices in the Interbank Market

Forward transactions in the interbank market are dealt on the basis of a swap that incorporates two simultaneous deals. In one deal, a currency is sold, while in the second, it is purchased. This process minimizes the amount of spot risk taken. An example transaction would be as follows:

1. Sale of DEM value spot

2. Purchase of DEM value one-month forward

When Bank ABC calls Bank XYZ to seek a forward price, the two traders work on the premise that they are trading the standard forward dates. Thus, a bid in the one-month market is one's rate to buy the one-month forward (and, therefore, sell spot); one's offer is to sell the one-month forward (and, therefore, buy spot).

In an interbank trade, a conversation may go as follows:

BANK ABC: "Bank ABC calling. One-month dollar-mark, please."
BANK XYZ: "Thirty; twenty-eight."

BANK ABC: "One dollar yours at thirty."

BANK XYZ: "OK, done. Let's use a spot of 2.0000 which is for value
April 20; my forward purchase will be at 1.9970 for value May 20."

In Bank ABC's first statement, the bank introduced itself and asked
for Bank XYZ's market on one-month forward points of USD against
the DEM.

Bank XYZ responded by stating that it would buy one-month forward
at 30 points discount and sell at 28 points discount.

Bank ABC liked Bank XYZ's bid and sold to Bank XYZ 1 million
USD one-month forward at 30 points discount.

The two banks agreed to the deal, wherein Bank XYZ bought the
one-month forward points. It did not buy USD outright; that is, Bank
XYZ did not buy USD which it would own forever if nothing else was
ever done.

In order for the two parties to settle the transaction, they agree on the
establishment of two foreign exchange contracts. The first is a contract
value spot and is priced at spot. The second is for value one month
hence and is priced at spot less the forward points of 30 discount. Bank
ABC sold the one-month, and thus the one-month forward contract will
represent a sale of USD to Bank XYZ. Moreover, the spot contract will
represent a purchase of USD value spot. Bank XYZ's contracts will show
a spot sale and a forward purchase of USD.

Note. In practice, 1 million USD is a small interbank trade and does
not usually occur. That amount is used here to help provide clarity in
the numerical calculations that follow.

Managing a Forward Position

If Bank XYZ does nothing as a result of the trade to offset it or manage
it, its cashflows would be as shown in Exhibit 7.14.

Bank XYZ will be short USD and long DEM from the spot value date
for a period of one month when the offsetting contract matures. Its net

Exhibit 7.14. Bank XYZ Cashflows on Swap Transaction—No Hedging

	USD, in/(out)	DEM, in/(out)	Exchange rate
Value spot	(1,000,000)	2,000,000	2.0000
Value one month forward	1,000,000	(1,997,000)	1.9970
Net	0	3,000	

cashflow as a result of the trades shows that it will be receiving 3000 DEM from Bank ABC. At first glance, this may seem to be a great trade. The other side of the coin, however, is that Bank XYZ had possession of DEM, which carried a lower interest rate than did the USD, the currency given up by Bank XYZ. The additional interest forgone (or paid) on the USD over what was earned on the DEM compensates for the net DEM inflow on the foreign exchange contracts.

If the forward trader for Bank XYZ sits on the contracts for the whole duration, there are several consequences. First, the bank itself is faced with additional DEM which it needs to properly employ. It must also source USD to fund the shortfall created by the contract. If, by chance, Bank XYZ has a natural shortage of DEM and a surplus of USD, the forward trader's position can fill the bank's own cash management needs. Internal trades are then consummated so that the forward trader evens his or her position and the bank is able to adjust its cash positions.

If the bank has no inherent interest in the trade from an overall cash-management standpoint, then investment of DEM and borrowing of USD by the forward trader have the impact of increasing both the assets and liabilities on the bank's balance sheet. As banks are often measured on a basis of return on assets, increasing the assets by means that bring little return results in a lower overall return on assets. Consequently, this type of investing and borrowing activity by forward traders is not actively pursued.

If the forward trader cannot or does not want to finance the position, he or she must seek other means of handling the cashflows that arise on the spot value date. An ideal way is for another bank (Bank OFFSET) to call and want to do a transaction on the other side of the market. In this case, Bank OFFSET would buy USD for DEM one month forward from Bank XYZ.

Offsetting Positions

BANK OFFSET: "Bank OFFSET calling. One-month dollar-mark, please."

BANK XYZ: "Thirty; twenty-eight."

BANK OFFSET: "One dollar mine at twenty-eight."

BANK XYZ: "OK, done. Let's use a spot of 2.0000 which is for value April 20; my forward sale will be 1.9972 for value May 20."

In this trade, Bank OFFSET liked Bank XYZ's offer and advised XYZ that it wanted to deal 1 million USD one month forward at 28 discount. Bank XYZ confirmed and established the related spot and forward

Exhibit 7.15. Bank XYZ Cashflows—Bid-and-Offer Spread Realized

Value date	Counterparty bank	USD, in/(out)	DEM, in/(out)	Exchange rate
Spot	ABC	(1,000,000)	2,000,000	2.0000
	OFFSET	1,000,000	(2,000,000)	2.0000
Net cashflow		0	0	
One month forward	ABC	1,000,000	(1,997,000)	1.9970
	OFFSET	(1,000,000)	1,997,200	1.9972
Net cashflow		0	200	

prices for the two contracts. In this case, Bank OFFSET is selling USD spot and buying USD forward; Bank XYZ is buying USD spot and selling USD forward.

With the two trades on the books, Bank XYZ's cashflow offsets nicely, and a trading profit of two basis points from its bid-and-offer spread is realized, as shown in Exhibit 7.15.

While the trader made 200 DEM in this example, two aspects should be borne in mind:

1. The spot rate could have moved in the time between the two trades, and if so, there would then be some working capital or cashflow impact on Bank XYZ for the month. For example, assume the deals with Bank OFFSET were done at a spot of 2.0500 and a forward rate of 2.0472, as shown in Exhibit 7.16.

   The overall net cashflow on the contracts continues to show a gain of 200 DEM. However, Bank XYZ was out of pocket for 50,000 DEM for the period of one month. The true result for the trader is thus

Exhibit 7.16. Bank XYZ Cashflows—Working Capital Shortfall

Value date	Counterparty bank	USD, in/(out)	DEM, in/(out)	Exchange rate
Spot	ABC	(1,000,000)	2,000,000	2.0000
	OFFSET	1,000,000	(2,050,000)	2.0500
Net cashflow		0	(50,000)	
One-month forward	ABC	1,000,000	(1,997,000)	1.9970
	OFFSET	(1,000,000)	2,047,200	2.0472
Net cashflow		0	50,200	
Overall net cashflow			200	

not a gain of 200 DEM, but a loss of 133 DEM, assuming the one-month financing cost of the DEM was 8 percent.

Trading gain	200	
Interest expense	(333)	(50,000 × .08 × 30/360)
Net gain/(loss)	(133)	

2. Bank OFFSET's trade was for exactly the same amount as that of Bank ABC. The position was perfectly offset; this coincidence, however, does not seem to happen very often in practice.

If Bank OFFSET did not call and Bank XYZ wanted to offset the position, there are different ways to try to do it. One is to call other banks and hope to deal at a price that makes money. If the other banks are also quoting markets of "30–28," no profit is possible under this alternative, as Bank XYZ would be hitting another bank's bid at 30 points discount, the same rate at which it bought.

Another way is to put prices for the desired volume into the brokerage market. In other words, Bank XYZ could instruct one or more interbank brokers to work 1 million USD in the one-month at 29 points discount.

Roll the Forward Position with Short-Dated Swaps

A trader will often want to hold a position for a period of time if his or her view is that it will be profitable to do so. The one-month forward contract has no payments or other obligations until it matures. However, the offsetting spot position cannot be ignored. If a trader wants to hold the one-month position, he or she will often manage the cashflows of the spot position by "rolling" it one day at a time. In the case of Bank XYZ, the bank is short USD for spot value. Consequently, the trader will buy USD spot and sell USD for value the next valid business day. This transaction is appropriately called a *spot-next* swap.

The spot-next swap is identical to a one-month forward swap in that the same amount of currency is bought and sold, but for different dates. The number of days between the maturity dates is much less on the "spot-next" (one day during the week, three or four days on a weekend), and thus the points on a spot-next deal are much smaller, at least usually, than on a one-month forward. Assume the spot-next deal was done at a "spot" of 1.9990 and a "next" rate of 1.9989, as shown in Exhibit 7.17.

Exhibit 7.17. Bank XYZ Cashflow—Rolling Position One Day via Spot-Next Swaps

Value date	Counterparty bank	USD, in/(out)	DEM, in/(out)	Exchange rate
Spot	ABC	(1,000,000)	2,000,000	2.0000
	SPOTNEXT	1,000,000	(1,999,000)	1.9990
Net cashflow		0	1,000	
Spot + 1	SPOTNEXT	(1,000,000)	1,998,900	1.9989
Cashflow to date		(1,000,000)	1,999,900	

The swap with Bank SPOTNEXT essentially moved the spot contract one day forward. In the example, the spot rates on the spot-next and one-month forward swaps differ slightly from the original spot value, and the trader is faced with the same working capital implications as demonstrated in Exhibit 7.16 for the deals with Bank OFFSET. When the second half of the swap settles, the working capital impact vanishes and the trader is left with a position for value the next day. The effective exchange rate is the original spot contract rate adjusted by the point(s) on the spot-next swap.

Original spot rate	2.0000
Spot-next points, 1-point discount	(.0001)
Effective exchange rate	1.9999

$$\text{Reconciliation} = \frac{1,999,900}{1,000,000} = 1.9999$$

In undertaking the swap, the trader has rolled the position one day forward at a 1 point cost. If this were done a number of times, the forward trader could roll the spot sale to the same maturity date as the forward contract. The two remaining contracts would then settle off against each other, and the position would be closed. The question remains, however, Was any money made?

If the spot contract position was rolled every day at a point per calendar day, the effective rate on the spot position would change from 1.9999, to 1.9998, to 1.9997, and so on. If the duration of the forward was 28 days, the effective rate on the last spot-next swap would be 1.9972. In this case, the forward trader would have made 2 points, or 2,000 DEM, as Exhibit 7.18 shows.

A simplified analysis of the forward dealer's strategy in this case is that the 28 points cost on the daily spot-next rollovers would be less

Exhibit 7.18. Bank XYZ Final Cashflows Utilizing Spot-Next Swaps

Dealing date	Counterparty bank	USD, in/(out)	DEM, in/(out)	Exchange rate
Original forward	ABC	1,000,000	(1,970,000)	1.9970
Roll of spot purchase	LASTROLL	(1,000,000)	1,972,000	1.9972
Net cashflow		0	2,000	

than the 30 points discount earned when the original deal on the one-month forward was made with Bank ABC.

In the cases shown here, the receipt of the profits in actual cashflow is uncertain. If the offsetting trade is done so that the spot rates generate working capital gains, the profit could be received on the original spot value date. Alternatively, the profits may not be received until later, possibly not until the final maturity date of the contract.

A forward dealer will usually have a myriad of contracts of different amounts and maturity dates. Although positions in the forward market are usually offset, it is not feasible to offset every position to the exact dollar, even if the trader so wished. The interbank market trades in round amounts, and so residual or leftover amounts and odd dates are not always perfectly offset. As a result, the forward trader will have these short-term cashflows, or "cash positions," to manage even if he or she wanted to be flat.

Spot Risk in the Forward Market

The forward market is essentially an interest-rate market that is traded through use of foreign exchange swap transactions. The key differences between the purchase and sale contracts in the swap are the different maturity dates and the differences in price which are the forward points. Moreover, as both the purchase and sale incorporate a spot component, the forward dealer would seem to have no direct risk on the spot market. In reality, however, there are three forms of spot risk.

As we have seen, forward points reflect the interest-rate differentials between two currencies. Moreover, the number of forward points is affected by the spot exchange rate of the two currencies. Consequently, movements in the spot rate will affect the forward market. In most trading institutions, the responsibility for managing the spot risk of the markets is borne by spot traders. The forward traders, on the other hand, do not usually trade the spot market. Rather, spot risk is eliminated wherever possible.

Movements in the spot rate can affect a forward trader in three ways:

1. Movements in spot can lead to changes in interest rates in one or both currencies. These changes will, in turn, cause the interest differentials, and therefore the forward points, to change.

2. Movements in the spot rate will result in changes in the number of forward points simply because there will be more or less principal on one of the currencies on which interest is "earned" or "paid."

3. Movements in the spot rate will result in working capital cash imbalances which generate interest expenses or revenues.

As we saw in Chapter 2, spot exchange rates can affect, and be affected by, interest rates. This interrelationship is a vital one to recognize, but it is only one of several factors affecting each market. To trade a forward book, forward traders should have an opinion on the future movements of the spot rate, just as they will have on other factors affecting the forward market. Their collective assessment of the relevant factors will determine the view about which way the market will move. Trying to gauge the impact of the spot market and developing a hedge for this risk are difficult, if not inappropriate, to do. The risk cannot be easily, if at all, quantified, and the trader should simply consider it as one of several factors.

The other two forms of spot risk can, however, be quantified, and hedges may be more appropriate to consider.

As an example of the second spot risk, consider Exhibit 7.19, which shows 90-day forward-rate calculations based on a spot rate of 2.00 DEM/USD, DEM rates of 8 percent, and USD rates of 10.5 percent.

If the spot rate moves 500 points to 2.05, the forward points will change from 122 to 112 points discount. This impact of spot movements will vary depending on the interest-rate differential and the term of the forward. If the interest-rate differential, for instance, is negligible or if the forward is short-dated (e.g., one week), movements in the spot rate will have no significant impact on forward points. Traders may decide simply to ignore this risk.

In this market scenario, a trader would have benefited from the spot movement if the trader had been long USD and short DEM in the forwards. Ignoring the impact of working capital for the moment, a 1 mil-

Exhibit 7.19. Calculation of 90-Day Forward Rates

STEP 1   Calculate the interest for each currency for the term:

$$\text{Interest} = \frac{\text{currency units} \times \text{interest rate} \times \text{term}}{\text{rate basis}}$$

$$\text{USD interest} = \frac{1.0000 \times .1050 \times 90}{360} = .02625$$

$$\text{DEM interest} = \frac{2.0000 \times .0800 \times 90}{360} = .0400$$

STEP 2   Determine the all-in forward exchange rate as follows:

$$\frac{\text{Unit amount currency B} + \text{interest on currency B}}{\text{Unit amount currency A} + \text{interest on currency A}}$$

$$\frac{2.0000 + .04000}{1.0000 + .02625} = 1.9878$$

STEP 3   Calculate the forward points:

Forward rate − spot rate = forward points

$$1.9878 - 2.0000 = .0122 \qquad \text{or 122 points discount}$$

---

lion long USD position would have resulted in a 1,000-DEM profit, as per Exhibit 7.20(*a*).

To hedge this risk on an outstanding forward position, a short USD spot position would be established. The size of the spot position is $20,000, as per Exhibit 7.20(*b*).

The type of hedge just shown is often viewed, however, in the context of the relationship between exchange rates and interest rates. In this case, the "standard" expectation would be that as the USD strengthens from 2.00 DEM/USD to 2.05, USD interest rates would tend to fall and DEM interest rates would tend to rise. This further widening of the interest-rate spread would tend to increase the forward points and could offset some or all of the 10-point decline that would otherwise result due to the spot movement. A trader may, therefore, want to incur the spot risk as a hedge against

Exhibit 7.20(*a*). Forward Profit Due to Impact of Spot Movement on Forward Points

USD, in/(out)	Exchange rate	DEM, in/(out)
1,000,000	1.9878	(1,987,800)
(1,000,000)	1.9888	1,988,800
		1,000

Exhibit 7.20(b). Net Result of Spot Hedge

USD, in/(out)	Exchange rate	DEM, in/(out)
(20,000)	2.0000	40,000
20,000	2.0500	(41,000)
		(1,000)

his or her forward position. Consequently, managing this spot risk is clearly an art, and not a science.

With the third form of spot risk, movements in spot rates can affect a forward position by generating cash surpluses or shortfalls when positions are opened and then covered at different exchange rates. As shown in Exhibits 7.15 and 7.16, this risk can be extremely significant and can quickly turn a profitable trade into an unprofitable one. Moreover, unlike the second form of spot risk which affects the forward points, the working capital risk exists whether the forwards are significant or nonexistent.

To hedge this risk, consider the examples in Exhibits 7.15 and 7.16. Recall that the trading gain of 200 DEM was turned into a net loss of 113 DEM because of the interest cost on the 50,000 DEM that the dealer was out of pocket for one month. The formula for calculating this loss is as follows:

$$\text{Loss} = \frac{\text{USD principal} \times \text{change in FX rate} \times \text{DEM interest rate} \times 30}{360}$$

$$= \frac{1,000,000 \times (2.00 - 2.05) \times .08 \times 30}{360}$$

$$= \frac{50,000 \text{ DEM} \times .08 \times 30}{360}$$

$$= 333 \text{ DEM}$$

To hedge this spot risk, one would establish a spot position that would generate a 333 DEM gain when the DEM/USD rate moved from 2.00 to 2.05. The size of this position can be calculated using the following formula:

$$\text{Hedge} = \frac{(\text{USD principal} \times \text{DEM interest rate} \times \text{days})/360}{1 + [(\text{DEM interest rate} \times \text{days})/360]}$$

$$= \frac{(1,000,000 \times .08 \times 30)/360}{1 + [(.08 \times 30)/360]}$$

$$= 6623 \text{ USD}$$

A reconciliation of this position shows the following:

6623 USD × 2.00	=	13,246 DEM
6623 USD × 2.05	=	13,577 DEM
Net		331 DEM

In this example, the forward dealer's original position was short USD on the near end of the swap. The dealer would lose if the USD strengthened. Therefore, the dealer would buy USD spot in the amount approximating $6600 to cover this risk.

If we look at the two elements of spot risk, a net hedge of short $13,377 USD should be established.

Risk	USD hedge, long/(short)
Movement in points	(20,000)
Working capital	6,623
Net spot hedge	(13,377)

In the overall context, the spot risk may or may not be viewed as a significant risk. However, if the forward position were $500 million, a position that is routinely held by major players in the market, the cashflow risks caused by spot movements may be well worth hedging. Moreover, it should be recognized that forward positions change on an ongoing position and the appropriate spot hedges would necessarily change as well.

Outright Forward Transactions

Commercial entities frequently sell or buy currencies on an outright forward basis. Pricing these deals involves determining the appropriate spot price and forward points.

Consider a purchase by Bank XYZ from Commercial A of 1 million USD against DEM one month forward. Following the market in Exhibits 7.14 and 7.15, assume the spot price is 2.0000 DEM/USD and the forward points are 30 discount.

To establish the spot risk and position, the spot dealer can enter the market and sell 1 million USD to Bank OFFSET; if the rate received is also 2.0000, the spot dealer breaks even, as can be seen in Exhibit 7.21.

Exhibit 7.21. Bank XYZ Spot Dealer Cashflows—Outright Forward Purchase

Value date	Counterparty	USD, in/(out)	DEM, in/(out)	Exchange rate
Spot	?	1,000,000	(2,000,000)	2.0000
	Bank OFFSET	(1,000,000)	2,000,000	2.0000
Net cashflow		0	0	

From a cashflow standpoint, Bank XYZ has to make a payment of 1 million USD value spot to Bank OFFSET. The spot trader does not receive the offsetting payment from Commercial A because Commercial A's deal calls for delivery one month hence. Instead, the USD is received from the forward trader.

From an overall bank standpoint, Bank XYZ has a purchase of USD from Commercial A at 1.9970, consisting of a spot rate of 2.0000 and 30 forward points discount. To segregate the deal from Commercial A into its component parts, the forward dealer "takes" the forward contract with the customer at 1.9970 and offsets the spot risk with a spot sale to the spot trader at a rate of 2.0000. The forward dealer delivers the 1 million USD to the spot dealer, which completes the spot trader's transaction cycle. The forward trader is left with only a one-month forward position at 30 points discount—the result that is supposed to occur.

By using this framework, the spot dealer will have a purchase from the forward dealer and a sale to Bank OFFSET. The dealer's cashflow and risk are offset. The forward dealer's cashflow will work as described in the preceding section. The one-month forward position can be offset immediately, rolled on a spot-next fashion for a few days, and then covered, or rolled for the entire period.

Cash Positions and Markets

On outright transactions, the spot dealer takes the spot risk, which calls for a standard delivery date. Outright purchases and sales made for value dates beyond spot incorporate a spot price adjusted by forward points. Outright transactions can also be dealt for value prior to spot value. Such transactions are termed *cash transactions,* and the pricing works much the same way as for forwards. The spot price is determined, and then an adjustment is made on the basis of the interest-rate differentials involved.

Exhibit 7.22. Summary of Market Prices

SPOT	1.2070–75	
O/N (overnight)	007–010	Reflects overnight swap from today until spot date. Market is 7 pips bid or 7/10 of one point. Offer is 10 pips or one point.
S/N (spot next)	006–009	Reflects overnight swap from spot value until next valid date. Market is 6 pips bid or 6/10 of point. Offer is 9 pips. As spot is next day on USD/CAD deals, it may also be labeled T/N (tomorrow/next).
S/W (spot a week)	05–07	Reflects swap points from spot to one week beyond. With holidays, one week may be more or less than 7 days.
1 Month	22–24	

To give the reader a challenge, let us change the market to a North American focus involving the USD and CAD. A summary of market prices is provided in Exhibit 7.22.

Consider a trade where Bank XYZ is to bid on (buy) 1 million USD from Commercial A value today (i.e., value cash).

Bank XYZ processes the deal via the following steps:

1. The Canadian dollar is quoted in Canadian terms, or the number of CAD per USD. The buying rate for USD is, therefore, the bid side, or 1.2070.

2. Delivery of the USD today, or one day ahead of spot, means the trader will receive a low-interest-rate currency (USD) and pay out a high-interest-rate currency (CAD) for a period of one day. To adjust for that cost, the spot price needs to be reduced to the client.

The basic adjustment can be determined by asking the question, What will it cost to unwind the cash position created by the deal? In this case, the trader would need to do a swap wherein he or she sells USD value today and buys USD value tomorrow. The intent is to buy on the far end of the swap and thus pay the offer on the overnight swap, which is 10 pips, or 1 point premium. This cost on the swap results in one point being *subtracted* from the spot price for Commercial A. A net price of 1.2069 is made.

These cash adjustments get quite tricky, and even experienced traders will sometimes have to stop and slowly think the process through.

One of the difficulties posed is the difference between handling cash points and forward points. In the CAD/USD market, where CAD interest rates have been historically higher than corresponding USD interest rates, a bid or buying rate for USD on a forward-rate results in adding the forward points on the bid side of the market to the spot rate. In a bid for value cash, the cash points on the offer side of the market are subtracted from spot.

Fixed Versus Option-Dated Forwards

The examples so far have assumed forward contracts maturing on a fixed date, i.e., March 21. Fixed-date forwards are used extensively. These contracts are ideal for hedging highly certain future cashflows, such as dividend and interest receipts or payments. Other cashflows, however, may be much less certain in timing and/or amount. In addition, other companies may have a large number of transactions which will result in inflows or outflows on a daily basis. Individual transactions may, however, be too small to hedge with individual forward contracts. One alternative way of hedging the risk is to combine them and hedge them with an option-dated contract.

The typical option-dated forward contracts allow the corporate cash manager to sell or buy a currency for delivery at any time during the option period. It is the cash manager's option when delivery takes place. Delivery, moreover, can typically be done in total on one day, or a number of partial deliveries can be made throughout the option period. By the last date of the option period, full delivery is required. On each delivery, the cash manager receives in return an equivalent amount of the countercurrency as determined by the exchange rate of the contract.

Consider an option-dated forward contract where Commercial A sells to Bank XYZ 1 million USD against CAD at 1.2000 for delivery during the period March 10–March 25. Commercial A makes three different deliveries over the period, as shown in Exhibit 7.23.

The majority of option-dated contracts cover a period of 31 calendar days or less. Longer-term windows are dealt but are much less frequent. With the option-dated contract, one must bear in mind:

1. The first and last dates of the contract must be valid business dates.

2. A minimum amount of a delivery will usually be required. For example, it is impractical to deliver $10.28.

3. Notice of delivery on larger amounts will often be required; e.g.,

Exhibit 7.23. Example of Deliveries on Option-Dated Forward Contract

Delivery date	USD delivered to Bank XYZ	CAD paid to Commercial A	Contract balance	
			USD	CAD
March 10	0	0	1,000,000	1,200,000
March 12	100,000	120,000	900,000	1,080,000
March 16	400,000	480,000	500,000	600,000
March 25	500,000	600,000	0	0

plans to deliver amounts of $1 million or more must be communicated to some banks on the preceding business day. A bank has uncertainty in its own cashflows on a daily basis, and considerable effort is usually made to forecast these flows. Notice of delivery helps the bank to manage its cashflows and positions more efficiently.

4. Forward points on fixed-dated forwards will change as the end maturity date changes. The option-dated contract will thus include a series of forward dates, each of which would usually have differing forward points associated with it. Because Commercial A could deliver on any date, Bank XYZ will tend to price the contract according to the date that reflects the poorest exchange rate for Commercial A. Thus, the flexibility of option-dated contracts tends to be offset by poorer prices.

Consider the example of Commercial A which wanted to sell USD for value March 10 and March 25. Fixed-dated contracts would have yielded the following, assuming a spot rate of 1.1990–1.1995.

	March 10	March 25
Forward points	10–12	15–17
All-in forward rate	1.2000	1.2005

Dealing a single option-dated contract covering the period March 10–March 25 would have resulted, barring competitive pressures, in a rate of 1.2000. This rate reflects the worst price from Commercial A's perspective during the option period. Quoting the "worst" rate does not reflect greed on the bank's part, but rather recognition of the fact that Commercial A could deliver on the entire contract on March 10, the first day of the contract period. The risk of this delivery on March 10 warrants a price for March 10.

Although the professional trading group faces uncertainty in its own corporate cashflow management, it is not feasible for the interbank market to trade option-dated contracts due to the active arbitrage that would inevitably take place. Fixed-dated contracts are the only practical way for that market to function.

Forward and Futures Markets

The forward market is the primary foreign exchange market that government and commercial clients use to hedge or cover foreign exchange exposure. The futures market also offers some hedging opportunities. It is similar to the forward market in a number of ways.

Futures markets are perhaps best known for commodity trading. However, futures in interest rates and exchange rates also exist and are a big part of today's financial markets. Exhibit 7.24 compares forwards and futures. Essentially, the markets are comparable in basic features and pricing. If prices were different, arbitrage would take place to bring them into line.

There are several differences, however, between futures and forwards. First, there is no flexibility in the futures market in amounts and delivery dates. Futures are also only available on a few major currencies and are more difficult to use for cross-rated deals. Futures contracts involve cash margin which most commercial clients can avoid when they deal forward contracts with their banks. Issuing checks to meet margin requirements during the life of a contract is a significant matter for many corporations. A forward-contract credit line, on the other hand, involves no such hassle for most firms. Forward markets can be dealt at any time of day, whereas futures cannot, although global linkages between exchanges are being established. Finally, forward markets have more liquidity, and large transactions can be dealt more quickly and at one price. For these reasons, most commercial and government accounts tend to rely on forward contracts.

Speculators are not as concerned about matching cashflows in terms of amounts or maturities as a commercial client seeking an exposure hedge. Futures markets are thus more suitable for the speculator and, in fact, these types of clients are the largest users of the futures market.

Exhibit 7.24. Comparison of Forward and Futures Markets

	Forward Markets	Futures Markets
Marketplace	Global network of players communicating by telephone, telex, or electronic dealing system.	Trading floor with players communicating face-to-face
Deal size	Nonstandard. Amounts are agreed to by the buyer and seller.	Standard contract size. Players deal in multiples.
Currencies traded	All currencies that can be traded	Most of the majors
Cross rates	Available in one contract	Usually requires two contracts
Price fluctuations	No daily limit in many currencies. Others have limits set by formal policy and/or central bank intervention.	Daily price limit is set by the exchanges. There are provisions to change the limits.
Maturity dates	Any valid business date. Date agreed to by the buyer and seller.	Standard dates. Usually one delivery date such as the third Wednesday of every third month.
Furthest maturity date	Open. Forwards have been dealt as far forward as 20 years.	12 months forward
Credit risk	Borne with dealing counterparty. Risk is usually covered by credit lines although margin is gaining more usage.	With the exchange. Risk is covered by initial margin adjusted by daily gains and losses on contracts and deals.
Cashflow	None until maturity date	Initial margin plus ongoing variation margin and final payment on maturity date
Hours of trading	24 hours a day	4–8 hour trading session. Exchanges connect together to make global links.
Eligible dealers	No formal restriction	Must be members of the exchange. Nonmembers use member brokers.

8

Currency Options

Executive Summary

Currency options are frequently suggested as an appropriate hedging tool because one can remove downside risk without limiting the upside potential. To some practitioners, the options products and markets may appear fairly simple. Conceptually, options are relatively simple. However, several aspects must be understood for the product to be used properly. This chapter outlines those key dimensions. It introduces the basic terminology and features of the product, addresses the factors affecting the premium, and reviews the concepts of probability, volatility, and expected value. The chapter outlines several common strategies that can be executed with options. It compares the options with forward contracts and demonstrates the technique of graphing options so that the true upside and downside risks are easily seen. Although this chapter will appear quite technical in some areas to a newcomer to options, in reality, it is basic in nature, which is an indication of the complexity of options.

Introduction

Chapter 7 discussed forward contracts under which a currency can be bought or sold for delivery in the future. A contract could stipulate delivery on a specific date, e.g., May 1, or during a specific period of time, e.g., May 1–31. The first contract is called a *fixed-dated forward contract,* and the second an *option-delivery forward contract.* In both cases, however, the counterparties are obligated to fully settle the contract when the maturity date is reached.

In a currency option, the single biggest difference is that one of the dealing parties, the holder, actually owns the rights to the contract and will decide whether or not the contract is to be exercised, i.e., settled. If desired, the holder or buyer of the contract can let the currency option contract lapse without delivery taking place. The seller or writer of the option, on the other hand, has no flexibility in deciding whether or not delivery will take place. The holder has total control of that decision.

The word *option* in an option-delivery forward contract means that one has the option of *when*, during the option period, the settlement(s) will take place. The word *option* in a currency option contract means that the holder has the option of making or not making delivery.

Option Terminology—Key Terms and Definitions

Calls and Puts

A *call option* is a contract that specifies the currency that the holder has the right to buy. A *put option* is a contract that specifies the currency that the holder has the right to sell.

If Commercial A buys a DEM call, it owns the right to decide whether or not to buy a specified amount of DEM at a specified rate. If Commercial A buys a USD put, it owns the right to decide whether or not to sell a specified amount of USD at a specified rate.

Foreign exchange deals are settled by paying out one currency and receiving another. If Commercial A's DEM call option specified the USD as the countercurrency, exercising the contract would result in the receipt of DEM and payment of USD. If Commercial A's USD put specified the DEM as the countercurrency, exercising the contract would also result in the receipt of DEM and payment of USD. Both deals, consequently, could be labeled as DEM calls or USD puts.

Because one currency can be priced vis-à-vis almost any other currency, it is necessary to specify which currency will be called and which will be put when the deal is originally being negotiated.

Exercise

The holder of the currency option has the right to decide whether or not the contract will be settled or will expire unexercised. If the holder wants to settle, or "exercise," the deal, the holder must contact the seller of the option before expiry and advise that the option is being exercised. More-over, the seller must be available for the holder to give notice.

Exercise Price or Strike Price

Prices on spot and forward contracts reflect prevailing market prices. In currency options, the rate at which settlement will take place is called the *strike*, or *exercise*, price. The strike price is determined when the deal is originally made and may be significantly different from current spot or forward rates. In fact, it can be whatever the holder wants it to be, provided he or she can find a seller of the option at that rate.

Exchange-Traded and OTC Options

Options can be traded on exchanges, such as the Philadelphia Stock Exchange or the Chicago Mercantile Exchange. In these markets, the options are traded in a standardized manner. The *over-the-counter* (OTC) market is essentially the market outside of the exchange-traded sector. Market makers are primarily banks and investment dealers.

A comparison of the two markets would prove similar to one made between forward markets and the futures market. As with forward contracts, the OTC is the dominant currency options market because of its superior liquidity; its increased flexibility on such aspects as amounts, currencies, expiry dates, and strike prices; and its reduced administration burden related to margin requirements.

From a pricing standpoint, the exchange-traded options and OTC options will be comparable. If significant differences exist, arbitrage between the two markets will usually take place. In fact, many market participants actively pursue price discrepancies, looking for the chance to arbitrage. Their dedicated focus on these markets keeps prices in one market in line with prices in the other. Having said that, there can be exceptions. For instance, consider a futures trader who has a small open position that he or she wants liquidated. Other traders simply have no interest in dealing an offset because it is too small. To unwind the position, the trader must, therefore, give a strong price incentive for another trader to deal.

Reversing or unwinding a position is usually feasible in both exchange-traded and OTC options. In the exchange-traded option market, offsetting an existing position results in the automatic cancellation of the option. In the OTC market, offsetting an option with the same bank or dealer that dealt the original option will often result in a netting or cancellation of the two deals. However, an offsetting position can be done with any market participant, including the exchange-traded option market. The two contracts offset from a risk standpoint, but, if exercised, cashflow settlements take place on both. Dealing with different entities can involve more cashflow administration, but the primary objective of offsetting the position is accomplished as effectively, and perhaps more so, from a pricing perspective.

Some market makers will also allow assignment of currency options that they sold. An option dealt with Bank A could thus be physically delivered and sold to Bank B. Bank A and Bank B then become the counterparties on the option. This practice is not overly common, largely because the hassles of an administrative, legal, and credit nature usually exceed the benefit.

Expiry Date

Currency option contracts have a final expiry date. The holder of the option must advise the writer on or before the designated expiry of the contract if the contract is to be exercised. The expiry will be specific as to the year, date, and time of day, e.g., 10:00 EST, November 18, 1992.

If the holder does not advise the writer of the intention to exercise the option before the contract expires, the writer is not legally bound to exercise the contract. Market etiquette frequently, but not always, gives some grace time in instances where it is clearly obvious that the holder would have exercised the option. This grace period should not be relied upon, however, and controls should be instituted by the holder to ensure that proper notification is always provided.

Furthermore, the writer *must* be available when the contract is due to expire so that the holder can exercise the contract if desired.

European and American Style

European-style currency options allow the contract to be exercised only on the expiry date. Actual settlement of the contract usually takes place either one or two business days later, in a manner consistent with the way in which spot transactions are dealt for the currencies in question.

American-style options can be exercised on any eligible business day as specified in the contract. Actual settlement again takes place one or two business days later. Most American-style options allow the owner to exercise the contract on any date between the original dealing date and the expiry date. Other contracts may specify a shorter period of time, such as the two weeks before the expiry date.

There is usually no reason for a holder of either an American or a European option to advise the writer earlier than necessary that the option will be exercised. Moreover, there is seldom any reason to exercise an American option before expiry. It is usually better to sell the option and deal the currency on a spot basis. As you will see later in the chapter, the only times when early exercise may be prudent is when the option is near expiry and has no extrinsic value, or when the option is deep in the money and its intrinsic value is greater than its option value.

At the Money

Exercise prices that equal the current spot price are termed *at the money—spot* (ATM-S). For example, both the exercise price and the current spot rate are 1.8000 DEM/USD.

Exercise prices that equal the current forward price corresponding to the contract's expiry date are termed *at the money—forward* (ATM-F). For example, both the exercise price and the three-month forward rate are 1.7500 DEM/USD.

In the Money

Exercise prices (1.5000 DEM put/USD call) that would provide the holder with a superior rate to that provided by the current spot rate (1.8000 DEM/USD) are termed *in the money—spot* (ITM-S).

Exercise prices (1.5000 DEM put/USD call) that would provide the holder with a superior rate to that provided by the current forward rate corresponding to the option's expiry date (1.7500 DEM/USD) are termed *in the money—forward* (ITM-F).

One way to determine if the contract is "in the money" at a given time is to calculate the result if the contract were exercised immediately and an offsetting spot or forward transaction were made. If a gain would result, the contract is in the money. (Exhibit 8.2, which appears later, provides a sample calculation.)

Out of the Money

Exercise prices (2.0000 DEM put/USD call) that would provide the holder with an inferior rate to that provided by the current spot rate (1.8000 DEM/USD) are termed *out of the money—spot* (OTM-S).

Exercise prices (2.000 DEM put/USD call) that would provide the holder with an inferior rate to that provided by the current forward

Exhibit 8.1. Example of ITM, ATM, and OTM Options

			Spot price	Forward price
Current market prices			1.8000 DEM/USD	1.7500 DEM/USD
Puts	Calls	Strike		
DEM	USD	1.5000	ITM-S	·ITM-F
		1.8000	ATM-S	OTM-F
		2.0000	OTM-S	OTM-F

rate corresponding to the option's expiry date (1.7500 DEM/USD) are termed *out of the money—forward* (OTM-F).

Consider Exhibit 8.1 which shows three USD calls (DEM puts) at different strike prices. The quotes are in currency terms, where the price reflects the number of DEM per USD.

It should be recognized that currency markets are often volatile and a currency option may be in the money at one moment and out of the money the next.

In Exhibit 8.1, the 1.5000 DEM/USD strike price is said to be "in the money" on both a spot and a forward basis for a USD call. To verify the classification, consider the hypothetical deal outlined in Exhibit 8.2, wherein one exercises the 1 million USD call and then sells the same amount of USD value spot.

In determining whether or not a contract should be exercised at maturity, the holder should compare the strike price with the current spot price. Consider Commercial A, which owns a USD call at a strike price of 1.8000 DEM/USD. It is 10 minutes before expiry, and the current spot rate is 1.5000. This is shown in Exhibit 8.3.

In this case, the spot purchase of USD is considerably superior to the USD call option, and the option would be allowed to expire unexercised. The flexibility of either exercising the contract or letting it expire unexercised is clearly beneficial to Commercial A.

On the other hand, consider Commercial A's situation should the spot rate be 2.2000 DEM/USD, shown in Exhibit 8.4.

Exhibit 8.2. Verification That Option Is In the Money

	USD, in/(out)	DEM, in/(out)
Exercise USD call	1,000,000	(1,500,000)
Sell USD spot at 1.8000 DEM/USD	(1,000,000)	1,800,000
Net gain/(loss)	0	300,000

Exhibit 8.3. Whether or Not to Exercise 1.8000 USD Call—
Spot at 1.5000

	USD, in/(out)	DEM, in/(out)
Exercise USD call	1,000,000	(1,800,000)
Buy USD spot at 1.5000 DEM/USD	1,000,000	(1,500,000)
Variance favoring spot purchase	0	300,000

Exhibit 8.4. Whether or Not to Exercise 1.8000 USD Call—
Spot at 2.2000

	USD, in/(out)	DEM, in/(out)
Exercise USD call	1,000,000	(1,800,000)
Buy USD spot at 2.2000 DEM/USD	1,000,000	(2,200,000)
Variance favoring USD call	0	400,000

The USD call is better than the current spot rate, and thus Commercial A would exercise the USD call. The option clearly was beneficial when compared with dealing on a spot basis. On the other hand, consider the plight of the writer of the option, shown in Exhibit 8.5. To highlight the writer's risk, assume the writer has no offsetting position and will, therefore, have to buy USD on the spot market to cover the option obligations.

Not surprisingly, the net loss of $400,000 incurred by the writer is the same amount by which the holder benefited from having the option (Exhibit 8.4). The writer clearly faces considerable downside risk. On the other hand, the writer would not benefit from the option, for if the option was out of the money (1.5000 as per Exhibit 8.3), the holder would let the option expire unexercised and would buy USD on a spot basis.

Exhibit 8.5. Losses Facing Writer on 1.8000 USD Call—Spot at 2.2000

	Writer's cashflow	
	USD, in/(out)	DEM, in/(out)
Commercial A exercises USD call	(1,000,000)	1,800,000
Buy USD spot at 2.20 DEM/USD	1,000,000	(2,200,000)
Net gain/(loss)	0	(400,000)

The writer will see the option exercised only when it suits the holder to do so. The writer faces an unknown loss that could be large. Option writers are not charitable players by nature, however, and for this risk, the writer needs to be compensated.

Premium

The premium on a currency option is the compensation paid by the holder to the writer. The premium must be adequate enough to justify the risk borne by the writer and yet, from the holder's standpoint, must be worthwhile paying. Let us return to the example above and assume the writer received a premium of 25,000 DEM for the option. If the option expired unexercised, the only cashflow that would have materialized would have been the premium paid by the holder to the writer. The writer's gain was thus a maximum of 25,000 DEM. However, if the option was exercised when the spot rate at expiry was 2.2000 DEM/USD, the net loss that would be incurred by the writer, assuming no offsetting hedge was in place, was still a significant, although a slightly smaller, 375,000 DEM, as Exhibit 8.6 shows.

The premium is nonrefundable. It is also usually paid up front, reflecting the fact that the risk has been incurred and payment for the risk is due. Payment can also be made at expiry date. Doing so effectively creates a loan from the writer to the holder. Consequently, the writer will demand the normal premium plus the interest on the loan, as outlined in Exhibit 8.7. This so-called *Boston-style option* can reduce the accounting problems associated with the up-front premium and may be just as cost-effective, especially for entities that are already borrowers of short-term money.

Premium Quotation

Premium can be quoted in terms of percentages or points. Market convention suggests that points are used when the premium is in one cur-

Exhibit 8.6. Losses Facing Writer after Receipt of Premium

	Writer's cashflow	
Spot market at 2.20	USD, in/(out)	DEM, in/(out)
Commercial A exercises USD call	(1,000,000)	1,800,000
Buy USD spot at 2.20	1,000,000	(2,200,000)
Premium received		25,000
Net gain/(loss)	0	(375,000)

Exhibit 8.7. Calculation of Premium on Boston-Style Option

Base premium for option	25,000
Interest on deferred payment of premium for 1 year at 10%	2,500
Total premium — Boston-style option	27,500

rency and the unit of account is in the other currency. In other words, if the premium is in DEM and is calculated on the basis of so many DEM per USD, the premium will be expressed in points, e.g., 250 points (.0250) per USD. If the currency of the premium and the unit of account are the same (e.g., both DEM), the premium is expressed in percentages, e.g., 2.5 percent per DEM. In the above example, the premium of 25,000 DEM would represent 250 DEM points.

$$\frac{25,000 \text{ DEM}}{1,000,000 \text{ USD}} = .0250 \text{ DEM/USD}$$

While options are usually quoted to corporate buyers in terms of regular foreign exchange points, there are different ways of quoting premium. Using the USD call option described above, the premium could be quoted in one of the following four ways:

1. DEM points per USD
2. DEM as a percentage of DEM
3. USD as a percentage of USD
4. USD points per DEM

To convert from one method to the next, one simply adjusts the premium by the spot rate, the strike price, or both rates. Consider the following calculations where the premium is 25,000 DEM and the contract amounts are 1,000,000 USD and 1,800,000 DEM. The current spot rate is 2.0000 DEM/USD.

1. If the premium is to be expressed as DEM per USD, it is calculated by dividing the 25,000 DEM premium by the USD amount in the contract. The result is 250 DEM points, or 25,000 DEM per million USD:

$$\frac{25,000 \text{ DEM}}{1,000,000 \text{ USD}} = .0250 \text{ DEM/USD}$$

2. The second method, DEM as a percentage of DEM, calculates the premium on the number of DEM in the contract. The option quote is determined by dividing the 25,000 DEM premium by the DEM

amount in the contract. The premium is, therefore, 1.39 percent per DEM, or 13,900 DEM per million DEM:

$$\frac{25,000 \text{ DEM}}{1,800,000 \text{ DEM}} = .0139 \quad \text{or } 1.39\%$$

3. The third method, USD as a percentage of USD, involves a change in the currency of the premium from DEM to USD. The premium is thus calculated by first dividing the DEM premium by the current spot rate of 2.0000 DEM/USD. This amount is then divided by the USD amount in the contract to generate a premium of 1.25 percent per USD, or 12,500 USD per million USD:

$$\frac{25,000 \text{ DEM}}{2.0000 \text{ DEM/USD}} = 12,500 \text{ USD}$$

$$\frac{12,500 \text{ USD}}{1,000,000 \text{ USD}} = .0125 \quad \text{or } 1.25 \text{ percent}$$

4. The final method, USD points per DEM, involves two steps. First, it involves a change in the currency of the premium from DEM to USD, which requires the 25,000 DEM to be divided by the current spot rate of 2.0000 DEM/USD. This USD amount is then divided by the DEM amount in the contract to determine the points (69.44, or 6944 USD per million DEM):

$$\frac{25,000 \text{ DEM}}{2.0000 \text{ DEM/USD}} = 12,500 \text{ USD}$$

$$\frac{12,500 \text{ USD}}{1,800,000 \text{ DEM}} = .006944$$

To verify that the conversions are correct, one can complete a quick and simple calculation, as shown in Exhibit 8.8.

Exhibit 8.8. Premium Comparison of Different Premium Quotations

Alternative	Points or %	Unit of account Currency	Unit of account Amount	Premium DEM	Premium USD
DEM per USD	.0250	USD	1,000,000	25,000*	
DEM as % of DEM	1.39%	DEM	1,800,000	25,020†	
USD as % of USD	1.25%	USD	1,000,000		12,500
USD per DEM	.00694	DEM	1,800,000		12,492†

*At a spot exchange rate of 2.00, the 25,000 DEM premium equals the 12,500 USD premium.
†The small differences are due to rounding.

Premium can also be expressed in currencies totally unrelated to the deal, such as GBP points per USD. It would certainly be unorthodox and most unusual, but still plausible. The method used for quoting points does not matter as long as all counterparties know exactly the parameters within which they are dealing.

Factors Influencing Premium

A number of factors determine the value or premium of an option:

1. Maturity date
2. Strike price
3. Current spot rate
4. Current forward rate or interest-rate differentials between the two currencies
5. Put or call
6. American or European style
7. Volatility
8. Risk-free interest rate (used for discounting expected value)

The next few pages will clarify why each of these factors affects the option price. However, many practitioners like to think of option value as simply consisting of two components, intrinsic and extrinsic value.

Intrinsic Value. The intrinsic value of a currency option is the amount by which an option is in the money. In other words, it is the difference between the strike price and the current market price. For example, a DEM put/USD call with a strike price of 2.0000 DEM/USD has 100 points (.0100) of intrinsic value with the current forward rate at 2.0100.

Current market rate to buy USD	2.0100
Strike price on USD call	2.0000
Intrinsic value	.0100

The premium for an option will be unlikely to trade at less than its intrinsic value. If it did, arbitrage would occur. For example, assume the premium on the USD call option is only 40 points (.0040). The risk-free trade could be executed as shown in Exhibit 8.9.

Exhibit 8.9. Arbitrage Where Option Premium Is Less Than Intrinsic Value

	Cashflow	
	USD	DEM
1. Buy USD call at 40-DEM points		
Premium (.0040 × 1,000,000)		(4,000)
Exercise USD call	1,000,000	(2,000,000)
2. Sell USD spot at 2.0100 DEM/USD	(1,000,000)	2,010,000
Net gain/(loss)	0	6,000

Extrinsic Value. The extrinsic value of a currency option is the total premium of an option less the intrinsic value. It is also known as *time value* or *volatility value*.

Total premium	.0360
Less: Intrinsic value	(.0100)
Extrinsic value	.0260

If an option is at the money or out of the money, it has no intrinsic value. If exercised immediately, the resulting position could not be offset in the market at a profit. Accordingly, the entire premium of at-the-money and out-of-the-money options is extrinsic value.

Intrinsic value is easy to understand. Its value can be easily calculated whether or not one knows the total value of an option. It is simply the amount that the option is in the money. The extrinsic value is also easy to understand and easy to calculate, provided one knows the total value of the option. To calculate extrinsic value without knowing the total value is not intuitively obvious.

The determination of an option's value is a fairly complex issue. One needs to take into account the various factors already mentioned to arrive at a price. The nature of an option is that the holder will exercise the option or let it expire unexercised, depending on the market rate at expiry. This uncertainty of the rate at expiry underlies the complexity of pricing options. To address it, probability analysis is used.

Probability and Expected Value. In life insurance, underwriters determine policy premiums on their estimate of the probability that the insured will die during the life of the insurance policy. With a large database, the underwriter is able to determine with reasonable accuracy the odds of this occurring for a particular person. Factors such as sex, age, smoker or nonsmoker, level of fitness, and history of family diseases help determine the probability that the insured will die by a particular age.

Assume there is a group of 1000 people. If each person has a 1 in 100 chance of dying during the next year, 10 members of the group are, therefore, expected to die in the next year.

Number of deaths = probability of death multiplied by the
number of people insured

= .01 × 1000

= 10

If each person has an insurance policy for $100,000, the company can expect to pay out $1 million in insurance claims in the next year:

10 × $100,000 = $1,000,000

To break even against this risk, the insurance company must collect $1 million in premiums.

Probability plays a similar role in pricing currency options. If we could know with absolute certainty whether or not an option would be exercised, the premium would reflect this certainty. For instance, if the option is in the money and is going to stay that way, the premium will equal the intrinsic value. The buyer will, in effect, have a forward contract and will not pay a premium higher than the intrinsic value.

The writer, moreover, will not accept anything less than the intrinsic value, as he or she will otherwise be arbitraged by the market and will suffer losses. The probability of exercise is either 100 percent or 0 percent in a world of certainty, and the premium will reflect these outcomes. Fortunately, or unfortunately depending on your perspective, markets with this degree of certainty do not exist.

In the case of currency options, predicting future outcomes, as far as market rates are concerned, is not quite as straightforward a process as insurance underwriting. The foreign exchange market is more volatile and uncertain, although some insurance companies might disagree!

Options pricing models analyze the range of outcomes that could occur and the frequency of each occurrence. The analysis shows the expected value of the option by using past results for future probabilities and multiplying the value associated with each possible outcome by the probability of its occurrence.

Exhibit 8.10 outlines a simplified expected-value calculation for an at-the-money 1.80 USD call/DEM put.

The historical analysis shows that the expected future spot price will be one of five prices. Each price has an estimated probability associated with it and, if it occurs, will produce a particular value vis-à-vis the option. If the

Exhibit 8.10. Expected Value of At-the-Money 1.80 USD Call/DEM Put

Future spot	Value at expiry	Probability, %	Weighted value at expiry
2.0000	.2000	10	.0200
1.9000	.1000	20	.0200
1.8000	0	40	0
1.7000	0	20	0
1.6000	0	10	0
Expected value (before discounting)			.0400

future spot is 2.0000 DEM/USD, the outcome has value, as it is superior to the 1.80 strike on the USD call by .2000. With a probability of 10 percent, the weighted value of that outcome is .0200 (.2000 × .1 = .0200). Similarly, a future spot rate of 1.6000 has no value for the 1.8000 USD call because the USD could be bought more cheaply at the 1.6000 level. The option would not be exercised. Overall, two possible outcomes are of value and collectively generate an option value of 400 points.

If the strike price was 1.9000 instead of 1.8000, the out-of-the-money option's expected value would only be 100 points, as per Exhibit 8.11.

Compared with the 1.8000 USD call, the reduced value of the 1.9000 USD call is due to a combination of only one outcome now having any value, the value of that outcome being reduced from .2000 to .1000, and the probability that the option will be exercised being reduced from 30 to 10 percent.

If the strike price was 1.7000, the in-the-money option would be worth 1100 points, as per Exhibit 8.12.

Compared with the 1.80 USD call, the increase in the value of the option is due to a combination of three outcomes now having value, the value of the outcomes being larger and the probability that the option will be exercised increasing from 30 to 70 percent.

Exhibit 8.11. Expected Value of Out-of-the-Money 1.90 USD Call/DEM Put

Future spot	Value at expiry	Probability, %	Weighted value at expiry
2.0000	.1000	10	.0100
1.9000	0	20	0
1.8000	0	40	0
1.7000	0	20	0
1.6000	0	10	0
Expected value (before discounting)			.0100

Exhibit 8.12. Expected Value of In-the-Money 1.70 USD Call/DEM Put

Future spot	Value at expiry	Probability, %	Weighted value at expiry
2.0000	.3000	10	.0300
1.9000	.2000	20	.0400
1.8000	.0100	40	.0400
1.7000	0	20	0
1.6000	0	10	0
Expected value (before discounting)			.1100

Armed with this historical information, the writer of an option has an estimate of the expected value of the option and what should be paid or charged at various strike prices. However, two points should be noted:

1. The above analysis is based on historical data. While history gives some terms of reference, it does not necessarily reflect what will happen in the future. Consequently, historical analysis is only a guide.

2. The range and number of outcomes are much larger than those presented here. Moreover, as mentioned before, many other variables affect an option's price. Incorporating all variables makes options pricing complex and essentially beyond the scope of manual calculations. An options pricing model is required.

A number of sophisticated mathematical models have been developed to price options. Two of the more common are the Black-Scholes model[1] and the Cox and Rubenstein model.[2] For the mathematically inclined, a detailed review of these models will show that each has strengths and limitations. However, both are used extensively in the marketplace.

Pricing models calculate the value of options based on the various criteria previously described. All the components except volatility are readily identifiable and can be easily included in the pricing model. The element which requires the most thought, and which prevents options pricing from being a purely mathematical exercise, is the volatility factor. Past and current market prices serve as guides, but they do not tell what volatility will be in the future.

Volatility. The historical analysis predicts the range of outcomes and the probability of each outcome occurring. This analysis is quantified in terms of volatility. If a currency is pegged to the USD at 1.50 units per USD, the currency has no volatility. As per Exhibit 8.13, there is no variation in prices at all. Conversely, a freely floating currency will have movements that can be relatively small (time 0–2) or extremely large (time 2–4).

Volatility in the context of options measures the extent by which ex-

Exhibit 8.13. Relative Movements of Pegged versus Floating
Currencies

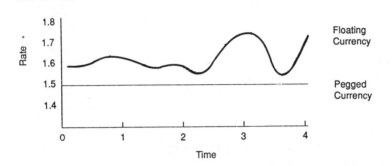

change rates move over a period of time. More specifically, volatility can be
defined as the annualized standard deviation of the current market price.
Using this definition, a 5 percent volatility means that there is a 2/3 probability that the future spot rate (one year hence) will be within 5 percent, or
one standard deviation, on either side of the current one-year forward
price. There is a 95 percent chance that the future spot rate will be within
10 percent, or two standard deviations, of the current forward rate. These
confidence limits assume a normal distribution. Exhibit 8.14 illustrates how
the range of expected outcome varies with volatility.

A summary of the volatility can also be shown in graphical form, as in
Exhibit 8.15.

Note. Normal probability distributions have particular properties
and are in the form of a bell curve; the curve to the left of the current
price line is a mirror image of the curve to the right of the current price
line. In options pricing, lognormal distributions are assumed, as there is
no chance of a negative exchange rate; but there is the possibility of extremely large exchange rate movements in the other direction. The natural log transformation helps to offset this inherent skewness in the
exchange-rate distribution.

Exhibit 8.14. Range of Expected Outcomes with Varying Levels of
Volatility

Volatility, %	Current forward	One Std. Deviation		Two Std. Deviations	
		Lower value	Upper value	Lower value	Upper value
5	2.00	1.90	2.10	1.80	2.20
10	2.0000	1.80	2.20	1.60	2.40
15	2.0000	1.70	2.30	1.40	2.60
25	2.0000	1.50	2.50	1.00	3.00

Exhibit 8.15. Probability Distribution with Varying Levels of Volatility

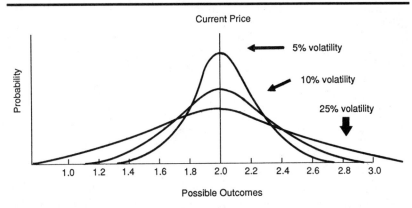

As the three graphs show, the higher the volatility, the flatter and wider the probability distribution. There are more possible outcomes at extreme levels, and the probability of any one outcome decreases. As the probabilities shift from fewer and smaller expected price changes (5 percent volatility) to more and larger price changes (25 percent volatility), the expected value of the option increases. This, in turn, results in a higher premium.

To verify this, we return to Exhibit 8.10, which had five possible outcomes and an expected value of .0400. If we add one more extreme outcome and change the probability distribution, we quickly change the expected value to .0510, as shown in Exhibit 8.16.

By itself, the additional outcome of 2.1000 increases the value of the option by .0150. However, the probability distribution for the other outcomes also changed, resulting in a net increase in value of only .0110.

The possible future spot rates at the maturity of an option are far less for an option with one week remaining to maturity than for an option that has one year to maturity. The expected value will, therefore, be dif-

Exhibit 8.16. Expected Value of 1.8000 USD Call with Increased Volatility

Future spot	Value at expiry	Probability, %	Weighted value at expiry
2.1000	.3000	5	.0150
2.0000	.2000	9	.0180
1.9000	.1000	18	.0180
1.8000	0	36	0
1.7000	0	18	0
1.6000	0	9	0
1.5000	0	5	0
Expected value (before discounting)			.0510

ferent, as will the premium. The time factor is a major component in determining the extrinsic value of an option and must be accounted for in the pricing of options in two ways.

1. The annualized measure of volatility must be adjusted for the actual life of the option. This is done in some pricing models by multiplying the annualized rate by the square root of the number of years that the option is outstanding. For example,

$$3 \text{ months} = 1/4 \text{ of } 1 \text{ year}$$

$$\text{Square root of } 1/4 = 1/2 \quad (1/2 \times 1/2 = 1/4)$$

$$\text{Standard deviation} = 5\% \times 1/2 = 2.5\%$$

Consequently, a three-month option at 5 percent volatility implies that there is a 2/3 chance that the spot rate at expiry will be within 2.5 percent, or one standard deviation, of the current forward rate. There is also a 95 percent chance that it will be within 5 percent, or two standard deviations, of the current forward rate.

This first adjustment is a mathematical adjustment built into the actual pricing models themselves. The user inputs the volatility and the term; the model makes the appropriate adjustments.

2. The volatility factor may differ for different option terms. A three-month option may be trading at 5 percent volatility, while a six-month option may be dealing at 8 percent volatility. This might occur, for example, from a forecast of a future change in volatility of the underlying exchange rate, perhaps because of the planned release of some relevant information at that time. Moreover, the current volatility rates on which the markets are trading can change significantly. Option traders and active hedgers must focus on these potential changes in volatility, known as *vega,* if they are to be successful. This forecast or call on the markets is where the human element comes into play and is the key to making money, assuming that the other aspects are also properly understood and controlled.

Implied Volatility.   When a volatility factor has been determined, the premium for a given option can be determined. Similarly, when the premium for an option is known, one can determine the volatility that would be required to generate that premium. This volatility calculated from premiums is called *implied volatility,* and it represents the market's assessment of possible market movements in the relevant future.

Interest Rates.   Interest rates play a role in the pricing of options in two ways:

1. The pricing of an option involves generating the expected value of the option at expiry. The expected value is the premium. As the premium is paid up front, the expected value must be discounted back to today's value. The interest rate used is usually the risk-free rate, such as that on federal government treasury bills. The formula for discounting investments is a straightforward present-value formula. Using the 1100 points in Exhibit 8.12 for expected value, and a 10 percent risk-free discount rate for a 90-day term, the present value of the expected value (i.e., premium) is 1073 points.

$$\frac{.1100}{1 + (.10 \times 90/365)} = .1073$$

2. Determining whether an option is in, at, or out of the money is a necessary part of options pricing. Comparison to the current spot market alone neglects the impact that forward points have on foreign exchange prices. Consequently, options pricing must incorporate either the forward points or the relevant interest rates for the two currencies.

Time Makes Options a Wasting Asset.   Increasing the term of an option gives volatility more time to affect prices. An option with a one-day expiry has a fairly narrow expected range of outcomes. An option with two days to expiry is outstanding twice as long and has a significantly larger range of possible outcomes. It still may be a relatively narrow range, but compared with the one-day option, it is much larger in percentage terms. A three-day option has an even larger range than a two-day option. However, the percentage change in time from two days to three days (50 percent) is smaller than the percentage change from one day to two days (100 percent).

As the time to expiry increases, the expected value increases significantly, especially in the first few weeks. With each passing day, however, the rate of increase in the premium decreases. Conversely, as an option approaches expiry, the rate of decline in its extrinsic value increases. This decline is known as *time decay*.

A representative summary of how the value of options increases and decreases with time is shown in Exhibit 8.17. The option prices are based on two currencies with identical interest rates. Moreover, all terms are based on 10 percent volatility.

A graphical summary of these values is portrayed in Exhibit 8.18.

Several observations arise from the results:

1. The value of deep in-the-money options is primarily intrinsic value, which in Exhibit 8.18 is 300 points (.0300). Time value has the smallest impact on in-the-money options and the largest impact on at-the-money options. The impact of time for out-of-the-money options is somewhere between the other two.

Exhibit 8.17. Summary of Option Premiums at 10% Volatility

Number of days to expiry	Option premiums at 10% volatility		
	Deep in the money	At the money	Far out of the money
1	.0300	.0013	0
2	.0301	.0025	0
4	.0302	.0037	0
8	.0304	.0053	.0001
16	.0311	.0075	.0002
32	.0327	.0110	.0008
64	.0363	.0160	.0028
128	.0423	.0230	.0074
256	.0511	.0327	.0152
364	.0568	.0389	.0207

Exhibit 8.18. Portrayal of Changes in Premium due to Changes in Term between ITM, ATM, and Options

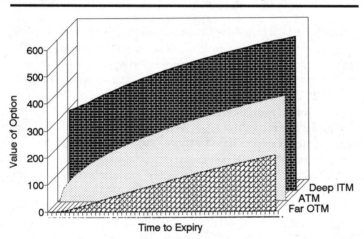

2. A deep in-the-money option with little time left to expiry, e.g., one day, is almost certain to be exercised. As time to expiry increases, the range of possible outcomes will increase, which enhances the value of the option beyond its current intrinsic value. However, the actual probability that the option will be exercised is reduced.

3. As an option nears expiry, the premium approaches the option's intrinsic value.

4. Far out-of-the-money options have a limited number of expected outcomes. As per Exhibits 8.17 and 8.18, however, additional time will increase both the number of possible outcomes and the overall probability

of the option being exercised. Consequently, the impact of time is greater on out-of-the-money options than on in-the-money options.

5. Additional time to expiry also increases the range of outcomes for at-the-money options. The probability of maturing in the money is essentially unchanged near 50 percent. However, it is still more likely to be exercised than out-of-the-money options. The combination of a greater probability of exercise and a larger range of possible outcomes causes time value to have more of an impact on at-the-money options than on out-of-the-money options.

6. A currency option can increase or decrease in value due to changes in either the underlying spot or forward foreign exchange markets. It can also increase or decrease due to changes in the options market such as when volatility changes. Moreover, an increase in the number of days to expiry will also tend to see an increase in the value of an option. Conversely, as each day passes, an outstanding option has fewer days left to expiry, and its value diminishes simply through the passage of time. As the option nears expiry, its value could, of course, diminish to zero value if it is at or out of the money. Accordingly, options are a wasting asset. Time decay works against holders of options, as time alone can cause erosion in an option's value. Conversely, time decay works in the favor of writers of options.

7. The speed at which the option wastes away will vary, depending on whether it is in, at, or out of the money. Intrinsic value is not affected by time, and the only element that wastes away is the time or extrinsic value. The further one goes in or out of the money, the smaller the time value. Consequently, the decline in value is slower for these options than for options that are closer to being at the money.

8. For almost all options with the exception of some options that are extremely far in or out of the money, time decay accelerates as one gets closer to maturity. The speed of the decay is measured by *theta*, which is the anticipated change in the premium of an option given a small change in time to expiry.

Days before Expiry	Premium
32	.0044
31	.0042
One-day theta	.0002

Starting about 35 days before expiry, time decay begins to accelerate significantly. Exhibit 8.19 provides a three-dimensional illustration of time decay.

Exhibit 8.19. Three-Dimensional Graph of Theta Plotted against Time and the Underlying Forward Market

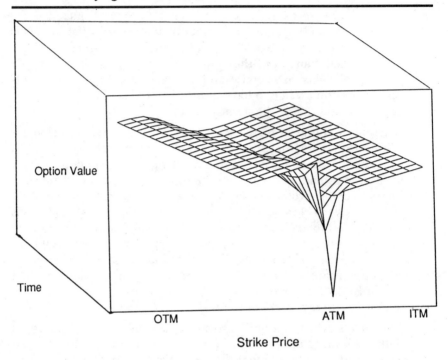

Strike Price

The three-dimensional graph shows that theta is largest for at-the-money options, especially as the expiry date approaches. Theta declines, on the other hand, as the strike price moves further in or out of the money and as time to expiry increases.

Premium—American versus European Option

A European-style option allows the holder to exercise the option on the expiry date. An American-style option allows the holder to exercise the option before the expiry date. If the currency that the holder of the option can call has a higher interest rate than the currency to be put, the holder enjoys a potential interest-rate gain by exercising the option early rather than waiting until expiry. This interest-rate advantage for the holder will cause the initial premium of an American-style option to be higher than a European-style option.

If the currency to be called is a lower-interest-rate currency, the

American-style option does not present the same interest-rate advantage to the holder. Instead, the interest-rate advantage of early exercise lies with the writer. The writer could conceivably reduce the premium for an American-style option below that of a comparable European option. However, the writer is unlikely to do so simply because the holder may not exercise the option early. Moreover, it should also be recognized that interest rates could change during the life of the option. Interest rates associated with the currency that the holder could call could move higher than the put currency. The potential interest-rate advantage could swing from the writer to the holder. In assessing the impact on premium, if the writer expects that the currency that the holder will call will remain as the low-interest-rate currency, the writer should charge the same premium for an American as for a European-style option. However, if the writer feels there is a reasonable risk that the interest-rate advantage could shift from the writer to the holder, an increase in premium is possible.

Exercising American-Style Options Early

When a holder has an American-style option, the ability to exercise before maturity would seem to be an attractive feature, especially if the currency to be called by the holder is the high-interest-rate currency. However, doing so may not be the best path to pursue. Assume the holder is faced with the scenario in Exhibit 8.20.

With the option in the money on both a spot and a forward basis, the holder has two alternatives:

1. The holder can simply exercise the USD call and take delivery of the USD at a rate of 1.2000 CAD/USD. In so doing, the option is exercised at 50 points better than the current spot rate. Consequently, .0050 of intrinsic value has been realized.

2. The holder can sell the USD call into the market. At 5 percent volatility, it would be worth approximately 120 CAD points per USD.

Exhibit 8.20. Example Market Scenario Facing Holder of American-Style Option

Currency option	Current market
1,000,000 USD call against CAD Expiry: 60 days Strike price: 1.2000 CAD/USD	Spot: 1.2050 60-day forward: 1.2090

Selling the option, however, does not give the holder of the option the USD that are desired. Consequently, a spot purchase of USD is made at the same time that the option is sold.

The effective rate for the USD buyer is now 1.1930, or .0070 better than the first alternative.

USD spot purchase	1.2050
Less: Premium received	(.0120)
Effective rate	1.1930

As summarized in Exhibit 8.21, the 70-point advantage arises because selling the option allows the holder to pick up the 30 points extrinsic, or time value of the option, and the 40 points of intrinsic value related to the forward points.

In this call option, the original purchase of the American-style option would have cost the same as a European-style option. If exercised early, the holder would have received the low-interest-rate currency (USD) and paid out the high-interest-rate currency (CAD). There was no disincentive to purchase the American option as opposed to the European-style option at the outset. However, 60 days before maturity, there also proved to be no advantage to having the flexibility to exercise the option early.

If the option was a CAD call instead of a USD call, the American-style option would have cost more initially because the holder has the right to take delivery of the high-interest-rate currency early. However, dealing spot and selling the option will still usually be the preferred alternative because the holder can realize any extrinsic value in the option.

Exhibit 8.21. Summary of Gains Achieved by Selling Option and Dealing Spot

Market price, 60 days forward	1.2090
Less: Strike price	(1.2000)
Total intrinsic	.0090
Less: Intrinsic realized when exercised early (1.2050–1.2000)	(.0050)
Net intrinsic recouped by selling option	.0040
Total premium	.0120
Less: Total intrinsic	(.0090)
Extrinsic or time value	.0030

While early delivery will not usually be beneficial, there may be occasions when it is prudent. Consider the following:

1. Ease of administration may justify doing so, especially when deals are small or when options are very close to maturity and the option value only reflects intrinsic value.

2. The bid-and-offer spreads in the market may eliminate the benefits of selling the option and dealing outrights.

3. If the option moves deep enough in the money, the interest-rate differential gained by early exercise may actually exceed the value of the option.

Delta

For foreign exchange options, the term *delta* represents the change in premium for a small change in the underlying exchange rate, everything else being equal. Delta also reflects the probability that the option will expire in the money. If the premium changes 1/2 point for a single-point change in the exchange rate, the delta is .5. If the premium changes by a full point for a point change in the underlying exchange rate, the delta is 1. Similarly, if the premium does not change at all, the delta is 0.

When an option is at-the-money forward, there is essentially a 50 percent chance that it will be exercised and a 50 percent chance that it will not. The market is just as likely to go one way as the other.

Consider a USD call (CAD put) option with an at-the-money strike price of 1.2000 CAD/USD. The premium is 200 CAD points per USD. Recall that the option premium is determined by the probability of the outcomes and the value associated with that outcome. In this case, there is a 50 percent chance that the option will be exercised.

If the market moves to 1.2001, the option at 1.2000 remains so close to being at the money that it still stands a 50 percent chance of being exercised. The difference in value for the option at the two market rates is the change in the underlying market multiplied by the probability of the option being exercised.

$$.0001 \times .5 = .00005$$

As a USD call is more valuable with the market at 1.2001 CAD/USD than it is at 1.2000, the option will be worth an additional 1/2 point (.0005), or .02005.

Exhibit 8.22 compares the premium of a 1.2000 USD call in several different market scenarios.

Exhibit 8.22. Calculation of Delta under Various Scenarios

	CAD premium for 1.20 USD call			
Forward rates	1.2000	1.2200	1.2400	1.2600
Intrinsic	0	.0200	.0400	.0600
Extrinsic	.0200	.0120	.0080	.0070
Total premium	.0200	.0320	.0480	.0670
Change in premium		.0120	.0160	.0190
Change in underlying rate		.0200	.0200	.0200
Ratio of change in premium to		.0120	.0160	.0190
change in underlying market				
rate (i.e., delta)		.0200	.0200	.0200
Delta*		.6	.8	.95

*Delta is usually calculated on small changes in underlying rates. The calculations in this exhibit are meant to clarify the concepts being discussed.

As strike prices move in the money, the intrinsic value will increase on a direct one-to-one relationship. However, the total premium does not increase on a one-to-one basis (delta does not equal 1) until the option is deep in the money. Until that point, two facts are worth noting:

1. The extrinsic value declines
2. A net value is "purchased" as the strike price is improved with a smaller amount of premium increase.

As shown in Exhibit 8.23, when strike prices are at the other extreme, that is, far out of the money, changes in spot prices may yield little or no change in the premium. Delta approaches 0.

The delta is a highly important piece of information when looking at an option. It represents the probability that the option will expire in or at the money. Alternatively, one could also say delta represents the elasticity of the premium against a particular change in the exchange rate.

Exhibit 8.23. Premium of 1.20 USD Call at Various Market Rates

Forward rates	1.2000	1.1800	1.1600	1.1400
Intrinsic	0	0	0	0
Extrinsic	.0200	.0120	.0060	.0020
Total premium	.0200	.0120	.0060	.0020
Change in premium		.0080	.0060	.0040
Change in underlying rate		.0200	.0200	.0200
Delta		.4	.3	.2

Bid and Offer

The options market features sellers and buyers in much the same way as other financial markets. When a corporate entity seeks a price from a market maker, it will specify the currency to be called, the currency to be put, the amounts, the strike price, the expiry date, European style or American style, and the way the premium is to be quoted. Market makers feed the relevant information into their pricing model and determine the price at which the option should be sold or bought.

From a trading standpoint, however, options traders tend to think of a long or short volatility (vega) position. Traders will go long volatility if they believe the volatility will increase. Moreover, if traders feel a currency will strengthen, they may go long a call on the currency. When that currency strengthens, the call will be closer to being in the money or will be deeper in the money than it was before. Its value will inherently increase, and will increase even more so if perceived volatility has also increased.

Option Strategies

There are a myriad of option strategies. To give the strategy some terms of reference, it is useful to look at the strategy in the following three ways:

1. Are you a buyer, a seller, or both a buyer and a seller?

2. What are the downside and upside risks being undertaken?

3. How do the results of the option compare with a forward or futures contract? Inherent in this final question is the determination of the breakeven point between the option and the forward or futures contract.

All three points go hand in hand in determining the benefits, risks, and features of the option strategy. Some people can answer these questions for complex strategies by simply taking a minute and thinking about the possible outcomes. The rest of us probably should physically lay out the strategy on a piece of paper, in either statistical or graphical form.

Consider a Canadian importer who needs to buy USD. The dollars can be bought forward with a forward contract at a rate of 1.1915 CAD/USD. Two basic alternatives using options are to buy a USD call option and to sell a USD put option. Two other alternatives include a strategy known as the "collar" and a variation of the collar called the ratio spread.

1. Buy a USD Call Option

The purchase of a USD call option gives the importer the right, but not the obligation, to buy USD at a specified rate by or on a specified date. A worst-case price equal to the strike price plus the premium has been established. This would occur if the option was exercised. The best case is not known at the outset because the company does not know what the future spot will be.

A statistical summary comparing three different strike prices to a forward contract at 1.1915 is given in Exhibit 8.24.

If the 1.2115 USD call is exercised (*a*), the worst price is the strike of 1.2115 plus the premium of .0036 for an all-in rate of 1.2151. Compared with dealing a forward contract at 1.1915, this out-of-the-money option, when exercised, is inferior by .0236, or 236 points.

The at-the-money forward USD call of 1.1915 (*b*) is also potentially inferior to the extent of the premium, 109 points. The deep in-the-money strike of 1.1715 (*c*) is only 36 points inferior, if exercised.

The ability to improve the strike price without a commensurate increase in premium shows the benefit of buying deep in-the-money options. This flexibility is only beneficial after the fact, however, if the option is exercised. Being deep in the money enhances the likelihood of the option being exercised. The greater the likelihood of exercise, the more the option tends to take on the characteristics of a forward con-

Exhibit 8.24. Comparison of Buying USD Calls to 1.1915 Forward Contract

Strike price	CAD premium per USD paid	Best situation possible		Worst situation possible	
		All-in FX rate	Variance to forward contract	All-in FX rate	Variance to forward contract
Forward contract		1.1915	0	1.1915	0
USD Call:					
a. 1.2115	(.0036)	The best price possible is the spot rate at the expiry date plus the premium paid.		1.2151	(.0236)
b. 1.1915	(.0109)			1.2024	(.0109)
c. 1.1715	(.0236)			1.1951	(.0036)

Exhibit 8.25. Comparison of Unexercised USD Calls to Spot Purchase at 1.1500

Strike price	CAD premium per USD paid	Spot rate	All-in FX rate	Variance to spot purchase
Forward contract		1.1500	1.1915	(.0415)
USD Call:				
a. 1.2115	.0036	1.1500	1.1536	(.0036)
b. 1.1915	.0109	1.1500	1.1609	(.0109)
c. 1.1715	.0236	1.1500	1.1736	(.0236)

tract. Moreover, as the option becomes closer to a forward contract, the relative attractiveness of the option decreases.

The major risk of going deep in the money is that the option may not be exercised. Exhibit 8.25 compares the USD calls if none of the options is exercised and the USD are bought at the spot rate of 1.1500 CAD/USD at expiry.

The effective rate when the USD spot is bought spot is the spot rate (1.1500 CAD/USD) plus the premium. As the deep in-the-money 1.1715 USD call (c) has the largest premium, it is also the most expensive alternative when the options are not exercised. The out-of-the-money option is the best alternative. An analogy would be to compare the 1.2115 USD call to having a large deductible on a fire insurance policy. If there is no fire, the policy will not be utilized and the homeowner is out of pocket the least amount of money. After the fact, a small deductible (i.e., the deep in-the-money option) provided no additional benefit when not exercised, and yet it cost more. Consequently, while buying deep in-the-money options provides for cheap purchase of intrinsic value, it also has the biggest downside risk when not exercised.

It should also be recognized that payment of the premium was not a waste of money when an option was not exercised. In fact, when an option was dealt, the importer would hope that the option would not be exercised in order that the USD could be purchased at levels superior to the strike price. The option should be viewed as having eliminated the currency risk for the importer in the same manner that a forward contract would. Moreover, the option proved superior in this case because it allowed the importer to take advantage of the strengthening CAD and buy the USD value spot at 1.1500 CAD/USD.

A graphic portrayal from the importer's perspective of the above 1.1715 USD call is provided in Exhibit 8.26.

Exhibit 8.26. Graphic Portrayal of In-the-Money 1.1715
USD Call

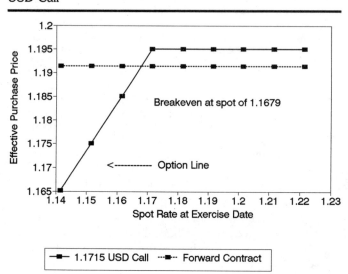

Exhibit 8.26 illustrates a few points:

1. The horizontal portion of the option line reflects the worst-case scenario. If exercised, the all-in cost of the option is the strike price plus the premium. It does not matter what the current spot is. The final effective rate of the option remains the same.
2. The distance between the forward contract line and the horizontal portion of the option line represents the amount by which the importer could be worse off by buying the USD call option than by buying USD on a forward contract. For an in-the-money 1.1715 USD call option, this distance of 36 points (.0036) is the extrinsic or time value of the call option when the option was initially purchased.
3. Moving from right to left, the downward-sloping line to the left shows that the final effective rate continues to decline as the USD weakens (CAD strengthens) from 1.1879 to 1.1400 CAD/USD. The call option allows the holder to let the contract expire unexercised and buy the USD spot at the current and more favorable spot rates. The final effective rate is the actual spot rate plus the premium paid. There is no restriction on the best price.
4. If the option is exercised, it will be more expensive (and less effective) than the forward contract. The breakeven between the two occurs when:

a. The option is not exercised.

b. The USD are bought spot at a level equal to the initial forward rate less the premium paid.

The breakevens for the three USD call options are as follows:

	1.1715 call	1.1915 call	1.2115 call
Initial forward rate	1.1915	1.1915	1.1915
Premium paid	(.0236)	(.0109)	(.0036)
Breakeven spot rate	1.1679	1.1806	1.1879

A graphical portrayal of the out-of-the-money 1.2115 USD call is given in Exhibit 8.27.

The same comments apply to the 1.2115 USD call option that were made concerning the 1.1715 option, with one exception. The distance between the forward contract line and the horizontal portion of the option line (.0236) consists of the extrinsic value of .0036 plus the amount by which the option is out of the money (.0200).

When the market has such a favorable move that the options are not exercised, the most advantageous alternative would be the out-of-the-money option (USD call at 1.2115). Much as deep in-the-money options tend to take on the characteristics of a forward contract, the far out-of-the-money options tend to become similar to spot contracts. The fur-

Exhibit 8.27. Graphical Portrayal of Out-of-the-Money 1.2115 USD Call

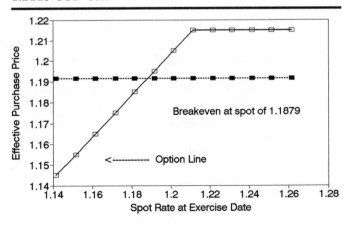

ther the option is out of the money, the smaller the premium and the less likely that the option will be exercised. Therefore, it will more likely result in dealing a spot transaction that generates an all-in price that is only slightly inferior to the spot rate.

At-the-money options are just as likely to be exercised as not. They tend to have a balance of the advantages provided by both spot and forward contracts.

2. Sell a USD Put Option

A second strategy available to the importer is to sell or write a USD put option. Premium is received which will reduce the final cost of the USD purchase. However, the importer has limited the best price to be the strike price on the option less the premium, and this will only occur when the buyer of the put option exercises the option. Exercise will only occur if the USD is weaker than the strike price. The worst case for the importer would be if the USD strengthened dramatically and the option was not exercised. The importer would then have to buy dollars on the spot market. A comparison of three USD puts to a forward contract is provided in Exhibit 8.28.

The best outcome for the writer is to have the USD weaken (CAD strengthen) and to have written the out-of-the-money put at 1.1715. Exhibit 8.29 portrays the results if the spot rate at expiry was 1.1800 CAD/USD.

If the USD had strengthened to 1.2500, the best strategy would certainly have been to buy forward. However, as outlined in Exhibit 8.30, if one did write an option, it would have been best to write the deep in-the-money option at 1.2115 to gain the most premium.

Exhibit 8.28. Comparison of Writing USD Puts to 1.1915 Forward Contract

Strike price	CAD premium per USD received	Best situation possible		Worst situation possible	
		All-in FX rate	Variance to forward contract	All-in FX rate	Variance to forward contract
Forward contract		1.1915	0	1.1915	0
USD Put:					
a. 1.2115	.0230	1.1885	.0030	The worst price possible
b. 1.1915	.0104	1.1811	.0104	is the spot rate at expiry less the premium received.
c. 1.1715	.0030	1.1685	.0230	

Exhibit 8.29. Comparison of USD Puts to Forward Contract with Spot at Expiry of 1.1800

Strike price	CAD premium per USD received	Spot rate	All-in FX rate	Variance to forward contract
Forward contract			1.1915	0
USD put:				
a. 1.2115	.0230	1.1800	1.1885	.0030
b. 1.1915	.0104	1.1800	1.1811	.0104
c. 1.1715	.0030	1.1800	1.1770	.0145

Exhibit 8.30. Comparison of USD Puts to Forward Contract with Spot at Expiry of 1.2500

Strike price	CAD premium per USD received	Spot rate	All-in FX rate	Variance to forward contract
Forward contract		1.1915	1.1915	0
USD put:				
a. 1.2115	.0230	1.2500	1.2270	(.0355)
b. 1.1915	.0104	1.2500	1.2396	(.0481)
c. 1.1715	.0030	1.2500	1.2470	(.0555)

A graphical portrayal of the 1.1715 USD put from the importer's perspective is shown in Exhibit 8.31.

Exhibit 8.31 illustrates some key points:

1. The importer has a firm best price, which is the dotted horizontal line on the left side of the graph. This price (1.1685) is the strike price (1.1715) less the premium received (.0030).

2. The distance between the forward contract line and the horizontal portion of the option line represents the maximum amount by which the importer can improve by writing the USD put rather than buying USD on a forward contract. For an out-of-the-money 1.1715 USD put option, this distance of 230 points (.0230) represents the extrinsic value of the put option when the option was initially sold (.0030) plus the extent to which the option is out of the money (.0200).

3. From left to right, the upward-sloping line shows that the all-in cost continues to increase as the USD strengthens (CAD weakens) from the 1.1715 CAD/USD level. The put option does not guarantee de-

Exhibit 8.31. Graphical Portrayal of Out-of-the-Money
1.1715 USD Put

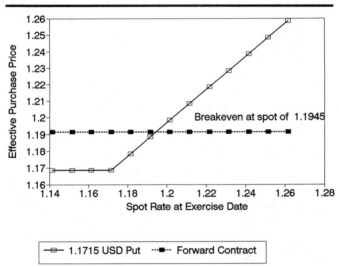

livery of USD, and if the USD is stronger than the strike price (i.e., at 1.1800 CAD/USD), the holder of the USD put will not exercise. In this case, the worst case will be the eventual spot rate less the premium received.

4. If the option is exercised, it will be cheaper (and more effective) than the forward contract. If not exercised, the put option may be a less favorable strategy. The breakeven spot rate at expiry equals the forward rate plus the premium received.

	1.1715 put	1.1915 put	1.2115 put
Initial forward rate	1.1915	1.1915	1.1915
Premium received	.0030	.0104	.0230
Breakeven spot rate	1.1945	1.2019	1.2145

A graphical portrayal of the 1.2115 USD put from the importer's perspective is shown in Exhibit 8.32.

The same comments apply to the 1.2115 USD put option that were made on the 1.1715 option, with one exception. The distance between the forward contract line and the horizontal portion of the option line (.0030) consists of only one element, the extrinsic value of .0030. In

Exhibit 8.32. Graphical Portrayal of Out-of-the-Money
1.2115 USD Put

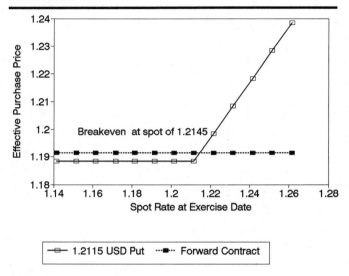

Spot Rate at Exercise Date

—▫— 1.2115 USD Put   ···■··· Forward Contract

other words, the importer can only improve upon the forward contract
by 30 points.

When the market has such a favorable move that the options are exercised, the most advantageous alternative would be the out-of-the-
money put option at 1.1715.

Comparing the Purchase of the USD Call to the Sale of the USD Put. The
USD call option that gives the USD buyer the best possible price is the
1.2115 USD call. The best possible price on the USD put can be
achieved through the 1.1715 USD put. A graphical comparison between the two is shown in Exhibit 8.33.

	Strike	Premium rec'd. (paid)	Best price	Worst price
USD call	1.2115	(.0036)	?	1.2151
USD put	1.1715	.0030	1.1685	?

Exhibit 8.33 portrays a number of key points:

1. The horizontal line on the USD call shows the worst price of 1.2151.
   The call has no best price.

Exhibit 8.33. Comparison of Purchase of 1.2115 USD Call and Sale of 1.1715 USD Put

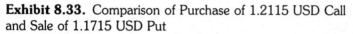

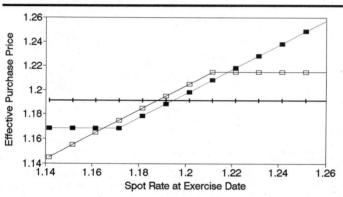

Spot Rate at Exercise Date

| ─□─ 1.2115 USD Call | ─■─ 1.1715 USD Put | ─┼─ Forward Contract |

2. The horizontal line on the USD put option line shows that the best price is 1.1685. The put has no guaranteed worst price.

3. The two alternatives will yield the same worst-case results if the USD is trading at a spot rate equal to the USD call's worst price plus the premium earned by writing the USD put.

Worst price of USD call	1.2151	(1.2115 + .0036)
Premium earned on USD put	.0030	
Breakeven rate	1.2181	

4. The two alternatives will yield the same best-case results if the USD is trading at a spot rate equal to the USD put's best price less the premium paid by buying the USD call.

Best price of USD put	1.1685	(1.1715 − .0030)
Premium paid on USD call	.0036	
Breakeven rate	1.1649	

5. In between these two breakeven points of 1.1649 and 1.2181, writing the USD put is advantageous because the premium was received and

not paid, as in the case of buying the USD call. If the spot rate is outside this range, the USD call option is advantageous because the importer can exercise the call if the USD strengthens, or let it expire unexercised if the USD weakens.

3. Collar—A Purchase and Sale of Options

Another strategy that may be considered by the importer needing to buy USD is the transaction known, among other labels, as the collar or limit forward. (See Exhibit 8.34.)

The collar involves the purchase of a USD call (for example, 1.2115) and a simultaneous sale of a USD put (for example, 1.1715). Both contracts have the same maturity date and the same principal amount. If the CAD traded to 1.2400 at expiry, the importer would exercise the USD call option and take delivery of USD at the strike price of 1.2115. Alternatively, if the CAD traded to 1.1600, the holder of the USD put would exercise and give the importer USD at the strike price of 1.1715.

If the CAD was trading between 1.1715 and 1.2115 at expiry, neither party would exercise its option and the importer would simply buy the USD spot. A firm best and worst scenario is thus created.

A graphical description of the collar is shown in Exhibit 8.35.

From the perspective of the USD buyer, a few more points should be noted about the collar.

1. The importer, a USD buyer, has a firm worst price defined by the USD call line (1.2121) and a best price defined by the USD put line (1.1721).

Exhibit 8.34. Comparison of Collar to Forward 1.1915 Contract

Strike price	CAD premium per USD, (paid)/rec'd.	Best situation possible		Worst situation possible	
		All-in FX rate	Variance to forward contract	All-in FX rate	Variance to forward contract
Forward contract		1.1915	0	1.1915	0
FX collar:					
USD call 1.2115	(.0036)				
USD Put 1.1715	.0030				
Net	(.0006)	1.1721	.0194	1.2121	(.0206)

Exhibit 8.35. Graphical Portrayal of a Collar with 1.2115 Call and 1.1715 Put

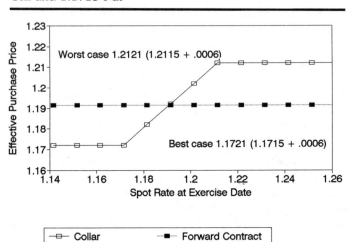

2. If the spot rate at maturity is between the two levels, the final effective cost is the spot price plus or minus the net premium. In this case, it is equal to the spot rate plus 6 points (spot + .0006).
3. If the USD call is exercised, the transaction will be more expensive than the forward contract by 206 points. If the USD put is exercised, it will be cheaper than the forward contract by 194 points.

    In doing such deals, one needs to determine this comparison of upside and downside risk. In this case, the importer can improve upon a forward contract by 194 points (.0194), but is risking 206 points (.0206). From a pure risk/reward standpoint, it would not seem to make sense to do this deal. One of the main reasons many collar structures contain more downside risk than upside risk is that one is paying the bid-and-offer spread to the market maker. In other words, the client is paying the offer side of the market on the option purchased (USD call), but is receiving only the bid side on the option sold (USD put).
4. Care must be taken in designing the collar to prevent both sides of the collar from being exercised and giving the importer double the amount of USD required. This risk can be overcome in two ways:

    a. The collar transaction is usually dealt on European-style options. If done on an American-style basis, a move to 1.2500 could see the buyer exercise the 1.2115 USD call. If the market subsequently moved to 1.1500, and the USD 1.1715 put had not been purchased back when the call was exercised, the holder of the put could exercise it. If the USD call was exercised, the USD buyer could buy back the USD put to prevent double delivery. If this was done, however, it begs the question of why the USD call was exercised. It would seem inconsistent to exercise the USD call at 1.2115 and then buy back a USD 1.1715 put for fear of the USD weakening (CAD strengthening) and getting exercised on the USD put. However, unexpected and large market movements are always possible; and to eliminate this risk, buying back the USD put may be done if the USD call was exercised.

b. The strike prices are established so that only one party would ever want to exercise at maturity. If the collar had a 1.1715 call and a 1.2115 put, a spot market at maturity in between those levels, i.e., 1.2000, would see both the put and call exercised. To prevent this, the strike price on the USD call would reflect a stronger USD (i.e., 1.2000) than on the USD put (i.e., 1.1800).

4. Ratio Spread

The ratio spread is a variation of the collar. The major difference is that the principal amount on the two options differs. With our importer who needs to buy USD, the USD put could be for $7 million, while the USD call is for $10 million.

To structure a deal so that the amount of the premium is eliminated or minimized, the strike price in either the put or call option or in both the put and call options needs to be changed from what it would be in a collar. This can be done in a few ways, two of which are as follows:

1. Making the USD call strike price more out of the money will reduce the premium paid.

2. Moving the USD put strike price closer to at the money will increase the premium received.

If we change the strike price on the USD put, for example, the results would be as follows if 30 of the 36 points premium on the 1.2115 USD call are to be offset:

Premium to be offset on $10 million 1.2115 USD call ($10,000,000 × .0030)	$30,000
Premium in points for $7 million USD put (30,000/7,000,000)	.0043

At a strike price of 1.1715, the USD put has a premium of 36 points. To generate 43 points, the strike price would need to improve to 1.1750.

To compare the ratio spread to the collar, first look at the common $7 million portion. The only difference on this core amount is that the strike price on the USD put was changed from 1.1715 to 1.1750. The importer gave up 35 points of upside risk on the $7 million. In exchange for the 35 points, the importer has effectively purchased a net 3 million USD call position at 1.2115.

Collar. If the USD weakened to 1.1400, the USD put in the collar would be exercised. The total cost for the purchase of USD is thus 11,721,000 CAD.

Exercise of 10 million USD put at 1.1715	$11,715,000
Net premium on collar	6,000
Total	$11,721,000

Ratio Spread. By comparison, the ratio spread would involve a total cost of $11,650,900.

Exercise of 7 million USD put at 1.1750	$ 8,225,000
Purchase of $3 million spot at 1.1400	3,420,000
Premium received on 1.1750 put (7,000,000 × .0043)	(30,100)
Premium paid on 1.2115 USD call	36,000
Total	$11,650,900

Because the ratio spread allowed the USD buyer to benefit from the USD weakening (CAD strengthening) on the 3 million USD portion, the total cost of the USD was reduced.

To compare the ratio spread to the collar, consider Exhibit 8.36.

If the spot rate was at 1.2500 at expiry, the USD 1.2115 call would provide the same protection for both the ratio spread and the collar.

At levels between 1.2115 and 1.1750, each point change in the underlying spot market changes the effective cost of the entire 10 million USD purchase by a full point for both the collar and the ratio spread. However, when the spot USD is weaker than 1.1750 (i.e., 1.1735), the 7 million USD put in the ratio spread would be exercised and the improvement in the rate below 1.1750 would only be experienced on the remaining $3 million. Consequently, each point improvement in spot below 1.1750 only generates a .3-point improvement in the effective cost of the ratio spread. Graphically, the change in improvement is witnessed by the reduction of steepness on the ratio spread line below the 1.1750 level.

The collar, on the other hand, would continue to reap point-for-point improvement all the way to the 1.1715 level, after which no further improvement would be achieved. Consequently, between 1.1750 and

Exhibit 8.36. Comparison of Ratio Spread to Collar

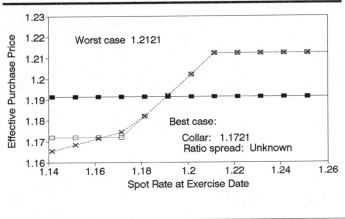

Spot Rate at Exercise Date

| --▫-- Collar | --×-- Ratio Spread | --▪-- Forward Contract |

1.1715, the collar achieves superiority in comparison to the ratio spread because it achieves a point-for-point improvement, while the ratio spread only achieves 30 percent of that improvement. After the 1.1715 level, however, the collar reaps no further gains. On the other hand, the ratio spread would continue its gains until, at some level, the ratio spread would prove superior. This breakeven rate of 1.1633 between the ratio spread and the collar can be calculated as follows:

Spot rate at which collar starts to gain advantage	1.1750
Spot rate at which collar starts to lose advantage	1.1715
Point span	.0035
Change in spot rate below 1.1715 required to breakeven (.0035/.3)	.0117
Breakeven rate between ratio and collar (1.1750 -- .0117)	1.1633

Many different option strategies could be discussed at length, but they are beyond the scope of this book. The purpose of the chapter is to provide a framework against which individual strategies can be evaluated. A few examples of other strategies are graphed and briefly described in the section that follows.

Other Options Strategies and Products

Understanding the basic elements in option pricing and the main issues involved in writing or buying a call or a put is essential to using options.

When this fundamental understanding is in place, the user can move into a selection of more complex options strategies. The collar and ratio spread are slightly more complex than a straight put or call, but they are nothing more than a combination of options with a few twists thrown in.

A few other strategies used by corporations are briefly reviewed in this section. Graphs are included, using the following basic format:

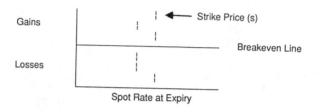

Straddle

A *long straddle* involves the purchase of both a put and call at the same strike price and expiry date. It is ideal for a quiet market that is expected to move sharply: the only uncertainty is which direction it will take. One buys volatility. Gains can be made from the actual market move or from increases in the volatility component in the options market. The maximum loss is the premium paid and occurs when the options expire at the money.

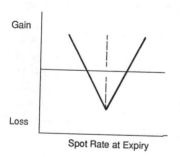

A *short straddle* involves the sale of both a put and a call, again at the same strike price and expiry date. It is suited for markets that are expected to stay near current levels. One is selling volatility. Gains are made from the time-decay process as well as from declines in the volatility component if the options are bought back. The maximum loss is unlimited.

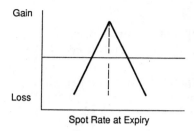

Strangle

A *long strangle* is similar to the long straddle except that the call and put are at different strike prices. Usually, both strike prices are out of the money, which reduces both the downside risk (less premium paid) and the potential gain (the market must move further before the option becomes profitable).

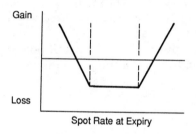

A *short strangle* is similar to the short straddle except that the call and put are at different strike prices. Both strike prices are out of the money, which again reduces both the potential gain (less premium received) and the downside risk (the market must move further before the option becomes profitable to the holder).

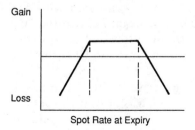

Spread

A *bull spread* involves a purchase of a call at a low strike price (A) and a sale of a call at a higher strike price (B). The strategy is used when the market is expected to rise slightly.

The sale of the calls limits the upside potential, and the premium received offsets part or all of the premium paid.

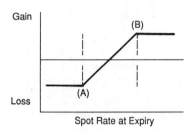

A *bear spread* involves a purchase of a put at a high strike price (A) and a sale of a put at a lower strike price (B). The strategy is used when the market is expected to decline slightly.

As with the bull spread, the sale of the put reduces the profit potential, and the premium received offsets part or all of the premium paid.

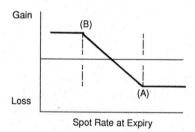

Synthetic Options

The basic purchase and sale of options can be combined with forward contracts to form synthetic options. For example, consider the purchase of a USD call at 1.20 CAD/USD and a forward sale of USD also at 1.20. Together, the contracts create a synthetic USD put at a 1.20 strike price. If the USD strengthens to 1.22 CAD/USD, USD are sold spot at 1.22. The USD call at 1.20 is exercised, with the proceeds used to deliver on the forward contract, which is also at the rate of 1.20 CAD/USD. If the USD weakened to 1.18, one would simply deliver on the forward contract and let the USD call lapse. When used together, the USD call and forward USD sale create the same functional properties as a USD put at 1.20.

In addition to these synthetic options, options and forwards can be combined in a number of other ways to create "products." Some of these products may help sell the concept of options internally, or they may simply minimize accounting problems. Consider the following:

1. A forward contract for purchase of DEM against USD is combined with an option to buy USD with AUD. The buyer of the forward has the option of buying DEM with either USD or AUD. The cost of the option is built into both the USD and AUD forward rates.

2. A forward contract for purchase of USD against DEM is combined with an option to buy additional USD against DEM. The buyer of the forward can now buy a base amount of USD, and more if so desired. The cost of the option is built into the forward rate and is collected when the base amount of the forward contract is settled.

3. An option is dealt that gives a buyer the right to buy or sell an option.

4. A forward contract is dealt at a price that is lower than the prevailing forward rate. However, the buyer of the forward contract also receives a separate option contract, premium-free.

5. A forward contract is dealt at a price that is lower than the prevailing forward rate. However, the forward contract can be canceled at a specific price at any time before its maturity. This ability to cancel the forward is, in effect, a built-in option with the premium paid for by the adjustment in the original forward rate.

6. A forward contract is dealt at a price poorer than the prevailing forward rate. Should the market move in the buyer's favor, both the buyer and the seller of the option share the gain. In effect, an option is purchased, but for only a part of the principal amount involved.

7. In a bid or tender situation, the contractor may take out an option on behalf of all entities tendering on the contract. The winning company is given the option.

Naked and Covered Options

The importer in the above example was using options to manage a future cashflow exposure. Other entities may have actual assets in foreign currencies such as stocks, bonds, or money-market assets. The portfolio manager may write call options on the currency of these assets at a strike price at which he or she would be comfortable selling the currency. If the currency is below the strike price at expiry, the option expires unexercised and the portfolio manager has generated extra income. If the option is exercised, the manager has liquidated at a desirable level.

Writing call options against assets owned (the currency in this case) is called *covered call writing*. Where one does not have the underlying asset but would like to buy the currency, an out-of-the-money put on the currency can be sold. If the currency declines below that level at expiry, the manager receives the currency at the desired level cushioned further by the premium.

When one writes calls and does not have the underlying asset, one is writing the call "naked." If the call is exercised, the writer will have to buy the foreign currency to deliver against the contract. Such trading works on the premise that the income from the option premium will more than offset any losses.

Usage of Options

While there are no golden rules for using options, there are a few considerations to bear in mind:

1. Options are usually the second best alternative behind either a spot or a forward contract. Consequently, if one had a strong opinion on future market direction, dealing spot or forward would likely be preferable to an option.

2. Options tend to be the best alternative when an option is written and the market is relatively stable. The writer earns premium, which enhances the effective rate and makes it a superior alternative to both the spot and forward contract alternatives.

3. Options tend to be the worst alternative when an option is purchased and the markets do not move.

4. Options are an alternative to, not a substitute for, spot or forward contracts.

5. Purchased options are an asset; sold options are a liability. Market movements can present attractive opportunities to either sell or buy back the option. Do not automatically wait until expiry before doing anything.

Having said the above, all strategies need to be viewed in light of why they were chosen. In a market that does not move, a purchase of an option could be viewed as the worst alternative. However, it should also be viewed as having reduced financial risk, something that dealing spot contracts, for instance, may not do. Accordingly, it is important for users of options to look beyond the product itself and consider the overall situation.

Since very little is certain in this world, currency options can be an effective and useful tool in the following instances:

1. Dealing in contract tenders that pose uncertainty about whether or not the exposure will arise and, if it does, when the exposure will actually materialize

2. Carrying out ongoing transactions that have exposures that are uncertain in terms of timing and/or amounts (e.g., sales made from price lists)

3. Hedging balance sheet translation exposures

4. Hedging previously unhedged foreign currency loans or investments

5. Making new foreign currency loans or investments using options as the hedge vehicle

6. Generating income on a foreign investment portfolio

7. Hedging known exposures that already have foreign exchange gains where some or all of the gains are used to buy options to guarantee a breakeven and provide the opportunity for additional gains

References

1. Black, Fisher, and Myron Scholes, "The Pricing of Options and Corporate Liabilities," *Journal of Political Economy*, May/June 1973, pp. 637–659.

2. Cox, J., and M. Rubenstein, "Option Pricing: A Simplified Approach," *Journal of Financial Economics*, September 1979, pp. 229–263.

9
Foreign Exchange and Interest-Rate Swaps

Executive Summary

Chapter 9 reviews a variety of foreign exchange swap transactions including rollover swaps used in trading, cash-management swaps, historical-rate rollovers, and foreign currency borrowing and investment swaps that are hedged with forward contracts or currency options. The chapter also briefly reviews currency swaps used in long-term financing, as well as interest rate swaps used in managing interest-rate exposure. The chapter is technical in nature.

Introduction

A basic foreign exchange swap is the simultaneous purchase and sale of one currency for another, where the two contracts have different value dates. At least, that is one definition that exists in the market. By itself, the term *swap* can have different meanings for different people, and one has to be careful that there are no misunderstandings among participants involved in a deal or discussion. The purpose of this chapter is to describe and explain the more common forms of swaps and show how they are used in the marketplace.

Rollover Swap

Trading the forward market uses swaps in both dealing forward transactions and trading the cash positions associated with forward trading. If you recall from Chapter 7, a purchase in the forward market will incorporate a sale for value spot. These spot sales create cash positions that are managed by rolling them over day by day, or week by week, until offsetting transactions materialize or until the forward contract matures. Because of the rollover practice, we refer to these types of swaps as *rollover swaps*.

Rollover swaps are frequently used by the interbank and professional trading community. The purchase and sale are usually for the same amount in one of the two currencies. In other words, if one contract is for 10 million USD, so is the other. In addition, both contracts usually mature within the spot/week time frame, i.e., within a week beyond the current spot date. A more detailed review of this use of swaps is covered in both Chapter 7 and Chapter 10.

Cash-Management Swap

Nontrading entities, such as corporations and governments, also use swaps extensively. Some may actively trade a forward book in the same way as an interbank dealer and will, therefore, use the rollover swap extensively. Others use the swap to realize efficient cash management or to adjust the maturity dates of existing forward contracts.

Handling Surplus and Deficit Cash Positions

The international scope of business conducted by both financial and nonfinancial organizations will often require the management of cashflows in more than one currency. From time to time, an entity will find itself with surplus cash balances in one currency and deficit balances in another currency.

Consider Commercial A, which has a surplus cash position of 1,000,000 USD and a deficit position in CAD of 1,200,000. These cash positions will exist for an estimated 30 days, at which time other cashflows will bring both currency positions to surplus status.

Current market rates are as follows:

Spot	1.2000
30-day forward	17–19
30-day interest rates:	
To invest USD	10%
To borrow CAD	12%
Commercial A's credit spread*	1%

*The credit spread is the rate that Commercial A pays to its bank for lending the money to Commercial A. The 1% spread is paid over and above the market interest rate.

Commercial A has different alternatives for managing these cash imbalances:

1. Invest surplus USD and borrow CAD for 30 days. This strategy involves treating the two cash positions totally independently of each other.

2. Via a swap, sell the USD spot and buy back the USD 30 days forward. This strategy uses the surplus currency to fund the deficit currency for 30 days. At the end of 30 days, the surplus USD and deficit CAD cash balances are restored. No foreign exchange risk is undertaken.

3. Sell USD spot and buy back the USD value day 30 at some future time. The third alternative involves creation of foreign exchange risk. In this case, Commercial A sells some of the surplus USD in order to fund the deficit CAD position. If this is done at 1.2000 and then the USD are bought back at 1.1800, the decision to take the risk would be the correct one. If the USD are bought back at 1.2500, it would not be a prudent decision. The issue of speculation is an important one and will be addressed in Chapter 16.

Exhibit 9.1 compares the first two alternatives.

The difference of $907 in favor of alternative 1 is equal to 9 forward points (907 CAD/1,000,000 USD). In other words, it would have taken 28 forward points, or a forward rate of 1.2028, for the two alternatives to generate the same basic results. The nine-point difference would seem large, since the forward market is supposed to closely offset the interest-rate differentials, especially in liquid markets such as the one-month CAD/USD market. Why did this significant variance occur?

Exhibit 9.1. Comparison of Investing USD and Borrowing CAD to Cash-Management Swap

	Cashflow in/(out)	
Alternative 1. Invest USD and Borrow CAD:	USD	CAD
1. Invest USD 1,000,000 for 30 days at 10%.		
USD interest earned $\left(\dfrac{1,000,000 \times .10 \times 30}{360}\right)$	8,333	
Convert USD interest to CAD via a forward contract (8333 × 1.2019).	(8,333)	10,015
2. Borrow CAD 1,200,000 for 30 days at 13% (12% market plus 1% credit spread).		
Interest paid $\left(\dfrac{1,200,000 \times .13 \times 30}{365}\right)$		(12,822)
3. Net cost of alternative 1	0	(2,807)
Alternative 2. Deal Cash-Management Swap:		
1. Sell USD 1,000,000 at 1.2000.	(1,000,000)	1,200,000
2. Buy USD 30 days forward at 1.2019.	1,000,000	(1,201,900)
3. Net cost of alternative 2	0	(1,900)
Net advantage of alternative 2 over alternative 1		907

Exhibit 7.6 in Chapter 7 describes a formula for calculating forward points, which is to multiply the spot rate by the interest-rate differential and then adjust this annualized result by the actual term of the forward. According to this formula, the forward points should be .0018.

$$\frac{\text{Spot} \times \text{interest differential} \times \text{term}}{\text{rate basis}}$$

$$= \frac{1.2000 \times \{.1200 - [(.1000 \times 365)/360]\} \times 30}{365}$$

$$= \frac{1.2000 \times (.1200 - .1014) \times 30}{365}$$

$$= .0018$$

The formula suggests that the forward points should be about 18 points, and 19 is close. Why then is 28 points the breakeven?

The reason for the discrepancy is that the interest rates underlying the forward rates are 10 percent for USD and 12 percent for CAD. The interest rates facing Commercial A are 10 percent for USD and 13 percent for CAD. Commercial A has to pay the 1 percent credit spread on top of the market rate. In dollar terms, this 1 percent credit spread is worth almost 1000 CAD, or an additional 10 forward points.

$$\frac{1{,}200{,}000 \text{ CAD} \times .01 \times 30}{365} = 986 \text{ CAD}$$

$$\frac{986 \text{ CAD}}{1{,}000{,}000 \text{ USD}} = .00099 \quad \text{or } 9.9 \text{ CAD points}$$

Consequently, because Commercial A's situation is different from the market's, it can benefit significantly by using the cash-management swap.

In many cases, governments, government agencies, crown corporations, and major corporations are able to borrow money at levels close to or even lower than those rates paid by major banks. In such instances, there is no credit spread issue to distort the picture, and the first alternative may be superior. The key point to remember is that different organizations face different financing costs and what works for one may not work for another.

If the foreign exchange market is not functioning properly, the swap transaction may not be possible. In such cases, optimum cash management may be hard or impossible to achieve. As a general rule, however, one can usually follow the premise that good cash management will involve eliminating situations in which a company has surplus cash in one currency and deficit cash in another.

In addition to the economics that are specific to the deal, use of a cash-management swap may also affect the borrowing capacity of the company. This can be a significant issue for organizations, as it can affect such balance sheet ratios as debt/equity, return on assets, current ratio, or quick ratio.

The cash-management swap can also be of value for organizations such as central banks. Consider the issue of foreign exchange intervention. If a central bank wanted to limit the upside strength of its currency, it could enter the foreign exchange market and sell its currency. Such intervention adds to the domestic money supply. Such increases could be offset by selling treasury bills; this withdraws money from the market and puts it in the hands of the central bank. However, it should be recalled that the intervention activities of the central bank would have increased its holdings of the foreign currency. Consequently, neutralizing the impact on the money supply could also have been accomplished by executing cash-management swaps, in much the same way that a corporation would manage its cash imbalances.

Netting of Foreign Exchange Exposures

Organizations will often face situations where there are offsetting foreign currency inflows and outflows. The ideal situation in most cases would occur if the amounts were equal and the cashflows materialized on the same day. That seldom happens, however, and mismatches in timing and amounts predominate. If the issue is timing, the problem is a cash-management issue similar to that illustrated in Exhibit 9.1. The company may invest the temporary surplus or borrow to fund the temporary deficit. Alternatively, it may do a cash-management swap. If the problem is not just timing of cashflows, but also different amounts of incoming and outgoing cash, then the cash manager may view the difference as one exposure and handle it using forward contracts, currency options, or spot contracts. The common amount could again be handled via investing the surplus, borrowing the deficit, and/or dealing a cash-management swap.

Swapping Forward Contracts Forward

Corporations often face considerable uncertainty in timing and/or amount when forecasting currency cashflows. Forward contracts that were dealt to hedge such flows may mature on a date that does not match the actual cashflow. In such cases, the maturity of the original forward contract creates cashflows for which there is no immediate offset. Once again, the cash manager can borrow to fund the deficit, invest the surplus, or execute a cash-management swap.

Consider Commercial A, which bought 1 million USD against CAD for value March 22 at a rate of 1.1000 CAD/USD. It is now March 21, and the USD is not expected to be paid out for 30 days. In this case, delivery of the forward contract on March 22 will create a surplus USD position and a deficit CAD position. Commercial A has three basic alternatives in handling this situation. The first two have been described before:

1. Deliver on the contract and manage the resultant cashflows independently. In other words, borrow CAD and invest USD for the 30 days.

2. Swap the contract for 30 days at market rates. This alternative involves selling the USD spot and buying them back value 30 days forward.

The choice between these first two alternatives can be made using the process outlined in Exhibit 9.1. Simply compare the cost of the forward points on the swap with the net interest expense and choose the least expensive method.

3. The third approach is a variation of the cash-management swap, wherein the contract is swapped for 30 days, but at historical rates.

Swapping Contracts at Historical Rates

This method involves dealing a swap in which the spot sale is dealt at a rate equaling the original forward contract rate. The new forward contract consists of the maturing forward rate adjusted by the current points and a working capital interest factor. In analyzing this third approach, and in particular the working capital interest factor, it is prudent to determine the cashflows when the contract is swapped at market rates. Exhibit 9.2 provides this summary based on the same market scenario used in Exhibit 9.1.

In terms of this swap dealt at market rates, a few points should be noted:

Exhibit 9.2. Cashflows Arising from Rolling a Contract at Current Market Rates

Market Scenario:		
Spot		1.2000
30-day forward		17–19
30-day interest rates		
To invest USD		10%
To borrow CAD		12%
Commercial A's credit spread		1%

	Commercial A cashflow	
March 21:	USD, in/(out)	CAD, in/(out)
Original forward contract	1,000,000	(1,100,000)
Sale side of swap at 1.2000	(1,000,000)	1,200,000
Net cashflow	0	100,000
30 days later:		
Buy side of swap at 1.2019	1,000,000	(1,201,900)
Total cashflow	1,000,000	(1,101,900)

1. The final effective rate consists of the original forward rate and the forward points on the swap.

Original forward rate	1.1000
Forward points on swap	.0019
Effective final rate	1.1019

2. There is a net cash inflow of 100,000 CAD on the original maturity date. The inflow is reported in many financial statements as a foreign exchange (FX) gain, but one should be careful in the interpretation of the word *gain*.

   In this example, the cashflow gain of 100,000 CAD is not a realized profit. The sale side of the swap shows the current market rate compared with the rate on the original USD purchase. The rate on the original forward contract is better than market by 100,000 CAD. However, the far date on the swap, which is the new forward contract covering the exposure, is also at the current, and higher, market rates. When this new forward purchase contract settles, Commercial A's net cashflow will consist of the original contract adjusted by the forward points on the swap. The swap is thus an interim mark-to-market measure that does not reflect a true FX gain, in spite of what the FX gain/loss account may show. Chapter 14 reviews this account in more detail.

3. The cash surplus generated on the original settlement date is a temporary item when one looks at the final cashflows. In essence, it is a working capital item that exists for the duration of the swap. In this case, Commercial A has 100,000 CAD in its hands for 30 days which it can use to reduce debt and save interest or invest to earn interest.

Commercial A originally bought USD forward at 1.1000. To swap it forward using historical rates, Commercial A would sell USD value spot at the original forward rate of 1.1000 CAD/USD and buy USD forward at 1.1019 (spot of 1.1000 plus the current forward points of .0019). The cashflows in this historical-rate swap are shown in Exhibit 9.3.

The swap carried out at market rates in Exhibit 9.2 gave Commercial A 100,000 CAD in working capital to use for a 30-day period. The historical-rate rollover, however, eliminates the working capital issue. In effect, Commercial A transfers the working capital gain to the bank. Commercial A is investing 100,000 CAD with the bank, which, at prevailing 30-day interest rates, is worth 12 percent.

A direct payment of interest to Commercial A may be difficult because there is seldom a specific investment instrument purchased. Con-

Exhibit 9.3. Cashflows Arising from Rolling a Contract at Historical Rates

	Commercial A cashflow	
March 21:	USD, in/(out)	CAD, in/(out)
Original forward contract	1,000,000	(1,100,000)
Sale side of swap at 1.1000	(1,000,000)	1,100,000
Net cashflow	0	0
30 days later:		
Purchase side of swap at 1.2019	1,000,000	(1,101,900)
Total cashflow	1,000,000	(1,101,900)

sequently, the "interest" is typically paid by adjusting the exchange rate on the new forward contract.

$$\text{Interest} = \frac{100,000 \text{ CAD} \times .12 \times 30}{365} = 986 \text{ CAD}$$

Interest in FX points = 986/USD amount in forward contract

= 986/1,000,000

= .000986

The interest compensation of almost 10 points (.0010) would be used to adjust Commercial A's new forward price to 1.1009.

Original forward rate	1.1000
Forward points on swap	.0019
Working capital interest factor	(.0010)
Adjusted forward rate	1.1009

Historical-rate rollovers have the same basic economics as market-rate swaps. They also eliminate the need for any cash settlements on the original maturity date and avoid the accounting problems frequently associated with the FX gain/loss account. On small forward contracts, the actual dollar amount of the net settlement may be small, and the costs of settling may be excessive given the amounts involved. In other cases, an entity may not have the cash to settle on the swap but still want the swap done. Another reason for using the swap is that an organization may have a true foreign exchange loss, and rolling the contract at market rates will reveal the loss, if it has not already been identified. The historical-rate swap, on the other hand, may successfully avoid reporting the loss. Such justification is highly questionable and gives support to the notion that any investments or loans created by the historical-rate swaps must be properly disclosed. As a general comment, usage of historical-rate swaps varies from market to market, but the swap is not a heavily traded transaction. One of the major reasons is its susceptibility to abuse.

Regular revaluation of contracts has a number of benefits in certain instances. Where routine mark to market is done, the actual rollover of the contract in a loss position will have already been highlighted. It will not generate any unusual accounting entries, and the appetite for historical-rate rollovers tends to be eliminated. From a cashflow and/or taxation standpoint, however, there may still be some benefit.

Investment Swaps

Investors in today's markets have a large number of fixed-income investment products from which to choose. Risk preferences range from low to high risk. Some investors require every investment dollar to be in highly liquid instruments, that is, investments that can be readily exchanged into cash. Some investors will want a portion of their portfolio to be highly liquid, while the remainder can be in less liquid assets provided they generate higher yields.

Investment swaps are investments in a foreign currency asset which have no foreign exchange risk. In most cases, the risk is eliminated by the execution of a foreign exchange swap. The most common investment swap is not liquid, although a semiliquid swap can be dealt. The appeal of the investment swap to the investor is a higher yield. Credit risk is usually comparable to other bank paper.

Consider Commercial A which has 10 million CAD to invest for 90 days. Commercial A typically buys banker's acceptances or investment swaps. A comparison of the two alternatives is provided in Exhibit 9.4.

In deciding whether to buy the investment swap, one must decide if an improvement of 4 basis points (.04 percent) in yield is worth the reduction in liquidity. For some investors, it may well be the case. For others, 10 to 20 basis points may be required before a swap is dealt.

Negotiable Investment Swaps

The underlying foreign currency investment vehicle in most swaps is a bank term deposit that is nonnegotiable. Because the underlying deposit is illiquid, the swap is also illiquid.

Exhibit 9.4. Comparison of Investment in BAs to an Investment Swap

90-day investment rates:		
CAD BAs	12%	
USD deposit	10%	
CAD/USD FX rates:		
Spot	1.2005–10	
90-day forward	55–57	

Banker's acceptance*:	USD	CAD
Interest earned		295,890

$$\left(\frac{10,000,000 \times .12 \times 90}{365}\right)$$

Investment Swap

Value day 1:

	USD	CAD
1. Buy USD at spot rate of 1.2010 (near date of swap).	8,326,395	(10,000,000)
2. Invest USD.	(8,326,395)	

Value day 90:

	USD	CAD
3. Redeem USD investment.		
Principal	8,326,395	
Interest	208,160	

$$\left(\frac{8,326,395 \times .10 \times 90}{360}\right)$$

	USD	CAD
4. Deliver USD principal and interest on forward contract (far date of swap) at 1.2065 (1.2010 + .0055).	(8,534,555)	10,296,940
Net cashflow (interest)	0	296,940

Effective yield on the swap is 12.04%.

$$\frac{(296,940 \times 365)/90}{10,000,000} = .1204$$

*Example ignores realities of discount pricing on BAs and assumes that the full 10,000,000 CAD is invested.

However, a swap could be done using a negotiable investment such as treasury bills, banker's acceptances, or commercial paper. In this case, the investment could be liquidated, although not as cleanly as straight CAD banker's acceptances. To liquidate the swap, the investor would sell the USD negotiable paper and unwind the outstanding forward contract by doing a foreign exchange swap.

Exhibit 9.5 is an example of a semiliquid investment swap made by

Exhibit 9.5. Steps Involved in Purchase of Negotiable Investment Swap

90-day investment rates		USD CP	10%
CAD/USD FX rates:		Spot	1.2005–10
		90-day forward	55–57

Value day 1:	USD	CAD
1. Buy USD at spot rate of 1.2010 (near date of swap).	975,610	(1,171,707)
2. Invest USD.	(975,610)	
Value day 90:		
3. Redeem USD investment. Principal	975,610	
Interest	24,390	
$\left(\dfrac{975,610 \times .10 \times 90}{360}\right)$		
4. Deliver USD principal and interest on forward contract (far date of swap) at 1.2065 (1.2010 + .0055).	(1,000,000)	1,206,500
Net cashflow (interest)	0	34,793

Effective yield on the negotiable swap is 12.04%.

$$\frac{(34,793 \times 365)/90}{1,171,707} = .1204$$

Commercial A. The underlying instrument in the swap was $1 million of 90-day USD commercial paper purchased at a yield of 10 percent. The proceeds required to buy the paper are 975,610 USD.

Liquidating a Negotiable Investment Swap

Assume that 30 days after dealing the swap, Commercial A needs the CAD cash and decides to liquidate the investment swap in a market that has remained relatively unchanged.

60-day USD commercial paper rate	10.13–10.10%
60-day CAD banker's acceptance rates	12.00–11.96%
CAD/USD rates:	
Spot	1.2045–50
60-day forward	34–36

To liquidate or unwind the investment, Commercial A has to sell the USD commercial paper and execute a foreign exchange swap.

STEP 1   Sell the USD commercial paper at 10.13% and receive proceeds of
          983,397 USD.

$$\frac{1,000,000}{1 + (1 \times .1013 \times 60)/360} = 983,397 \text{ USD}$$

NOTE: The interest actually earned while holding the USD commer-
        cial paper is the amount received on liquidation less the orig-
        inal investment: 983,397 − 975,610, or 7787 USD. The ef-
        fective yield on the commercial paper was 9.58%.

$$\frac{(7787 \times 360)/30}{975,610} = .0958$$

STEP 2   Execute the foreign exchange swap.
          a. Sell the 983,397 USD that were received from the sale of the
             commercial paper value spot at 1.2045 CAD/USD.
          b. Buy 1,000,000 USD value 60 days forward at 1.2081 (spot of
             1.2045 + .0036 forward points).

A summary of the cashflows is provided in Exhibit 9.6.

In determining the effective interest rate earned from day 1 to day
30, one cannot simply look at the net cashflow of 12,794 CAD generated from day 1 to day 30. One has also to account for the net cashflow
resulting from the closing of the original 90-day forward contract. One

Exhibit 9.6. Cashflows Arising from Liquidation of Negotiable Investment
Swap

Day 0:		USD	CAD
Purchase of USD		975,610	(1,171,707)
Invest in USD commercial paper		(975,610)	
Net cashflow		0	(1,171,707)
Day 30:			
Sell USD commercial paper		983,397	
Sell USD spot		(983,397)	1,184,501
Net cashflow:	Day 30	0	1,184,501
	To date	0	12,794
Day 90:			
Original sale of USD		(1,000,000)	1,206,500
Purchase of USD on Day 30		1,000,000	(1,208,100)
Net cashflow:	Day 90	0	(1,600)
	Total	0	11,194

can do so by determining the present value on day 30 of the 1600 CAD that will be paid out on day 90. With a discount rate of 12 percent, the 1600 CAD outflow on day 90 is worth 1569 on day 30.

$$\frac{1}{1 + [(1 \times .1200 \times 60)/365]} = .9806555$$

$$1600 \times .9806555 = 1569$$

The USD investment can now be evaluated as follows:

Day 1:	
Original investment	(1,171,707)
Day 30:	
Spot sale of USD	1,184,501
Value of outflow on day 90	(1,569)
Net interest earned	11,225

Effective yield for the 30-day investment is 11.66%.

$$\frac{(11,225.00 \times 365)/30}{1,171,707} = .1166$$

Liquidating the investment before maturity results in a yield of only 11.66 percent, which is certainly less than desirable. However, the decision whether to liquidate the swap should not be driven off the issue of what the effective rate of investment will be on the 30 days that have already gone by. Commercial A needs to raise cash, and the real decision facing Commercial A is how to raise cash in the cheapest manner. One alternative is banker's acceptances at 13 percent, given a market rate of 12 percent and a stamping fee of 1 percent. The other alternative is to unwind the swap. To calculate the effective financing rate, one can simply look at the cashflows.

Cash originally scheduled to be received on day 90	1,206,500
Less: Cash received on day 30 through the liquidation of the investment	(1,184,501)
Plus: Cash to be paid out on liquidation of forwards	1,600
Equals: Interest effectively paid	23,599

$$\text{Effective interest rate} \quad \frac{(23,599 \times 365)/60}{1,184,501} = .1212, \text{ or } 12.12\%$$

Compared with issuing BAs at 13 percent, the liquidation of the investment swap was superior by .88 percent and clearly justifies doing the transaction.

Negotiable swaps are an alternative investment vehicle that can provide a degree of liquidity as well as a higher yield than other comparable investments. Such swaps can also provide good trading opportunities, depending on how the underlying forward market and negotiable paper markets have moved during the term of the investment.

Borrowing in Foreign Currencies

Borrowers in today's markets have a variety of ways of raising money. Some borrow in foreign currency because they have revenues in that currency which are used to service the debt. Others borrow in another currency because they believe that the currency being borrowed will weaken, thereby reducing the overall cost of borrowing.

Other borrowers in foreign currencies have no offsetting revenues and do not want to incur any foreign exchange risk. They will fully hedge their foreign borrowings by means of a foreign exchange swap transaction in much the same way investors hedge their foreign fixed-income investments.

Consider Commercial A which would like to borrow 10 million CAD for 90 days. Commercial A can borrow via prime, banker's acceptances, or USD Libor. Current market rates are as follows:

CAD prime	14%
90-day rates for borrower:	
CAD BAs	12%
USD Libor	10%
Credit spread:	
BAs	1%
Libor	1%
CAD/USD rates:	
Spot	1.2010–15
90-day forward	55–57

Commercial A will be unlikely to borrow on a prime basis mainly because it is the most expensive alternative and is subject to increase during the 90-day period. However, prime may be chosen if Commercial A believes that rates are headed sharply lower in the very short term. If this view is not held, the company will look at the banker's acceptances and fully hedged Libor options.

Banker's acceptances:	
Base yield	12%
Credit spread	1%
Total cost	13%

Issuance of 10 million CAD in BAs at a 12 percent yield will generate a price of 97.126 and proceeds of 9,712,600.00 CAD.

$$\frac{100}{1 + [(1 \times .1200 \times 90)/365]} = 97.126$$

The Canadian convention on CAD BAs is to express the price in terms of $100, rounded off to three decimal places. The credit spread or stamping fee is also usually paid on the date of issuance of the BAs and is calculated on the face value or maturing amount of the BAs, adjusted by the term of the BAs. The cashflow for the BA option is shown in Exhibit 9.7.

The base yield of 12 percent and the 1 percent credit spread would imply a yield of 13 percent to Commercial A. The effective yield is 13.06 percent and occurs for two reasons:

1. The credit spread is calculated on the full 10 million CAD of BAs, whereas the 12 percent yield is based on the net proceeds received.

2. The credit spread was paid up front on day 1, whereas interest is normally paid in arrears. The effect of compounding increases the true cost of the spread from 1 percent to 1.03 percent.

Exhibit 9.7. Cashflows of Issuance of CAD Banker's Acceptance

Day 1:	CAD, in/(out)	USD, in/(out)
Issuance of BAs	9,712,600	
Payment of stamping fee	(24,658)*	
Net proceeds	9,687,942	
Day 90:		
Repayment of BAs	(10,000,000)	
Interest	(312,058)	

Effective CAD yield = 13.06%

$$\frac{(312,058 \times 365)/90}{9,687,942} = .1306$$

$$* \frac{.01 \times 10,000,000 \times 90}{365}$$

$$.01 + \frac{.01 \times .12 \times 90}{365} = .0103$$

Fully hedged Libor loans differ from BAs in four key respects:

1. The credit spread is paid in arrears and is normally based on the actual proceeds drawn down.

2. When a long-dated Libor such as a three-year deal is made, interest is paid quarterly, semiannually or annually. In a 90-day loan such as in this example, however, the interest is paid on day 90.

3. USD Libor transactions are typically done on one day for settlement two days later. CAD BAs are usually dealt for same-day settlement.

4. USD Libor loans can be unwound at a gain or cost to the borrower, dependent on market conditions. The notes issued by the BA borrower, on the other hand, are bearer in nature and could be held by any number of investors. Finding these notes in an attempt to redeem them is difficult, if not impossible. One exception is that the notes may be held in a form of escrow account.

If Commercial A dealt a fully hedged Libor loan, the following simultaneous steps would occur:

1. Borrow USD Libor. *Note:* In order to compare the cashflows between the Libor and BA alternatives, the amount of the Libor is calculated so that it generates the same net CAD proceeds on day 1:

   $9,687,942 CAD/1.2015 = 8,063,206 USD

2. Sell Libor proceeds of 8,063,206 USD for CAD based on the spot rate of 1.2015 CAD/USD.

3. Buy USD forward to repay Libor principal, interest, and credit spread. The forward rate is 1.2072 (spot of 1.2015 plus forward premium of 57 points).

The fully hedged Libor cashflows are detailed in Exhibit 9.8.

The interest paid on the fully hedged Libor is 1584 CAD more than that paid under the BA facility. If finding the lowest-cost debt was the only consideration, the BA option would be chosen.

In addition to BAs and USD Libor, many Canadian entities will also issue commercial paper in USD as well as other currencies. This multicurrency and multiproduct flexibility that is available to major borrowers in most developed countries enhances the possibility of finding cheaper financing than that provided by their domestic market alone. The basic methodology for evaluating these alternatives is the same as

Exhibit 9.8. Fully Hedged Libor Loan Cashflows

Day 1:	USD, in/(out)	CAD, in/(out)
Issuance of Libor	8,063,206	
Sell USD for CAD	(8,063,206)	9,687,942
Net proceeds	0	9,687,942
Day 90:		
Repayment of Libor:		
Principal	(8,063,206)	
Base interest	(201,580)	
Credit spread	(20,158)	
Total Libor payment	(8,284,944)	
Purchase USD forward at 1.2072	8,284,944	(10,001,584)
Total interest (9,687,942 − 10,001,584)		(313,642)

Effective CAD yield = 13.13%

$$\frac{(313,642 \times 365)/90}{9,687,942} = .1313$$

above. Again, in any investment or borrowing decision, determining the amount and timing of cashflows will allow one to determine the effective principal proceeds, the true amount of interest, and, therefore, the effective interest rate.

It is important to note that the cost of fully hedged debt can be significantly increased or decreased with a relatively small move in foreign exchange points. A single-point decline in the CAD (from 1.2072 to 1.2073) increases the debt repayment outlined in Exhibit 9.8 by 829 CAD. The effective cost of debt increases by more than .03 percent, from 13.13 percent to 13.164 percent, over a 90-day period.

Furthermore, the extra debt to repay is strictly a function of the amount of USD to repay, whether the debt is 90 days or 365 days in duration. However, the change in effective interest rates from an 829 CAD increase in interest is four times as much on a 90-day borrowing as it is on a 360-day borrowing. Forward points represent annualized interest differentials, and a single-point change can significantly change the appeal of a fully hedged transaction, especially in the short-term area.

Swaps Using Currency Options

The examples of investment swaps and fully hedged Libor examined transactions in foreign currencies in which foreign exchange risk was

Exhibit 9.9. Market Scenario for USD Investor

CAD/USD FX rates:		
Spot	1.2010–15	
90-day forward	55–57	
Currency options	Strike price	USD premium, Boston style
Buy 90-day CAD put	1.2067	1% of USD
Write 90-day CAD call	1.2067	.95% of USD

eliminated by the use of foreign exchange swaps. The near date of the swap involved a spot sale (or purchase), while the far date involved a forward purchase (or sale). An alternative to a forward contract is a currency option. Consider a USD investor that is currently earning 10 percent on USD fixed-income investments. The investor wants to bear some exchange risk and decides to invest in 90-day CAD commercial paper which is currently yielding 12 percent. The foreign exchange markets available to the investor are outlined in Exhibit 9.9.

In managing the foreign exchange exposure, three principal alternatives are available:

1. The first alternative is simply to leave the exposure unhedged for the time being. The 2 percent interest differential works in the investor's favor, and as each day passes, the forward points that the investor would have to pay will decline, all else being equal. However, doing nothing has considerable risk which may be beyond the risk that the investor wants to assume.

2. A second alternative is to use forward contracts. Doing so, however, will only generate a return similar to the 10 percent currently being earned on straight USD investments.

3. The third alternative is currency options. Two basic strategies, the purchase of a CAD put and the writing a CAD call, will be briefly discussed.

Purchase ATM CAD Put at 1.2067
CAD/USD

The purchase of the CAD put option gives the investor the right, but not the obligation, to sell the CAD principal and interest at the strike price of 1.2067 CAD/USD. The strike price can vary considerably, but for illustrative purposes, an at-the-money forward strike of 1.2067 is used. Moreover, the options are Boston style (i.e., premium paid at expiry), and the premium is a percentage of the USD amount. Based on

Exhibit 9.10. Worst-Case Scenario If Purchase ATM CAD Put

Value day 1:	USD, in/(out)	CAD, in/(out)
1. Buy CAD at spot rate of 1.2010.	(1,000,000)	1,201,000
2. Invest CAD in commercial paper.		(1,201,000)
Value day 90:		
3. Redeem CAD investment.		
Principal		1,201,000
Interest		35,536
$$\frac{(1{,}201{,}000 \times .12 \times 90)}{365}$$		
4. Deliver CAD principal and interest on option contract at 1.2067.	1,024,725	(1,236,536)
5. Pay for currency option premium.	(10,247)	
Net cashflow (interest)	14,478	0

Worst-case effective yield is 5.79%

$$\frac{(14{,}478 \times 360)/90}{1{,}000{,}000} = .0579$$

the option being exercised, a worst-case or minimum yield of 5.79 percent is guaranteed, as detailed in Exhibit 9.10.

The 5.79 percent minimum yield is considerably less than the 10 percent yield that would be available under a basic USD investment. As the strike price is the same as the prevailing forward rate when the deal was originally done, the lower return is entirely due to the premium paid. However, once the premium has been recouped, the profit potential on buying CAD puts can be significant. To expand on this point, the investor benefits from a strengthening CAD in that the investor is not obliged to exercise the CAD put option at 1.2067 CAD/USD. If the CAD can be sold (or USD can be bought) in the market at a better price than the strike price on the option, the option will be allowed to lapse. If the CAD, for example, was at 1.10 CAD/USD, the investor would let the option expire unexercised and sell the maturing CAD principal and interest at the 1.10 spot rate as opposed to exercising the option at 1.2067.

Based on the spot rate of 1.10 CAD/USD, the maturing proceeds of 1,236,536 CAD would yield proceeds of 1,124,124 USD. After paying the premium of 10,247 USD, the net interest proceeds are 113,877 USD. An effective yield of over 45 percent would be realized:

$$\frac{(113{,}877 \times 360)/90}{1{,}000{,}000} = .455, \text{ or } 45.5\%$$

The prospect of limited risk, but unlimited profit potential, makes this strategy a reasonably popular one for international portfolio managers. However, many investors prefer to write options.

Write ATM CAD Call at 1.2067
CAD/USD

Writing a CAD call does not limit the downside risk for the investor. If the CAD weakens to 1.2500 CAD/USD, the buyer of the 1.2067 CAD call option will let the option expire unexercised. As a result, the investor will be faced with selling the CAD at the 1.2500 level, which will, in fact, result in a negative return of .41 percent, as shown in Exhibit 9.11.

In terms of upside risk, the best exchange rate available to the investor will be 1.2067. If the CAD is stronger than that level at expiry, for example, 1.2000 CAD/USD, the buyer of the option will exercise it and take delivery of the CAD.

The risk profile of writing the CAD call is clearly quite different from buying the CAD put. Writing the CAD call does not protect the downside risk, and it limits the upside risk. However, writing the option generates premium income that can improve the yield over what it might otherwise be. The best-case return for the investor, for the initial 90-day period at least, occurs if the option is exercised. As shown in Exhibit 9.12, this return is 13.74 percent.

Exhibit 9.11. Example of Downside Risk If Write CAD Call

Value day 1:	USD, in/(out)	CAD, in/(out)
1. Buy CAD at spot rate of 1.2010.	(1,000,000)	1,201,000
2. Invest CAD in commercial paper.		(1,201,000)
Value day 90:		
3. Redeem CAD investment.		
Principal		1,201,000
Interest		35,536
4. Deliver CAD principal and interest		
on spot contract at 1.2500.	989,229	(1,236,536)
5. Receive currency option premium.	9,735	
Net cashflow (interest)	(1,036)	0

Effective yield is a negative .41%:

$$\frac{(-1{,}036 \times 360)/90}{1{,}000{,}000} = -.004144$$

Exhibit 9.12. Best-Case Return If Write CAD Call

Value day 1:	USD, in/(out)	CAD, in/(out)
1. Buy CAD at spot rate of 1.2010.	(1,000,000)	1,201,000
2. Invest CAD in commercial paper.		(1,201,000)
Value day 90:		
3. Redeem CAD investment.		
Principal		1,201,000
Interest		35,536
4. Deliver CAD principal and interest	1,024,725	(1,236,536)
on option contract at 1.2067.		
5. Receive currency option premium.	9,735	
Net cashflow (interest)	1,034,460	0

Best-case effective yield is 13.74%:

$$\frac{(34,360 \times 360)/90}{1,000,000} = .1374$$

At expiry, if the CAD is trading at the strike price of 1.2067, the purchase of the CAD put will provide a worst-case yield of 5.79 percent, while the writing of the CAD call will yield a best-case 13.74 percent. Clearly, the writing of the option is advantageous when the market has no net movement, for the simple reason that the option premium is received instead of paid out. Premium income can be quite significant and, therefore, an attractive carrot for many portfolio managers. As investors may be prepared to unwind foreign investments when certain returns can be achieved, they will often write options that, if exercised, will produce the desired returns. If the options are not exercised, the investor has gained premium income that increases the overall return beyond what would otherwise have been earned.

The strategies that investors or borrowers can use with options are comparable to these for the hedging of basic exposures, which were discussed in Chapter 8. Ratio spreads, collars, straddles, and strangles are but a few of the strategies available.

Moreover, an option is a tradable asset with an inherent value of its own. An option position bought can be sold before maturity; similarly, an option position sold can be bought. An option, therefore, can be successfully used in conjunction with the forward market to lock in profits or close out an exposure. For instance, assume the investor purchased a CAD put at 1.2067 when the CAD investment was made. Subsequently, the CAD strengthens to 1.1750. The USD investor could sell the CAD principal and interest forward at that level and lock in a substantial profit on the CAD investment. The option is still outstanding and could be sold at any time during its remaining life.

Currency Swaps

The term *currency swap* (also referred to as *cross-currency swap*) generally applies to transactions in which two entities effectively exchange two long-dated borrowings that are denominated in different currencies. This process and the example that follows appear fairly simple. However, this market has a number of dimensions that are beyond the scope of this book, and this section should be viewed as an introductory overview.

Consider two companies, Australian Corporate AUST and French Corporate FREN. Corporate AUST wants to borrow French franc (FRF) debt, and Corporate FREN wants to have Australian dollar (AUD) debt. Their respective costs of borrowing in each currency are as follows:

	Corporate AUST, %	Corporate FREN, %
AUD	15	16
FRF	11	10

In their home currency, each company has a 1 percent borrowing advantage. Corporate AUST, for example, can borrow AUD at 15 percent, or 1 percent below what Corporate FREN would have to pay to borrow AUD in its own name. Similarly, Corporate FREN can borrow FRF at 10 percent, or 1 percent less than Corporate AUST can issue long-term FRF debt. It is this relative advantage that allows the currency swap to materialize.

The currency swap process is as follows:

1. Corporate FREN borrows FRF at 10 percent and Corporate AUST borrows AUD at 15 percent.

2. The two companies then exchange the debt with each other so that Corporate AUST has FRF debt at 10 percent and Corporate FREN has AUD debt at 15 percent.

Each party reduces its borrowing cost by 1 percent. However, it is difficult for most corporation and government borrowers to locate others that want to do an offsetting transaction at the same time and for the same amount. They also face credit risk with each other, a risk they may not want. Consequently, swaps dealt directly between nonfinancial entities are not common, although capital adequacy and credit issues within the financial-markets sector may make the currency swap market move in that direction from time to time.

The volume of currency swap transactions increased significantly in the 1980s. In most swaps, a corporation or government would deal with a market maker such as a bank, investment dealer, or insurance company. The market maker might warehouse the deal into its own position if it was not able to simultaneously deal an offsetting transaction. The market maker provides an intermediary role and takes on credit risk with both counterparties. In exchange for the service, the market maker will take part of the savings involved in the swap. Consequently, the net savings of the swap for Corporate AUST and Corporate FREN will be somewhat less than 1 percent.

As an example, consider the spot FRF/AUD exchange rate to be 5.0 FRF per AUD. A two-year deal based on 100 million AUD is executed. Normally, currency swaps are much longer, but the two-year time frame is used for ease of presentation. In order for the swap to work, it is essential that the amounts be the same value. The deals are in two different currencies, and to equate value, the current spot rate is used. At a spot rate of 5.0 FRF per AUD, a 500 million FRF issue is needed to work the swap against a 100 million AUD issue.

Exhibit 9.13 summarizes the cashflows related to the FRF financing.

In the example, Corporate FREN raised debt at 10 percent, which it used to swap for AUD debt. The market maker took the FRF debt and fully offset Corporate FREN's payments to the initial investors or buyers of the two-year notes. When dealing with Corporate AUST, however, the market maker increased the effective interest rate in order to generate a profit for itself. Corporate AUST's effective cost of FRF debt is not 10 percent, but 10.20 percent.

$$51/500 = 10.20\%$$

The cashflows on the 15 percent AUD debt are outlined in Exhibit 9.14.

The market maker offset Corporate AUST's obligations on the AUD 15 percent debt issue and, in turn, charged Corporate FREN a slightly higher yield of 15.20 percent.

$$15.2/100 = 15.20\%$$

Corporate FREN could have borrowed AUD directly at 16 percent or issued FRF debt and swapped it for AUD debt at 15.2 percent. Similarly, Corporate AUST could have borrowed FRF debt at 11 percent or else is-

Exhibit 9.13. FRF Cashflows on Currency Swap
(Millions FRF)

Time	Payment	Corporate FREN	Intermediary market maker	Corporate AUST
0	Original loan proceeds	500		
	FREN to market maker	(500)	500	
	Market maker to AUST		(500)	500
	Net	0	0	500
Year 1	Interest payments:			
	AUST to market maker		51	(51)
	Market maker to FREN	50	(50)	
	FREN to investor	(50)		
Year 1 cashflow		0	1	449
Year 2	Interest payments:			
	AUST to market maker		51	(51)
	Market maker to FREN	50	(50)	
	FREN to investor	(50)		
	Net interest	0	1	(51)
	Principal payments:			
	AUST to market maker		500	(500)
	Market maker to FREN	500	(500)	
	FREN to investor	(500)		
	Net principal	0	0	(500)
Year 2 cashflow		0	1	(551)
Total net cashflow		0	2	(102)

sued AUD debt and swapped it for FRF debt at 10.2 percent. The currency swap allowed both companies a significant reduction in the cost of their borrowings, which is clearly to their advantage. The market maker facilitated the transaction by finding the necessary counterparties, by assuming the credit risk between them, and by handling much of the paperwork and cashflows involved in the deal. For its expertise and role, the market maker benefits through the generation of profit.

Currency swaps involve a major utilization of credit. In this deal, the market maker has credit exposures of interest and principal with both Corporate AUST and Corporate FREN. If Corporate AUST went bankrupt, the market maker would still have to honor all future payments to Corporate FREN. Corporate FREN would still have to make its payments to the market maker, but uncertainty exists about how the

Exhibit 9.14. AUD Cashflows on Currency Swap
(Millions AUD)

Time	Payment	Corporate FREN	Intermediary market maker	Corporate AUST
0	Original loan proceeds			100
	AUST to market maker		100	(100)
	Market maker to FREN	100	(100)	
	Net	100	0	0
Year 1	Interest payments:			
	FREN to market maker	(15.2)	15.2	
	Market maker to AUST		(15.0)	15
	AUST to investor			(15)
Year 1 cashflow		(84.8)	.2	0
Year 2	Interest payments:			
	FREN to market maker	(15.2)	15.2	
	Market maker to AUST		(15.0)	15
	AUST to investor			(15)
	Net	(15.2)	.2	0
	Principal payments:			
	FREN to market maker	(100)	100	
	Market maker to AUST		(100)	100
	AUST to investor			(100)
	Net principal	(100)	0	0
Year 2 cashflow		(115.2)	.2	0
Total net cashflow		(30.4)	.4	0

bank would be positioned to use those AUD inflows from Corporate FREN to fund the FRF payments in return. Since the owners of Corporate AUST debt want repayment, as do other creditors, resolution of the situation could be complicated. The possible outcomes of a contract default will not be explored here, as the intent is only to outline the credit risk to the market maker, as well as to both corporations. One of the consequences of these risks is that bank capital adequacy requirements may cause market makers subject to such requirements to seek a larger return on currency swap transactions.

Interest-Rate Swaps

Interest-rate swaps are transactions involving only interest payments. They are primarily used by borrowers to change debt from fixed rate to floating rate or, vice versa, from floating to fixed. Such swaps typically occur in the same currency. However, basis swaps are routinely done in which, for example, floating-rate USD Libor debt is swapped to floating-rate New Zealand dollar debt. Moreover, unlike currency swaps, interest-rate swaps can be used by investors who want to change the risk profile of their portfolio without changing the actual investments they own.

There are many interest-rate swap variations and arrangements. The next few pages will illustrate a basic and straightforward interest-rate swap and discuss the underlying framework for the market.

Consider the following market environment and swap transaction: Company AAA wants to borrow USD at floating rates. Company B wants USD fixed-rate financing. Their respective borrowing costs are as follows:

	Company AAA	Company B	Difference
Five-year fixed	11%	13%	2%
Credit spread for short-term Libor	1/2%	1%	1/2%

Company AAA has a 2 percent rate advantage in the five-year debt market but only a 1/2 percent advantage in the short-term markets.

If Company AAA raised long-term debt at 11 percent and gave it to Company B at 12 percent, Company AAA would earn 1 percent. In addition, if Company B raised short-term Libor debt and gave it to Company AAA at Libor plus 1/2 percent, Company AAA ends up with floating-rate debt at a net cost of Libor minus 1/2 percent. Exhibit 9.15 summarizes the swap rates, using an assumed Libor rate of 9 percent.

As shown in Exhibit 9.16, Company B can raise five-year money at a rate of 12.5 percent, or 1/2 percent less than the cost of raising it in its own name.

This swap transaction reduces the cost of borrowing for both Company AAA and Company B. It also changes Company AAA's fixed-rate debt into floating-rate debt. At the same time, it transforms Company B's short-term or floating-rate debt into five-year fixed-rate financing.

In the plain vanilla cross-currency swap example, there was an ex-

Exhibit 9.15. Company AAA's Cost of Short-Term Debt

Rate paid on long-term debt issued		11%
Rate received on long-term debt		(12%)
Rate paid on short-term Libor debt	Libor + 1/2%	9.5%
Effective rate paid on short-term debt	Libor − 1/2%	8.5%

Exhibit 9.16. Company B's Cost of 5-Year Debt

Rate paid on long-term debt		12.0%
Rate paid on short-term Libor debt	Libor + 1%	10.0%
Rate received on short-term Libor debt	Libor + 1/2%	(9.5%)
Effective rate paid on long-term debt		12.5%

change of both principal and interest. Some currency swaps may involve only one or even no principal payments. However, the standard swap does have exchange of principal. The interest-rate swap, on the other hand, does not involve any exchange of principal. Doing so would accomplish nothing except increase the workload and the settlement risk for both parties. Consequently, interest-rate swaps only involve the exchange of interest payments based on a specified notional amount of principal.

To appreciate this market more fully, one needs to reexamine the tiering of interest rates. The borrower with the best credit risk (i.e., least likely to default) should pay investors the lowest interest rate. In most cases, federal or national governments will enjoy this status.

Interest rates applicable to other borrowers will be correspondingly higher depending on their perceived creditworthiness.

	5-year Rates, %	180-day Rates, %
Government	10.75	11.00
Corporate AAA	11.00	11.10
Corporate B	13.00	11.70

Issuing long-term debt is more feasible for borrowers with better credit than for those with poorer credit. The longer the term of a debt issue, the greater the risk that the borrower will run into financial difficulty. Consequently, some corporates can issue short-term debt, but have difficulty issuing long-term debt. On the other hand, if a borrower is able to raise long-term debt, it should have no trouble issuing short-term debt.

In the interest-rate swap market, borrowers that provide the underlying fixed-rate financing to the market are those that can raise long-term debt relatively inexpensively. Those that use the swap market in order to fix their debt are those that cannot raise long-term debt at all or, if they can, are only able to do so at relatively high interest rates.

In the simple example just given, Corporate AAA was a supplier of fixed-rate money to Corporate B. The matching of two borrowers with a financial institution serving as the intermediary was the norm in the market's early years in the 1980s. As time passed, the inefficiency of back-to-back dealing encouraged dealers to trade the market and to warehouse the risk in much the same way as they would in the foreign exchange market.

The underlying market for the swap is federal government bonds. This is the lowest cost of funds and is the foundation on which other interest rates are determined by the markets. Suppliers of fixed-rate money are often governments, although the supply is limited by their debt requirements, their own needs for fixed-rate financing, and the proportion of readily marketable securities outstanding in the public domain. Consequently, other suppliers of fixed rates are required for the market to function properly.

The swap market has evolved to a point where there are two main interest-rate components on the fixed portion of the swap. The first component is the current rate on federal government bonds for the term in question. The second component is called the *swap spread,* which essentially represents the spread over government bonds that is required for debt to be issued by the lowest-credit quality supplier of fixed rates to the swap market. For instance, market conditions may be such that the only issuers of debt are essentially AA credit quality or better. If AA debt is issued at 50 points over government debt, the swap spread would normally be at least 50 points. If the spread was less than the 50 points, there would be a disincentive for an AA company to swap its debt. It would simply issue short-term debt directly. If the swap spread was significantly larger than 50 points, additional long-term debt would be issued and swapped in order to get cheaper short-term funding. See Exhibit 9.17.

A supplier of three-year fixed-rate money to the market would "sell" it to the market maker at the bid rate of 10.05 percent plus .70 percent. A taker or buyer of fixed-rate money would "buy" it from the market maker at the offer rate of 10.10 percent plus .75 percent. If this happened, the market maker would make the 10 cents bid-and-offer spread.

If the supplier of fixed-rate money was able to raise three-year debt at 20 basis points (.20 percent) over government debt, the supplier would gain a net 45 points.

Exhibit 9.17. Market Maker's Interest-Rate Swap Market

	3-year	5-year
Government bond yield	10.05–10.10%	10.35–10.42%
Swap spread	.70–.75%	.75–.80%
All-in swap rate	10.75–10.85%	11.10–11.22%

Rate paid on long-term debt	10.30%
Rate received on swap	(10.75%)
Net gain	.45%

The other half of the swap involves the supplier of fixed rates paying a floating rate to the market maker. While various floating rates can be utilized, the most common rate used in USD swaps is the six-month Libor setting at 11 a.m. GMT. If it is six-month Libor, the Libor rate for the swap is established every six months. In the early 1990s, Reuters page LIBO was primarily utilized as the six-month Libor rate.

The market maker and the supplier make these payments to each other every six months. To further simplify matters, the two payments are frequently netted, and a net payment is made by one party to the other. Consider Exhibit 9.18, which summarizes the scenario from the perspective of the supplier of fixed-rate funds.

The volatile interest-rate environment portrayed in the exhibit shows that the supplier of fixed rates incurred net interest expense at rates varying from 5.55 to 13.55 percent. In all cases, the rates were .45 percent below the prevailing six-month Libor rate in effect on the rollover date.

The taker of fixed-rate funds in the above market would generate its actual cash by issuing six-month Libor loans that are rolled over for the term of the swap. The interest rates facing the payer are shown in Exhibit 9.19. Note that the rollover of the Libor debt involves not only a

Exhibit 9.18. Interest-Rate Flows for Supplier of Fixed Rates
(Who Takes Floating-Rate Debt in Return)

Month	6-month Libor, %	Instrument	Interest payments received/(paid)		
			Fixed portion	Floating portion	Net
6	10	To bondholders	(10.30)		(10.30)
		(To)/from swap	10.75	(10.00)	.75
		Net cost	.45	(10.00)	(9.55)
12	14	To bondholders	(10.30)		(10.30)
		(To)/from swap	10.75	(14.00)	(3.25)
		Net cost	.45	(14.00)	(13.55)
18	6	To bondholders	(10.30)		(10.30)
		(To)/from swap	10.75	(6.00)	4.75
		Net cost	.45	(6.00)	(5.55)

Exhibit 9.19. Interest Rate Flows for Buyer of Fixed Rates
(Who Gives up Floating-Rate Debt in Return)

Month	6-month Libor, %	Instrument	Interest payments received/(paid)		
			Fixed portion	Floating portion	Net
6	10	Libor market rate		(10.00)	(10.00)
		Libor credit spread		(1.00)	(1.00)
		(To)/from swap	(10.85)	10.00	(.85)
		Net cost	(10.85)	(1.00)	(11.85)
12	14	Libor debt		(14.00)	(14.00)
		Libor credit spread		(1.00)	(1.00)
		(To)/from swap	(10.85)	14.00	3.15
		Net cost	(10.85)	(1.00)	(11.85)
18	6	Libor debt		(6.00)	(6.00)
		Libor credit spread		(1.00)	(1.00)
		(To)/from swap	(10.85)	6.00	(4.85)
		Net cost	(10.85)	(1.00)	(11.85)

market rate, but also a credit spread, which is assumed to be 1 percent in this example.

For the payer of fixed-rate debt, the interest-rate swap offsets the rates incurred on the underlying Libor debt. The volatile rates do not affect the payer's cost, which is fixed at 11.85 percent, consisting of the market rate of 10.85 percent plus the 1 percent credit spread incurred on the short-term Libor loans.

10

How Price Makers Trade the Markets

Executive Summary

Chapter 10 reviews the environment in which the professional foreign exchange dealer works. The chapter focuses on the interbank dealers and investment dealers who are the primary price makers and who do most of the global foreign exchange trading. The chapter provides an overview of pricing and trading the spot, forward, and currency option markets. For the corporate practitioner, the chapter should provide some ideas on managing a trading operation, as well as on executing deals and using foreign exchange products. Chapter 10 is fairly technical in some sections.

Introduction

In foreign exchange trading, every trader can call the market right, after the movement has occurred. Some traders are skilled enough to consistently call market movements correctly before they actually occur. Trading the markets successfully is a challenging and stressful job.

Active trading is necessary to provide foreign exchange markets with liquidity. Trading requires training, tools, and discipline, among other things. This chapter outlines the role of the market makers, and the environment in which they work.

Dealing in the Interbank Market

Reciprocity

As mentioned in Chapter 6, the primary price makers deal on a basis of two-way prices. When Dealer A asks Dealer B for a price, Dealer B responds with both a buying and a selling price; in other words, he or she provides a bid and an offer. Similarly, when Dealer B calls Dealer A for a price, Dealer A will make a two-way price.

To be shown two-way pricing is a privilege that must be earned, not a right. If Dealer A did not make two-way prices, he or she would not receive them in return. Or if he or she made two-way prices, but with a wide bid-and-offer spread, wide pricing would be received in return. Or if he or she made good prices in terms of the bid-and-offer spread, but the prices were good for only small amounts, the same treatment could be expected in return.

In all these cases, the market conditions need to be considered. In a very thin market or in a market that has just been hit by a major shock, the bid-and-offer spread can be very wide. If the market can just as easily go up 100 points as it can go down 100 points in the next few seconds, dealers have to protect themselves by quoting wide prices. If they do not, they can find themselves buying at "current" prices, only to immediately find they are offside 100 or more points.

The relationships between interbank dealers are typically one on one. Banks A and B, for instance, may make spot markets on a 3-point bid-and-offer spread for up to $25 million. Banks A and C may also trade on a 3-point spread, but only for up to $2 million.

Warehousing versus Back-to-Back Pricing

If Dealer A is asked to price a deal by Dealer B, Dealer A can handle the situation in two ways. First, he or she can call another market maker, Dealer C, and ask for a price. Dealer A can then show Dealer C's price to Dealer B. If Dealer B deals, Dealer A immediately offsets the deal with Dealer C.

The other method of dealing is for Dealer A to price the transaction using whatever information is available and then take the deal into his or her own position and handle it accordingly. The dealer does not have an immediate offset.

If a client asks Dealer A for his or her selling price on a currency that the dealer does not actively trade, such as Norwegian kroner, he or she will often work on a back-to-back basis. Dealer A will not seek two-way prices from Dealer C because he or she does not want to reciprocate with two-way prices in Norwegian kroner to Dealer C in the future. Dealer A may simply approach Dealer C with the information that a client would like a price to purchase kroner. Dealer C faces no uncertainty about the amount and whether or not it is a question of buying or selling. In effect, Dealer C treats Dealer A like a client and shows a one-sided price for Dealer A to buy the kroner.

There are dealing relationships in which Dealer A could expect two-way prices in kroner, however, without having to reciprocate in kroner. For instance, Italian-based Dealer A could have a working relationship with Norwegian-based Dealer C, under which Dealer C will make two-way prices in Norwegian kroner to Dealer A as long as Dealer A will reciprocate and make two-way prices to Dealer C in Italian lire.

If a dealer wants to deal actively in a market, he or she cannot operate on a back-to-back basis. It is too cumbersome and slow. Clients want fast pricing, and if one has to call out all the time for prices, response time will not be fast enough. It not only does not facilitate any form of reciprocity, but also will tend to result in uncompetitive prices and limit any opportunities to make any profits. Dealing on an interbank basis requires risk taking and a willingness to inventory deals in one's position.

Establishing and Cutting Positions

If a dealer believes the USD is going to appreciate or strengthen against the Swiss franc (CHF), he or she will want to own or be "long" the USD. A dealer can take a long position in different ways.

Assume the market is 1.5000–1.5010 CHF/USD. The bid of 1.5000 represents the market rate to buy USD, and the offer rate of 1.5010 is the market rate to sell USD.

1. The dealer can buy USD by paying the offer in the street at 1.5010.

2. The dealer can make a market to one or more brokers at 1.5005–1.5015. In so doing, he or she knows it is not the best offer, and thus he or she will be unlikely to sell any USD at 1.5015 when there are offers at 1.5010. However, 1.5005 is the best buying price in the market at that time. If another dealer is selling USD, that dealer may quite likely hit the bid of 1.5005.

3. If another dealer calls for a price, he or she could make a two-way price such as 1.5005–1.5015, which again provides incentive for a seller of USD to deal and a buyer of USD to pass on the price.

4. If a client of the dealer calls looking to sell USD, the dealer may again move the bid inside the rest of the market to, perhaps, 1.5005.

Different dealers will have different interests at any one time. Buyers of USD will tend to show higher bids, and sellers of USD will tend to show lower offers. As a result, the market may show several different prices at any one time.

Alternatives 2, 3, and 4 allow the dealer to get long USD, but at cheaper prices than alternative 1. However, just because a dealer has the best price, it does not automatically mean he or she will be able to buy USD. There may simply be no interested sellers at that moment. If a dealer wants to buy sizable USD in a hurry, he or she will not be worried about saving a few points by trying to entice other dealers to hit his or her bids. The dealer will simply pay the offers.

Dealing rooms work as a team. If a dealer wants to buy a large amount of USD quickly, he or she can contact one or more brokers and pay the offers, indicated by the word *mine*; i.e., he or she will buy USD based on the offers being shown by the broker. Alternatively, or in addition, the dealer can ask a number of fellow dealers to simultaneously call other market makers for prices. As these other market makers reflect their prices, the dealer will decide which offers to pay and which to pass. In this form of team dealing, a large number of trades can be done almost simultaneously.

The same basic alternatives face the dealer when he or she wants to liquidate a long USD position. There are a number of approaches, and the size of the position, the profit in the position, and the market conditions will all influence how a dealer handles the situation.

Dealing off Own Prices

If a dealer always dealt on the prices given by the market, positions established by the dealer would usually start out in a loss position. For instance, if Dealer A bought USD by paying the offer of 1.5010, selling the position out immediately would see Dealer A hitting the market bid at 1.5000. As shown in Exhibit 10.1, Dealer A would lose 10 points, or 1000 CHF, for every $1 million USD traded.

Exhibit 10.1. Costs Incurred When Paying away the Bid-and-Offer Spread

	Cashflow	
	USD, in/(out)	CHF, in/(out)
Purchase of USD at 1.5010	1,000,000	(1,501,000)
Sale of USD at 1.5000	(1,000,000)	1,500,000
Net cashflow	0	(1,000)

Exhibit 10.2. Gains Achieved When Earning the Bid-and-Offer Spread

	Cashflow	
	USD, in/(out)	CHF, in/(out)
Purchase of USD at 1.5000	1,000,000	(1,500,000)
Sale of USD at 1.5010	(1,000,000)	1,501,000
Net cashflow	0	1,000

In order for Dealer A to break even by dealing off the market's prices, he or she has to see the market move to the extent of the bid-and-offer spread. In this case, a 10-point move is required.

If Dealer A were able to deal off his or her own prices, there would be a much better chance of making money. For instance, if he or she bought the USD at 1.5005, Dealer A is starting off only 5 points away from the market bid, i.e., the rate at which the USD could be sold.

If Dealer A had two other dealers dealing off his or her prices at the same time, with one "hitting" the bid (1.5000) and the other "paying" the offer (1.5010), Dealer A would, in fact, make the bid-and-offer spread as profit, as Exhibit 10.2 shows.

Transacting deals off one's own price is clearly advantageous, as it makes the bid-and-offer spread work for, instead of against, you. Continually making market prices is also important in order to find out what other market players are doing.

Market Amounts

The global foreign exchange markets trade hundreds of billions of dollars' worth of currencies every full trading day. Transactions less than 1 million USD equivalent in almost any currency are usually viewed as small. An interbank trade of this size is typically done when a bank has no active involvement in that particular currency and is simply offsetting a customer transaction.

Typical market amounts can vary dramatically, depending on the currency and the market. The largest standard market amounts exist in the forward market where prices are regularly made for amounts of 50 million USD equivalent and more. Market amounts for currency options transactions are in the $5 million–$10 million range, while standard spot transactions can range within a $2 million–$50 million range, depending on the currency, financial center, and counterparties. From a customer standpoint, the size of these base volumes is important for the following reasons.

1. Dealing a small amount makes it difficult for the dealer to cover the risk on an interbank basis. Consequently, the dealer would typically have to warehouse the deal, until additional deals either offset the original deal or are combined to give the dealer a market amount to trade. Pricing on small amounts, therefore, should not be expected to be on the straight market bid or offer that relates to larger deals.
2. Care must be used in handling larger deals. Consider Company ABC, which has 20 million USD to sell for MEX. Assume the market is 3034.00–3050.00 MEX/USD and the peso floats freely in global foreign exchange markets. If the company makes simultaneous calls to five banks for competitive prices, one of two situations is likely to develop.
   a. A dealer could be short USD and, wanting to buy the USD, will show an aggressive bid (such as 3034.30). He or she will probably win the deal. Company ABC sells the USD at a good price and is happy with the transaction. The dealer has covered all or part of a short position and is also pleased.
   b. No dealer has a particular interest in buying. As the dealers want to protect themselves in case they win, they immediately sell some USD into the market by hitting the 3034.00 bids. If all five banks sell $10 million, a total of $50 million USD will be sold into the market. The market bid will undoubtedly move from the 3034.00 level down to, perhaps, 3030.00 or lower unless support from sources such as the central bank enters the market.

If one dealer had initially shown a price of 1.1950 and the company came back to deal, the dealer would have probably reduced the price to reflect the new level of the market. By shopping, the company has thus moved the market against itself.

Misquotes

Dealers can make mistakes in pricing. If the price is clearly a mistake, market etiquette suggests the calling party ask the dealer to double-check the price. This allows the quoting dealer to verify the price and, indeed, if there was an error, to change the price. If the quoting dealer stands by the price, then a deal will be done even if there was an error. If the two parties have a good relationship, the calling dealer may go so far as to explain why there appears to be an error and discuss what the basic prices should be. In this situation, the dealer perceives the relationship to be important and is taking steps to ensure that a good relationship is maintained.

Notwithstanding this market etiquette, a dealer's word is his or her bond, and a dealer is obligated to stand by the price, unless the price is totally ludicrous. Barring that, however, a trader can get stuffed by a wrong price. The implication for the party who took advantage of the situation and dealt unfairly on the price is that he or she will get no sympathy when the shoe is on the other foot.

Credit Lines

Chapter 15 outlines the various credit risks involved in dealing foreign exchange. These risks, in turn, result in the establishment of various limits for dealing with each and every counterparty. For example, usually limits are placed on the amount of forward contracts that can be outstanding with a particular counterparty. A maximum term may be set on forward contracts. Also, limits may be put on the maximum amount of contracts settling on any one day with a particular counterparty. In addition to the credit limits for foreign exchange, there may also be "house limits"—the total aggregate credit risk that can be outstanding at any one time with a counterparty. In other words, the foreign exchange credit risk can be $100 million, and the house limit may be $400 million.

Foreign exchange is only one form of business with credit implications transacted between dealers. A deposit by a bank into another bank is, in effect, a loan and constitutes hard-dollar credit risk. Interest-rate swaps, cross-currency swaps, forward-rate agreements, and money-market trades of other banks' paper, such as banker's acceptances, all have credit implications, even though there may be no initial cash provided to the counterparty.

Limits are set for each counterparty. The trader will determine how much credit is needed. Staff skilled in the credit and banking areas assess the creditworthiness of the counterparty and will determine how much credit risk can be taken. Traders do not always get the credit lines that they would like. If and when enough transactions are dealt that the maximum credit limits are reached, internal approval for additional lines must be granted before any additional deals can be done. In some cases, additional dealings may be limited, not because the foreign exchange limit has been reached, but because the overall house limit has been reached. Consequently, the forward dealer may be unable to deal additional contracts until some of the overall credit availability has been restored.

Credit lines are set not only by banks and investment dealers. Corporations should also have limits with their counterparties, as they face the same kind of credit risk as do the banks and dealers. Moreover, if a company receives any amount of credit it wants from a bank, it should establish its own internal limits so that the bank is not, in fact, too "easy" on credit and, therefore, in trouble if the economy deteriorates. Credit is a resource; it should be managed as such and not simply taken for granted.

Position Limits

Traders manage risk for profit. The amount of risk taken should determine the amount of profit expected. Profits are not guaranteed, however, and the amount that could be lost by assuming a particular level of risk must also be taken into consideration. An experienced trader is much more likely to make money than is a rookie. Losses will also probably be smaller; accordingly, senior traders will be given larger amounts of risk to trade. Naturally, profit expectations are correspondingly higher. In turn, the seasoned trader expects higher compensation.

Control of the trading risk is done in several ways. A spot trader may be allowed to go long or short $50 million in a particular currency. If the trader trades several currencies, there may be limits on each currency, with a combined short or long position not to exceed $150 million. These limits may apply to the regular working day when the trader is actively dealing the markets. Outside of these hours, the limits are usually reduced.

Each bank, investment dealer, and trading corporation is probably different in terms of its approach to foreign exchange trading, the involvement of management, its customer base, its financial resources, its global network, and the skill and depth of its traders. Some are fairly cautious and have smaller limits. Others take spot positions that can exceed over a billion USD equivalent at a given time.

In the forward book, which is the composite of all outstanding forward contracts, limits are also established. The forward market is quite different from the spot market. The forward market is driven off the interest-rate differentials between the currencies. If a forward is outstanding for one day, the interest differentials are only at work for one day, which is not very significant. In a six-month contract, the differentials are in effect for 180 times as long. Bearing this in mind, forward limits may include the following:

1. Long and short positions can exist anywhere from a single day until several years into the future. A $10 million long position in the six-month range has a much larger risk attributable to it than a $10 million short position in the one-month area. While the positions offset in nominal terms, the actual risk is significantly different. A simple way of quantifying the risk is to weight the position to annual terms using the framework outlined in Exhibit 10.3.

Exhibit 10.3. Weighting Forward Positions

Term, months	Amount, millions	Base position, long/(short)	Weighted position*
1	10	(Short)	(.8)
6	10	Long	5.0
	Net	Long	4.2

*Weighted position $= \dfrac{\text{No. of months} \times \text{amount}}{12 \text{ months}}$

The actual weighting can be done by different methods, but a daily weighting is the most precise if this methodology is used.

2. The above limit tends to quantify the risk from a macro-perspective. However, it is also prudent to establish a limit for the net long or short position for a given day. If a bank has a massive short position on Monday and a similarly large long position on Tuesday, the weighted forward position could show a nil position. Moreover, while all the contracts are outstanding, the cash position of the forward book would not be greatly affected.

   When the contracts mature, the short-dated mismatch could create a significant cash imbalance on the Monday, which the trader would have to resolve. If something happens in the markets that causes a temporary distortion, the dealer could find the mismatch expensive to resolve. It must also be recognized that the forward dealer's actions in these markets can have an impact on the bank's overall cash-management activities. Caution must be taken to keep such activities within reasonable limits.

3. Limits can also be imposed on term. The maximum long or short position in the one-month area may be different than it is in the one- or five-year area.

In the case of currency options, holders of options risk losing the premium. Limits may thus be placed on how much premium can be at risk at any time. When writing options, the risks primarily revolve around changes in the underlying currency and in its volatility. Quantifying these risks is essential for proper control, and limits may be constructed on the basis of how much one can lose over the next day given expected maximum changes in the spot rate, forward points, volatility, or all three. There may also be limits placed on the number of contracts or the amount of calls or puts outstanding. As with spot and forward trading, these limits can be assigned to individual currencies as well as on an aggregate basis.

Terminology

Interbank trading is often done with a minimum of communication between dealers. Market participants know the customs of the market and can talk in extreme brevity. A few of the more common terms are as follows:

1. *"Hit the bid/yours/given."* When Dealer A asks for a price and wants to deal on Dealer B's bid, Dealer A may simply say: "At 55, I give you 10 USD." Dealer A can be said to have *hit the bid*. Dealer B is said to have been *given*.

   Conversations tend to be even more abbreviated when dealing with brokers where several banks may be attempting to deal on a price simultaneously. Consequently, a dealer may simply say: "Yours, ten," to let the broker know that the dealer wants to hit the bid for 10 million USD.

2. *"Take the offer/mine/paid."* When Dealer A asks for a price and wants to deal on Dealer B's offer, Dealer A may simply say: "At 65, I take 10 USD." Dealer A can be said to have *taken or paid the offer*, and Dealer B is said to have been *paid*.

   Using the broker, the dealer would simply say: "Mine, ten."

3. *"Long/short."* A dealer is *long* a currency when he or she owns it. A dealer is *short* a currency when he or she has sold it without owning it beforehand. As foreign exchange involves two currencies, a deal that puts a dealer long one currency makes him or her short the other currency.

4. *"Bullish/Bearish."* When dealers believe the price or value of a currency will rise, they are *bullish* on the currency. When the currency is expected to decline in value, dealers are *bearish* on the currency.

5. *"Two-Way Price/Bid, Offer/Choice Price."* Dealers usually make a market in which they will give a price at which they will buy and another at which they will sell. This is referred to as a *two-way price*. The difference between the two prices is referred to as the *bid-and-offer spread*. If the two prices are the same, the dealer is said to have made a *choice price*, i.e., "Here is my price. You can either buy or sell on it."

Orders

Dealers and corporates can deal at any time by a variety of means. They can wait for certain levels, and when reached, they can contact other market participants, seek prices, and deal. Alternatively, they can leave standing instructions that if certain changes take place, a deal is to be done. A dealer, in effect, can thus have other market participants watch the market and execute trades on his or her behalf. Such orders can exert more discipline on many traders. There is sometimes a tendency when a desired market level is reached to turn around and decide that "The market is going my way; I will wait a bit longer." Of course, the market then seems to move the other way far too often, and the desired price, which became available, was missed.

Orders which dictate the rate and the parameters under which the deal is to be executed are as follows:

1. *Limit order.* A price is specified at which the order is to be done. Sometimes, only part of an order can be dealt at the specified price at a given time. Thus, the order should specify whether it can be dealt in pieces or whether all of it must be done at the same time (see orders 9 and 10).

2. *At-the-market order.* The deal is to be done immediately at the best available price.

3. *Stop-loss order.* A dealer who may be long or short a currency wants to limit the potential losses. Defensive in nature, a stop-loss order is triggered when the market trades at the specified price. The price at which the order is executed is the next available price which may or may not be that specified in the order. Moreover, the order may not be totally executed at the next available price, and more than one price may be applied.

4. *Take-profit order.* A dealer who is long or short a currency may also want to close out the position if a certain profit level is reached. Similar to a stop-loss order, a take-profit order is activated when the market trades at the specified level. The price at which the order is executed is the next available price (or prices), if the order cannot be totally completed at one price.

5. *Open or good-until-canceled orders.* Such orders remain in effect until they are executed or canceled by the dealer leaving the order.

6. *Good-until-specified-time orders.* Orders are automatically canceled if not executed by a certain expiry time.

7. *Day/night orders.*   Day orders are good until the close of that business day. Night orders are good until the opening of business the next business day.

8. *Fill or kill orders.*   Usually the order is for a very short period of time. Moreover, instructions could be to fill all or any part of the order. The balance that is not filled within that short time frame is to be canceled.

9. *Any-part orders.*   At the specified price, any part of the order that can be filled is to be filled. The remaining portion is in effect until it is also filled or canceled.

10. *All-or-none orders.*   At the specified price, either all the order must be filled, or nothing is to be done.

11. *Either/or orders.*   These kinds of orders involve two orders. If one order is done, the other is canceled. For example, a trader may establish both a take-profit and stop-loss order on a position. If the trader's take-profit order is executed, the stop-loss order is no longer needed and is automatically canceled.

Trading Foreign Exchange

Trading a market is a demanding job, regardless of which market it is. Trading causes considerable mental stress in the continuous attempt to determine what is happening in the markets and where rates are going. Profits generate tremendous enthusiasm and excitement. Losses create feelings of frustration, anger, and disappointment. Hours tend to be long, and for some traders, the job takes essentially 24 hours a day. Calls in the middle of the night are routine, and some traders even have Reuters, Telerate, or Knight-Ridder terminals at home so that they can keep better abreast of market developments. A trader may specialize in one currency, but if that currency is stable and providing few profitable trading opportunities, the trader will usually look to trade another currency in order to generate the required profits for his or her organization.

Almost every person who has ever traded has made some great trades and reaped good profits. More likely than not, other people know about these successes. There are also probably some notable losses, but fewer people may know about them, unless the losses are very large. To consistently make money over a long period of time is difficult. Traders typically need a fairly healthy ego and some self-confidence that they can make money, i.e., that they can beat the market. At the same time, the market is always right, and dealers have to be realistic and sensible enough to admit when they are wrong. They must be willing to cut out losing positions early before the losses become too large.

Individual traders should also be aware of their environment. A trader working for a German bank will usually have a greater advantage trading the DEM than will a DEM trader working for an Australian bank. The German bank should have more customer business providing more market intelligence on transaction flows as well as increased volume dealt on its prices. The bid-and-offer spread would be expected to work for the German bank's trader and against the Australian bank's trader. Many traders forget the natural advantage they may have. Only when they trade a currency in which their employer does not have a competitive advantage, do they truly test their trading skills.

Sources of Profit

There are three basic methods for generating profits, each of which is briefly described below using the spot market as the base market.

1. Positional profits can be generated by taking a position in a currency, waiting for the market to move, and then liquidating the position, with profit making the goal.

   For example, 5 million USD are bought at a rate of 1.6500 DEM/USD. The market moves to 1.6600, whereupon the dealer sells the USD back to the market. A profit of .0100 per USD, or 50,000 DEM (5,000,000 × .01), has been realized.

2. Spread profits are generated when transactions are priced off market.

   For example, assume the market is 1.6500 DEM/USD. A sale of 5 million USD is made at a rate of 1.6501. A basically risk-free gain of .0001 per USD, or 500 DEM, has been made.

3. The trader is a market maker who has other participants trading off his or her prices. The bid-and-offer spread works in his or her favor rather than against it (see Exhibit 10.2).

Categorizing the ways to make money is fairly simple. Actually making the money is not quite so easy. While the next section is not intended to demonstrate all the ways to trade profitably, it will provide a flavor of how dealers trade the spot, forward, and options markets.

Spot Trading

Spot trading occurs in what is frequently a fast-moving market. Positions are typically taken with a short-term view, and a trader can be long a currency one minute and short the same currency the next minute. An interbank dealer is faced with making prices throughout the day to other dealers. Dealer A may want to be long a particular currency, but if other dealers call and "pay" Dealer A's offers, Dealer A could be at least temporarily forced into a short position. Only through heavy buying on Dealer A's part, does he or she maintain or get back into the desired long position.

A primary market maker can establish a position that is independent of the regular trading book and will "sit on it" as long as considered appropriate. In many organizations, these positions are driven by management and are appropriately called *management positions*.

Spot markets are heavily influenced by short-term supply-and-demand factors. Rumors, large deals, central bank intervention, unexpected news, and economic statistics can all affect a market quickly and sharply. Movements caused by such surprises are often over in a matter of minutes or even seconds. The spot trader has to be quick to react in order to survive. Markets are also global and trade 24 hours per day. Traders have overnight positions which they pass on to their counterparts in other markets to manage. However, they still have to decide the price levels at which currencies are bought and sold. As market conditions change, active traders are frequently called in the middle of the night for market updates and queries.

Many dealing rooms operate in a structure where there is a chief dealer who is the primary decision maker. Because trading by consensus is time-consuming, there can only be one decision maker when trading a fast-moving market. A dealer can also have responsibility for more than one currency. If there is a team of dealers, the decision maker's focus is clearly on the market. If the decision maker wants to do something in the markets, he or she often relies on associates to execute the deals. The leader maintains an overall perspective on what is going on, much like a general leading troops into battle. The assistant dealers will also be focusing on the market, but they will have the primary responsibility for fielding incoming calls, making outgoing calls for prices, writing tickets, and keeping track of the positions.

Arbitrage describes the practice of executing simultaneous and offsetting transactions in two different markets to earn a risk-free profit. Such activities in the foreign exchange market can occur in different forms. In years gone by, one could sometimes buy in London and sell at a higher price in Melbourne at the same time. Risk-free profits were thus feasible. Arbitrage of this nature is no longer common in the spot market for major currencies. Arbitrage between the interbank market and the futures markets can occur, but price differences are small. There are two main reasons for the reduction in significant arbitrage opportunities. First, communication systems are extremely effective, and arbitrage opportunities are readily identified. Second, arbitrage opportunities are sought by a large number of dealers, who quickly take advantage of even the smallest price discrepancies. Sophisticated computer systems in many banks alert dealers and ensure that market gaps do not last very long.

The value of a currency is really its spot value. Sometimes a currency appears to be valued largely on sentiment. Although it may be hard to determine or justify the reason for the sentiment, it can be quite obvious that the market wants either to buy or to sell. Market psychology at times is quite amazing. Sometimes the market seems only to care about the bad news, while the good news is ignored. At other times, the good news is everything and the bad news is "not a factor." Its relevance is not totally ignored; it is simply discounted.

Calculating Profits and Losses on Spot Trading

Profits and losses on spot trading can be calculated easily. Since all contracts mature within the next couple of days, the net cashflows related to those contracts will provide a fairly good estimate of the profit and loss generated. However, this process has some delays and is open to abuse. Consequently, a more structured process is appropriate.

Consider the spot DEM/USD transactions dealt by Bank ABC that are detailed in Exhibit 10.4.

The settlement of the above contracts two days in the future would result in Bank ABC's being long 500,000 USD and short 1,010,000 DEM. This, in itself, does not readily reveal whether the trader made a profit. To find out, the net position at the end of the day is compared with closing

Exhibit 10.4. Example Spot Transactions

Day	Transaction	DEM amount	Rate	USD amount
1	Bought USD	(2,000,000)	2.0000	1,000,000
	Sold USD	1,990,000	1.9900	(1,000,000)
	Bought USD	(1,000,000)	2.0000	500,000
	Net	(1,010,000)		500,000

Exhibit 10.5. Calculating Spot Profit and Loss Based on a Closing Rate of 2.0100

Day	Transaction	DEM amount	Rate	USD amount
1	Bought USD	(2,000,000)	2.0000	1,000,000
	Sold USD	1,990,000	1.9900	(1,000,000)
	Bought USD	(1,000,000)	2.0000	500,000
	Revaluation	1,005,000	2.0100	(500,000)
	Net	(5,000)		0

rates, and a profit and loss analysis is done on the basis of what would have resulted had the position been liquidated at the closing rates.

Assume the closing rate was 2.0100 DEM/USD. The profit and loss would be a loss of 5000 DEM, as outlined in Exhibit 10.5.

Given a closing rate of 2.0100 DEM/USD, the trader lost 5000 DEM. However, it must be recognized that the revaluation does not change the actual position of the trader, which is long 500,000 USD. The revaluation simply serves to determine the trader's profit and loss up to that point. Based on that revaluation rate, the trader lost money on the day.

The rate chosen for the revaluation is significant in that differing rates will generate different profit and loss results. For example, a closing rate of 2.0200 would show the trader breaking even. However, it must be remembered that the rate at which a position is revalued at the end of one day is also the rate at which the trader's position is valued at the start of the next day's trading. A revaluation at 2.0100 is less favorable than a rate of 2.0200 for the trader from the standpoint of today's profit and loss (P&L). However, it is equally more favorable when the next day's results are determined. To prevent games from being played, revaluation of daily P&Ls should be done using a consistent source of rates. While traders can have input into the revaluation rate, they should not be able to unilaterally set the rate.

One risk of allowing traders to set their own revaluation rates is that they could artificially hide losses for an extended period of time. In addition, if a trader in a major loss position tries to get out of it without anybody knowing, the losses usually seem to increase, instead of decrease. An objective and consistent revaluation system is thus warranted. Industry practice is usually to obtain the revaluation rates at the same time of day every day from the same sources, whether they be the closing rates from selected Reuters pages, selected broker(s), other banks, or the central bank.

A further dimension of the spot trader's P&L concerns the overnight position. In the above case, the trader went home on day 1 long 500,000

Exhibit 10.6. P&L Impact on Spot Dealer due to Rolling of Spot Position

Swap side	Value date	Rate	USD, bought/(sold)	DEM, bought/(sold)
Sell	Day 3	2.0100	(500,000)	1,005,000
Buy	Day 4	2.0099	500,000	(1,004,950)
Net			0	50

USD value day 3, or two days hence. When the next business day commences, the position is held for value day 3, or one day before the new spot date, day 4, as shown in Exhibit 10.6. To bring the position into line with the market, the spot trader effectively rolls the position one day forward similar to a forward trader rolling the cash position.

In practice, the spot position in most shops is taken into the forward dealer's cash position, and the management of the roll is handled by the forward dealer. The gains or costs in handling the rollover of the position are, however, usually credited or charged to the spot dealer.

In this case, the dealer is long USD, which carries a higher interest rate than the currency the dealer was short, the DEM. Consequently, the dealer will be paid the interest differential of 50 DEM.

Forward Trading

Forward market pricing is driven off the interest-rate differentials between the two currencies. Forward transactions are dealt so that direct spot risk is minimized. When a forward dealer buys forward, the main element of spot risk is largely eliminated by selling the same amount of underlying currency on a spot basis. Forward trading thus involves dealing via swaps. The only differences between the buy and the sell sides of the swap are the value dates and the rates on each date. The differences in the rates are the forward points on which the forward trader is really trading. However, as outlined in Chapter 7, three forms of spot risk are inherent in forward trading, two of which warrant taking spot positions to hedge the spot risk.

Trading the forward market has a number of dimensions. While Chapter 7 has already touched on some of the issues that follow, a complete review is given here to provide a perspective of forward trading. Consider Exhibit 10.7, which shows the forward dealer establishing a short USD position in the three-month area.

There are a number of ways the dealer can make money with this forward position.

Exhibit 10.7. Example of Forward Swap Transactions

Swap no.	Swap side	Value date	Rate	USD, bought/(sold)	DEM, bought/(sold)
1-b	Buy	Spot	1.8000	1,000,000	(1,800,000)
1-s	Sell	3 months	1.7700	(1,000,000)	1,770,000
	Net		.0300	0	(30,000)

Covered Interest-Rate Arbitrage. The first way is for the dealer to invest the USD for three months and borrow DEM for three months. If the net interest earned on the USD investment exceeds the net 30,000 DEM paid out on the swap, the dealer can lock in a profit. This kind of forward transaction, which allows a dealer to lock in a profit on a risk-free basis, is known as covered interest arbitrage.

From a pure profit standpoint, covered interest arbitrage may seem to be an attractive transaction. However, from an overall corporate or bank perspective, these trades involve creation of additional liabilities (USD deposit) and assets (DEM loan). The balance sheet is inflated. For some organizations, but especially for banks, one measure of performance is return on assets. Target numbers for individual banks vary, but it is not uncommon to see banks trying to generate overall returns of 100 basis points on total assets. Financial markets are quite efficient, and returns of this magnitude are seldom available through covered interest-rate arbitrage.

On the other hand, if one area of the bank is deficit USD and another area is surplus DEM, the forward dealer could undertake covered interest arbitrage without a net increase in the bank's overall assets. The forward dealer invests his or her surplus USD with the area short of USD and borrows DEM from the area that is surplus DEM. The internal transactions help all three areas within the bank to meet their desired objectives.

Dealing Exclusively in Foreign Exchange Markets. If we restrict the forward dealer to dealing exclusively in the foreign exchange markets, the dealer can take one of two actions, or a combination of both:

1. Roll the cash position using swaps.
2. Deal an offsetting forward contract.

Dealing Spot-Next Swaps. The first alternative—rolling the cash position created by the contract with a spot value—can be done by rolling the contract forward one day at a time, using "spot-next" swaps. Alter-

Exhibit 10.8. Rolling Cash Position One Day Using a Spot-Next Swap

Swap No.	Swap side	Value date	Rate	USD, bought/(sold)	DEM, bought/(sold)
1-b	Buy	Spot	1.8000	1,000,000	(1,800,000)
2-s	Sell	Spot	1.8000	(1,000,000)	1,800,000
	Net			0	0
2-b	Buy	Spot+1	1.7996	1,000,000	(1,799,600)

natively, it can be rolled forward for a week or even a month at a time, if the dealer so chooses. Using a daily roll, the swap would consist of a spot sale of USD (2-s) at 1.8000 DEM/USD and a spot-next purchase of USD (2-b) at 1.7996. The results are shown in Exhibit 10.8.

In doing this swap of selling spot and buying the day after spot, the dealer has rolled the 1 million long USD cash position from spot value to one day beyond spot. However, the dealer is long USD at a lower rate of 1.7996, which amounts to a gain of 4 points (.0004). If this daily roll was done for the 90-day period until the maturity date was reached on the forward sale contract, the long USD position would have an effective rate of 1.7640.

Original rate	1.8000
Less: Gains on daily rolls (90 × .0004)	.0360
Effective rate on long USD position	1.7640

As shown in Exhibit 10.9, when the final purchase ticket with an effective rate of 1.7640 that is generated with these daily swaps settles against the original three-month sale at 1.7700, a 6000 DEM profit will have been made.

In looking at the example, a few points should be noted.

1. The daily rolls are not likely to be 4 points every day. The interest differentials applicable to this spot-next swap are the interest rates

Exhibit 10.9. Rolling Cash Position 90 Days Using a Spot-Next Swap

Swap No.	Swap side	Value date	Rate	USD, bought/(sold)	DEM, bought/(sold)
90-b	Buy	3 months	1.7640	1,000,000	(1,764,000)
1-s	Sell	3 months	1.7700	(1,000,000)	1,770,000
	Net			0	6,000

for one day, two business days hence. There can be significant changes in this differential on a day-to-day basis.

2. The daily swaps will be based off the current spot rate. As the spot rate moves, there will be working capital adjustments that can affect the profitability of the position. This spot risk can, however, be hedged through the establishment of spot positions.

3. The distortions in cashflow due to the differing rates used on the daily spot-next swaps make it hard from a cashflow standpoint to determine if a profit or loss is being made on the position. As a result, daily mark-to-market profit and loss calculations must be done.

4. As previously mentioned, the forward dealer could roll the cash position by using longer-dated swaps, such as one week or one month. If a one-week swap was at 35 points discount, for instance, the numbers would suggest to go that route. Daily swaps would only generate a discount of 28 points (7 days × 4 points per day).

Dealing Offsetting Forward Contracts. The second way of managing the forward position is, of course, for the dealer to deal an offsetting forward immediately, and try to make money basis the bid-and-offer spread. With a swap in which the three months are bought at 310 points discount, the cashflows and profit are 1000 DEM, as shown in Exhibit 10.10.

The dealer originally sold the USD at 300 points discount and subsequently bought them at 310 discount.

In this situation, the daily profit and loss statement will show that the dealer made 10 points, or 1000 DEM. The dealer, however, does not

Exhibit 10.10. Deal Offsetting 90-Day Swap and Make Bid-and-Offer Spread

Swap no.	Swap side	Value date	Rate	USD, bought/(sold)	DEM, bought/(sold)
1-b	Buy	Spot	1.8000	1,000,000	(1,800,000)
2-s	Sell	Spot	1.7950	(1,000,000)	1,795,000
	Net			0	(5,000)
1-s	Sell	3 months	1.7700	(1,000,000)	1,770,000
2-b	Buy	3 months	1.7640	1,000,000	(1,764,000)
	Net			0	6,000
	Net Profit			0	1,000

collect the profit for three months. Moreover, the different spot rates on the two swaps resulted in the dealer's being out of pocket 5000 DEM for the three months. While this working capital outlay is recouped when the three-months forward contracts are settled, there is an interest cost that is borne by the dealer, if the dealer does not have an appropriate spot position established. When the present value of the profit and the interest costs on the 5000 DEM are factored in, the effective profit is only 896 DEM.

Book profit on day 1	1000 DEM
Less: Interest on 5000 DEM shortage	(88)
$\dfrac{(5000 \times 7\% \times 90)}{360}$	
Adjusted profit 3 months in the future	912 DEM
Present value	896 DEM
$\left[\dfrac{912}{1+(.07 \times 90)/360}\right] = 896$	

In long-dated forwards, the present value of the profits will be much less than the nominal amount. With a 10 percent discount rate on a five-year forward contract, for instance, a profit of 1000 DEM received five years hence is worth only 621 DEM today. If the dealing bank also had to pay taxes on the income in the year the deal was done and had a tax rate of 50 percent, 500 in current DEM would be paid out in taxes. With only 621 present-day DEM coming in and 500 DEM going out, the true net profitability is far less than the reported 1000 DEM. One of the consequences of the impact of the time value of money is that these medium- and long-dated forwards are increasingly being dealt through capital markets transactions, such as currency swaps. The bid-and-offer spreads have also widened out over time as market practitioners focused on the real overall return and not the nominal accounting results.

Forward positions are proactively taken when the dealer has a view that the forward points are going to move in a certain direction. If the dealer thought the three months could go to over 400 points discount in a short period of time from the current 300 points discount, he or she would take advantage of this expected move by initially selling the three-month forward. The cash position would then be rolled using spot-next transactions for a few days. After the market had moved, the dealer would then buy forward to cover the three-month short position. Consider Exhibit 10.11 which outlines a position es-

Exhibit 10.11. Forward Position Using Both Spot-Next and Forward
Contracts

Swap no.	Swap side	Value date	Rate	USD, bought/(sold)	DEM, bought/(sold)
1-b	Buy	Day 3	1.8000	1,000,000	(1,800,000)
2-s	Sell	Day 3	1.8200	(1,000,000)	1,820,000
	Net			0	20,000
2-b	Buy	Day 4	1.8195	1,000,000	(1,819,500)
3-s	Sell	Day 4	1.7900	(1,000,000)	1,790,000
	Net			0	(29,500)
3-b	Buy	Day 90	1.7500	1,000,000	(1,750,000)
1-s	Sell	Day 90	1.7700	(1,000,000)	1,770,000
	Net			0	20,000
	Net Profit			0	10,500

tablished, rolled for one day, and then covered via an offsetting forward. The contracts dealt are as follows:

Day 1:
  Sell three months at 300 points discount; tickets include a spot purchase
  at 1.8000 (swap 1-b) and a three-month sale at 1.7700 (swap 1-s).

Day 1:
  Roll the cash position one day at 5 points discount; tickets include a spot
  sale at 1.8200 (swap 2-s) and a spot-next purchase at 1.8195 (swap 2-b).

Day 2:
  Buy three months, less a day, at 400 points discount; tickets include a
  spot sale at 1.7900 (swap 3-s) and a three-month purchase at 1.7500
  (swap 3-b).

The 10,500 DEM profit consists of the following:

1. Gain on initial spot-next swap
   $[1,000,000 \times (1.8200 - 1.8195)]$ 500

2. Gain on movement in forward points
   $[(.0400 - .0300) \times 1,000,000]$ 10,000

                                                         10,500

Forward Trading—Some General Comments. Taking the positions
outlined above involves a forecast of a change in the interest-rate dif-

ferentials. The ability to anticipate these changes in the market is essential to making money when trading forwards. Rolling the cash positions and obtaining bid-and-offer spreads can certainly help the profit picture, but these are usually inadequate by themselves.

Forward trading does not usually have the volatility of spot-rate dealing. Interest rates do not normally move to the same extent as spot currency prices, and thus forward trading takes on a different dimension. In stable economic conditions, interest rates can be quite steady, leading to little movement in forward points. Moreover, when rates move, they tend to go in one direction and then plateau for a while. They usually do not rise and then fall significantly. Consequently, if a trader misses a move or is on the wrong side of a move, there are fewer opportunities to make up for the losses or the lost opportunity.

Forward trading does not lend itself to the rapid trading often found in the spot markets. A forward dealer does not flip from short to long and vice versa throughout the day, unless he or she is the beneficiary of counterparties dealing on his or her prices and the bid-and-offer spread is being gained. A basic position is established and tends to be held for longer periods of time.

Another constraining factor in the forward market is the fact that forward contracts involve credit lines with counterparties. Excessive dealing can fully utilize credit lines, and when caught in this position, a dealer can be handicapped in future dealings. Preferred counterparties may be unavailable because of lack of credit availability; thus the dealer, forced to deal within a smaller market, is inhibited in his or her ability to deal.

Spot trading is something like poker. Several different sources affect the supply of and demand for a currency in the short term, and one's ability to read these pressures will determine how successful one is at trading the market. Every day provides the dealer with a new market, which is likely to be sufficiently volatile to provide adequate opportunities to make or lose money.

In contrast, the forward market can be viewed as a chess match. There are numerous factors to consider, including the spot market, but it usually takes longer for the significant movements to materialize. A market can remain basically the same for several days, weeks, or months. Unlike spot trading, therefore, a new game does not start every day, and one's perspective is longer term in nature.

Profits on Forward Trading

As with spot trading, forward dealers will end the trading day with a net position that is either long or short. This net position, however, is likely to include an assortment of net long and short positions on many of the forward dates that the dealer has traded. The forward book's P&L can be estimated in different ways. One way is to determine the gain or loss if every outstanding contract were liquidated. On a manual system, this would be onerous and inefficient, but on a computer system, it can work quite well.

One method of liquidation utilizes closing outright forward rates. If there were no transactions of any kind on that day, the profit or loss for the day would be the difference in the liquidation value today versus what the liquidation value was on the previous day. Exhibit 10.12 gives an example showing a revaluation process on a CAD/USD forward book. Consider the following:

1. In the example, the dealer bought USD value May 3 at 100 points premium for an all-in forward rate of 1.2000. The spot side of the swap is for value February 3 at a rate of 1.1900.

2. On the February 1 revaluation, the forward points for May 3 increased to 110. The dealer was long that position and thus made 10 points, or $1000.

3. On the February 2 revaluation, the forward points for May 3 declined to 90. Compared with the contract rate where the forward points were 100, the dealer now has a net loss of $1000. For that particular day, however, the loss was $2000, reflecting the forward point decline from .0110 at the close of business on February 1 to .0090 at the close of business on February 2.

The dealer in the example in Exhibit 10.12 is long USD value May 3 and has an offsetting spot position value February 3. On February 3, assume the dealer rolls or swaps the February 3 contract to February 4. The revaluation process takes on a new twist because the two contracts maturing on February 3 are no longer outstanding.

Assume the swap contract was dealt as follows:

Purchase	1,000,000 USD value February 3 at 1.2000 CAD/USD.
Sell	1,000,000 USD value February 4 at 1.20004.

On February 3, the maturing contracts would have generated the following cashflow:

	Rate	USD, in/(out)	CAD, in/(out)
Original swap	1.1900	(1,000,000)	1,190,000
Rollover swap	1.2000	1,000,000	(1,200,000)
Net		0	(10,000)

Exhibit 10.12. Revaluation of the Forward Position via Liquidation of Contracts

Revaluation Day	Maturity date	Contract amount	Contract rate	Revaluation rate	Canadian Equivalent		Daily gain/(loss)	Month-to-date gain/(loss)
					Contract	Revaluation		
Feb. 1	Feb. 3	(1,000,000)	1.1900	1.2000	1,190,000	(1,200,000)	(10,000)	
	May 3	1,000,000	1.2000	1.2110	(1,200,000)	1,211,000	11,000	
					(10,000)	11,000	1,000	1,000
Feb. 2	Feb. 3	(1,000,000)	1.1900	1.2000	1,190,000	(1,200,000)	(10,000)	
	May 3	1,000,000	1.2000	1.2090	(1,200,000)	1,209,000	9,000	
					(10,000)	9,000	(1,000)	
							(1,000)	
							(1,000)	
							(2,000)	(1,000)

1. February 2 total revaluation gain/(loss).
2. Adjusted by reversal of previous day's revaluation.
3. Daily gain/(loss).

289

Exhibit 10.13 shows that the revaluation process of the remaining contracts outstanding at the close of business on February 3 yields a significant profit of $10,040. The large revaluation profit occurs because the revaluation does not include the $10,000 cashflow loss on the contracts settled on February 3. The original contract for value February 3 at 1.1900 has matured and is no longer included in this revaluation process. It has been replaced in the revaluation calculations by the new contract arising from the rollover transaction. The remedy to the revaluation problem is simply to incorporate the effect of the contracts settling that day. In this case, the revaluation gain of $10,000 is exactly offset by the contract settlement cashflow loss of $10,000.

The revaluation rates in Exhibit 10.13 also show that the forward contract on May 3 is worth .0100 premium. This value is exactly the same as that existing when the position was established. Consequently, the cumulative gain or loss should be limited to whatever gains or losses were incurred on the near-dated swaps that were dealt to roll the cash position. The example only had one rollover swap generating a gain of $40, which, indeed, is the dealer's profit for the three days of trading.

An alternative method to revaluation based on the outright forward prices is to revalue forward positions using the forward points, instead of the outright forward price. Given that the forward market is essentially traded on points, it makes sense to value them as well on this basis. The basic concept is the same as the outright approach, but there are a few nuances that could be explored to make the process clear. Because these details are beyond the scope of the book, however, they have been excluded.

Trading Currency Options

Trading currency options requires the skills of a spot trader, a forward trader, a mathematician, and more. It is a complex area, and the objective of this section is to provide an appreciation of trading and the complexity involved.

As with any market, but especially with options, the trader must be able to quantify the risks involved in trading. In order to do that, the trader has to have an intimate understanding of options pricing. As explained more fully in Chapter 8, the value of an option is usually expressed as a premium. The premium, which is a function of several factors, has two components, intrinsic and extrinsic value. Intrinsic value reflects the benefit, if any, if the option could be exercised immediately. Extrinsic or time value is what is left over.

Exhibit 10.13. Revaluation of Existing Contracts plus Contracts Previously Settled

Revaluation Day	Maturity date	Contract amount	Contract rate	Revaluation rate	Canadian equivalent		Daily gain/(loss)	Month-to-date gain/(loss)
					Contract	Revaluation		
Feb. 2				(per Exhibit 10.12)				(1,000)
Feb. 3	Feb. 4	(1,000,000)	1.20004	1.2000	1,200,040	(1,200,000)	40	
	May 3	1,000,000	1.2000	1.2100	(1,200,000)	1,210,000	10,000	
					40	10,000	10,040	

1. February 3 revaluation gain/(loss) — 10,040
2. Adjusted by reversal of previous day's revaluation — 1,000
3. Plus or minus current day's net settlement — (10,000)

4. Daily gain/(loss) — 1,040   40

291

The factors which collectively determine the premium, and which the trader needs to consider, include the following:

1. Maturity date

2. Strike price

3. Current spot rate

4. Current forward rate or interest differentials between the two currencies

5. Put or call

6. American or European style

7. Volatility

8. Risk-free interest rate (used for discounting the future expected value)

One of the rules of trading is that you should always know how to get out of a position before you get into it. Thus, while one may know the value of an option, one needs to be able to hedge or unwind the risk, if so desired. Consequently, prices in options market may differ from what sophisticated pricing models say the option is worth because there may simply not be a ready market for that particular option. A brief review of some of the hedging alternatives for currency options follows.

Hedging Options Positions

The only way one can truly hedge or exactly offset an option is with another option. An alternative method that can be used successfully, and sometimes unsuccessfully, is delta hedging.

Delta is the amount by which an option premium changes given a small change in the underlying exchange rate. A delta for at-the-money options is approximately .5 (known as 50 delta). That is, for a small change in the spot exchange rate, the premium will change by approximately half that amount. Consider a purchase of an at-the-money CAD put/USD call at a strike price of 1.2000 CAD/USD:

$$\text{Principal} \times \text{points} = \text{premium}$$
$$10,000,000 \text{ USD} \times .0135 = 135,000 \text{ CAD}$$

If the market moves 10 points, the premium will change 5 points, or 5000 CAD.

$$\text{Principal} \times \text{change in market} \times \text{delta} = \text{change in premium}$$
$$10,000,000 \text{ USD} \times .0010 \times .50 = 5000 \text{ CAD}$$

The same $5000 result could be achieved if we adjust the principal amount of the position by the delta and then multiply this risk-adjusted principal by the change in points.

$$10,000,000 \text{ USD} \times .5 \times .0010 = 5000 \text{ CAD}$$

The risk-adjusted principal of the option can be used to determine the change in premium due to a change in the market. Consequently, we can forget delta for now and focus on the risk-adjusted principal of 5 million USD as the position to hedge.

The above USD call could be hedged in several ways, three of which are:

1. Sell an identical call. This is the only way of achieving a true hedge.
2. Sell other calls that generate the same amount of risk-adjusted principal. For instance, calls could be written with different strike prices, different maturity dates, and/or different principal amounts.
3. Sell USD in the spot market in an amount equal to the risk-adjusted principal.

Hedging with Matching Options

Selling an identical call option creates a perfect offset to the call option that was purchased. As the market moves, the value of each option will move in unison, and the trader suffers no market risk. This alternative is not always available at a price that the trader likes. Consequently, the trader may look to other alternatives to hedge the position.

Hedging with Options on Risk-Adjusted Amounts

This alternative essentially involves selling other USD calls which can have different strike prices, different expiry dates, and/or different principal amounts. For instance, an out-of-the-money 20 million USD call and a delta of .25 should provide a risk-adjusted hedge, at least at that precise time.

$$20,000,000 \text{ USD} \times .25 = \text{risk-adjusted principal}$$
$$= 5,000,000 \text{ USD}$$

To verify this, recall that for a 10-point movement in prices, the long USD call position would see a 5000 CAD change in the value of the option. The sale of the 20 million USD call at a delta of .25 will also generate a corresponding, but opposite, change in value of 5000 CAD.

$$\text{Principal} \times \text{change in market} \times \text{delta} = \text{change in premium}$$
$$20,000,000 \text{ USD} \times .0010 \times .25 = 5000 \text{ CAD}$$

One of the difficulties with such a hedging strategy is that as the underlying spot market changes, the deltas of the two options will also change. If the 20 million USD call that was sold becomes at the money, its delta is now .5. The risk-adjusted principal is now 10 million USD.

$$20,000,000 \text{ USD} \times .5 = 10,000,000 \text{ USD}$$

On the other hand, the delta on the original call that was purchased may have only improved to .75. The risk-adjusted principal on the long call option is thus only 7,500,000 USD, and the hedge of 10,000,000 USD risk-adjusted principal is now excessive. Consequently, a well-hedged option position one day may not be well hedged the next day. The options trader needs to be constantly aware of these actual or possible changes and be prepared to adjust his or her portfolio accordingly.

Hedging Options Using the Spot Market

A third way to hedge the USD call is by selling the risk-adjusted principal of 5 million USD on the spot market. If the USD declines by 10 points, the impact is as follows:

CAD loss on USD call:	
.0010 × .5 × 10,000,000 USD	= (5000) CAD
(points × delta × USD amount)	
CAD gain on USD spot short:	
.0010 × 5,000,000 USD	= 5000 CAD
(points × USD amount)	
Net gain/(loss)	0

The delta determines the risk-adjusted principal. If delta were stable, the initial hedge could be left in place and the trader could sit back and relax. However, such is not the case. As outlined in the second hedging alternative, delta will change as the option goes further in or out of the money. It can also change as the option gets closer to expiry. Changes in volatility can also change the delta. Delta hedging is thus dynamic and requires the trader to adjust the amount of the spot hedges almost constantly. Consider, for example, if the market moves to 1.19 CAD/USD from 1.20 and the delta changes to .45.

The spot hedge of 5,000,000 USD should be reduced to 4,500,000 USD and is accomplished by the dealer buying back USD at 1.19. In so doing, the trader profits on the 500,000 USD originally sold but now bought back:

	Dealing price	CAD cashflow, in/(out)
Sale of 500,000 USD	1.20	600,000
Purchase of 500,000 USD	1.19	(595,000)
Net CAD gain/(loss)		5,000

The offset to the gain is the option that is worth less than when it was purchased. If the USD strengthened thereafter, the trader would be back in the market selling more USD. Over the life of an option, the trader could conceivably be buying and selling on many occasions. It could work to the dealer's advantage, as in the above example, but that is not always the case.

If the above scenario were changed so that the trader wrote the USD call instead of buying it, the delta hedge would have consisted of a purchase of USD. The subsequent move to 1.19 CAD/USD would have resulted in a cash loss on the sale-back of the 500,000 USD. The option is further out of the money, which is to the writer's advantage, but part of the initial premium received is now gone.

While another option is the best hedge, the delta works well against this basic kind of market movement. It is commonly used and is especially useful when a trader first deals an option and needs to hedge the market risk quickly. As offsetting options are dealt, the delta hedges in the spot market are unwound.

One of the biggest weaknesses facing delta hedging is that it does not hedge against decreases or increases in volatility. If the only change in the market was a reduction in volatility, the trader would be long an option that has declined in value. Because the delta hedge has had no offsetting gain, the trader is in a net-loss position. Consequently, the adage that the only way to truly hedge an option is with an option is quite appropriate.

Having seen some different ways of hedging options, let us now review some elements of options trading. If a trader has one contract, it is relatively easy to keep track of the risk profile of the contract. However, options traders typically trade a portfolio of options; the risk assessment on a portfolio of options is highly complex and can only be properly handled by computers. In addition, assessing future hedging and trading strategies is greatly enhanced when traders can do a "what if" type of analysis on their portfolio.

The next section briefly reviews some second-level concepts of options: delta, gamma, theta, vega, and rho.

Delta

Delta represents the change in premium for a *small* change in the underlying spot market exchange rate. It also reflects the probability that the option will expire in the money. Delta ranges from 0.0 for far out-of-the-money options to 1.0 for deep in-the-money options. Delta is obviously affected by the relationship of the strike price to the current market rate; it can also be affected by the volatility of the option market and the time to expiry.

1. The intrinsic value of an option is the degree to which the option is currently in the money. The intrinsic value is a known amount and is not affected by changes in volatility, only by market movements.
2. If the volatility of an option increases, the premium will typically increase, with three primary exceptions:
    a. The option is extremely deep in the money, and the premium is strictly intrinsic.
    b. Too much time has lapsed, and the option is so close to expiry that the premium is purely intrinsic.
    c. The option is far out of the money and still remains essentially worthless.

    The extent of the premium increase due to increased volatility is, consequently, purely extrinsic in nature.
3. Delta is also affected by the time remaining to expiry. If an option is far out of the money, but has a long time to expiry, there still may be a chance for it to expire in the money. The premium may thus include some extrinsic or time value and have a small delta. However, as time to expiry nears, the chances of an out-of-the-money option expiring in the money decrease, until the market's assessment is that there is virtual certainty that it will expire unexercised. When this happens, the option is worthless, the premium is zero, and, of course, delta is zero.

    Similarly, in-the-money options have a delta anywhere from slightly over .5 to 1.0. As expiry draws near and it appears certain the option will expire in the money, the option premium is totally intrinsic and delta is 1. The option essentially becomes a forward contract. Delta is subject to change from market movements, changes in the volatility component, and time decay. Using delta hedging techniques involves using a moving target which can take significant and often unexpected moves. It can help minimize the risk, but it is an imperfect hedging strategy.

Gamma

Mathematically, the measure of change in the delta due to a given change in the underlying spot market is known as *gamma*. It is essentially the delta of the delta.

If one hedges an option portfolio with other options, changes in gamma are often largely offset. By contrast, hedging with spot or forward contracts has no offset, as the delta is always 1.0 and gamma is always 0 for those contracts. Again, it is worth repeating that hedging options with options clearly has advantages over hedging with spot, forward, or futures contracts.

From a trading standpoint, strategies that have low gammas reflect deltas that are stable. Stability in this context reflects a more conservative strategy than one that has a high gamma or a delta that is subject to more significant changes. Consider the following:

1. Options with the highest gammas tend to include at-the-money options. Recall that intrinsic value is not influenced by volatility. Only extrinsic, or time, value is influenced by volatility. As at-the-money options have the largest amount of time value, they are, therefore, most influenced by volatility. At-the-money options, consequently, also have the highest gamma.

2. As options near expiry, all else being equal, time decay erodes their extrinsic value at an accelerating pace. Volatility plays a smaller role in the makeup of the option's value, and the underlying market movement plays an ever-increasing role. As a result, gamma increases as expiry approaches, especially in the last 45-day time frame.

3. From the standpoint of value, in-the-money options are sensitive at expiration, as their value will change directly with every movement in the underlying spot rate. They, in fact, essentially become spot contracts. At-the-money options are also extremely sensitive to movements in the spot rate in terms of changes in both value and gamma. Assume a dealer is long a USD call option at a strike of 1.1900 CAD/USD. It is two minutes to expiry. With spot at 1.1899, the option is out of the money and has no value. If the spot rate moved to 1.1900, the value of the option would still likely remain at zero. Delta is, therefore, zero. Gamma is also zero. If the spot rate then moved to 1.1901, the option would have an intrinsic value of .0001. Delta would be 1.0, and gamma would also be 1.0.

Increases in volatility have mixed impact on gamma. Short-term out-of-the-money options will experience an increase, while at-the-money and in-the-money options experience gamma decreases. Longer-term options see gamma decrease with increased volatility.

Management of gamma is clearly complicated and challenging. Many practitioners do not look at gamma in their trading activities. Others may feel it is fine-tuning the process too much.

Theta

An option is a wasting asset. Time decay gradually erodes the value of an option until, at some time, the only value of an option is its intrinsic value. A trader cannot ignore the impact of time decay, whether he or she is long or short options. *Theta* is the anticipated change in the premium of an option or portfolio of options given a change in time to expiry. In other words, if one day goes by, what is the change in the premium of the option or portfolio of options?

The time value of an option is nil at expiry for all options. Consequently, as time value is the largest for at-the-money options, time decay must also be largest for at-the-money options.

Knowing how time decay works is important in establishing strategies. If one is short options, one would like to structure the deal so that time decay is faster rather than slower. Similarly, if one is long options, one will tend to avoid strategies with rapid time decay, all else being equal.

The three-dimensional graph at the top of page 299 shows time decay for options in, at, and out of the money.

Vega

Considerable discussion has taken place on the importance of volatility in the options market. Measuring the impact of small changes in volatility is done by determining an option's vega.

Whereas theta measures the impact of time on an option or portfolio of options, *vega* measures the impact due to changes in the overall volatility.

Rho

The determination of an option's value is essentially the future expected value. This future expected value is then discounted in the pricing model to current dollars to generate the premium. If the interest rate used in the pricing changes, the premium will also change. This

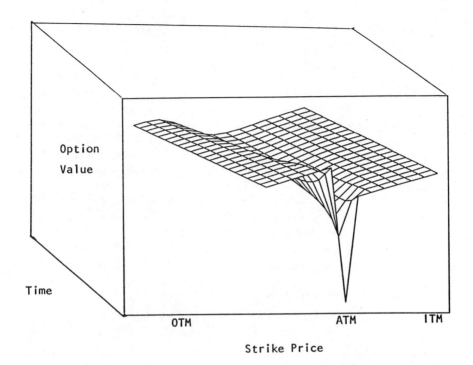

Option
Value

Time

OTM   ATM ITM

Strike Price

risk is, in relative terms, a small risk for short-dated options, but it increases as the term increases. The ratio of the change in option value for a change in the discount interest rate is known as *rho*.

Pricing and Control Models

Pricing decisions must often be made quickly on a variety of currencies, expiry dates, strike prices, or combinations thereof. For a market maker to succeed in today's competitive environment, it is essential that traders have computer tools to give them the information they need.

From a business perspective, these tools are necessary to generate revenue. Perhaps even more important, however, is that the tools identify the risks and facilitate proper management, so that losses are attributable to wrong opinions on the market, and nothing else.

From a corporate perspective, aggressive trading of options is no different. Investment in technology and systems is essential for active and large-scale trading. If one trades a few options at a time with a strategy of dealing only when major market moves are expected, the tools need not be nearly as elaborate. In fact, manual systems may work well. Nevertheless, the trader/hedger should still know the risks faced due to a change in the market, be it volatility, spot or forward market movements, or time decay.

Executing Interbank Transactions in Options

The importance of volatility in options cannot be overestimated. In fact, the professional dealing market trades on the basis of volatility. Consider the following example conversation, where spot DEM/USD is 1.7975–1.7980 and one-month forwards are 30 points premium.

> DEALER A: "Dealer A calling. Market on at-the-money forward, one-month calls on the dollar against the mark, please."
>
> DEALER B: "9.8 to 10.2."
>
> DEALER A: "At 9.8, I can do 10 dollars."
>
> DEALER B: "Ok, that's done. I buy a 10 million USD call against the mark, at-the-money forward, expiry one month. How about a strike of 1.8010 with a 49 delta on a spot of 1.7977?"
>
> DEALER A: "That's fine. So I buy from you 4,900,000 USD value spot at 1.7977. I would like my premium in percentage of USD which I calculate to be .75 percent, or $75,000."
>
> DEALER B: "Agreed."

Dealer A begins by introducing himself and asks for Dealer B's market for options on USD calls against the deutsche mark expiring in one month. The "at the money" refers to the strike price being at the money in relation to the prevailing forward rate.

Dealer B responds by showing her prices in terms of volatility. Her bid for USD call options is 9.8 percent volatility, and her offer is 10.2 percent volatility.

Dealer A likes the market and hits Dealer B's bid at 9.8 percent for 10 million USD.

Dealer B confirms the deal is done and the details of the transaction. Dealer B also suggests the at-the-money strike price which, of course, is based on current market spot and forward prices. In the initial discussions, the two dealers never mention the actual market rate or the strike price. They focus on the relationship of strike to market, on the time to expiry, on the amount, and on the volatility. When the deal is actually done, they agree on the actual strike price for the contract, as well as the amount and currency of the premium. Note that the premium is expressed in percentage terms as opposed to foreign exchange points.

It should also be noted that when Dealer B suggested a strike price, she also suggested a delta and a spot rate. When an options deal is done, both dealers face two key market risks. The first is that the spot market will move against them. The second is that volatility may change. The risk of spot movement can be temporarily offset through delta hedging. As the two dealers have offsetting spot risks, there is a benefit to the two parties to deal a spot transaction with each other. In fact, market practice calls for a spot transaction to be done, unless the calling bank asks for a live price, indicating that no spot transaction is desired. In this case, the spot transaction is wanted. When the spot deal is done, the rate is usually the middle of the market, and the amount is equal to the principal amount of the deal multiplied by the delta of the option. In this case, Dealer A would buy 4,900,000 USD value spot at 1.7977.

Options Trading Strategies

In trading options, the volatility component is usually the part that makes or breaks a trader.

There are two forms of volatility to be aware of:

1. Historical volatility calculates the actual price volatility over a specific period of time. It can be calculated for any time frame from hours to days, weeks, months, and years. If calculated over a number of years, historical volatility will indicate what volatility levels represent a good sale and what levels represent a good purchase.

   Calculations of historical volatility covering the most recent trading period give the trader assistance in pricing deals in the current market environment. This does not automatically provide a good forecast, because market conditions in the past may not be the same in the future. However, it gives the trader additional information on which decisions can be judiciously made.

2. Implied volatility represents the market views on future price movements from where the market is now trading. If recent historical volatility has been 10 percent, but the implied volatility is only 7 percent, the market clearly believes volatility will trend down.

The individual trader needs to develop his or her own view about what will happen. If the trader's expectations of volatility are the same as or differ from the market's, he or she would establish the positions that reflect that view.

On the one hand, option pricing is a science that uses sophisticated mathematical analysis and elaborate pricing models. However, pricing is also an art, because it is the trader's opinion on volatility and market direction that will generate the trading profits. Forecasting market movements and using effective strategies form the essence of options trading.

Many actual trading strategies can be used to take advantage of movements in a particular direction, the lack of market movement in any direction, increases or decreases in volatility, or time decay. Chapter 8 covered some of the basic strategies, including buying and writing puts and calls, straddles, strangles, and bull or bear spreads. A few others are as follows:

1. Buy or write calls or puts based on the expected direction in a currency. Leverage is high on purchased options because one benefits from the entire principal amount of the option, but only risks a small portion (i.e., the premium).

2. Buy longer-term options and write shorter-term options to take advantage of different rates of time decay.

3. Trade the volatility curve by buying short-dated options and selling long-dated options when volatility increases significantly with time to expiry (i.e., the volatility curve is positively sloped). As the longer-dated options move closer to expiry, the volatility component declines, thereby reducing their value. If the declines on the long-dated options more than offset the declines on the short-dated options, profits can be realized. However, this strategy is more complex than it might appear. For instance, time decay is a significant factor, especially on the short-dated options, and could more than offset the gains made by riding down the volatility curve.

4. Trade in terms of a portfolio of currencies. For instance, a trader could buy options on currencies whose volatilities are currently low by historical standards and sell options whose current volatility is high according to historical standards. However, one must always remember that there is a reason for volatility to be what it is. Simply comparing current volatility to historical volatility does not guarantee success.

General Rules for Trading

There are many rules that traders use. Some general guidelines developed over the years and frequently followed by practitioners are given below. Some may seem contradictory, while others may be almost too obvious. Experience with profits and losses will identify those rules of most value.

1. Getting into positions requires three prices: the entry price, the price to take profits, and the price to take losses.

2. A price maker's best price should be the price at which he or she can get out of the position at that moment.

3. If you take a position, make sure you can get out.

4. Positions are bought to be sold and are sold to be bought. Do not hang on forever.

5. You will never go broke taking profits.

6. Every market has its day; do not overstay it.

7. Let your profits run, but cut your losses.

8. Never wait for that extra point; profits are not at the top or the bottom, but in between.

9. Bulls make money; bears make money; pigs get slaughtered.

10. When in doubt, do nothing.

11. If everybody believes the market is going one way, do the opposite.

12. Bullish markets get overbought, and bearish markets get oversold.

13. If the market does not rise, it will decline.

14. Deal on the rumor; close out on the fact; this strategy is also known as "buy the rumor and sell the fact."

15. Rumors are mostly an exaggeration of fact.

16. If a large move in a market has caught your eye, chances are the move is largely over.

17. Market factors can only fuel a market for so long. Fresh fuel is needed to keep it going.

18. Do not make the same mistake twice. If you do, figure out why.

19. If you forget the past, you are doomed to see it again.

20. Never buck the trend; this strategy is also known as "the trend is your friend."

21. Do not second-guess the market; you will go broke trying to prove it wrong.

22. Base your decisions on facts and ideas, not your emotions.

23. If the profit or loss is yours, the decision must also be yours.

24. A market decision is the trader's decision; second-guessers should either trade or be quiet.

25. Never trade positions you do not watch.

26. Markets are global. Go home flat; go home with stop-loss and/or take-profit orders or instructions to call; but do not ignore your position.

27. Profit expectations rise with the amount of risk taken.

28. The threat of intervention is often more significant than the intervention itself.

29. Use technical analysis in conjunction with fundamental analysis.

30. Fundamentals define the market; technical factors are for timing.

PART 3

Corporate Foreign Currency Exposure and Management

11

Transaction Exposure

Executive Summary

Chapter 11 is the first of four chapters that identify and explain the specific types of corporate foreign exchange exposure. The chapter begins with a brief description of all the exposures and then proceeds to examine transaction exposure. Examples are used to demonstrate how to measure transaction exposure. The chapter then deals with the management of transaction exposure, first looking at methods that do not involve financial market hedging and covering activities. The chapter closes with a discussion of the use of financial-market contracts, and of the influence of currency price forecasting and risk aversion on the selection of an appropriate hedging strategy.

Introduction

Exposure is defined as the possibility of a change in shareholder wealth arising from a movement in the foreign exchange rate. The three basic types of corporate exposure, which are called transaction, economic, and translation, can be distinguished by their relation in time.

1. *Transaction exposure* refers to a potential gain or loss arising from business transactions that are planned, are currently in progress, or have already been completed. However, the actual gains and losses are based on current foreign exchange transactions. Examples include a signed, but not shipped, sales contract; a foreign-currency-

denominated receivable or payable; and a collected, but not converted to local currency, receivable.

2. *Economic exposure* is defined as a change in future earning power and cashflow as a result of currency adjustment. In effect, it represents a change in competitive position.

3. *Translation exposure,* also called *accounting exposure,* concerns the past. Gains or losses can result from the process of translating the financial statements of foreign subsidiaries and affiliates from the local currency to that of the parent firm. This translation must be done in order to consolidate the statements. Gains or losses may also occur in the translation of foreign currency assets and liabilities that are on a parent or subsidiary company's statements.

Economic exposure and transaction exposure are related in that they both involve a change in real cashflows, as opposed to the change in accounting or reported earnings and equity associated with translation exposure. We will leave the past and the future to subsequent chapters and concentrate in this chapter on the present, which involves transaction exposure.

Defining Transaction Exposure

As indicated, transaction exposure involves the possibility of gain or loss on deals booked or in progress. In fact, any planned foreign-currency-denominated payment or receipt of cash would involve exposure. Examples include:

1. A foreign currency asset or a liability already on the balance sheet, or a contract or agreement requiring a future foreign currency cashflow.
2. Planned, but not contractual, cashflows. These cashflows may arise from various activities, such as:
   a. Publication of a price list for goods which guarantees the price for several months. The amount of goods to be sold is uncertain.
   b. Submission of bids or tenders on projects in a foreign currency. A contingent exposure is created, dependent on whether or not the contract is won.
   c. Funds held in foreign currencies as margin for commodity futures contracts.

At the limit, any anticipated foreign currency receipt or payment resulting from any business operation is a source of transaction exposure.

One of the simplest examples is a receivable in a foreign currency, such as pound sterling. If not hedged, the dollar value of the receivable will fall if the pound devalues relative to the dollar during the collection period. This potential decline in value represents the exposure. Other exposures are not quite so easily defined and measured. The balance of the chapter will explore, with examples, the measurement and management of transaction exposure.

Measuring Transaction Exposure

A good point to start measuring corporate transaction exposure is with an analysis of the balance sheet. At this level, only completed deals, represented by an asset or a liability, are included. In order to identify foreign-currency-denominated accounts, it is first necessary to specify the home or counting currency, which is usually the primary shareholders' currency. In the example that follows, we will consider two situations using the same balance sheet.

Case A: A Canadian Firm, Canadian Shareholders

In the first case, shown in Exhibit 11.1, we will assume a Canadian corporation owned by Canadian shareholders. Clearly, the home or count-

Exhibit 11.1. Case A: Canadian Firm, Canadian Shareholders

(In Thousands)

	Balance sheet in CAD	Currency denomination of accounts expressed as CAD value		
		CAD	DEM	USD
Cash	200	200		
Receivables	1000	600	200	200
Inventory	500	500		
Fixed assets	2000	2000		
Total	3700	3300	200	200
Payables	250	50	100	100
Long-term debt	1000	500		500
Equity	2450	2450		
Total	3700	3000	100	600
Currency exposure		Nil	+100	−400

ing currency is Canadian dollars. In the second case, our company will be a subsidiary of an American parent, and the home currency will be U.S. dollars. The purpose is to measure the potential gain or loss in shareholder wealth caused by currency revaluation.

We can see from this very brief exposure report that our firm has foreign-currency-denominated receivables, specifically 200 CAD worth of deutsche marks (DEM) and 200 CAD worth of USD. Similarly, there are DEM and USD payables and some U.S.-dollar-denominated debt. If we sum the exposure by currency, the business is long 100 CAD worth of DEM and short 400 CAD worth of USD. If the exchange rate between Canadian dollars and either of these other two currencies changed before these particular accounts were settled, there would be a corresponding change in shareholder wealth. There is, of course, no currency exposure from the CAD-denominated accounts because the counting currency in this case is Canadian dollars.

Case B: A Canadian Subsidiary of a U.S. Parent

Now let us assume that the Canadian firm is a subsidiary of an American parent. Exhibit 11.2 shows the exposure of this same balance sheet measured from the point of view of the American corporate share-

Exhibit 11.2. Case B: Canadian Subsidiary of an American Parent
(In Thousands)

	Balance sheet in CAD	Balance sheet in USD*	Currency denomination of accounts, expressed as USD value		
			CAD	DEM	USD
Cash	200	160	160		
Receivables	1000	800	480	160	160
Inventory	500	400	400		
Fixed assets	2000	1600	1600		
Total	3700	2960	2640	160	160
Payables	250	200	40	80	80
Long-term debt	1000	800	400		400
Equity	2450	1960	1960		
Total	3700	2960	2400	80	480
Currency exposure			+240	+ 80	Nil

*Exchange rate = .8 USD/CAD.

holder. The balance sheet is first translated into USD because the counting currency is now U.S. dollars. We have assumed an exchange rate of .8 USD/CAD for this purpose.

Case B measures the balance sheet transaction exposure of the same Canadian firm, seen from the position of an American parent. The DEM exposure remains, only now it is measured in USD. There is no longer USD exposure because the counting currency is USD. However, CAD exposure is now of concern, for it has the potential to affect USD shareholder equity.

Although the exposure reports reflected in case A and case B are a good beginning, they are by no means complete. They show only transactions booked as assets or liabilities. Other business deals may have been made which will produce either definite or highly probable foreign currency cashflows and are, therefore, a source of transaction exposure. For example, only the principal of the USD debt is acknowledged in the balance sheets. The interest will presumably also have to be paid in a known and certain schedule over time. Management may, however, have executed forward contracts to hedge the principal and/or interest on the USD debt. Such contracts would not show on the balance sheet, but will certainly produce foreign currency cashflows on maturity and, therefore, should be considered in measuring the exposure.

In addition, there may be other less certain, but still highly probable, foreign currency cashflows in the future. These would include sales or purchases of goods or services, dividends, royalties, and management fees.

Funds Flow Mapping

Inclusion of all these scheduled or forecast future cashflows requires modification of the preceding report, which was based solely on the balance sheet. In addition, the balance sheet format gives no real indication of when these obligations may fall due.

To include both the amount and timing of the planned and forecast transactions, a foreign exchange exposure report, broken down by day, week, month, or quarter, needs to be developed. It would show the net currency position by time period. The process is called *funds flow mapping*. How far the report goes into the future is often a function of the ability to forecast future cashflows. Some flows, like principal and interest payments on foreign currency and fixed-rate debt, will be known with certainty for the life of the financing. Forecasts of operating cashflows, on the other hand, will be derived from operating budgets and projections. They will necessarily become less

Exhibit 11.3. Five-Quarter Exposure Report, by Currency
(Flows of USD, in Thousands)

	Q1	Q2	Q3	Q4	Q5	Q5+	Total
Swiss franc	+200		+200		+200	+800	+1400
	−50	−70			−100		−220
Net CHF	+150	−70	+200		+100	+800	+1180
Pound sterling	+450	+400	+300	+250	+250	+1100	+2750
		−760		−400			−1160
Net GBP	+450	−360	+300	−150	+250	+1100	+1590

exact as one moves further into the future. However, as a working document, an exposure report using forecast information can be very useful in monitoring and managing transaction exposure. Such a report might take the form shown in Exhibit 11.3. The example is based on two currencies and the next five quarters.

For the five quarters specified, these forecast cashflows should include all the anticipated cashflows from any source in each of the two currencies. This is a mix of contractual flows and flows estimated from budgets and forecasts. At some point the latter become too uncertain to be useful; they are simply beyond the planning horizon. It may then be useful simply to summarize the remaining contractual flows. Some of these flows may not occur for several years; an example would be payments on long-term debt. This is done above in column Q5+ in Exhibit 11.3.

The choice of five quarters is, of course, arbitrary. The Total column summarizes the entire period. It is similar to what the case A and case B balance sheet reports shown earlier would do, except the total now includes all forecast or anticipated flows within the next five quarters, as well as the contractual or booked flows beyond quarter 5. The expanded report is not only more complete, but also provides information on the timing of the obligations over the next five quarters and beyond.

The preceding report would show the exposure for a particular business unit. The multinational corporation would, on the other hand, have operations in several, and perhaps many, countries. In that case, a final step would involve summing the individual business unit reports by currency from all the operations on a worldwide basis. If the management of transaction exposure is centralized, such a report would provide an invaluable position statement, which is, of course, one of the critical initial steps in exposure management.

Managing Transaction Exposure without Financial-Market Contracts

Transaction exposure management frequently involves the use of money-market hedges, currency options, and spot and forward contracts. However, there are other less obvious, but often equally effective, methods by which to approach the problem. Before automatically hedging the exposure using financial-market products, it is useful to explore ways to build exposure management into the basic business practice. Doing so may sharply reduce the exposure, and any remaining exposure can be handled, if necessary, with a foreign exchange or money-market hedge. We will first consider the exposure generated from operations and then examine exposure produced by financing activities.

Managing Exposure from Operations

Risk Shifting. On the operational side, a common objective is to avoid exposure on receivables and payables. The simplest way to accomplish this, if the bargaining power is available, is to do the business in your own currency in the first place. Such a practice shifts the currency risk to the trading partner. If you have a strong bargaining position (for example, as the only supplier of the product), such risk shifting can be the best strategy to follow.

In other cases, even though possible, it may not be the best strategy. For instance, consider a Canadian importer of a specialty product from Australia. If the deal is struck in CAD, it would appear that the Australian exporter bears the foreign exchange risk. However, if the CAD depreciates significantly against the AUD and the Australian company has not hedged the CAD receivable prior to the goods being shipped, the vendor may want the price renegotiated before shipment will occur. If the importer must have that product and the price is increased to compensate for the weaker CAD, it is the importer (the CAD-based company) that effectively has the risk. Dealing in your own currency does not always eliminate risk. As discussed in more detail in Chapter 13, this fact is especially true when dealing in commodities.

In other cases, where bargaining power is less pronounced, shifting the risk in this way may require concessions equal to or greater than the currency risk, and the effort may not be worthwhile. This may occur, for example, on long-dated receivables in a foreign currency that is experiencing a high rate of inflation. Everyone is aware of the currency risk, and the question becomes, Who bears the risk and at what cost?

Leading and Lagging. If you are required to book foreign-denominated trade accounts, it may be possible to alter the timing of the payments in your favor. If possible, the classic rules to follow are these:

1. Accelerate payment of payables in currencies that are expected to strengthen and delay payment in currencies that should weaken.

2. Accelerate collection of receivables denominated in "weak" currencies and delay receipt of those in "strong" currencies.

There are, however, three main problems with these rules:

1. They ignore a basic principle in cash management, which is to collect receivables as quickly as possible and to delay payment of payables as long as possible after due consideration of discounts and interest penalties. However, the objective should be to increase interest revenue and/or reduce interest expense.

2. The rules imply that foreign currency deals are done on a spot basis. In other words, the foreign exchange deal is to be done when the cash is received or paid out. One should be careful to distinguish between proper cash management and proper risk management.

3. The rules assume that your trading partners do not share your view of the currency exposure. As in the case of risk shifting, if everyone has the same opinion of the relative strengths and weaknesses of the currencies involved, it may be very difficult to aggressively manage the timing of your receivables and payables.

In some cases, cash-management and exposure-management practices can be limited by regulatory issues. Many governments facing foreign exchange shortages will restrict imports. They may also specify the maximum acceptable leads and lags in payments for both imports and exports. Consequently, while leading and lagging techniques may be useful concepts in the management of exposure, they can be severely restricted in their application.

Netting and Reinvoicing Centers. A third approach to managing exposure without the use of financial-market contracts involves netting of individual transaction exposures. For example, a DEM receivable can be used to offset a DEM payable. Moreover, because some currencies such as the Dutch guilder (NLG) are closely linked to the DEM, an effective netting from a risk standpoint could be achieved by having DEM receivables offset NLG payables.

For most companies, some netting of individual transaction exposures can usually be achieved. For multinational corporations, an expanded version of netting can be accomplished through the establishment of reinvoicing centers. Such centers are offices that purchase product from the various operational units of the multinational for resale to other units or to the ultimate customer. They have several advantages. Transaction exposure is centralized and netted on a corporatewide basis. For example, if unit A is long sterling and unit B is short sterling, the reinvoicing center would recognize that the corporate position is neutral or square, and would do nothing. Individual units, unaware of the offsetting positions elsewhere in the company, would be inclined to (unnecessarily) cover their own positions independently.

Reinvoicing centers also permit operational units to do business in their own currencies, removing currency gains or losses from unit returns and simplifying performance evaluation. The use of a center also permits consolidation of expertise in the management of currency exposure.

On the negative side, extra expense is incurred in the center's operation, even though the product is shipped directly to the customer. Furthermore, with increasing sophistication of tax legislation and enforcement, there is little remaining scope to reduce corporate tax liability with other than fair-market transfer prices.

Managing Exposure from Financing Activities

Transaction exposure can be avoided in financing activities if the only currency borrowed is the accounting or shareholder currency. At a second level, a foreign currency can be borrowed to offset or hedge a "long" currency position acquired through operations. For example, if a corporation has a fairly constant and predictable revenue stream in DEM, it might be useful to look for DEM debt structured in such a way that the principal and interest payments absorb a large part of the DEM revenue cashflow.

There are also situations in which it is necessary or desirable to borrow a foreign currency with no offsetting operational cashflow. If the currency is fully convertible, hedges can be put in place quickly to neutralize the exposure. Sometimes, however, it is necessary to raise funds in a currency that is experiencing high rates of inflation or that is not fully convertible, or both. Back-to-back or parallel loans have been used for some time in these circumstances.

Parallel Loans.   Parallel loans became popular around 1970 when the Bank of England was imposing fairly stringent currency controls in an attempt to support the pound. It was difficult for British firms to convert pounds for export to finance subsidiaries abroad. Under a parallel loan arrangement, an American firm would lend dollars to the American subsidiary of a British parent, and the British parent would lend pounds to the English subsidiary of the American parent. No money was converted or crossed borders. Credit risk was controlled by the right to offset: if your subsidiary defaults on its loan from me, I will authorize my subsidiary to suspend payments on its loan from you. Topping-up provisions were also frequent. In the event of a currency realignment exceeding some preset limit, partial repayment would be required on the part of one of the borrowers, so that the value of the credit extension remained roughly equal. Without this provision, the right to offset could lose its capacity to control credit risk over time. With the relaxation of currency controls in the last decade, parallel loans have become less useful.

Credit Swaps.   Credit swaps through the banking system are used primarily in situations involving controlled currencies, which are also considered likely to devalue. Once again, a multinational may wish to provide financing for a subsidiary operating in such a currency, but is reluctant to convert a "hard" currency for this purpose. Typically, the corporation places its currency on deposit with the bank, and the bank, through its branch or affiliate in the subsidiary's country, makes a local currency loan of equal value to the subsidiary. The parent may forgo interest on its deposit, but at maturity of the loan arrangement the parent does receive its "hard"-currency principal back intact, while the subsidiary simply repays the local currency loan.

Currency Swaps.   The currency swap is, by far, the most common method for hedging currency exposure in long-dated foreign currency financing. A currency swap is an arrangement under which borrowers effectively exchange the cashflows from both principal and interest on the debt. The exchange rate used for all principal exchanges is the rate in effect when the swap deal is done. The interest payments are determined by the interest rate on the date multiplied by the outstanding balance, just as in any form of financing. The rates, of course, may differ between the two currencies.

For example, if a Swiss corporation swaps Swiss francs for U.S. dollars, it may pay 11 percent for the dollars and receive only 7 percent for the francs. However, through the swap, U.S. dollars have been borrowed by a Swiss franc-based company, without currency exposure. The swap market is a readily traded market that can be used to hedge existing foreign debt. It can also provide windows or opportunities to borrow fully hedged foreign currencies at an all-in cost less than that of the domestic market. A detailed analysis of the swap market is beyond the scope of this book; however, Chapter 9 provides more information and a brief example.

Managing Transaction Exposure Using Financial-Market Contracts

We have examined a series of business-management methods to avoid or reduce currency exposure arising both from operations and from financing activities. However, if the exposure is necessary in order to meet other objectives, and the currency involved is fully convertible, there is also a range of financial arrangements that can be used to reduce or eliminate the exposure. These arrangements include contracts on the forward and futures markets, borrowing and investing on the money markets, and currency options. The choice depends on the nature of the exposure, the decision maker's risk preferences, market forecasts, and the access available to the various markets. The procedures can best be explained in the context of a brief example.

Example Problem

Assume the following situation: The receipt of 1 million GBP is expected in one year's time. It represents pure transaction exposure, and no offsetting currency transactions are planned or expected. The GBP cashflow could be a dividend payment, repayment of a loan, liquidation of an investment position, or even a long-dated trade receivable. For our purposes, however, we will assume there is virtual certainty associated with its receipt. We will specify our counting currency as U.S. dollars, and assume the following accessible market conditions.

Spot exchange rate	1.60 USD/GBP
1-year forward rate	1.56 USD/GBP
1-year interest rates	
USD	9.0%
GBP	11.8%

Notice that for clarity we have conveniently omitted the bid-and-offer spread on these quotations. Let us also assume the availability of a GBP put option as follows:

Maturity	1 year
Strike price	1.54 USD/GBP
Premium	.08 USD/GBP

How should this transaction exposure be managed? With access to all these market alternatives, our choice may depend on how much risk we wish to take, which decision, in turn, can depend on our (subjective) expectations concerning the future USD/GBP exchange rate. As discussed in Chapter 3 and elsewhere, the forward rate of 1.56 USD/GBP serves as a benchmark value of the future spot rate. Our degree of risk aversion and our own forecast, if any, of the future spot rate in comparison to the current forward rate will influence our choice of a risk-management method.

Risk Aversion and Market Forecasts

If we have no expectation concerning the future spot rate, and we are willing to take the foreign exchange risk, we may well choose to do nothing. No risk aversion in this instance means that we value the last dollar in a million dollar loss or gain as much as the first dollar of the loss or gain. For most individuals, and perhaps many companies, this would be inconceivable, but for large corporations it is quite possible. As we shall see, given our market-condition assumptions, and the lack of any forecast of our own of the future spot, hedging or covering in either the forward or the money markets does not change the expected value of the receivable (except for minor transaction costs). These contracts will only remove the uncertainty.

If we have no risk aversion for payoffs of this magnitude, then the uncertainty does not bother us, and we would be unwilling to commit the resources or pay whatever costs are involved in hedging the exposure. In most cases, the transaction cost involved in setting up the hedge or cover transaction is the bid-and-offer spread, which, in our example, we have assumed away. In practice, it could be significant, especially for smaller transactions. However, if the foreign currency is converted on a spot basis, the same basic bid-and-offer cost remains. Consequently, the incremental cost of doing the hedge is not likely to be a critical factor in the hedging decision.

On the other hand, we may decide to take the risk if:

1. Our forecast of the future spot differs from the hedge rate available in the forward market.

2. *And* we have a strong degree of confidence in this forecast.

3. *And* we are not burdened by aversion to risk.

In fact, if all the preceding conditions hold, we may choose to go beyond simply attempting to hedge or cover a given position and actually create net new currency exposure in the financial markets. The rationale for a policy decision to create exposure for profit is explored in Chapter 16. The point to be noted is that transaction exposure management:

1. Starts with a good measurement of current and anticipated currency exposure

2. Proceeds with a determination of the degree of risk aversion on the part on the decision makers

3. Requires a forecast or a view of future currency and money-market conditions, if any degree of risk is to be assumed

The forward rate can be used as a benchmark estimate of the future spot, or the decision-making group can develop its own forecast.

We can now turn to the specifics in choosing a hedge for the long GBP position assumed earlier. To illustrate how the willingness to develop an independent forecast of future market conditions and the willingness to take risk both affect the hedging decision, we will assume four different combinations of these variables.

Scenario 1: No Forecast of the Markets; Very Risk Averse. In this case, we believe we have enough risk exposure in normal business operations, and we want to avoid, if possible, all currency exposure. In addition, we have no particular forecasts for the currency and money markets. For our purposes, these markets are efficient, in the sense that all available (at least to us) information is already reflected in current market prices. We have the following choices, which we might assess as follows:

Forward-Market Hedge. We could sell the GBP forward at 1.56 USD/GBP and realize 1,560,000 USD in one year's time. The "loss" compared with the value available, if we had the GBP now, is apparent. It is the difference between the 1,600,000 USD value at the spot exchange rate and 1,560,000 USD one year hence, available through the forward contract. On the other hand, we cannot gain possession of the GBP for a year, and the contract at least removes all doubt about the USD value of the GBP when we do get them. Given our risk aversion and lack of a forecast, this alternative looks good unless another choice produces a higher yield with equal certainty.

Money-Market Hedge. We could create a money-market hedge. That is, we could establish a currency position in the money market with a payoff position as a function of the future spot exchange rate exactly opposite that of our current pound exposure. As our current exposure is long GBP, we would, therefore, go short GBP on the money market by borrowing GBP and exchanging them for USD on a spot basis. To compute an exact cost for this transaction we will assume that we have no need for the USD realized and, therefore, will invest them for a year at the available money-market rates. This assumption will produce a result that can be compared with the forward contract above because both will make USD available at year end.

The cost of the money-market hedge under our assumptions is simply the difference in interest rates. We borrow GBP at 11.8 percent, convert to USD, and invest the USD proceeds at 9 percent. It appears that we pay a price to remove the risk. However, if we believe the current forward price is a reasonable estimate of the future spot (at least to the extent that we are unwilling to make our own forecast), and we cannot realize the GBP for a year, then the money is lost even if we do nothing, and the money-market hedge provides the risk removal at no extra cost. Actually, it is not quite free; remember that we have assumed away market transaction costs in this example.

It might be useful to compare the actual USD cost of the forward- and money-market hedges. Both arrangements remove the exchange exposure. The only problem in cost comparison is our assumption of the investment of the USD proceeds of the converted GBP loan in the money market. We will relax this assumption shortly.

The cost of the forward cover is as stated. It is the difference between the 1,600,000 USD value, if the receivable could be converted at the current spot exchange rate, and the 1,560,000 USD value from the forward contract when it matures in one year. Since the 1,600,000 USD value is common to both the money-market and forward-market hedging alternatives, our preference depends on whether the money-market hedge can produce value in excess of 1,560,000 USD one year hence. Let us find out by specifying the money-market hedge transactions.

1. Borrow just enough GBP so that the GBP receivable when due will exactly repay principal and interest on the loan. Since the loan rate is 11.8 percent, we would borrow 894,454 GBP:

Principal	1,000,000/1.118	=	894,454
Interest	$\dfrac{894,454 \times .118 \times 365}{365}$	=	105,546
Principal and interest			1,000,000

2. Convert the loan proceeds to dollars at the spot exchange rate of 1.60 USD/GBP:

$$894,454 \text{ GBP} \times 1.60 \text{ USD/GBP} = 1,431,126 \text{ USD}$$

3. Invest the USD at the USD money-market rate of 9 percent to produce a value in one year's time of 1,559,928 USD.

$$1,431,126 \times 1.09 = 1,559,928 \text{ USD}$$

This value is only 72 USD less than that produced by the forward-market contract; 72 USD on 1.6 million USD is not likely to sway the decision one way or another.

In practice, the money-market hedge may not be as attractive for most corporations as the forward market. One reason is that the forward rate is based on the deposit (offer) rates in GBP and USD. In the above case, the company would thus be paying the bid-and-offer spread on the GBP loan (made at the bid rate). In addition, most companies borrow from their banks and pay a credit spread. These spreads vary depending on the credit risk of the borrower, but, in general, they range between .25 and 2 percent. The bid-and-offer spread and the credit spread thus make the money-market alternative less attractive to this group of companies. However, many governments and some larger companies can raise funds at lower rates than can the major banks, and, therefore, they may have a natural advantage in using the money-market hedge rather than the forward market.

In addition, the money-market hedge gets cash into the hands of the company more quickly than does the forward contract. The corporate reinvestment rate on cash is often much higher than the money market investment rate (9 percent in this case). If so, the economics may favor the money-market hedge. Cash could also be realized more quickly using the forward-market hedge, if the receivable was used as collateral for a dollar loan. However, the loan cost, including the credit spread cited above, would rarely be less than the effective cost of the cash realized early under a GBP loan associated with the money-market hedge.

In addition to the economics of the transaction, it should be recognized that the money-market deal will show on the balance sheet and increase the debt-to-equity ratio, neither of which may be desirable. The forward contract is typically footnoted only. For reporting purposes we may prefer the latter.

Do Nothing. We could forget both the forward market and the money market and simply do nothing about the 1 million GBP receivable. We would then accept the pounds when available in one year's time and sell them for dollars at the spot exchange rate at that time.

Under scenario 1 this alternative is less attractive than either of the preceding two because of our assumed aversion to risk and because of our lack of a specific forecast of the future value of the pound to justify acceptance of the exposure.

Buy a GBP Put Option.   We can also buy a GBP put option which, in this case, gives us the right, but not the obligation, to sell the GBP when received one year hence, at 1.54 USD/GBP. The option cost assumed in this example is .08 USD/GBP. If the GBP is worth less than 1.54 USD/GBP when we collect the receivable, we would clearly exercise the option and sell the GBP at 1.54, netting 1.46 USD/GBP. Remember that we have already paid and cannot recover the .08 USD/GBP premium. In addition, conventional options require payment of the premium when the option is purchased. Strictly speaking, therefore, the net proceeds would be less than 1.46 USD/GBP, given the cost of financing the premium.

The relative value of the GBP put option lies in the result we enjoy if the future spot is above 1.64 USD/GBP. Recall that the 1.56 value is available from both the forward- and money-market alternatives. In order to break even against these alternatives, the spot at expiry must equal 1.56 plus the .08 premium cost. The breakeven spot rate is, therefore, 1.64 USD/GBP, plus the small cost of financing the premium. For a price, the downside risk is removed, but the upside potential is still there.

In addition, we must note that markets can be quite volatile and that the GBP could be considerably stronger at some point between now and collection of the receivable. Should this occur, the company could sell the GBP forward and lock up the higher rate. Having done this, the company would no longer need the option for hedging purposes. The option could possibly be sold to recover a small part of the original premium or utilized in a more aggressive trading approach. Options, in general, are very versatile, and they lend themselves to a wide variety of trading strategies. Chapters 8 and 10 provide more detailed information on this product.

In this case, however, we do need a future spot greater than 1.64 to improve on the forward- and money-market hedges. In the absence of a strong market forecast, and given substantial risk aversion, the put option may not be attractive under scenario 1.

Let us now see how our alternatives compare under slightly more aggressive scenarios.

Scenario 2: Our Own Forecast; Very Risk Averse.   Many managers may fall under this category. It is difficult to work with currencies and the problems caused by their value changes without forming some sort of opinion regarding future currency values. Moreover, most of us are risk-averse.

We know what we can do with options, forward contracts, and money-market deals. These opportunities are outlined above and elsewhere in the book. What we choose depends on the balance between our confidence in our forecast and our degree of risk aversion.

Forward contracts and money-market hedges produce square positions. They essentially take the player out of the game; the only residual risk is that of failure on the part of the hedged cashflows themselves to materialize on schedule. Option-dated forwards or cash-management swaps can be used if timing is the only issue, and currency options work well in instances where there is doubt about the cashflows themselves. These alternatives would be entirely appropriate for managers whose forecasts are worse than the forward price. In the preceding example, the forward price will guarantee 1.56 USD/GBP. If a manager's forecast is for a future spot substantially lower than 1.56, a hedging strategy is clearly indicated.

Managers may be risk-averse and still choose not to cover, if they believe there will be better rates in the future at which to hedge the exposure or if they believe the eventual payoff will justify the risk. The distinguishing behavior under this scenario is a willingness to take the risk. The position should be closely monitored, with the expectation that prices will move in the right direction. If they do, more value can be locked in later with a contract. If they do not, some loss may result before the position can be closed. In order to control the exposure, policy guidelines may set limits on how far the position can deteriorate before the forecast is abandoned and hedges are put in place.

Scenario 3: No Forecast; No Risk Aversion. As indicated earlier, if we have no risk aversion at these payoff limits, and we have no strong beliefs about future values of the spot rate, there may be no point in covering the transaction exposure. We are free to choose on the basis of expected value, and the expected value of the uncovered position is as high as any. Given scenario 3, we would do nothing.

Scenario 4: A Forecast Different from the Forward Rate; No Risk Aversion. This scenario would once again change our choice of exposure-management methods. At the limit, to the extent that we really have no risk aversion and are highly confident in our forecast, the door is wide open to trading or speculating in the financial markets. Let us work through a short example, with a particular forecast for the spot one year hence of 1.52 USD/GBP.

If we really believe the future spot will be 1.52 USD/GBP, and we want to avoid any "loss" on the original sterling receivable by realizing the full value of 1,600,000 USD which would be available at the current spot rate, the forward market offers us an opportunity. For instance, we could sell forward 2 million GBP, or twice as many as we expect to receive one year from now, at the available forward price of 1.56 USD/GBP. If our forecast is correct, we can buy back 1 million GBP at spot for 1.52 USD/GBP at contract maturity, deliver them against the contract, and make .04 USD per GBP. This gain is then added to the 1.56 rate achieved on the forward contract for the actual receivable, and an effective rate of 1.60 is achieved.

This happy result may appear better than it is. It is only going to happen if the market moves as expected. We really are net short 1 million GBP, and if the GBP strengthened, we could have a loss on the speculative 1 million GBP position, which would reduce the effective hedge rate.

To go a step further with this scenario, there is no need to wait for operations or financing activities to produce transaction exposure. You can generate it for yourself. If you really believe a currency is going to move in a certain direction, positions can be taken in options, in forward contracts, in futures contracts, or on a spot basis. Basically, these positions result where the "strong" currency is purchased and invested or the "weak" currency is borrowed.

Before we sell the business and embark on a career of currency speculation, it might be useful to ask where our competitive skills and talents lie. The answer is probably in the product and/or service markets in which the firm is engaged. The business may sell insurance or manufacture computer chips, and currency positions are simply a result of that activity, or a means to accomplish it more efficiently. In almost all cases, this is as it should be, notwithstanding the fact that a growing number of major corporations are developing and expanding in-house currency trading operations. Even though these trading functions may be done on a profit center basis, they should clearly be regarded as a means to an end. That is, the trading activities should be carried on as a means to gain more sophistication and efficiency in trading currencies in order to reduce the risks and costs of carrying on the organization's primary business. Having said this, if managers have specific forecasts, and feel comfortable with controlled currency and interest-rate exposure, there are ongoing opportunities to bet on the market.

Other Examples of Transaction Exposure

The preceding discussion of transaction exposure was concerned with measuring the overall exposure position of the organization, and thinking about appropriate responses, given available currency forecasts and management attitudes toward risk. It may also be useful to look at some particular types of business activities that give rise to transaction exposure, in addition to the basic trade accounts and financing activities discussed earlier. Three such areas are the maintenance of a futures contract margin, publication of price lists, and submission of project tenders. In addition, Chapter 13 deals with exposure measurement and management in commodity transactions.

Margin Requirements on Commodity Futures Contracts

If futures contracts are used consistently over a long period of time to hedge commodity positions, the core margin requirements on the contracts could be viewed as an actual investment of funds. At the very least, it certainly represents use of working capital. On the other hand, if hedging is sporadic or if the hedged amount changes frequently, a company can be faced with significant cashflow volatility.

For American corporations dealing on USD-based margins, the margin requirements do not pose any direct foreign exchange risk. They are simply a cash-management issue. For companies whose primary currency is not the USD, the USD margin may create foreign exchange exposure. If the company has extensive involvement in USD transactions, the margin may simply be part of the company's overall USD cash- and exposure-management activities. For companies that have no USD cashflow to provide a natural way of financing the margin, the margin can be of concern from a foreign exchange standpoint.

If margin is needed for extended periods of time, the company may view the margin as an investment and simply buy USD outright. This strategy is attractive if the company forecasts that the USD will strengthen against the company's home currency. If the USD is expected to weaken, however, then the company may prefer instead to borrow USD to finance the margin requirement. In either case, as the USD can have significant swings over time, the company should review the method for funding the margin to see if another alternative is more appropriate.

If some or all of the margin is needed for intermittent periods of time, one method for handling the exposure is to deal a cash-management swap. The company buys USD spot to fund the margin and simultaneously sells USD forward. If the margin is still required when the forward contract matures, the position is rolled forward via another swap. If the margin requirements decline, the surplus USD cash position can be invested in a USD investment vehicle or else swapped back into the company's home currency.

Price Lists

Many businesses buy and sell products using price lists. Consider an Australian company that has no real competition in the widget business. It buys its widgets from a nearby manufacturer and distributes them in the domestic market. All revenues and expenses are in local currency. In this environment, price lists could be used without foreign currency exposure.

If, however, the company's price list is "guaranteed" for several months and a foreign-currency-based supplier is involved, the company's profit margins could get squeezed. This situation could easily arise, for instance, if the supplier is in Germany and the DEM appreciates. From the Australian company's standpoint, if the goods are purchased in DEM, this "price increase" in the DEM could be avoided for the duration of the price list by buying DEM on a forward basis or by buying DEM calls. If the Australian company is paying for the widgets in AUD, it could hope that the DEM supplier sold the AUD forward, which would similarly preserve the exchange rate on the business. If the business is done in AUD, and if the supplier does not hedge, and also makes it known that any foreign exchange losses are for the buyer's account, the AUD company has several choices.

1. First, it could again buy DEM forward and then sell them back after the DEM strengthened. This type of hedge is not frequently seen, as there is the risk that the DEM could weaken and the German supplier might not reduce its AUD price. If so, the Australian company would have a foreign exchange hedge loss but would not receive the offsetting benefit on the widget price.

2. A second arrangement that would be desirable, but is not typical, is a price agreement under which the Australian company could purchase the widgets in either DEM or AUD. This arrangement effectively incorporates a currency option, which of course has considerable benefits. However, the cost of the option would have to be built into the base cost of the widgets.

3. A third tactic is to match the terms of purchase with the terms of sale so that any price changes on the purchase side are passed on to the sales side, that is, to the Australian company's clients. If this is feasible, one could question if there really is a foreign exchange risk for the Australian company.

4. A fourth strategy is to have alternative suppliers on a global scale so that the AUD company has access to the lowest-cost producer(s) in the world at all times. Again, this may or may not be practical.

With some imported products, such as fresh produce, the inventory turnover is rapid. Price lists are changed very quickly, as they must take into account the price of the commodity as well as exchange-rate movements. Canada imports a considerable amount of fresh produce from the United States, and prices are volatile. Although competition is strong, considerable benefits can accrue if a Canadian distributor can gain a price advantage through buying USD at better rates. Conversely, considerable disadvantages can occur if one is less competitive on the foreign exchange front.

Foreign exchange management can be a key element in the competitiveness of companies in many industries besides food. If the industry as a whole hedges on a spot basis, an individual company can do the same and try to be successful on its operating and marketing strengths. Alternatively, it may try to use aggressive foreign exchange management as a vehicle to gain a competitive advantage. There are track records to show that this strategy has indeed proved successful over long periods of time. The question is whether management is comfortable with the exposure and whether it is able and willing to commit the required resources to this activity.

Project Tenders

Tendering is widely used to award contract work. Except for cost plus projects, almost all projects involve uncertainty with respect to profitability. Future base costs and completion schedules cannot be known with certainty. However, once the project has been won, the winning company should be able to look forward to making a reasonable return. In tendering international projects, though, the economics of the tender can change dramatically because of adverse foreign exchange price movements. Net revenues could decline if there is a weakening in the foreign currency in which the receivables are denominated. Alternatively, expenses could increase if the currencies in which they are denominated rise. Automatically hedging such contingent risks is not the answer either. Consider the following situation.

The project, if won, will result in AUD revenues for a British company. Almost all expenses will be in GBP. One way the company could protect itself during the tendering process is to sell AUD forward. If the project is won, the AUD will be delivered on the contracts, and all is well. However, if the tender is not successful, the company will have to buy back the AUD it sold. If the AUD strengthens, the company will lose. In effect, the forward contract changes the risk from being long AUD if the project is won to being short AUD if the project tender is lost. Deciding which risk to take requires a forecast of both the future spot and the probability that the tender will be won.

A second alternative is to buy AUD put options. If the tender is won, the option can be used as protection against the AUD receivable, as in the case of any other foreign currency receivable. If the tender is lost, the company is only at risk for the amount of the put premium. Moreover, the option could still have residual value which would reduce the loss. In fact, if the AUD weakened, the put could be worth more than it originally cost, and the company could make money even if the tender is lost. The drawback, however, is that the options can be expensive.

If a company submits many tenders, it may take a portfolio view in two ways:

1. It might "self-insure" the risks by paying the premium on options to itself. This pool of premiums may then be used to offset any foreign exchange losses that arise on tenders that are won.

2. It might use one option as a hedge against a series of tenders. For instance, consider a company whose track record is to win 1 in 5 tenders. If there are 10 tenders outstanding with a value of 10 million USD each, an option portfolio of 20 million USD could be established as a hedge against the 100 million USD in tenders.

$$10 \times 10,000,000 \text{ USD} \times .2 = 20,000,000 \text{ USD}$$

Tenders involving foreign exchange risk should usually be bid accordingly. Premiums for options can be included, or some form of pricing protection can be built into the project costs. The company awarding the project may find that it can best provide the currency protection during the tendering phase and thus may buy options on behalf of the various companies submitting bids.

12
Economic
Exposure

Executive Summary

Economic exposure refers to the effect that a real move in a foreign exchange rate may have on the future operating cashflows of a business. These cashflows are important because the market value or worth of a business is the present value of all its future cashflows. This chapter will show, with specific numerical examples, how a move in the real foreign exchange rate can change the cashflows and value of a firm, and will indicate some types of business operations that are particularly subject to economic exposure. The chapter closes with some guidelines for managing this exposure.

Defining Economic Exposure

Economic exposure is a measure of the reduction in cashflow and value that a business may experience as a result of a real adjustment in the foreign exchange rate. Before we work through some examples, however, let us consider the process. Cashflow and value depend on profitability, while profitability depends on prices and volumes, and particularly on the competitive position of the business. If another firm can sell your product in your market for considerably less money than you can, your business could be in trouble. A real change in a currency exchange rate may enable a competitor to do just that.

Foreign Exchange Rates and Prices

Foreign exchange rates are really just prices. The exchange rate as a price becomes relevant when the extent of import and export activity in most markets, and the increasing degree of globalization of business operations, is considered. If your prime competitor is in another country, a move in the exchange rate may make a real and permanent change in its cost structure compared with yours.

A classic example of the indirect effect on competitive position is that of an electric utility in the United States selling to domestic steel and automobile manufacturers. One might assume that because all the utility's sales and factor costs were denominated in dollars and made in the United States, the utility should have no economic exposure to an exchange-rate move. However, if the dollar climbs sharply against the yen, the utility's customers may fall on very hard times indeed. Export opportunities for steel and cars from the United States may be sharply reduced, and even the home markets of these customers may become less profitable due to the presence of cheaper imports secured from off-shore suppliers. As a result, the sales volumes and prices of the utility will come under a great deal of pressure, even though it is, at first glance, an entirely domestic business operation. Its future cashflows will be affected, as will the value of the firm itself.

We mentioned earlier that to constitute economic exposure, the move in the foreign exchange rate had to be real. As discussed more fully in Chapter 2, a real exchange-rate move is one that is not offset by a corresponding inflation differential in the two countries whose exchange rates are involved.

In a highly simplified example, if the dollar/mark rate is 2.00 DEM/USD, and this rate changes to 1.818 DEM/USD, it would seem that a price change had occurred. With this dollar devaluation, American exporters should enjoy windfall gains in the German market (the deutsche mark revenues are worth more dollars), and German exporters should suffer substantial losses (the dollar revenues are worth fewer deutsche marks), at least in the American market. However, in the case of the German exporters, the loss could be offset if the dollar prices could be increased. If the American economy experienced considerably higher inflation than the German economy, it is possible that the dollar price levels might rise by enough so that both exporters would be unaffected. If this were the case, there would be no real move in the exchange rate, and no change in competitive position.

Adjusting Foreign Exchange Rates for Inflation

Specifically, suppose the American inflation was 10 percent, while there was no German inflation at all. What would be the real or effective adjustment in the exchange rate, given that the nominal, or observed, rate moved from 2.00 DEM/USD to 1.818 DEM/USD?

To answer this question, we must adjust the move in the observed exchange rate for the inflation differential. Price levels in the United States went up by 10 percent, while price levels in Germany did not change at all. As a result, our German exporter has more dollars from the export sales in the United States, with no change in unit volume, and, therefore, no change, we assume, in deutsche mark costs. The extra dollars received will just offset the decline in the deutsche mark value of each dollar. The new exchange rate multiplied by the "extra" dollars just equals the old exchange rate:

$$1.818 \text{ DEM/USD } (1.1/1.0) = 2.00 \text{ DEM/USD}$$

In this case, nothing has changed. We can see why there has been no change in competitive position. United States producers have raised their dollar prices with American inflation, and so have the German producers exporting into the American market. The German producers' deutsche mark proceeds from the dollar sales have not changed, nor have their deutsche mark costs. The American producers' increased dollar prices have just been offset by the inflated domestic costs. Neither competitor is better off. This leads us to an important conclusion, as suggested at the beginning of this section. Economic exposure results only from a real change in exchange rates, and a real change in a exchange rate results when a nominal or observed change is not offset by a proportional difference in rates of inflation.

Real Adjustments in the Exchange Rate

Before we go on to look at what happens to business when a real adjustment in the exchange rate occurs, it is useful to remember that real moves in the exchange rate do happen. Exhibits 2.1 through 2.5 show both the nominal and real rate changes for the U.S. dollar against the yen, the mark, sterling, and the Canadian dollar for the period 1974–1990. In each case, the nominal rate is the reported rate, and the real rate is the nominal rate adjusted for the inflation differential as measured by the consumer price index. Real moves in the exchange rate do, in fact, occur, and the size of the moves is large enough to cause a substantial shift in competitive position for firms affected by the resultant price changes.

Examples of Economic Gains and Losses

Examples of winners and losers abound. In the late 1970s, Laker Airways, a U.K. company, was a profitable and rapidly growing airline. However, the very strong dollar in the early 1980s discouraged American holidays for Britons, and also made the firm's unhedged U.S. dollar debt, incurred to finance the aircraft, prohibitively expensive.

About the same time, this real strength of the dollar against the yen initially gave Japanese auto manufacturers a big lift in their efforts to capture market share in the United States. By the time the dollar subsequently declined, Japanese exporters had had time to set up North American manufacturing plants and to upgrade the luxury and quality of their products. The redesigned products were more able to absorb dollar price increases, without a loss in unit volume.

Finally, we can look at the Canadian dollar exchange rate, and observe that even though Canadians have, from time to time, professed concern about their "weakening" currency, and American producers have objected to an undervalued Canadian dollar, the reality is otherwise. Over the last decade (1980–1990) the Canadian dollar, adjusted for differential inflation, has gained, not lost, strength against its American counterpart.

Measuring Economic Exposure: Scenario Building

Exposure is the size or scope of a potential loss; risk is the probability that the loss will occur. When we consider economic exposure, the risk is measured as the probability of a move in the foreign exchange rate, and the exposure is the amount of financial loss that will occur if the rate move occurs. In this section we will take the rate move as a given, and explore ways to calculate the size of the ensuing loss. Chapter 4 has discussed exchange-rate forecasting methods (risk estimation), and the last section of this chapter will look at ways to manage the overall exposure.

We mentioned earlier that a move in the foreign exchange rate, unaccompanied by a corresponding degree of differential inflation, is a real price change. Suppose a ton of a particular product costs 200 DEM in Germany and 100 USD in America, and the exchange rate is 2 DEM/USD. Clearly, the product is the same price in both countries. Now suppose the exchange rate moves to 1.818 DEM/USD with no change in price levels (inflation) in either country. A German buyer could purchase 100 USD for 181.80 DEM and use the dollars to purchase a ton of the product, realizing a saving of almost 20 DEM per ton. If we assume no transportation costs, tariffs, duties, or other barriers to trade, this situation could not exist for long, because no well-informed buyer would purchase the product at the 200 DEM price in Germany. In other words, in our hypothetical world of no trade barriers and perfect information, a given article must have the same price in all places and, in particular, in all currencies.

This conclusion suggests that when a real currency move causes a price difference for a product between countries, the product price in one of the countries will have to change, or both prices will adjust somewhat to eliminate the difference. The critical issue for business firms operating in this environment is: Which price will change, how fast will it change, and how will that change affect the business? These questions are at the heart of economic exposure. We will consider them separately and then combine them in the numerical example that follows.

Price Makers and Price Takers

The price change issue really depends on the location of the marginal producers and consumers of the product in question. They are the price makers, as opposed to the price takers. The actions of these parties determine the equilibrium price for any good or service. Price takers are the producers or consumers whose transactions are more or less independent of price; they have no choice, or their volumes are so small that their participation or lack of it will have a negligible effect on the market price. In the DEM/USD product-pricing case above, if the price makers are in Germany, then the new dollar price will be the old DEM price expressed in dollars at the new exchange rate:

New USD price = 200 DEM (1/1.818 DEM/USD) = 110 USD

This would be the result, for example, for a German designed and manufactured product, of which only a very small part of the volume was exported. In addition, perhaps the exporting was done on an opportunistic basis. That is, the manufacturer did not care about the export business and simply filled the occasional export order, on receipt, at domestic German prices. In this case, the price adjustment is all for the account of dollar-based businesses; such businesses would see their dollar costs rising if the product were purchased or their dollar revenues rising if the product were sold.

If, however, the price makers are in America, the exchange-rate move will not affect the dollar price. The new dollar price would equal the old dollar price of 100 USD. It is the DEM price that would adjust. The new DEM price would be the old dollar price at the new exchange rate:

New DEM price = 100 USD (1.818 DEM/USD) = 181.80 DEM

Of course, in this case the DEM-based businesses would feel the price shock and would have to make changes to accommodate the real DEM price change.

Currency of Determination

These are extreme examples. We have assumed that the product is priced entirely in one currency, the currency of determination. This is rarely, if ever, the case, and particularly not if the currencies in question are both major trading currencies. For example, oil and many other commodities are traditionally priced in USD. Theoretically, a real change in the dollar/mark or the dollar/yen exchange rate would not affect the dollar price for oil. However, both Germany and Japan are major consumers of oil, and a change in the deutsche mark and yen oil prices might change their purchase volumes enough to affect the dollar price. In such a case, some of the adjustment to the price change would be made by the dollar-based businesses and some by the deutsche-mark- and yen-based businesses.

In summary, abstracting from transport cost and government interference, tradable goods tend to cost the same in real terms around the world. When a real move in the foreign exchange rate occurs, initially the product price will differ by currency. A real change in the product price, as expressed in one or both of the currencies, will occur. Which price changes, and by how much, will depend on which is the currency of determination, or the currency of the price makers. In the extreme case, players based in this currency will notice no change; their counterparts working in the other currency will make all the adjustment.

Price Elasticity of Demand

The second and equally important dimension of exposure is how the price change will affect a particular business. The answer depends in part on the change in volume which occurs as a result of the price change. Consider an American business that is exporting product to Germany. If the USD devalues and the currency of determination for that product is dollars, then there will be a real decline in the DEM price. This situation offers the exporter both a problem and an opportunity. The problem is to determine a new optimum DEM price, and the opportunity is to consider the price elasticity of demand for the product; that is, by how much will the volume increase when the price is reduced? Elasticity (E) is usually expressed as the percentage change in volume divided by the percentage change in price:

$$E = \frac{\text{change in volume/old volume}}{\text{change in price/old price}}$$

If E is greater than 1, a price reduction will increase revenue, because the loss in unit price will be more than made up by the volume increase. For example, if a price of 10 USD produces a volume of 100 units, and a price of 8 USD (a 20 percent reduction) produces a volume of 160 units (a 60 percent increase), then E would equal 3 (60/20), and following the reduction, revenue would increase from 1000 USD to 1280 USD.

	Volume		Price		Revenue
Old	100	×	10	=	1000
New	160	×	8	=	1280
Change	+60		−2		
Percent change	60%		20%		
Elasticity	60/20 = 3				

The adjustment may or may not be good news, depending on the change in contribution or profit margin per unit, but the real DEM price decline offered by the exchange-rate movement, together with the concept of demand elasticity, offers the exporter an opportunity. In the case of a relatively inelastic demand, the best choice may be to keep the DEM price where it was and simply accept the increased dollar receipts afforded by the more favorable exchange rate. We will see, in a numerical example, that assumptions about elasticity of demand are critical when measuring the degree of economic exposure, assuming a real move in the exchange rate. In other words, we have to know, or at least have an opinion about, what will happen to volumes when the prices change.

The Exposure Measurement Process

We now have the building blocks in place to measure economic exposure. We know the exchange-rate move has to be real. For a given currency, in any particular economic environment, we can think about the probability or likelihood of this happening. In addition, for any given rate move, we can assess the financial loss or gain for the business by anticipating the nature of the subsequent product price and volume adjustments. These adjustments will depend on which currency is the currency of determination for the product in question, and on the price elasticity of demand.

The preceding sounds like a long and difficult process, which would at best yield uncertain results. However, in practice, it is often much easier than it seems. Managers familiar with product markets know which currency is the currency of determination, and good marketing people understand very well what will happen to volumes given a particular price change. Forecasting the exact timing and size of an exchange-rate adjustment is not easy and, in fact, may be impossible. However, all we need is the prior likelihood, and a sense of the direction, of an impending move. Managers can then usefully estimate the gains or losses that would result, given that move, and change their corporate strategy or tactics accordingly.

Importers, Exporters, Domestics, and World Businesses

We must also consider the basic activity of the business unit in question. Broadly speaking, for our purposes, we can group businesses in four categories: importers, exporters, domestics, and global businesses. The activities of importers and exporters are self-explanatory. A domestic is defined as a firm whose activities are restricted to the geographical boundaries of its own country. Global businesses are the truly international companies, which both manufacture and market product in many different countries.

Defining the primary business activity helps in anticipating the gain or loss following a currency move. For example, a real currency devaluation would represent a serious situation for an importer of a product if that product's currency of determination was the domestic (devalued) currency and the demand was elastic. High elasticity of demand would result from the presence of highly competitive domestic products, or readily available substitutes. In this case, the importer would have no opportunity to raise the domestic currency price, and the domestic currency cost of importation would increase by the extent of the devaluation. If, on the other hand, the currency of determination was abroad and the demand was inelastic, the domestic currency price would rise with the devaluation, because customers would have no alternative source of supply, and no substitutes, for a required product. Our importer would then be no better or worse off than before the devaluation.

The fate of the exporting firm is, of course, the mirror image of that of the importing business, given a real currency move. How a domestic business would fare is more complex; it depends on how the currency change will affect both the firm's competition and its customers. An entirely domestically oriented vacation resort can lose even its domestic customers if its operating currency increases sharply in value, and its former customers decide to take less expensive vacations abroad. Or, in a more familiar example, a domestic firm can simply be forced out of business by a "low-cost" imported product, following real increases in the domestic currency value. This occurs because the competition's production costs are in currencies that give them a competitive advantage. One possible result is offshore product sourcing by the domestic firm as a survival strategy, either by importing or by manufacturing abroad.

Shifts in competitive position occur because of changes in productivity as well. For example, the struggle for the North American automobile market has been characterized by both productivity differences and currency swings. We do note, however, that the North American producers are now marketing substantial amounts of product that has been produced abroad.

The global business usually has more flexibility to deal with a single currency change. The firm may avoid economic loss if it can sell in different markets, or source product from different countries, quickly and easily in response to a currency move. The economic exposure is still there, and the potential for serious loss still exists. However, with good planning and management, the problems can be handled more effectively than, for example, those of single-business importing or exporting enterprises. The last section of this chapter will consider ways and means of managing economic exposure.

Foreign and Domestic Ownership

The issue of foreign, as opposed to domestic, ownership of the business also affects the measurement of exposure, because it determines the currency of account; that is, in which currency are we measuring results or corporate performance? The answer is, most frequently, the currency of the majority of the shareholders. For a domestically owned firm, economic exposure measurement stops with an assessment of the impact of the currency change on the local currency operating cashflows. In the case of a foreign-owned business the analysis must go one step further and consider also the effect of the currency move on the parent currency value of these domestic currency cashflows. This second-level valuation can either increase or reduce the exposure as measured in the domestic currency. For example, an importing firm's local currency returns may be improved by a strengthening local currency, and this improvement may be reinforced if these cashflows are converted to a parent's relatively weaker currency.

An Example of Exposure Measurement

Finally, let us now look at a numerical example of the measurement of economic exposure. The purpose is to show that useful estimates of the size and direction of the cashflow and value changes, which would result from specified exchange-rate moves, can be made. Such estimates are possible even though knowledge of the underlying relationships is far from perfect.

The ownership issue can be explored by assuming a Canadian subsidiary of an American parent. First, we will measure the economic exposure in local currency (LC), as if the firm were a Canadian-owned enterprise. We will then do the conversion into USD (foreign currency, FC), as would be the case if there were an American parent.

The effect of the currency of determination and elasticity-of-demand factors can be examined by assuming three examples, or scenarios, involving different corporate product lines. The effect of the type of business operation will be explored by assuming a firm that exports half its output and that imports raw material worth about one-quarter of its direct product costs. The business is, therefore, a blend of the importer/exporter/domestic categories specified above.

In order to construct consistent financial statements, we will make the following assumptions:

Cash	5% of sales
Accounts receivable	90 days of sales
Inventory	90 days of sales at direct cost
Accounts payable	90 days of purchases

Exhibit 12.1 shows our base-case balance sheet and income statement, stated in the local (and, we assume, operating) currency, which in our example would be Canadian dollars.

Our base-case exchange rate will be 1.2 CAD/USD, and we will measure the economic exposure of our business assuming a real 20 percent devaluation of the Canadian dollar, to a new exchange rate of 1.5 CAD/USD. The exposure will be measured under each of three product-type scenarios. The three scenarios are:

Exhibit 12.1. Base-Case Balance Sheet and Income Statement

Balance Sheet			
Cash, LC	200,000	Accounts payable, LC	250,000
Accounts receivable	1,000,000		
Inventory	500,000	Long-term debt	1,000,000
Net fixed assets	2,000,000	Equity	2,450,000
Total assets	3,700;000	Total liabilities	3,700,000

Income Statement			
	Units	LC per unit	
Domestic sales	10,000	200	LC 2,000,000
Export sales	10,000	200	2,000,000
Cost of sales			
Labor		50	1,000,000
Domestic raw material		25	500,000
Imported raw material		25	500,000
Cost per unit		100	
Operating income			2,000,000
Fixed cash operating cost		LC 600,000	
Depreciation expense		300,000	
Interest		100,000	
Total fixed cost			1,000,000
Net income before tax			1,000,000
Income tax			400,000
Net income			600,000
Add back depreciation			300,000
LC cashflow from operations*			LC 900,000
FC value of cashflow [(1.2 LC)/(FC)]			FC 750,000

*Assumes no net change in noncash working capital.

1. A global product (currency of determination abroad) with inelastic demand
2. A domestic product (currency of determination Canadian dollars) with inelastic demand
3. A global product with elastic demand

For the imported raw materials the currency of determination will be abroad, in all three scenarios. The currency of determination of the locally supplied raw materials is, in all cases, the local currency. The volume of raw material purchases will reflect changes in total sales vol-

Exhibit 12.2. Scenario 1: Producing a World Product (e.g., Steel);
Importing a Raw Material (e.g., Energy, Oil)

	Export sales	Domestic sales	Imported raw material	Domestic raw material
Currency of determination	Abroad	Abroad	Abroad	Domestic
Price elasticity of demand	Inelastic	Inelastic		
LC price change, given LC devaluation	Up 25%	Up 25%	Up 25%	No change
Unit volume change	None	None	None	None

umes. We can summarize these scenario attributes in Exhibits 12.2,
12.3, and 12.4.

Given the market structure suggested in scenario 1, the devaluation is
clearly good news. With product pricing based in the foreign currency
and with inelastic demand (no substitutes), the local currency product
price rises to offset the devaluation exactly, with no change in unit volumes. As shown above, the increase in the effective local currency price
is 25 percent. We now receive (and pay) 1.5 local currency units, rather
than 1.2, for each unit of foreign currency arising from business transactions. Our company's cost structure is affected by the increased cost of
imported raw materials, but not nearly enough to offset the increase in
revenue, because all the other local currency costs have not changed.

In scenario 2, the company's production is really designed for the domestic market, even though a high proportion (half) of the unit sales
are exported. Had there been significant import competition, our busi-

Exhibit 12.3. Scenario 2: Producing a Domestic Product (e.g., High-
Fashion Clothing); Importing a Raw Material (e.g., Textiles)

	Export sales	Domestic sales	Imported raw material	Domestic raw material
Currency of determination	Domestic	Domestic	Abroad	Domestic
Price elasticity of demand	Inelastic	Inelastic		
LC price change, given the LC devaluation	None	None	Up 25%	None
Unit volume change	None	None	None	None

Exhibit 12.4. Scenario 3: Producing a Global Product (e.g., Recreational Boats); Importing a Raw Material (e.g., Fittings and Parts)

	Export sales	Domestic sales	Imported raw material	Domestic raw material
Currency of determination	Abroad	Abroad	Abroad	Domestic
Price elasticity of demand	Elastic	Elastic		
LC price change, given the LC devaluation	Up 19%	Up 19%	Up 25%	Up 5%
Unit volume change	Up 20%	Down 10%	Up 5%	Up 5%

ness might have captured market share with the rising cost of the imports. However, under our assumptions, the only change attributable to the devaluation is an increased cost for the imported raw materials. To the extent that we are unable to substitute domestically sourced raw materials, the business will suffer with the devaluation. Note that there is no increase in export unit volumes in spite of a reduction in foreign currency prices. This reflects our assumption of a completely inelastic demand curve.

Finally, scenario 3 relaxes some of the restrictive assumptions of the first two scenarios. We again consider a global product, with an offshore currency of determination, but now we assume some price elasticity of demand; that is, the demand for our product will vary inversely with price.

Our highly competent management team has raised both domestic and local currency export prices by 19 percent, to LC 238 per unit. Translating this price to foreign currency at the new exchange rate produces a price about 5 percent less than the old foreign currency price.

$$\text{Old FC price} = \frac{\text{LC } 200}{1.2 \text{ LC per FC}} = \text{FC } 167$$

$$\text{New FC price} = \frac{\text{LC } 238}{1.5 \text{ LC per FC}} = \text{FC } 158$$

$$\text{Percent price decrease} = \frac{167-158}{167} = .054 \text{ or about } 5\%$$

With some domestic competition assumed in the home market, the 19 percent price increase there results in (by assumption) a 10 percent volume loss. We have taken the benefit of much greater price elasticity abroad, and shown a 20 percent export volume increase. Such a volume increase would be consistent with a very small share of that market.

On the raw material cost side, we have assumed that the full devaluation is added to the import cost and that our domestic suppliers have some access to foreign markets. They have, therefore, chosen to raise domestic prices by 5 percent on the grounds that, if we do not want it, they can quite possibly sell it abroad.

The overall results for scenario 3 are good. Because of the demand elasticities we have assumed, our revenues are up almost 25 percent compared with those of the base case. Since higher LC costs for imported materials raise our cost by less than 13 percent, the contribution improves accordingly. The observed result is, of course, highly dependent on the demand elasticities. However, this more realistic scenario suggests the best opportunity for management to alter strategy or tactics to minimize losses, or maximize gains, from an exchange-rate change.

The numerical results for each of the scenarios are shown in Exhibit 12.5. The results are expressed as both the annual local currency cashflow from operations and the equivalent foreign currency cashflow, with conversion made at the new exchange rate. These results can be compared with the base-case cashflows as follows:

	Base case	Scenario 1	Scenario 2	Scenario 3
LC cashflow ($000)	900	1410	810	1323
Exchange rate, LC/FC	1.2	1.5	1.5	1.5
FC cashflow ($000)	750	940	540	882

Two more steps are required to complete our assessment of economic exposure in this example. First, the cashflows shown are from operations only. To these we must add or subtract any working capital changes (first year only) caused by any change in volume or pricing following from the exchange-rate move. We have assumed that the unit volume changes shown can be accommodated with no change in fixed assets.

In addition, we must place a value on these total cashflows for the base case and for each of the three scenarios, if we want to measure economic exposure as the change in value of the business resulting from an adjustment in the currency exchange rate.

Using the balance sheet assumptions specified earlier, Exhibit 12.6 shows the first-year working capital changes for the three scenarios. Note that these changes are caused entirely by the exchange-rate move. The current asset increases are, to some extent, offset by the increases in accounts payable, but for scenarios 1 and 3, the first-year operating cashflows will be reduced by increased working capital requirements.

Exhibit 12.5. Scenarios 1, 2, and 3

	Scenario 1			Scenario 2			Scenario 3		
	Units (000)	LC per unit	LC (000)	Units (000)	LC per unit	LC (000)	Units (000)	LC per unit	LC (000)
Revenue									
Domestic sales	10	250.00		10	200.00		9	237.50	
Export sales	10	250.00		10	200.00		12	237.50	
Total revenue			5,000			4,000			4,987
Cost of sales									
Labor		50.00			50.00			50.00	
Domestic raw material		25.00			25.00			26.25	
Imported raw material		31.25			31.25			31.25	
Cost per unit		106.25			106.25			107.50	
Total cost of sales			2,125			2,125			2,257
Operating income			2,875			1,875			2,730
Fixed cash operating cost		LC 600,000			LC 600,000			LC 600,000	
Depreciation		300,000			300,000			300,000	
Interest expense		125,000			125,000			125,000	
Total fixed cost			1,025			1,025			1,025
Income before tax			1,850			850			1,705
Income tax			740			340			682
Income after tax			1,110			510			1,023
Add back depreciation			300			300			300
LC cashflow from operations			LC 1,410			LC 810			LC 1,323
FC value of LC cashflow ($\div$ 1.5)			FC 940			FC 540			FC 882

Exhibit 12.6. First-Year Working Capital Changes
(Local Currency)

	Scenario 1	Scenario 2	Scenario 3
Cash	50,000	0	49,375
Accounts receivable	250,000	0	246,875
Inventory	31,250	31,250	64,375
Accounts payable	(31,250)	(31,250)	(51,875)
Net change	300,000	0	308,750

The final step, set out in Exhibit 12.7, shows changes from the base case in annual operating cashflows, in working capital requirements, and in the dollar value of the business. The results are measured in both local currency and foreign currency units, and the percentage changes in value are calculated. For valuation purposes, operating cashflows are capitalized at 20 percent, and the result is adjusted for the dollar working capital change in all cases.

Given the market structures and the exchange-rate move assumed in this example, the economic exposure is substantial. The change in the value of the business ranges from a plus 50 percent (scenario 1, local currency value) to a minus 28 percent (scenario 2, parent currency value). There is, of course, nothing magical about this particular set of numbers, and, in practice, an exposure analysis will be more complex. The purpose is not to come up with an exact change in the value of the

Exhibit 12.7. Change from Base Case due to Devaluation
(Percent or Thousands of Dollars)

		Scenario 1	Scenario 2	Scenario 3
Change in annual	LC	+510	−90	+423
cashflow	FC	+190	−210	+132
Change in working	LC	+300	0	+309
capital, first year	FC	+200	0	+206
Change in dollar value	LC	+2250	−450	+1806
of corporation*	FC	+750	−1050	+454
Relative change in	LC	+50%	−10%	+40%
value of corporation	FC	+20%	−28%	+12%
from base case†				

*Dollar value is five times annual cashflow less increase in working capital.
†Base-case value of corporation: LC 900 × 5 = 4500; FC 750 × 5 = 3750.

business for a given exchange-rate move, but to examine the sensitivity of the business value to possible exchange-rate movements. The required analysis may also be at least partially justified by the benefit derived from occasionally thinking through the market structures and from developing optimum pricing policies assuming a particular movement in the foreign exchange rate.

Measuring Economic Exposure: Regression Analysis

For those who balk at building the preceding type of model based on assumptions about elasticities and currencies of determination, there is another way to examine the degree of economic exposure of a firm. This approach uses only real data, about which there is no argument. The problem is that the data are historical, and their relevance requires the assumption that the future will resemble the past. With this caveat, however, it does offer a useful alternative approach to exploring the sensitivity of corporate cashflows to exchange-rate adjustments.

Very briefly, regression analysis provides a means of measuring the degree of association between a proxy for corporate success and the movements in one or more foreign currency prices. With this method, the success measure (dependent variable) is usually change over time either in operating cashflows or in stock price. Change intervals of three months are common, and all data should be adjusted for inflation. The independent or explanatory variable(s) would be the exchange rate of one or more currencies, using the change in the rate in the appropriate time period. A stock price index is sometimes added as an explanatory variable, when the success measure used is change in corporate stock price. With quarterly data, a total time span of five years would give sufficient degrees of freedom. Using only one foreign currency exchange rate, a typical cashflow model would be as follows:

$$\text{Cashflow}(t) = a(0) + a(1)\text{exchange rate}(t) + u(t)$$

where cashflow and exchange rate are the percentage change in the variables in period t, $a(0)$ is a constant, $a(1)$ is a regression coefficient, and $u(t)$ is an error term. A stock price model would be similar, with the possible inclusion of the stock index data as an independent variable. In both models, the regression coefficient(s) of the exchange-rate variable(s) indicates the historical relationship between the success variable and exchange-rate adjustments.

Managing Economic Exposure

If economic exposure is the change in the value of corporate cashflows (measured in the owners' currency), in response to a real change in a foreign exchange rate, then it follows that a key objective in the management of this exposure would be to insulate the cashflows from the exchange-rate moves. If this is the goal, we would seek a situation in which the cashflows, and, therefore, the value of the firm, were independent of any or all exchange-rate movements. While it is obvious that complete independence is unachievable, well-informed and competent management can gain much of this objective.

Duration of Exchange-Rate Adjustment

It is useful to consider the probable duration of a real move in the foreign exchange rate. If the move is considered temporary, there may be much less incentive for a specific response from management.

As a basis for forming *long-run* expectations about exchange-rate adjustments, purchasing-power parity (PPP) has proved to be a useful guide. As indicated in Chapter 2, PPP suggests that exchange-rate adjustments will accompany, or follow, inflation differentials. To the extent that such adjustments offset the inflation differentials, the exchange-rate movement is nominal, not real, and no economic exposure follows. Therefore, a real exchange-rate move is one in which the exchange rate moves out of step with the relative inflation rates, or it can be a movement back toward equilibrium with differential inflation following a prior real move in the exchange rate in the opposite direction.

When assessing the likely permanence of an observed rate move, a move back toward equilibrium is considered more permanent than an exchange-rate movement away from equilibrium, that is, one that is moving out of step with inflation. In practice, many of the latter, or "disequilibrium," exchange-rate moves, can be attributed to governmental interference in the foreign exchange markets. This interference may be undertaken, perhaps, for reasons outlined in Chapter 2. On the other hand, the adjustments back toward equilibrium are usually associated with free-market forces.

Policy on Exposure Management

What management elects to do about economic exposure, once it has been identified and measured, depends on the nature of the anticipated change in cashflows and on management's tolerance for risk. If the exposure measurement is based on a forecast that includes the timing, direction, and magnitude of the rate move, and if the anticipated cashflow change is in the corporation's favor, management may well choose to do nothing. However, this degree of specificity in currency forecasting is not usual or, at least, not often highly successful. Management must usually be content to work with a forecast that says a particular currency is expected to experience a specified degree of volatility in the near future, with possibly a longer-term-trend forecast. To the extent that the direction is unclear, rational exposure management may mean minimizing sensitivity to any rate change.

Minimizing sensitivity to an exchange-rate movement may seem a passive approach. The more aggressive posture would be to accept a forecast of a future rate move and take positions accordingly. There are at least two problems with the latter approach, even though it may sound like more fun. As indicated, the direction, timing, and extent of a rate move are very hard to predict accurately, all at the same time, in a forecast. In addition, in economic exposure management, the positions to take to translate these forecasts into favorable changes in operating cashflows would almost always be highly illiquid. Major commitments to foreign sources of product, foreign markets, or even physical plant and equipment for foreign production cannot be easily recovered or reversed. Therefore, actively taking a position on a currency forecast is much more easily done through the financial markets, with, for example, a forward or futures contract.

The second problem, or reason not to be overly proactive with respect to managing operating cashflows given currency risk, concerns the source of the business operation's competitive advantage. What kind of business is it, and how does it earn its way in the world? For nonfinancial corporations, the competitive advantage almost always lies in the production and marketing of real goods or services. Taking foreign currency positions, for purposes other than the protection of the operating cashflows measured in the shareholders' currency, is, therefore, usually outside the corporate mission. If this is true, the passive approach to foreign currency exposure management is the most appropriate. Therefore, we will assume in the recommendations that follow that the objective is to minimize the sensitivity of operating cashflows to exchange-rate movements.

Diversification and Flexibility

There are two key elements in the implementation of a passive approach to economic exposure management: diversification and flexibility. As indicated earlier, multinational or global businesses usually have greater scope in the effort to reduce the sensitivity of operating cashflows to exchange-rate moves. As adjustments in the real exchange rate shift competitive advantage between and among the players in any given market, the effective corporate response almost always involves changes in marketing and production strategies.

On the marketing side, pricing or promotional strategies may be altered. As we have seen in the numerical example, a new pricing policy would have to allow for demand elasticities, with a view to maximizing total product contribution, measured in shareholders' currency. The permanence of the rate move would also have to be considered. If the move was considered temporary and likely to be soon reversed, the original local currency pricing structure might be maintained, to hold market share and preserve customer relations, at the expense of short-run margins. If the move is considered of a more permanent nature, then it may be necessary to alter the product in some way, perhaps to make the demand less price-sensitive, or even to withdraw from the market.

Production changes to offset an anticipated or actual currency change include finding new sources of supply, increasing productivity, and shifting the whole production operation to an operating currency that affords more competitive production costs. These types of changes are not trivial. They are both expensive and risky, and they consume a great deal of management time. As a result, they require careful planning, and it is important not to undertake them in an atmosphere of haste and confusion. Certainly, line management must be involved in both the planning and implementation; economic exposure management is not purely a corporate finance function responsibility. It must involve, on an ongoing basis, the most senior operating managers. The activity could best be described as continual contingency planning, in this case with respect to the possibility, in fact the probability, of material real movements in the exchange rate.

The corporate finance function does have a role to play, although an ancillary one, relative to the marketing and production functions. For example, cashflows to shareholders are net of debt charges in both foreign and home currencies. Some of the volatility in these net flows, caused by exchange-rate movements, can be offset by financing the operations with appropriate foreign currencies, to the extent that those currencies are available. Such a currency hedge can directly reduce the sensitivity of net cashflows to exchange-rate fluctuations and thus can contribute to economic exposure management.

A secondary, but also very useful, corporate finance function is that of monitoring the current net position, providing guidance regarding

Exhibit 12.8. Economic Exposure Summary

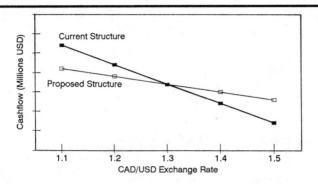

exposure-management options, and assessing the effectiveness of particular actions, if taken. This can be done by measuring, on an ongoing basis, the sensitivity of cashflows to movement in the exchange rates of primary interest to the corporation. The process would require constructing cashflow forecasts from current operations and from possible modifications of current operations, and showing the effect of specific exchange-rate moves on each of these cashflows. For example, a summary chart could be prepared, as shown in Exhibit 12.8, which would clearly illustrate the essence of the current economic exposure and indicate the way a major contingency plan would likely affect that exposure.

13

Foreign Exchange Exposure in Commodity Transactions

Executive Summary

Chapter 13 focuses on the nature of foreign exchange risk that can exist in the commodity sector. Using oil markets as an example, it discusses the concept of the inherent, or primary pricing, currency for commodities and the risk incurred when trading oil in currencies other than the USD. The chapter suggests a risk-management procedure for identifying and hedging foreign exchange risk. It gives an agricultural-market example of contracts priced against futures markets. The chapter concludes with a discussion on the issue of commodity reserves owned by organizations and the risks surrounding their foreign exchange management.

Introduction

In Chapters 11 and 12, we looked at transaction and economic exposure, and treated them as if they were separate and distinct forms of currency exposure. They are not. In fact, some managers will maintain that transaction exposure is really only a subset or a specific form of economic exposure. While it is often easier to explain and describe corporate foreign exposure by breaking it down into bite-sized pieces, there are areas where the distinction is blurred. This lack of clarity is often the case when an organization is involved with commodities.

Inherent Currency Risk

Most commodities are traded on a global basis. Prices, regardless of the currency being used in an individual transaction, must be similar, or goods will be purchased from the cheaper source until prices are properly realigned. As a result, there is usually a benchmark price in a particular currency that is deemed to reflect the global market's assessment of the commodity's value at that particular time. Most major commodities have an inherent value in the USD. In other words, the USD is the currency of determination, or the primary pricing currency. Oil, for instance, is a USD-inherent commodity. Oil's global price in USD does not change with every change in the USD against other currencies. Instead, as shown in Exhibit 13.1, the price of oil in other currencies will change.

In Exhibit 13.1, the only market factor that changed was the DEM/USD exchange rate. There was no short-term impact on the USD price of oil, but there was a very direct impact on the DEM price of oil. In the longer term, small movements, like the ones in the exhibit, are unlikely to affect the amount of oil consumed in Germany. However, if the DEM fell dramatically to 6.0000 DEM/USD, the DEM price of oil would increase from 40 to 120 DEM per barrel. Such a large increase in price would tend to reduce demand in Germany, which, in turn, would put some downward pressure on the global price of oil.

If the USD is strong against the DEM, it may also be strong against many other major currencies as well. Higher oil prices in these other countries will also lead to reduced demand. Collectively, the reduced demand from a number of countries could lead to a lower USD price of oil. The extent of the decline in demand and in oil prices is difficult to predict with any degree of accuracy. Currency realignments are only one of many factors that affect the price of oil. However, the point re-

Exhibit 13.1. Changes in Non-USD Prices of Oil due to Changes in Exchange Rates

	Day 1	Day 30	Day 60
Price of oil, USD per bbl	20	20	20
Exchange rate, DEM/USD	2.00	2.10	1.90
Price of oil, DEM per bbl	40	42	38

mains that, while oil is considered to be USD-inherent, the USD price of oil is still responsive to movements in global exchange rates. Consequently, it can be argued that dealing in commodities results in a blend of economic and transaction exposure.

Most major commodities are USD-inherent for one or more of the following reasons:

1. The USD is the major currency of the world, not only in foreign exchange markets, but for international trade and services as well.

2. The United States is home to many of the dominant futures markets for commodities. While foreign exchange markets do not look to the futures markets for benchmark pricing, many commodity markets do. Given that these futures markets are in the United States, the pricing, of course, is in USD.

3. The United States is almost always a major consumer of any given commodity. In addition, the United States can be a major direct supplier of commodities. Moreover, U.S. firms either own the resources or are heavily involved in developing many resources in other countries, and so add much more to the supply side in an indirect manner.

Dealing Commodities in a Local Currency

If a German company bought and sold oil in DEM, it would incur foreign exchange risk, if the two deals were not done simultaneously. The price of oil could move from 42 DEM per barrel to 40 DEM per barrel only because of foreign exchange movements. If an oil trader anticipated this foreign exchange movement, he or she could short (sell without owning) the oil at 42 DEM. When the oil declined to 40 DEM, the trader could buy back the oil and make 2 DEM on every barrel traded. However, contrary to appearances, the oil trader is not really trading oil markets. The oil trader is trading the currency markets. To eliminate the exchange risk from these transactions in local currencies, the trader should alter the DEM purchase price to a USD purchase price and the DEM sales price to a USD sales price. This can be done using spot, forward, or currency option contracts.

Consider, for example, a purchase of a barrel of oil at 40 DEM based on oil at 20 USD and a 2.00 DEM/USD exchange rate, shown in Exhibit 13.2. Because the purchase of the oil is in cash, the trader is out of pocket 40 DEM. In effect, the trader can be said to be long oil (owns oil) and short DEM (the purchase countervalue). The trader wants to create a synthetic USD purchase price and does so by buying 40 DEM at the

Exhibit 13.2. Changing the Purchase Price from DEM to USD

	Oil position	DEM, in/(out)	USD, in/(out)
Purchase of oil	1 barrel	(40)	
Establish USD purchase price by selling USD at 2.00 DEM/USD		40	(20)
Net position	1 barrel	0	(20)

2.00 DEM/USD exchange rate. The trader is now short 20 USD, which constitutes the USD purchase price of oil.

The trader flattened, or brought to zero, the short DEM position and established a short USD position. In doing so, the trader has established a USD purchase price for oil and is faced with managing the risks associated with the USD oil market only. He or she no longer faces the direct price risks posed by the foreign exchange market.

In Exhibit 13.2, the cashflows happened immediately; it is easy to see how a trader could eliminate the foreign exchange risk and create a USD purchase price. But what if the purchase is for delivery several days, weeks, or months into the future?

The same principles apply, except that the USD purchase price is created by selling USD on a forward basis. Consider Exhibit 13.3, which shows changes in both the underlying USD price of oil and the DEM/USD exchange rate.

Exhibit 13.3. Oil Transactions and Foreign Exchange Hedges with Changes in USD Oil Prices and DEM/USD Exchange Rates

Market scenario	Day 1	Day 30
Oil, USD per bbl	20.00	22.00
DEM/USD exchange rate	2.00	1.80
Oil, DEM per bbl	40.00	39.60

	Oil transactions	Foreign exchange hedges
Day 1	Buy oil at 40 DEM; payment in 60 days.	Sell 20 USD 60 days forward.
Day 30	Sell oil at 39.60 DEM; payment in 30 days.	Buy 22 USD 30 days forward.

Exhibit 13.4. Oil Trading Results When USD Purchase and Sales Prices Are Established

	Cashflows on day 60	
Day 1 transactions	USD, in/(out)	DEM, in/(out)
Payment for oil purchase	0	(40.00)
FX hedge at 2.00 DEM/USD	(20.00)	40.00
Net cashflow	(20.00)	0
Day 30 transactions		
Receipts from oil sale	0	39.60
FX hedge at 1.80 DEM/USD	22.00	(39.60)
Net cashflow	22.00	0
Day 60 net cashflow	2.00	0

The trader bought oil on day 1 when oil was at 20 USD per barrel and sold it on day 30 when oil was at 22 USD. If the foreign exchange risk was eliminated, the trader should have made 2 USD per barrel. Exhibit 13.4 shows the results.

If the foreign exchange risk was not eliminated, the trader would have bought oil at 40 DEM and sold it at 39.60 DEM. The trader would, therefore, have turned a 2 USD profit on oil trading into a .40 DEM loss, a loss entirely due to foreign exchange losses.

Clearly, dealing in a commodity in a currency other than the commodity's inherent currency results in foreign exchange exposure. A simple model by which the exposure and basic foreign exchange hedges can be determined, when selling commodities in both the inherent currency and other currencies, is outlined in Exhibit 13.5.

Exhibit 13.5. Foreign Exchange Risk-Management Model When Selling Commodities

		Inherent currency of commodity	
		USD	Other currency
Currency of transaction	USD	No FX Risk	Have FX risk Sell USD and buy inherent currency
	Any currency other than USD	Have FX risk Sell other currency and buy USD	No FX risk if inherent currency and currency in the deal are the same If they differ, sell the currency in deal and buy inherent currency

Exhibit 13.6. Foreign Exchange Hedges in Sales of Commodities

			Required FX hedge	
Commodity	Inherent currency	Currency in transaction	Currency to buy	Currency to sell
Oil	USD	DEM	USD	DEM
Oil	USD	USD		
Wheat	USD	CAD	USD	CAD
Canola	CAD	USD	CAD	USD
XYZ	AUD	JPY	AUD	JPY

The model basically advises that if you sell a commodity in a currency other than its inherent currency, buy the inherent currency and sell the currency in the transaction. A few examples are shown in Exhibit 13.6.

For buying commodities, the same basic premise applies. If you buy a commodity in a currency other than its inherent currency, the foreign exchange hedge is achieved by selling the inherent currency and buying the currency of the transaction. Exhibit 13.7 outlines a foreign exchange risk-management model when buying commodities in both the inherent currency and other currencies.

Exhibit 13.6 outlined the hedges required when selling various commodities in different currencies. Exhibit 13.8 outlines the hedges using the same framework except that the commodities are purchased, not sold.

Exhibit 13.7. Foreign Exchange Risk-Management Model When Buying Commodities

		Inherent currency of commodity	
		USD	Other currency
Currency of transaction	USD	No FX Risk	Have FX risk Buy USD and sell inherent currency
	Any currency other than USD	Have FX risk Buy other currency and sell USD	No FX risk if inherent currency and currency in the deal are the same If they differ, buy the currency in deal and sell inherent currency

Exhibit 13.8. Foreign Exchange Hedges in Purchase of Commodities

			Required FX hedge	
Commodity	Inherent currency	Currency in transaction	Currency to buy	Currency to sell
Oil	USD	DEM	DEM	USD
Oil	USD	USD		
Wheat	USD	CAD	CAD	USD
Canola	CAD	USD	USD	CAD
XYZ	AUD	JPY	JPY	AUD

Multiple Inherent Currencies

If the inherent currency is not easily discernible, life can get more complicated. Physical commodities face competition from other suppliers
and other commodities. For instance, canola, which is also know as rape
seed, produces an edible oil when crushed. Canola is produced in several countries, with Canada being the major producer. Surprisingly, the
United States is both a relatively small producer and consumer. Canola
seeds have more than double the oil content of soybeans, which are
used to produce the world's leading edible oil. If the world has a shortage of canola or canola oil, the markets that want canola oil for its
unique taste will continue to buy canola and/or canola oil even if their
prices relative to the prices of soybeans and soybean oil seem unusually
high. There is a core demand that is not price-sensitive. The CAD price
of canola may thus not be tied directly to soybeans, which are USD-
inherent; therefore, foreign exchange movements on a day-to-day basis
against the USD may be basically irrelevant.

On the other hand, if the supply-and-demand situation changes to
produce an ample supply of canola, the USD price of canola may be
closely tied to that of soybeans and soybean products. In this case, the
daily movements in the CAD/USD exchange rate may directly influence
the CAD price. Canola is not a perfect substitute for soybeans for reasons other than the taste. Consider the following characteristics:

	Canola	Soybeans
Oil content, %	40	20
Meal content, %	60	80
Protein content in meal, %	38	46

Exhibit 13.9. Example Market Price Scenarios of Soybeans

	Scenario 1			Scenario 2		
	Price of product	% of beans	Bean price	Price of product	% of beans	Bean price
Oil	20	.2	4	30	.2	6
Meal	10	.8	8	10	.8	8
Total			12			14

Soybeans' value is basically the value of the oil and meal that is generated on crushing the beans. Consider Exhibit 13.9 which outlines two pricing scenarios.

In both scenarios, the price of meal is 10 USD. The price of oil, however, increases to 30 USD in scenario 2, which causes the overall price of soybeans to increase 2 USD to 14 USD. The relative price increase of canola will be even greater because of its higher oil content. All else being equal, the price of canola in the two scenarios would be similar to that shown in Exhibit 13.10.

The price of canola increases 4 USD, compared with the 2 USD increase for soybeans. While the change is not due to changes in foreign exchange rates, the price movement could create a new form of foreign exchange risk for a trader, namely, trading profits or losses. For example, if a Canadian-based trader sold canola at 14 USD and had to cover the short position at 18 USD, the trader would suffer a loss of 4 USD. The USD loss represents a foreign exchange exposure. In commodity transactions, foreign exchange exposures are not necessarily restricted to the commodity itself. Consider the following:

Exhibit 13.10. Market Price of Canola When Closely Tied to Soybean Market

	Scenario 1			Scenario 2		
	Price of product	% of canola	Canola price	Price of product	% of canola	Canola price
Oil	20	.4	8	30	.4	12
Meal	10	.6	6	10	.6	6
Total			14			18

1. Transportation across oceans incurs freight charges, usually payable in USD.

2. Loading and unloading the commodity at terminals in foreign ports can incur expenses in a foreign currency.

3. Governments may levy various tariffs, which are usually payable in local currency.

4. The commodity may be insured during transportation, the premium for which can be in various currencies, but is usually in USD for commodities being transported across oceans.

5. Letters of credit that guarantee payment on delivery will incur fees, which may or may not pose foreign exchange risks.

6. As discussed in Chapter 11, futures margin requirements can pose foreign exchange risks depending on the futures exchange, the nature of the transaction, and the home currency of the organization.

7. The actual gains or losses generated on the business transaction may materialize in a foreign currency, giving rise to a foreign exchange exposure.

Arbitrage

In foreign exchange, price differentials in different markets are usually quickly offset as a result of arbitrage. Currency transactions do not involve a physical movement of money from one country to another. If a European entity sells USD to an Australian entity, the USD are not moved from Europe to Australia. The USD remain in the United States. Only the ownership of the USD changes as the European entity instructs its U.S. bank to debit its USD account and credit the Australian entity's USD account, which could be at the same American bank or at another American-based bank. Arbitrage is facilitated because money is so easy to deliver.

In commodities, price discrepancies can occur for a number of reasons:

1. Commodities cannot be transported as easily as money. Moreover, there can be significant costs for transportation, handling, and insurance.

2. Physical constraints such as winter freeze-ups, port limitations, lack of ocean freight availability, lack of railcar capacity to move the prod-

uct to or from the ports, or lack of pipeline capacity in the oil and gas sector can also limit the ability to do what would seem easily done, at least on paper.

On the other hand, price discrepancies and price movements of commodities are limited by the fact that there are substitutes for most commodities. Palm oil, corn oil, coconut oil, and canola oil, for instance, can all be used in place of soybean oil. Wheat and barley can be used in place of corn as a feedstock. Gas and coal can often be used instead of oil. While few commodities have a perfect substitute, there are levels of price discrepancy at which substitution is deemed worthwhile by the end user. This ability to substitute one commodity for another limits the price movements of commodities, and while price discrepancies will occur, they are contained within a reasonable range.

Trading commodities involves a number of risks and costs. There can be market risks on the underlying commodity, on freight, on foreign exchange, and on other areas. Moreover, costs could be incurred in a number of currencies. A Canadian entity could buy the grain from the farmer in CAD, sell the product to Japanese interests in JPY, and incur USD expenses on ocean freight. Each component should be analyzed from a risk standpoint and managed as deemed appropriate.

Pricing Related to Futures in Foreign Currency

Some commodity transactions are sold on an unpriced basis; the sale is made today, but the price is not finalized. The initial price agreement can take several forms, one of which could be so many dollars over a particular futures price. The buyer has the option to finalize the price whenever it wants, until an automatic pricing mechanism kicks in. For instance, a quantity of commodity XYZ could be sold for delivery to Frankfurt for 300 DEM over the September USD futures price. If the USD futures remain at the current level of 200 USD when the buyer "prices the deal," the price will be 500 DEM. If the futures are 225 USD, the price will be 525 DEM.

If the seller buys the commodity for 200 USD and has transportation and other costs equal to 40 USD, the trader needs to sell it at the equivalent of 240 USD to break even. Based on an exchange rate of 2.00 DEM/USD, the breakeven DEM price is 480 DEM. If the sale is made at 300 DEM over the futures price, which was at 200 USD, the trader should make 20 DEM, or 10 USD.

Futures price	200
Plus: Spread over futures	300
Total DEM selling price	500
USD equivalent at 2.00	250
Less: USD cost of goods	240
Net USD profit	10

Exhibit 13.11 shows the results if futures prices increase or decrease and no hedge is put in place. In scenario 1, if USD futures drop to 100 USD and the buyer "prices" the deal, the trader would receive 400 DEM. At an exchange rate of 2.000 DEM/USD, only 200 USD would be received. A 40 USD loss would be incurred.

If futures increased to 300 USD as per scenario 2, the DEM selling price would be 600 DEM, which is equal to 300 USD. A profit of 60 USD would be made.

To protect against this risk, the seller could sell the September futures contract at 200 USD. When the deal is priced at the time that the futures are at 100 USD, the futures hedge contracts are immediately bought back at 100 USD as well. In this case, there is a profit on the futures of 100 USD. The loss of 40 USD in scenario 1 has now been transformed into a profit of 60 USD. Conversely, if futures go to 300 USD as per scenario 2, the futures loss of 100 USD turns a 60 USD profit situation into a 40 USD loss.

The futures hedge served to offset the basic risk, but, unfortunately, created another risk that was just as unacceptable. Unprofit-

Exhibit 13.11. Impact on Unpriced Contracts due to Shifts in Futures Prices

	Scenario 1 (futures priced @ 100)		Scenario 2 (futures priced @ 200)	
	USD in/(out)	DEM in/(out)	USD in/(out)	DEM in/(out)
Base cost of commodity	(200)	0	(200)	0
Other transactions costs	(40)	0	(40)	0
Selling price:				
Futures price	–	100	–	300
Premium over futures	–	300	–	300
Conversion to USD price	200	(400)	300	(600)
Net gain/(loss)	(40)	0	60	0

able situations became profitable, while profitable situations became unprofitable.

In this deal, every single USD decline in the futures price reduced the selling price by 1 DEM. On the other hand, it generated a USD profit of 1 USD on the futures. Since 1 USD gained is worth more than 1 DEM lost, the trader actually improved the profit picture. In scenario 2, however, the reverse is true, and the trader loses money with the futures hedge. The reason for this imperfect hedge is that the exchange rate between the DEM and the USD is not at parity, i.e., not one for one.

To compensate for this lack of parity, the size of the futures position is adjusted by the exchange rate. Consequently, the futures position in this case is 1/2.00, or one-half of the transaction size. Therefore, the number of USD gained or lost on the futures hedge is one-half of the number of the DEM lost or gained on the underlying transaction. However, because the USD is worth twice as much, the USD gains and losses should offset the DEM losses and gains.

Exhibit 13.12 uses the same scenario as outlined in Exhibit 13.11. Assume there were 10 units sold. The futures hedge is, therefore, 5 units. A futures decline of 100 in scenario 1 thus would create a USD loss of 500 USD. Similarly, a futures increase of 100 USD in scenario 2 would generate a gain of 500 USD.

A gain of 100 USD was made in both scenarios. The adjusted futures

Exhibit 13.12. Results of Using Futures Hedge Adjusted by Exchange Rate

	Scenario 1 (futures priced @ 100)		Scenario 2 (futures priced @ 200)	
	USD in/(out)	DEM in/(out)	USD in/(out)	DEM in/(out)
Base cost of commodity	(2000)	0	(2000)	0
Other transactions costs	(400)	0	(400)	0
Selling price:				
Futures price	–	1000	–	3000
Premium over futures	–	3000	–	3000
Conversion to USD price	2000	(4000)	3000	(6000)
Net gain/(loss) before futures hedge	(400)	0	600	0
Futures gain/(loss)	500		(500)	
Total gain/(loss)	100	0	100	0

hedge actually worked and achieved the 10 USD margin per unit that was expected when the transaction was initially booked.

In practice, this perfect hedge rarely seems to work out. For instance, the above examples assume that the DEM proceeds were converted to USD at an exchange rate of 2.00 DEM/USD. There are two weaknesses in that assumption:

1. The exchange rate could have moved to 3.00 DEM/USD by the time the DEM cashflow was received. If not hedged, the USD received would have been reduced by one-third in both scenarios; and losses, not a 100 USD profit, would have resulted. To overcome this risk, forward contracts could have been dealt, wherein DEM would be sold for USD at 2.00 DEM/USD.

2. The second weakness is that there is uncertainty about the number of DEM that will be received. It is fine to hedge the DEM receipts on a forward basis as just recommended above, but the risk remains that the amount hedged may differ significantly from the amount actually received.

To manage this known exposure, which has an unknown amount, the trader might use a combination of forward contracts and currency options as follows:

1. Sell forward the minimum amount of DEM that are likely to be received.

2. Buy DEM puts for the balance of the DEM that could possibly be received.

Movements in the exchange rate will also require some adjustment in the futures position as well, if everything is to be kept in perfect balance. Such fine-tuning may seem warranted, but often it is impractical to do.

This type of commodity transaction has various risks. If it requires constant manipulation of hedges in order for a slim profit margin to be preserved, the deal is questionable from the beginning. Consequently, either it should not have been undertaken, or it should have been priced differently.

Commodity Reserves

Another issue on commodities is the situation facing companies that own reserves located in countries outside the United States but that are

USD-inherent. Oil reserves in the North Sea, copper reserves in Chile, coal reserves in Australia, and potash reserves in Canada are all basically USD-inherent reserves. Foreign exchange exposure exists on these reserves at all times. Dealing with these risks involves some questions that can be difficult to answer:

1. Should the company focus on the USD exposure on the asset, or should it focus on the local currency expenditures required to bring the asset to market?

   If the company focuses on the local currency exposures, the company may want to conduct its business on the premise that it is a USD company. Financial statements, budgets, and other reports should all be done in USD terms.

2. Over what time frame should hedging be contemplated? If a company has hundreds or thousands of years of reserves, what amount of those reserves from a foreign exchange perspective should be hedged at any point?

   Some companies have five-year plans that are used for hedging. Other companies will work on a fiscal-year basis with hedging activities based on trying to control key variables in the budget.

   Some companies consider the moment the sale is made as the moment the foreign exchange exposure occurs, and hedging the USD exposure is warranted. The time of sale does favorably affect the sales revenue component and the profitability of the income statement. It also creates a receivable on the balance sheet. However, the receivable is tempered to a degree, in that the reserves are depleted and there is a corresponding asset reduction on the balance sheet. From an overall economic standpoint, the sale effectively changes the asset from a raw resource material to an accounts receivable. The receivable is closer to cash than is the raw material, and if there was any doubt about having an exposure beforehand, there certainly should be no doubt now.

3. If the company owns a USD-inherent commodity, but all sales are made domestically, generating revenues in the local currency, what should the company do?

   There is no USD cashflow. In this case, the sale of the commodity constitutes a fundamental change, as it transforms a USD asset (reserves) into a CAD asset (accounts receivable). This is a form of economic exposure, and the sale transaction incorporates a foreign exchange transaction. The base price for the sale is the USD value of the commodity, which is adjusted by current exchange rates to give a CAD sales price.

The hedge on this type of exposure is really centered on the reserves themselves. USD debt can act as an effective hedge against the reserves. Alternatively, if there are, say, 120 million USD worth of product sales expected, a company may sell USD forward for a portion or all of the 120 million USD. As the product sales are made in CAD, the equivalent amount of USD is bought back in order to effectively create a USD selling price. Consider the following examples where a total of 120 million USD has been sold forward, 10 million USD for delivery each month, at a rate of 1.20 CAD/USD.

The product sales for the month of July are as follows:

1. Sales of 6,000,000 USD equivalent, when spot was at 1.15 CAD/USD, to yield a selling price of 6,900,000 CAD
2. Sales of 4,000,000 USD equivalent, when spot was at 1.22 CAD/USD, to yield a selling price of 4,880,000 CAD.

Exhibit 13.13 shows the results from a cashflow perspective.

In terms of the above hedging strategy, the company successfully achieved its 1.20 exchange rate. With that strategy and decision in mind, a few other aspects should be noted:

1. If there was a change in the pricing wherein the sales were struck in USD, the company would simply take the USD proceeds and deliver on the forward sale contracts.
2. The same principles could be used to lock in the price on the commodity using futures contracts. If sales contracts for the entire year

Exhibit 13.13. Cashflows from Using an Economic Hedge

Transaction	USD, in/(out) (000)	CAD, in/(out) (000)
Initial forward hedge	(10,000)	12,000
First product sale:		
Proceeds from sale		6,900
Unwinding of hedge	6,000	(6,900)
Second product sale:		
Proceeds from sale		4,880
Unwinding of hedge	4,000	(4,880)
Net cashflow	0	12,000

could be made, then both market risks could be looked after in a simple and straightforward fashion.
3. Forward hedging is simple to do in conceptual terms. Forecasting the amount of future receivables to hedge often poses some difficulties because there can be considerable uncertainty about:
   a. The amount of product to be sold
   b. The price of the product
   Long-term volume contracts combined with hedges on the actual commodity all help to fine-tune the foreign exchange hedging process.
4. Foreign exchange is but one market risk the company is facing. The same process and considerations should basically be made on the underlying commodity as well as on foreign exchange, interest rates, and other significant exposures. The decision may be to hedge one and not another, but the same decision-making process should prevail.
5. If the company focuses on the local currency costs, this issue may be facilitated to the degree that the cost amounts are known with more certainty.

14

Accounting and Translation Exposure

Executive Summary

Financial statement translation exposure is important because it can cause substantial changes in reported profit and shareholder equity. The changes in reported profits and equity result from translation of the foreign currency statements of affiliates and subsidiaries. The process used to account for foreign-currency-denominated transactions also matters, because bad practice can lead to incorrect assessments of these transactions. Misjudging the benefits of foreign currency transactions and hedging activities can follow from a basic misunderstanding of the foreign exchange gain/loss account. This chapter explains and explores both of these issues.

Defining Accounting Exposure

Strictly speaking, accounting exposure is the potential for change in value of the consolidated corporate earnings or equity accounts, as the result of a change in the foreign exchange rates used to translate the foreign currency statements of subsidiaries and affiliates.

Conceptually, the idea is simple. For example, if you make an investment in a foreign currency (that is, you first buy some foreign currency and then buy some "foreign currency assets") and that currency falls in value relative to your own, all else being equal, your wealth has declined. Even though the foreign-currency value of the assets has not changed, the value of these assets in your own currency will be less, when measured at the new exchange rate. Practically, for a corporation, it is difficult both to measure the true change in (shareholder) wealth caused by a translation gain or loss and to show the effect of the change in the corporate financial statements.

Because the change in reported wealth is not reflected in a cashflow (it is unrealized), it is also difficult to interpret the meaning of the reported change in wealth. However, the amounts of earnings and equity reported to shareholders do matter, and in some circumstances there may eventually be a real (cash) gain or loss. Therefore, the measurement and management of accounting or translation exposure merit our attention.

In this chapter, we will look at two dimensions of translation exposure. First, we will examine the more conventional aspect mentioned above, that is, the problem of translating foreign currency financial statements. We will then consider a more frequent, but less widely recognized, problem: how to measure the foreign currency gains or losses on the foreign-currency-denominated activities of a domestic firm. These activities typically include foreign-currency-based sales, purchases, and loans.

Measuring Accounting Exposure

Subsidiaries and affiliates operating in foreign currency environments usually produce financial statements in the local currencies. Consequently, these statements must be translated into the parent firm's currency in order to consolidate them with the parent statements. Corporations without foreign affiliates may still undertake transactions denominated in foreign currencies (for example, imports, exports, or foreign currency debt), and the impact of these activities must be assessed in the shareholders' currency. The primary issues arising in the translation process are:

1. At what exchange rate should the translation of each statement account be made?

2. Should the resultant gain or loss be taken into current income, deferred to a special equity account, or closed directly to shareholders' equity?

The answers to these questions depend on the circumstances of the transaction. The objective is to have the consolidated statements provide information that fairly reflects the firm's exposure to changes in the foreign currency rate.

Translation Rules

The accounting profession has developed rules to govern the actual translation process. Historically, foreign currency balance sheets were usually translated by one of two rules. Basically, for balance sheet translation, the current/noncurrent rule translates current assets and current liabilities at the exchange rate at balance sheet date; it translates the other assets and liabilities at the rate in effect when these amounts were booked. The monetary/nonmonetary (temporal) rule translates current assets except inventory, current liabilities, and long-term debt at the current rate and translates all other asset and liability accounts at the historical rates. The example in Exhibit 14.1 illustrates the effect on reported shareholders' equity of translation under each of these two rules.

Variations of these rules were possible and often practiced. During the era of the Bretton Woods Agreement and pegged exchange rates, translation exposure was much less a problem than it is today, and attracted less attention. However, when the major trading currencies floated following the breakdown of the Smithsonian Agreement in

Exhibit 14.1. Balance Sheet of Affiliate

| | Translation rule | | | | |
| | FASB 8 (temporal) | | | Current/ noncurrent | |
	Local currency	Rate*	Home currency	Rate*	Home currency
Cash	200	C	160	C	160
Receivables	1000	C	800	C	800
Inventory	500	H	500	C	400
Fixed assets	2000	H	2000	H	2000
Total assets	3700		3460		3360
Current liabilities	250	C	200	C	200
Long-term debt	1000	C	800	H	1000
Equity	2450		2460		2160
Total liabilities and equity	3700		3460		3360
Gain/(loss) in reported equity			10		(290)

*C = current exchange rate, LC .8 = HC 1.
H = historical exchange rate, LC 1 = HC 1.

1973, the extent of the exchange-rate adjustments began to produce material changes in the financial statements. In October 1975, the accounting profession in the United States responded with the "Statement of Financial Accounting Standards Number 8." The issuing authority was the Financial Accounting Standards Board, and the rule became known as *FASB 8*.

FASB 8, also known as the temporal translation method, was really the monetary/nonmonetary method, except when inventories were carried at current market values. If carried at market, as opposed to cost, inventories were to be included with the monetary assets and translated at current rather than historical exchange rates. Further rule development has taken place; we will look at the current rule shortly. First, let us see the kind of problems that prompted these more recent developments.

The process of choosing which assets and liabilities will be translated at current rates and which at historical rates should be guided by the objective of maximum disclosure. The choice is, however, constrained by the need to be consistent with prior years, and with the approach used in other firms, in order to maintain comparability. A similar trade-off arises in single-currency situations, when accounting for fixed assets under conditions of inflation. In dealing with inflation, accounting practice usually chooses consistency and shows fixed assets at historical cost, even though these amounts may be far from current market values. Recent practice occasionally supplements this approach by providing two statements, to show these assets both at historical and at estimated market values.

Balance Sheet Translation Exposure: An Example

Balance sheet exposure to currency fluctuation under any rule is simply the net exposed assets multiplied by the exchange-rate adjustment expressed as a percentage. The rule chosen defines the net exposed assets. The simple balance sheet in Exhibit 14.1 shows the exposure under each of the two rules mentioned earlier. First is shown the affiliate's balance sheet expressed in the local currency of the affiliate (LC). This balance sheet is then translated under each of the two rules to the home currency of the parent (HC). We have assumed a local currency initially at parity with the home currency (LC 1 = HC 1), and show how a devaluation of the LC of 20 percent (LC 1 = HC .8) affects the HC value of the shareholders' equity in the affiliate.

As indicated, the translation rule determines which accounts are translated at current and which at historical exchange rates. The balancing item is the owners' equity. Given that we started with currency parity, the translated equity values can be compared directly with the original local-currency value of the equity (2450) to see a measure of the home currency shareholders' gain or loss on translation. Under FASB 8 a gain of 10 HC units is recorded. What we have gained by restating the current liabilities and long-term debt at the new exchange rate more than offsets the loss on restatement of the cash and accounts receivable.

We could have reached the preceding result directly by multiplying the net exposed position by the rate move. Exposed accounts are those translated at current exchange rates. In our example, under FASB 8, exposed assets total 1200 (cash of 200 and accounts receivable of 1000), and exposed liabilities are 1250 (current liabilities of 250 and long-term debt of 1000). We are short the local currency (liabilities greater than assets) by 50 units, and this amount multiplied by .2 units of HC per unit of LC (the devaluation) produces the translation gain of 10 units of home currency, as shown. In other words, we owed more local currency than we owned, and when that currency declined in value relative to our own, we made a gain.

The situation would be much more serious under the current/noncurrent rule. In this case, the net exposed position is long 1450 units of the local currency (current assets less current liabilities; all long-term accounts are translated at historical rates). On translation, the long position produces a loss of 290 HC, which is charged directly to equity, as shown in Exhibit 14.1.

Translation Gains and Losses

The meaning of a gain or loss on translation, and, therefore, what, if anything, to do about it, is not entirely clear. Certainly no immediate cashflow is involved, and there are no tax effects; in that sense nothing has changed. The devaluation may have either increased or decreased the HC value of the affiliate's operating cashflows; this issue is addressed in Chapter 12, which examines economic exposure. On the other hand, the accounting process attempts to measure owners' equity, at least based on book values, in a consistent and comparable manner, and reported equity has changed. Therefore, it would be hard to argue that nothing at all has happened to shareholder wealth as a result of the exchange-rate adjustment.

FASB 8 assumed a direct relationship between translation gain or loss and operating results, and required the foreign exchange gain or loss to be included in the current period's income. Exchange-rate fluctuations could and did result in material changes in reported earnings of the parent. This was true, even though there was no apparent trend or permanent move in the exchange rate. Even random fluctuations in the rate produced the increased volatility in reported earnings, which was not welcomed by the reporting organizations. In addition to the issue of earnings volatility, firms objected in principle to reporting a translation loss as a reduction in income when no cash loss had occurred.

A classic example of the type of problem caused by FASB 8 concerns Noranda Inc., a major Canadian resource company. In the early 1970s, Noranda built an aluminum smelter in Missouri to serve the U.S. market, and to take advantage of relatively inexpensive Tennessee Valley Authority electricity. Since the project revenues would be in U.S. dollars, U.S. dollar financing would provide a natural currency hedge. The U.S. dollar revenues would be available to retire the U.S. dollar debt. This was done, and at that time the Canadian and American dollars were very close to parity. Noranda showed on its consolidated balance sheet the asset and the U.S. dollar debt liability, both translated into Canadian dollars. The project was completed without incident, and came on stream producing the U.S. dollar revenues as forecast.

Shortly after completion, however, the Canadian dollar devalued sharply against its American counterpart. Under FASB 8, Noranda was required to translate the asset at the historical exchange rate (the rate in effect when the asset was booked) and to translate the U.S. dollar loan at the current rate. The result would have been a charge to income in the period, equal to the increased Canadian dollar value of the U.S. dollar debt, even though the plant was entirely on budget. One could even argue that the rate move had increased the Canadian dollar value of the project's U.S. dollar operating cashflows and profits, and, therefore, a gain should be reported, not a loss. In any event, Noranda management objected very strongly to the application of the rule in this circumstance. Similar objections by many major corporations in the United States persuaded the Financial Accounting Standards Board to reconsider the rule.

FASB 52

FASB 52 became effective for fiscal years beginning on or after December 15, 1981, and is currently in use by U.S. corporations. In its most frequent application, asset and liability accounts are translated at the exchange rate in effect on the balance sheet date. Any gain or loss on translation is closed to a special equity account, usually called something like "cumulative translation variance" (CTV). The gain or loss is not included in period income and will not be recognized as income until the investment in the affiliate is liquidated, at which time it will be netted against gain or loss on disposal of the asset. Because all assets and liabilities are translated at the current exchange rate, the net exposed position is equal to the equity account.

The preceding application is intended for translation of statements of self-sufficient, stand-alone affiliates, whose operating currency (called the *functional* currency) is other than U.S. dollars. The assumption is that a change in the exchange rate between U.S. dollars and the functional currency will not necessarily affect the U.S. dollar value of the affiliate, at least not in the short term—hence the deferral of the translation gain or loss in a special equity account.

Foreign affiliates may be closely tied to the parent. If the operating or functional currency of the affiliate is, in fact, U.S. dollars, then FASB 52 reverts to the temporal approach used by FASB 8, including the requirement that gains or losses be taken into current income. The assumption here is that the affiliate is really an extension of the parent, and the exchange rate directly and immediately affects its, and therefore the parent's, value. An example of such an affiliate might be a manufacturing subsidiary in a Taiwanese free trade zone which imports all its raw materials from the United States and exports all its product back to the United States, to be sold for U.S. dollars.

The other exception to the use of the current exchange rate for translation under FASB 52 concerns the statements of affiliates in high-inflation economies. High-inflation economies are defined by the rule as economies that have experienced a cumulative inflation of more than 100 percent in the last three years. If such is the case, then once again FASB 52 uses the temporal translation method. The rationale here is the desirability of using a historical exchange rate to translate fixed or long-term assets, along with the accumulated depreciation, given:

1. The assumed decline in the exchange rate of the local currency
2. The inability to restate the local currency value of the assets to allow for the inflation

To use the current exchange rate for translation would see the value of the assets, as measured in the parent's currency, continually eroded. Thus, the book value expressed in the parent's currency would reflect neither original cost nor current market value. Using the historical exchange rate will show the original cost in a consistent manner.

In summary, FASB 52 generally uses the current-rate method for balance sheet translation and defers translation gain or loss to a special equity account. Exceptions are made for affiliates that are an extension of the parent and for affiliates that operate in high-inflation economies.

Translation of the income statement is done in a similar manner. FASB 52 essentially translates all income statement line entries at an average exchange rate for the period. FASB 8 differs, using historical (when the asset was booked) exchange rates for cost of goods sold and depreciation, and effectively average rates for the other line entries. FASB 52 forces a balance with the creation of a new equity account (the cumulative translation variance account), while FASB 8 shows a new line entry on the income statement (gain or loss on translation), which adjusts retained earnings for the gain or loss.

Financial Statement Translation Exposure: An Example

Exhibit 14.2 shows the translation of both the balance sheet and the income statement, under FASB 8 and FASB 52, for our example firm.

Exhibit 14.2. Statements of Affiliate

| | Statements of affiliate in local currency | Statements of affiliate translated into home currency, using | | | |
| | | FASB 8 (temporal) | | FASB 52 (current rate) | |
	LC	HC/LC	HC	HC/LC	HC
Cash	200	.80	160	.80	160
Receivables	1000	.80	800	.80	800
Inventory	500	.95	475	.80	400
Fixed assets	2000	1.00	2000	.80	1600
Total	3700		3435		2960
Payables	250	.80	200	.80	200
Long-term debt	1000	.80	800	.80	800
Equity					
Common	1850	1.00	1850	1.00	1850
R/E	600		585	.90	540
CTV					(430)
Total	3700		3435		2960
Sales	4000	.90	3600	.90	3600
Cost of sales	(2000)	.95	(1900)	.90	(1800)
Depreciation	(300)	1.00	(300)	.90	(270)
Other	(700)	.90	(630)	.90	(630)
Trans. gain/(loss)			175		
Profit before tax	1000		945		900
Tax	(400)	.90	(360)	.90	(360)
Profit after tax	600		585		540

We have assumed that the inventory and cost of goods sold were booked when the exchange rate was HC .95 = LC 1, and that the equity in the prior example is divided into LC 1850 of common stock at the beginning of the period, supplemented by LC 600 in retained earnings from the period covered by the income statement.

Note that in Exhibit 14.2 the CTV line entry under FASB 52 is HC 430 units. This is the balancing entry and reflects the accumulated translation loss to date, which in our example reflects only one accounting period. Under FASB 8 the balancing entry is the reported gain on the income statement of HC 175 units. This gain, together with the actual taxes paid, produces the retained earnings of HC 585 required to balance.

It is not clear which of these two rules best reflects reality. Both rules adjust the home currency value of earnings and equity in response to the exchange-rate adjustment. FASB 52 shows a loss while FASB 8 shows a smaller gain. The problem is that only subsequent events will reveal the true size of these adjustments.

A final observation: Unlike the temporal method, use of the current method of translation (FASB 52) produces HC statements with no significant change in the key statement ratios (debt to equity, profit to sales, etc.), following a move in the foreign currency rate.

CICA 1650

In Canada, the relevant accounting authority is the Canadian Institute of Chartered Accountants (CICA). The evolution of the rule in Canada governing translation of foreign currency transactions, and the financial statements of foreign affiliates, has followed a pattern similar to that in the United States. CICA 1650 in the *CICA Handbook* currently specifies how the translation shall be done. This rule was last revised in 1983 and became effective in its current form for all fiscal periods beginning on or after July 1, 1983.

Rule 1650 takes a "situational" approach and makes a distinction between three kinds of activities:

1. Foreign currency transactions

2. Integrated foreign operations

3. Self-sustaining foreign operations

Typical foreign currency transactions are imports, exports, and foreign currency borrowing and lending. Foreign currency sales and purchases are translated at the exchange rate when the order was booked, and monetary balance sheet items associated with all these transactions are translated at the rate in effect at the balance sheet date. Nonmonetary accounts (i.e., inventory carried at cost) are translated at historical rates.

Integrated foreign operations are defined as an extension of the parent firm's activities, and generally would cease without the parent's active involvement. A sales or distribution outlet established abroad, even though incorporated as a legal entity in the foreign country, would be typical of this category. Under CICA 1650, the statements of this and similar affiliates would be translated using the temporal method. This treatment is similar to that of affiliates of American firms under FASB 52 when the functional currency of the affiliate is U.S. dollars.

Self-sustaining foreign operations are those that enjoy a substantial degree of operational independence from the parent, so much so that they could continue in their own right without further association with the parent. Statements of these operations are to be translated using the current-rate method. The American counterpart is a foreign affiliate with a functional currency other than U.S. dollars. Also in keeping with FASB 52, statements of self-sustaining Canadian affiliates operating in high-inflation economies must be translated using the temporal method. CICA 1650 does not specify exactly what "high inflation" is. However, the interpretation in practice has been similar to that under FASB 52.

CICA 1650 does have a major difference from FASB 52. It concerns the treatment of long-term monetary assets and liabilities with fixed and ascertainable maturity dates. CICA 1650 prescribes that any translation gain or loss on these items will be deferred and amortized over the remaining life of the asset or liability. This is true for all three types of foreign-currency-denominated activities specified earlier. Under FASB 52, using the current-rate method, these gains or losses would be closed to the CTV account, with no income statement effect until the affiliate was sold or liquidated, while the temporal method would include the gains or losses in period income.

Rule 1650 has yet another minor exception. If a foreign currency borrowing can be construed as a hedging activity for a foreign currency revenue flow, then any gain or loss on translation of the balance sheet entry for the borrowing can be deferred as long as the hedge is in effect. For Canadian corporations with U.S. dollar revenues, the "revenue hedge" approach provides complete deferral of the translation gain or loss on associated debt, as opposed to the amortization of the gain or loss over the remaining life of the liability that would otherwise be required for a monetary liability with a fixed and ascertainable life. The difference in reported income could be substantial in the case of a relatively short-term loan.

In summary, CICA 1650 and FASB 52 are quite similar, certainly in intent, and also in practice. The functional currency distinction produces much the same result as the situational approach in categorizing affiliates and in choosing between the current and the temporal methods. CICA 1650's differences seem designed to ease the reporting requirements of firms with substantial foreign currency debt. Both rules are mandatory for the jurisdictions to which they apply.

Managing Translation Exposure

In order to find ways to manage translation exposure, it is first necessary to be clear about the objectives. There are basically three approaches to the issue. The choice is strongly influenced by management's attitude toward risk. These approaches can be termed aggressive, risk-neutral, and risk-averse.

Hedging Strategies

The aggressive approach appeals to those who are willing to forecast a future exchange-rate scenario and take a position based on this forecast. This group is really speculating ("investing" would be a softer term) in the foreign exchange markets and is simply using the vehicle of the available corporation as a means to an end. Such activity is certainly not sinful, but it may not be smart; the markets may be sufficiently efficient to preclude consistent worthwhile profits, and the comparative advantage of the firm is more likely to be found in the management of activities in the firm's traditional product and service markets. However, major corporations do trade currencies at levels far in excess of that required for normal hedging practice, and because they stay in the markets, we can only assume they are making money. This activity, however, is more than exposure management.

The risk-neutral management approach would follow from the assumption of an efficient market. A market is efficient when all available information is incorporated in the current price. Under these conditions, the expected value of the gain or loss from any new position is zero, and for hedging activities the net expectation is slightly negative due to the transaction costs. If management can tolerate the volatility in wealth or value implied by random or unexpected market moves (the efficient-market assumption implies that "expected" moves are already reflected in the current prices), then the best strategy is to do nothing explicitly to hedge either transaction or translation exposure.

Hedging activity is really for risk-averse management. For these managers, the harm of a loss is of more consequence than the benefit of a gain of the same magnitude. As the size of a prospective gain or loss increases, most of us would eventually join this group. If this is the case, management should be willing to pay a small, but explicit, cost to reduce the variability of future wealth positions. This is the textbook definition of a hedge. The purpose of the translation exposure hedge is, therefore, to offset the influence of exchange-rate movement on reported shareholder wealth. The reported wealth is, of course, measured in the shareholders' currency.

Translation Exposure Hedges

Given that a decision has been reached to hedge translation exposure, the issue becomes how to do it. There are two basic approaches:

1. Adjust the assets and liabilities so that the balance sheet of the affiliate has zero net exposure under the particular rule with which it will be translated.

2. Use foreign exchange contracts to offset the translation gain or loss.

The approaches can be combined; however, each approach has its drawbacks.

Balance Sheet Neutrality. Assuming that the affiliate has been conducting its operations in the optimal manner before considering translation exposure, then any changes in asset or liability management will be unattractive from an operations standpoint. The more common methods include borrowing local currency and shifting the proceeds to another currency, leading or lagging receivables or payables, and changing the currency of purchases or sales transactions.

If local governments and trading partners subscribe to the notion that markets are efficient, or hold opposing views in the market, some of the suggested activities may be possible at acceptable cost. However, if managers seeking hedges hold particular views or expectations regarding future currency moves, and if these same views are widely held, then everyone will want to do the same thing at the same time. The cost of achieving balance sheet neutrality may be prohibitive. For example, if a given currency is widely considered to be likely to devalue, no one will want to hold receivables denominated in that currency, and the interest cost associated with borrowing that currency could be very high. In this case, the cash operating costs of bringing the net balance sheet position to zero under the relevant translation rule may be unacceptable.

Forward Contracts. Another alternative for translation exposure hedging involves using profit or loss from foreign exchange contracts to offset a gain or loss on translation. There are, however, several possible problems. The first is that the translation exposure to be hedged is unknown at the time the contracts must be negotiated; the exposure is based on the end-of-period statements, which are as yet only available as a forecast. For this reason it is very difficult to achieve a zero-position hedge.

In addition, the forward price may already be part or all of the way from the current spot to where the future spot will be. Since the gain or loss on the contract depends on the difference between the forward and the future spot prices, it will be necessary to position many more units of currency in the forward contract than are exposed on translation. If this is the case, then the hedge will only produce a zero outcome if the future spot turns out to be exactly as forecast. The success of the hedge depends, therefore, on forecasting (speculation) with respect to the future spot.

For example, assume the exposure of a U.S. dollar-based company is a net asset (long) position of 1 million French francs (FRF), as forecast for the end of the accounting period, one year hence. Consider the three market scenarios shown in Exhibit 14.3.

In scenario A the hedge is straightforward. Sell 1 million FRF forward at .30 USD/FRF. No matter what the future spot turns out to be, the pretax hedge result per FRF sold will offset the translation gain or loss per FRF exposed.

Now let us look at scenarios B and C, and assume that the future spot turns out to be .26 USD/FRF as forecast. Under scenario B, .02 USD will be gained on each FRF in the forward contract, and .04 USD will be lost on each FRF in the exposed position. In scenario C, the hedge contract will produce no gain at all, while the translation loss is again .04 USD/FRF. Assuming our future spot of .26 USD/FRF, and using a 1

Exhibit 14.3. Scenarios A, B, and C

	Scenario A USD/FRF	Scenario B USD/FRF	Scenario C USD/FRF
Current spot	.30	.30	.30
1 year forward	.30	.28	.26
Forecast of spot in 1 year	.26	.26	.26

Exhibit 14.4. Hedge Results for Scenarios A, B, and C

	Scenario A, USD	Scenario B, USD	Scenario C, USD
1-year forward price	.30 USD/FRF	.28 USD/FRF	.26 USD/FRF
Day 1 place hedge	300,000	280,000	260,000
Sell 1,000,000 FRF forward			
Day 365:			
Buy 1,000,000 FRF Spot at .26 USD/FRF	(260,000)	(260,000)	(260,000)
Hedge pretax gain	40,000	20,000	0
Translation loss: (.30 − .26) USD/FRF			
× 1,000,000 FRF	(40,000)	(40,000)	(40,000)
Net result, pretax	0	(20,000)	(40,000)

million FRF hedge, the results for all three scenarios are shown in Exhibit 14.4.

If the forward price is not the same as the current spot, as in both scenarios B and C, the hedge is not perfect. In scenario B, if the pretax gain on the hedge is to offset exactly the loss on the exposure, it is necessary to forecast correctly the future spot and sell forward an amount of FRF different from the exposure. If we are willing to bet on our forecast of .26 USD/FRF, we should double the size of the hedge at the available forward price of .28 USD/FRF. If, and only if, the forecast is true, we will make .02 USD/FRF on each of the 2,000,000 FRF sold forward, producing a gain of 40,000 USD, exactly equal the 40,000 USD exposure loss. However, we will have assumed a net short position of 1,000,000 FRF in the process, and any error in our forecast of .26 USD/FRF will produce a forward contract result unequal to the exposure outcome. For example, if the FRF strengthened to .32 USD/FRF, the net pretax result for scenario B would be a loss of 60,000 USD, as shown in Exhibit 14.5.

Finally, under scenario C, the forward contract will produce neither a gain nor a loss *if the forecast is correct* and, therefore, will not help with the exposure. However, risk reduction may still be achieved. If the contract amount equals the exposure, in scenario C the overall loss will be 40,000 USD *regardless of the value of the future spot*. This result is shown in Exhibit 14.6.

In summary, if the forward price is not equal to the current spot, then an accurate forecast of the future spot is needed and a net exposed position must be maintained, if the pretax contract result is to equal and

Exhibit 14.5. Scenario B Result with Spot of .32 USD/FRF

	Scenario B
Spot	.30 USD/FRF
1 year forward	.28 USD/FRF
Spot 1 year hence	.32 USD/FRF
Day 1 place hedge:	
Sell 2,000,000 FRF forward at .28 USD/FRF	560,000
Day 365:	
Buy 2,000,000 FRF spot at .32 USD/FRF	(640,000)
Hedge pretax loss	(80,000)
Translation gain:	
(.32 − .30) USD/FRF × 1,000,000 FRF	20,000
Net result, pretax	(60,000)

Exhibit 14.6. Scenario C Result with Three Future Spot Rates

	USD		
Forward, per FRF	.26	.26	.26
Future spot (assumed) per FRF	.20	.26	.30
Contract result per FRF	.06	0	(.04)
Result for 1,000,000 FRF contract	60,000	0	(40,000)
Current spot	.30	.30	.30
Future spot (assumed) per FRF	.20	.26	.30
Exposure result per FRF	(.10)	(.04)	0
Result for 1,000,000 FRF exposure	(100,000)	(40,000)	0
Net result, pretax	(40,000)	(40,000)	(40,000)

offset the translation gain or loss. Because of the forecasting require-ment, this activity may be more like speculation than hedging. However, if the contract amount equals the forecast exposure, the forward con-tract hedge can be used to lock in a pretax net gain or loss, regardless of the value of the future spot. Risk reduction of this nature is the real purpose and value of a hedge.

There is another, more fundamental, problem with the forward con-tract as a translation hedge. In most jurisdictions, the tax treatment of the gain or loss on the contract will probably be different from that of the gain or loss on translation. The contract gain or loss is realized; it is an actual cashflow. The translation gain or loss is unrealized; it may change reported income under some circumstances, but it will usually not attract tax until realized. As a result, if the objective is to produce a zero exposure hedge in after-tax units of shareholder currency, the problem becomes even more formidable. Notwithstanding the difficulty, when FASB 8 was the rule, many corporations used forward or futures contracts in an attempt to reduce the impact of translation exposure on reported income.

As described above, the opportunities for hedging translation exposure sound rather bleak. However, there are at least three rays of hope:

1. With the adoption of FASB 52 and the revised CICA 1650, it is now possible in many cases to defer translation gain or loss, as opposed to reporting it in current income. In this sense, the problem has diminished.

2. Larger corporations, with activities in several currencies, may enjoy a natural diversification effect, which, in turn, may reduce the net effect of currency fluctuation on shareholder wealth.

3. It may be possible to appeal directly to the shareholders with an explanation of the nature of translation gains and losses, and ask the shareholders, creditors, and others to look beyond the accounting conventions and cease to be alarmed at translation-induced volatility in reported earnings. For many privately held firms, the problem may be easily resolved in this fashion.

Learning to Live with the FX Gain/Loss Account

The preceding discussion of translation exposure concerned the problem of consolidating the foreign currency statements of subsidiaries and affiliates with the parent's home currency statements, and determining what to do with any gain or loss measured annually in the process. Many firms do business in foreign currencies without the benefit of a foreign currency subsidiary to act as a sort of gain/loss holding tank until year end. These firms have a similar and related problem. In this case, the reporting cycle may be much shorter (monthly, for example), and the "holding tank" becomes an account usually called something like "foreign exchange (FX) gain/loss account."

One problem with the latter system is that the foreign exchange gain/loss account balances offer wide scope for misinterpretation. This is usually because the account may report only part of the relevant information concerning a particular transaction. A second problem is the timing of the report; the gain or loss when reported may or may not be realized. As a result, the assessment may be premature and in the long run prove incorrect. Such incorrect assessments could, in turn, lead to some bad management decisions.

The account itself is really a catchall account. It is frequently used to keep a running total of gains or losses on outstanding transactions involving foreign currencies. The account is closed periodically to the profit and loss statement. The entries arise in the process of translating foreign currency revenues, expenses, assets, and liabilities for inclusion in the home currency statements. It is necessary and worthwhile to do this, and the foreign exchange gain or loss account provides the means. However, as indicated, it is also useful to understand the problems and pitfalls involved in interpreting the account.

To this end we will now outline the mechanics of three different types of transactions and see how these deals could be reported in the FX gain or loss account. The suggestion is that foreign exchange deals sometimes absorb a lot of unfair, and perhaps quite incorrect, evaluation. Our three example transactions are:

1. A foreign-currency-denominated sale with 90-day terms

2. A hedge of a foreign-currency-denominated account receivable

3. A cash-management swap, as opposed to separate loan and investment transactions

In all three cases, U.S. dollars will be assumed to be the foreign currency and Canadian dollars the reporting currency. However, the assumed currencies could be reversed, or other currencies used, because the accounting procedures shown are widely followed. Finally, the section will close with a brief example of the amortization of foreign currency gains and losses on outstanding debt, as specifically prescribed by CICA 1650. FASB 52 does not have a similar provision for firms reporting in the United States.

A Foreign Currency Sale with 90-Day Terms

Consider a Canadian corporation that exports fidgets to the United States. The company makes sales of 100 USD per month and collects the cash in three months' time. The company hedges half of the sales on a forward basis at time of sale and deals the balance on a spot basis when the cash is received.

The trail of accounting entries that follows assumes the following market scenario:

USD sales	100
Average FX rate:	CAD/USD
Month 1	1.30
Month end FX rate:	
Month 1	1.32
Month 2	1.36
Month 3	1.28

Fifty dollars, or one-half of the sale, was hedged forward in month 1 at 1.3200. The balance was sold spot in month 4 at 1.3000. Exhibit 14.7 summarizes the relevant accounting entries as of the end of the first month.

The company would show sales of 130 CAD, based on 100 USD sales, converted at the average rate of 1.30 CAD/USD. The differential between the USD and CAD revenue items is 30 CAD and is charged to the FX gain/loss account. When the USD receivable is converted at month end, the conversion at 1.32 gives a net gain due to foreign exchange movements of 2 CAD. Note, however, that 50 USD of the 100 USD sales were sold forward at 1.32, and 1 CAD of the 2 CAD FX gain is a gain that will be realized. However, the CAD proceeds to be received from the other 50 USD are not yet known, and the gain should be viewed as possible, but not realized. Exhibit 14.8 shows the entries for the following month, and the effect of the exchange-rate adjustment when the CAD weakens to 1.36 CAD/USD.

The exchange rate at the end of month 2 was 1.36 CAD/USD. The revaluation of the USD account receivable resulted in a net gain in the FX gain/loss account of 4 CAD. The offset on the balance sheet is a CAD accounts receivable 4 CAD higher than at the end of month 1.

Exhibit 14.7. Accounting Entries—Month 1

	USD accounts			CAD accounts			
	Income statement	Balance sheet		Income statement		Balance sheet	
	Revenue	Accounts receivable	Cash	Revenue	FX gain/(loss)	Accounts receivable	Cash
1. USD sale is recorded	CR 100	DR 100					
2. USD revenue converted to revenue at month 1 average rate of 1.30	DR 100			CR 130	DR 30		
3. USD accounts receivable converted to CAD A/R at month end rate of 1.32		CR 100			CR 32	DR 132	
Net entries	0	0		CR 130	CR 2	DR 132	

Exhibit 14.8. Accounting Entries—Month 2

	USD accounts			CAD accounts			
	Income statement	Balance sheet		Income statement		Balance sheet	
	Revenue	Accounts receivable	Cash	Revenue	FX gain/(loss)	Accounts receivable	Cash
1. Reversal of prior month-end entries		DR 100			DR 32	CR 132	
2. USD accounts receivable converted to CAD receivable at month-end rate of 1.36		CR 100			CR 36	DR 136	
Net entries		0			CR 4	DR 4	

This gain of 4 CAD is, however, overstated by at least 2 CAD, because 50 CAD of the sales were sold forward at a rate of 1.32 CAD/USD.

If one wanted to prevent such FX gains or losses from being overstated, one could revalue the outstanding forward contract that is specifically related to the receivables that are being revalued. The revaluation would consist of the following steps:

	USD amount	Revaluation rate	CAD equivalent	Gain/(loss), basis previous rate
Forward contract	50	1.32	66	
Month-end rate:				
Month 1	50	1.32	66	0
Month 2	50	1.36	68	(2)

In doing this revaluation, the 2 CAD loss on the revaluation for month 2 would reduce the FX gain to 2 CAD, which is indeed appropriate, as the 50 USD in unhedged sales would generate this gain if hedged at 1.36. Exhibit 14.9 shows the revaluation for month 3 when the CAD strengthened to 1.28 CAD/USD.

The CAD strengthened over the course of month 3 from 1.36 to 1.28 CAD/USD. The reduction in the value of the receivables generated an 8 CAD FX loss. However, half of that loss is misreported because the forward hedge was put in place. If the forward contract had been revalued at month end, a 4 CAD gain on the contract would have been reported [50 USD × (1.36 − 1.28) = 4 CAD].

Exhibit 14.9. Accounting Entries—Month 3

	USD accounts			CAD accounts			
	Income statement	Balance sheet		Income statement		Balance sheet	
	Revenue	Accounts receivable	Cash	Revenue	FX gain/(loss)	Accounts receivable	Cash
1. Reversal of prior month-end entries		DR 100			DR 36	CR 136	
2. USD accounts receivable converted to CAD receivable at month-end rate of 1.28		CR 100			CR 28	DR 128	
Net entries		0			CR 8	DR 8	

Finally, Exhibit 14.10 reflects the collection of the receivable and the final disposition of the account. The exchange rate assumed at this time is 1.30.

A 3 CAD FX gain is reported because the two contracts on which the USD were delivered were superior to the previous month-end revaluation rate. A reconciliation is as follows:

Forward contract	50 USD × (1.32 − 1.28) = $50 × .04 =	2 CAD
Spot contract	50 CAD × (1.30 − 1.28) = $50 × .02 =	1 CAD
Total		3 CAD

Exhibit 14.10. Accounting Entries—Month 4

	USD accounts			CAD accounts			
	Income statement	Balance sheet		Income statement		Balance sheet	
	Revenue	Accounts receivable	Cash	Revenue	FX gain/(loss)	Accounts receivable	Cash
1. Reversal of prior month-end entries		DR 100			DR 28	CR 128	
2. USD cash collected		CR 100	DR 100				
3. Delivery on forward contract at 1.32			CR 50		CR 16		DR 66
4. Delivery on spot contract at 1.30			CR 50		CR 15		DR 65
Net entries		0	0		CR 3	CR 128	DR 131

A summary of the FX gains and losses for the four months is as follows:

Month	FX gain/(loss)
1	2
2	4
3	(8)
4	3
Total	1

A reconciliation of the net 1 CAD FX gain is as follows:

Conversion method	USD amount	Rate	CAD equivalent
Forward contract	50	1.32	66
Spot contract	50	1.30	65
Total cash proceeds	100		131
Less: Revenues as per financial statements	100	1.30	130
Net FX gain	0		1

The FX gain/loss account reports unrealized foreign exchange gains or losses, which can be especially misleading when there are hedges in place, such as the forward contract, which were not revalued.

A Hedge of a Foreign Currency Account Receivable

Consider another instance in which the FX gain/loss account should be viewed with caution. Assume Company Hedge-It makes a policy decision to hedge its anticipated sales at the prevailing rate of 1.30. The company's results are as follows:

Sales revenue	100 USD
Operating expenses	10 USD
Operating expenses	40 CAD
Forward sale	90 USD at 1.30 CAD/USD

If the company, for accounting purposes, converts its sales based on the average monthly rate, consider the results under these two scenarios in Exhibit 14.11.

Exhibit 14.11. Monthly Average Rates and Reported Performance

	Scenario A	Scenario B
Monthly average rate, CAD/USD	1.30	1.40
Sales revenue	130	140
Expenses:		
USD based	(13)	(14)
CAD based	(40)	(40)
Margin	77	86
FX gain/(loss)	0	(9)
Net margin	77	77

The net margin in both cases is 77 CAD, which is what one would expect by hedging the net 90 USD exposure. The 9 CAD foreign exchange loss in scenario B arises because the revenue is converted at the monthly average rate that existed when the sale was finally made. The policy to hedge at 1.30 CAD/USD is not reflected in the revenue line item, where it could be argued that it belongs. Instead, revenue is overstated because the USD sales were converted at the 1.40 exchange rate. The offset is shown as a foreign exchange loss.

Notwithstanding the inconsistency of the policy and the accounting treatment, the FX loss of 9 CAD does show the opportunity loss incurred by hedging on a forward basis as opposed to leaving the exposure unhedged. Often, it is this explicit measurement of opportunity gains and losses that causes a foreign exchange policy, and hedging practice, to come under close scrutiny. Everyone likes to see hedging gains, but many in management have a tendency to look at hedging losses as evidence of bad practice, and justification for not hedging in the future. The original rationale behind the decision to hedge is sometimes forgotten.

The results of hedging other market risks, such as commodity prices, do not show up in the financial statements in the same way as foreign exchange gains and losses, and thus management may or may not be as aware of the opportunity costs. Any management policy to hedge risks should be measured and evaluated on a regular and consistent basis. Because of the accounting treatment, foreign exchange activities frequently come under closer scrutiny than most other aspects of risk management.

A Cash-Management Swap as Opposed to a Separate Loan/Investment

The treatment of forward points (the difference between the spot and forward prices) is another typical problem area when assessing the significance of a reported loss in the foreign exchange gain/loss account. Chapters 7 and 9 discuss forward points and swap transactions in considerable detail. One type of swap is the cash-management swap, which can be used to make the most effective use of cash. Consider the following situation for Company Cashbest:

Cash position:
  Surplus 10,000,000 USD for 1 month
  Deficit 12,500,000 CAD for 1 month

Interest rates:
  USD deposit rate, 7%
  All-in CAD borrowing rate, 11%

Exchange rates:
  Spot   1.2500
  1 month forward   1.2538

Alternative A. This alternative involves investing the USD at 7 percent and borrowing the CAD at 11 percent. The net "cost" is determined by converting the USD interest earned to a CAD equivalent basis, as Exhibit 14.12 shows.

Alternative B. This alternative, shown in Exhibit 14.13, involves taking the surplus USD and swapping them into CAD for one month. At the end of the month, Company Cashbest still retains ownership of the USD and is in the same position as it would be under alternative A.

Exhibit 14.12. Invest USD, Borrow CAD

	USD	Exchange rate	CAD
1. Invest USD.	58,333		
$\left(\dfrac{10,000,000 \times .07 \times 30}{360}\right)$			
2. Sell forward the USD interest.		1.2538	73,138
3. Borrow CAD.			
$\left(\dfrac{12,500,000 \times .11 \times 30}{365}\right)$			(113,014)
Net cost			(39,876)

Exhibit 14.13. Deal a Cash Management Swap

	USD	Exchange rate	CAD
a. Convert USD spot at 1.25.	(10,000,000)	1.25	12,500,000
b. Buy USD forward at 1.2538.	10,000,000	1.2538	(12,538,000)
Net cost			(38,000)

Advantage of the Cash-Management Swap

The cash-management swap would save the company 1876 CAD (39,876 − 38,000). In many companies, the result, as reported in the financial statements, of doing the swap versus investing and borrowing would be as follows:

1. Reduced interest expense	113,014
2. Reduced interest revenue (CAD equivalent)	(73,138)
3. Increased FX loss	(38,000)
Net impact	1,876

Company Cashbest is $1876 better off by doing the swap; yet the financial statements show a significant foreign exchange loss. This implies that the cash manager is doing something wrong, when, in fact, a good business decision has been made.

Forward points represent interest differentials, and it is critical to report these transactions properly. In this case, the 38,000 CAD "loss" should probably be charged to interest expense. Consider another case. Assume the company did not have surplus USD and found it cheaper to borrow CAD via fully hedged USD Libor compared with CAD banker's acceptances. Any forward points incurred or paid would be the result of the borrowing decision. The points should, therefore, be charged to interest expense and not the foreign exchange gain/loss account. If they are shown in the FX account, distortions are created in both the interest expense and the FX gain/loss account.

Foreign exchange swaps can be used for other purposes as well, and care should be taken to handle the accounting entries properly. Consider the following two situations:

1. A company with no USD cashflow has to fund a USD futures margin. It funds the margin by swapping local currency into USD. This

is clearly a cash-management transaction, and forward points should be an interest item.

2. Maturing forward contracts can be rolled forward using swaps. The correct accounting treatment of these transactions can be less than obvious, depending on the situation. If the cashflow related to the contract has not arrived, is the subsequent rollover charged to the FX gain/loss account (i.e., the FX manager) or to another account? If payment is late because the credit or sales department is being too generous with collections or terms, the FX gain/loss account should not be charged or credited.

Clearly, the FX gain/loss account can be a catchall and confusing account. If the performance of an FX manager is measured by this account, the manager can become far too involved with transactions and items that are inappropriate or unnecessary from an overall company standpoint. The manager needs to be motivated to do what is best for the company, and not to try to make a particular line item look better at the expense of the company or other line items. Consequently, measuring an FX manager's performance on an overall hedging and cash-management basis requires a form of shadow accounting system. This approach is discussed more fully in Chapter 16.

Explanations for the FX Gain/Loss Variances

As examples of the sources of variance in the FX gain/loss account, consider the following, all of which assume a Canadian company exporting to the United States.

1. The rate at which sales are converted into revenues may differ from the month-end rate at which the account receivable is converted.
2. If accounts receivable at one month end remain uncollected at the next month end, the difference in the two month-end rates will cause a variance.
3. If accounts receivable are collected, the impact can be one of several:
    a. If the cash remains in USD, the variance will be the difference between the two month-end rates.
    b. If the cash is converted to CAD, the difference between the month-end rate and the conversion rate(s) will cause a variance.
    c. If the cash was used to pay for USD expenses, the difference between the month-end rate and the expense rate will cause a variance.

4. The forward points on swap transactions can lead to variances. If the second part of the swap is outstanding over the month end, any revaluation based on the month-end rate and the new contract rate could cause a variance.

Accounting for FX Gains/Losses on Outstanding Debt

As a final example of foreign exchange gain/loss reporting in Canada under CICA 1650, consider the treatment of foreign currency long-term debt. Foreign exchange gains and losses on long-term debt are included in full in period income in some countries, while in others, such as Canada, the gains and losses are amortized over the remaining life of the debt. Exhibit 14.14 shows how the amortization would be done.

In year 1, the loss is 1,000,000 CAD in total, but only 200,000 CAD of the loss is taken into income. The remainder is set up as a deferred item that will be amortized over the remaining four years in equal amounts of 200,000 CAD per year.

In year 2, the year-end exchange rate is unchanged from year 1, and thus no additional exchange loss is incurred. Accordingly, the exchange loss on the financial statements is again 200,000 CAD, with a corresponding reduction of the deferred item.

Exhibit 14.14. Amortization Schedule: Long-Term Debt FX Gains and Losses

(CAD 000)

Time 0	Amount of USD debt issued						
	Term				5 years		
	Original conversion rate				1.4000 CAD/USD		

			Amortized gains and (losses) recorded					
	Year-end exchange rate	Exchange gain/(loss) incurred	Year					
Year			1	2	3	4	5	Total
1	1.41	(1000)	(200)	(200)	(200)	(200)	(200)	(1000)
2	1.41	0		0	0	0	0	0
3	1.38	3000			1000	1000	1000	3000
4	1.38	0				0	0	0
5	1.40	(2000)					(2000)	(2000)
Exchange gain/(loss) per financial statements			(200)	(200)	800	800	(1200)	0

Note: Amount of USD debt issued = $100,000,000

In year 3, a gain of 3,000,000 CAD is achieved [100,000,000 CAD × (1.4100 − 1.3800)]. Amortized over three years (the current year and the remaining two years), the gain is 1,000,000 CAD per year. On the financial statements, the net gain is only 800,000 CAD, reflecting the losses being amortized from prior years.

Since year 4 brings the same year-end exchange rate as year 3, there are no further amortization entries. The net gain is again 800,000 CAD.

At year 5, the closing rate is the same as the original conversion rate of 1.40. Given this, the overall gains and losses over the life of the debt should net each other out. Compared with the previous year end, there is a 2,000,000 CAD loss for the year which, combined with the net amortization amount from prior years, yields a net loss for year 5 of 1,200,000 CAD. The net gain/loss for all five years is indeed zero.

Amortizing the gains and losses over time tends to smooth out the impact on the financial statements. However, as the debt nears maturity, the "reduction" due to amortization is less and less because of the fewer number of years remaining over which the debt can be amortized.

15

Credit Risks in Foreign Exchange Transactions

Executive Summary

Chapter 15 addresses the issue of credit risk that can occur in foreign exchange transactions. The chapter focuses primarily on the two most prevalent forms of credit risk in foreign exchange transactions, namely settlement risk and replacement risk. It also briefly describes related credit risks such as payments risk, third-party payments, and country risk, and finally it touches on issues such as netting of contracts and centralized clearinghouses.

Introduction

The preceding chapters have discussed various foreign exchange products and transactions. Involvement in these transactions will often incorporate a degree of credit risk. Organizations that have difficulty in obtaining credit lines may have limited access to products such as forward contracts, which could, in turn, impair their ability to manage their financial risks properly. For organizations that can easily obtain credit, access to the products is not a problem. However, it should be remembered that there is credit risk for both parties in most transactions, and all parties, whether of weak or of unquestioned creditworthiness, should be aware of the risks involved and ensure that the credit risk they are extending to their counterparty is known and controlled.

A significant number of foreign exchange transactions are accommodated by credit lines. To date, most credit lines have not had a fee attached. As there is no apparent direct cost to the credit lines, some organizations may not even be aware of their existence. However, it is a credit facility and is part of the overall credit extended by a counterparty. In addition, use of credit for foreign exchange or interest-rate dealings can reduce credit availability for other aspects of the organization's business. Consequently, proper management of this scarce resource should be proactively pursued.

Categories of Risk

There are two main categories of risk in foreign exchange transactions:

1. *Settlement risk* is incurred when a payment is made to a counterparty on a foreign exchange contract before the countervalue payment has been received. The risk is that the counterparty's payment will never be received.

2. *Replacement risk* is the risk of having to absorb the cost of replacing a foreign exchange contract at prevailing market rates if the counterparty fails to honor the contract.

Settlement Risk

Settlement risk exists when funds are paid to a counterparty before the countervalue is received. All foreign exchange contracts, whether cash, spot, or forward contracts, eventually settle. The process of settling foreign exchange transactions is conceptually quite simple: you pay me, and I pay you. In reality, a single foreign exchange settlement is part of a network of payments systems located throughout the world, in different time zones, involving many different currencies, and totaling hundreds of billions of dollars each business day.

Settlement of a foreign exchange transaction requires that each counterparty tell the other party where to make payment. Existing payments systems are not linked globally so that payments would occur instantaneously. Rather, payments are likely to be manually handled one or more times during the whole process. This element, plus the impact of time zones, often requires that the payment be initiated one or two days before the settlement date in order for the settlement to be properly executed. For example, a wire payment for a spot deal is prepared and sent usually on the same day, but for value one or two days hence. This delay should not be surprising. After all, the spot dates for foreign exchange deals are either one or two days hence because of the payments systems.

Exchange of payments in paper form, such as money orders or drafts, does not constitute same-day value if it is a foreign currency. Physical exchange of payments would be extremely onerous and impractical from a security and logistical standpoint. Consequently, wire transferring of funds is the only practical method of settling most foreign exchange transactions. As a result, settlement risk is largely unavoidable. In addition, because of the delays between the initial sending of the pay message and the final receipt of the payment by the counterparty, settlement risk is often borne by both parties in a transaction.

In the case of interbank trading, an active bank can have hundreds and thousands of payments to make each day to the many customers and dealing counterparties. No bank wants to undertake settlement risk unnecessarily, but it is a necessary risk to take if one wants to be in the foreign exchange business. To control the amount of risk undertaken, credit lines are usually established for each customer and trading counterparty.

The amount of settlement risk incurred on a particular transaction is the amount of currency expected but not yet received. If the counterparty is not considered worthy of receiving a credit line, the only way business can be done is to have receipt of the countervalue before the outgoing payment is made. For example, consider Bank A which does not have a settlement risk line for Company B and will not take settlement risk. If Company B sells 10 million USD to Bank A in exchange for 20 million DEM, Bank A will only deal on the condition that it will pay out the DEM after the USD have been received. Company B, on the other hand, would continue to incur the settlement risk.

Replacement Risk

The nature of replacement risk can be best explained using an example. Consider the following transaction involving a forward contract:

Day 1   *a.* Company XYZ sells 1 million USD to Bank A at a rate of 1.3000
            CAD/USD for delivery 60 days forward. The component prices
            are a spot rate of 1.2950 and forward points of .0050 premium.

        b. Bank A now has both a spot and a forward position which are
            managed independently of each other. (Chapters 7 and 10 cover
            this in detail.) For the sake of simplicity, assume Bank A covers its
            purchase from Company XYZ by selling 1 million USD to Com-
            pany ABC at 1.3000, also for delivery 60 days hence. The end re-
            sult is two offsetting forward contracts for Bank A.

Day 60 *a.* Company XYZ does not honor its contract with Bank A. Because
            of the default, Bank A is now short 1 million USD in its trading
            position. To remedy that, Bank A replaces its purchase from
            Company XYZ with a new purchase of 1 million USD from Bank
            C at current market rates of 1.3500 CAD/USD.

        b. Bank A honors its contract with Company ABC and delivers
            1,000,000 USD to ABC in exchange for 1,300,000 CAD.

A summary of the cashflows for Bank A that materialize on settlement of the contracts on day 60 is shown in Exhibit 15.1. The end result
is that Bank A loses 50,000 CAD as a result of the default by Company
XYZ.

The frequency of losses due to default on foreign exchange forward
contracts is extremely low given the large amount of transactions that
are dealt. The principal reason is that if an organization starts to get
into financial difficulty, its counterparties will reduce or terminate any
further forward dealings. Once the outstanding forward contracts have
settled, the replacement credit risk is removed. Nevertheless, losses
could occur, and the potential loss if a counterparty defaults must be
measured and established as a credit risk.

It is, however, unlikely that any counterparty will default on a contract if the contract rate is better than the prevailing market rate. If a
company was in receivership, the receiver would most likely deliver on
the contract and deal an offsetting contract in the market in order to
realize the current gain. Moreover, if there are losses on some contracts

Exhibit 15.1. Replacement Risk Cashflows for Bank A

Counterparty	Deal type	Dealing date	USD, cashflow in/(out)	CAD cashflow, in/(out)
Bank C	Cash purchase	Day 60	1,000,000	(1,350,000)
Company ABC	Forward sale	Day 1	(1,000,000)	1,300,000
Profit/(loss)			0	(50,000)

and gains on others, it should not automatically be presumed that the losses can be offset against the gains. Consequently, to be conservative, it is appropriate to view such credit risk as having only downside risk and no upside potential or benefits at all.

Measuring Replacement Risk

Two methods are commonly used to measure replacement risk:

1. The *deemed-risk approach* assesses a percentage of risk to each type and maturity of foreign exchange product.

2. The *mark-to-market approach* recalculates the credit risk on a regular basis, usually daily, by determining what it would cost to liquidate the contract at current market rates.

Deemed-Risk Approach

If we refer to the example, the loss on the contract defaulted on by Company XYZ was limited to the movement in the exchange rate. In this case, the market moved .0500 against Bank A, or 3.8 percent of the USD contract amount. Predicting what the actual gain or loss will be if a counterparty defaults in the future is impossible to do. If that were possible, we would hold the golden key to forecasting the markets. Consequently, estimates of the credit risk are made. These estimates can be based on practical experience of losses or derived from an analysis of actual daily market movements over time.

If loss experience is used, the risk may be understated if the losses incurred were small. In addition, losses could have been minimized because credit lines were only extended to good credit risks. Consequently, completing a historical analysis of markets may be more appropriate in quantifying the type of risk that a forward contract may pose. Completion of this kind of analysis provides two key results:

1. Higher levels of credit risk are experienced for longer-term transactions.

2. Different currencies have different degrees of risk.

The longer time period simply provides more time for adverse rate movements to occur. In addition, while the financial well-being of a counterparty does not usually change dramatically in the short term, the possibility of a significant deterioration occurring over a five-year period is much greater. The increased business risk and market-

Exhibit 15.2. Example Replacement Risk Factors

Currency	< 90 days, %	91–365 days, %	1–5 years, %	Over 5 years, %
CAD	4	10	20	40
DEM	7	25	40	75
FRF	7	25	40	75
JPY	7	25	40	75

movement risk with increasing term need to be considered as part of the risk of forward contracts.

Different currencies have different degrees of volatility. The CAD is tied closely to the USD and has less volatility against the USD than it does, for example, against the DEM. Similarly, the currencies within the European Economic Community all move against each other within a fairly small band. Consequently, the risk of a particular forward contract will also depend on the two currencies in the contract.

Exhibit 15.2 is an illustration of how risk factors might be assigned to a contract according to term and currency, assuming all transactions are valued against the USD.

When using the information contained in Exhibit 15.2, short-dated forwards between the USD and CAD are shown as having a risk content of 4 percent. In dollar terms, the 4 percent deemed risk on the contract between Bank A and Company ABC would be $40,000 USD (1,000,000 USD × .04), or 52,000 CAD (1,000,000 USD × 1.3000 CAD/USD × .04). The actual loss for Bank A is 50,000 CAD, which is almost the extreme maximum loss deemed to have been undertaken.

When using the historic analysis approach to establish the replacement risk factors, a specified level of certainty will usually be used. For instance, if a 90 percent certainty level is desired, the most extreme 10 percent of market movements is removed from the database. While still a possibility, these movements are viewed as market aberrations and not relevant to the calculation of risk. To date, no common risk-factor framework for forward contract replacement risk is used by the marketplace. Each market participant has tended to establish its own risk factors, which can vary significantly. However, the issue of capital adequacy will probably lead to a more consistent base of risk factors in the marketplace.

Three main arguments support the deemed-risk approach:

1. A detailed assessment of historical movements should provide an adequate foundation for assigning risk factors.

2. The control system requires very low maintenance once it is operational.

3. Credit exposure is easily identified and contained within any imposed limit.

If an organization has a manual control system, a deemed-risk approach is the only practical way to go. Moreover, a standard risk factor for all contracts is almost a necessity for the system to work reasonably well and not be an administrative nightmare. For that reason, a 10 percent risk factor has historically been a commonly used factor.

Critics of the deemed-risk approach have four primary concerns:

1. If the market moves in excess of the deemed-risk content, then the loss on a defaulted contract would be in excess of the amount allowed for under the credit line. Normally, one contract does not consume an entire credit facility afforded a counterparty, but it could.

2. Historical-rate analysis does not guarantee that it is representative of future market movements.

3. During any crisis, the actual losses facing an organization can only be estimated. The true risk can only be done via a mark-to-market calculation. If computer systems are not in place to do this function, the time required to complete the task manually could be quite lengthy.

4. Not all transactions necessarily incur credit risk, or if they do, they incur far less risk than is associated with the risk factors. Consequently, utilization of credit lines may actually be overstated.

Mark-to-Market Approach

The mark-to-market approach recalculates the credit risk attached to transactions using actual market rates. The process is usually completed at the end of every trading day, and sometimes more frequently than that.

There are two principal criticisms of mark to market:

1. The mark-to-market analysis on a particular day may show that there would be no loss if the existing contracts were defaulted upon and had to be replaced. The lack of credit risk at that time would naturally provide credit room for considerably more transactions with the same counterparty. If the market then moved significantly so that the contracts were in a loss or credit-risk position, the combination of the market move and the additional contracts could quickly result in the credit line being exceeded for that counterparty.

2. Without sophisticated digital feeds of daily market rates, the process of inputting mark-to-market rates into the system could be extremely laborious.

Whether an organization uses the deemed-risk approach or the mark-to-market approach depends on a number of factors. The number of transactions, number of counterparties, variety of products and currencies dealt, credit capacity, and credit risks of counterparties and others will all play a role. In some organizations, such as banks, which heavily trade the markets, it may be prudent to have a system that incorporates elements of both systems.

Collateralized Credit Lines

In some transactions, the credit risk is not accommodated by credit lines. Instead, cash or its equivalent is used as collateral for the transaction. The futures market is a good example. In the case of futures, initial cash margins, treasury bills, or letters of credit must be pledged *before* entering into transactions. The margin is sufficient to ensure the futures exchange against losses if the transactions entered into by the party are subsequently not settled. Moreover, these contracts are marked to market on a daily basis, and if the contracts are at a loss, the party must supply additional margin, known as *variation margin,* so that the total margin provides adequate collateral against the contracts.

A similar situation exists in the over-the-counter market where forward contracts or currency options are supported by margin. Margin is often used by market participants who do not have the financial strength to support a credit line and by private companies who do not wish to reveal their financial statements to their counterparties. Margin may also be used by entities who have fully utilized their existing credit lines and yet want to do additional deals.

Investment swaps can also have a degree of credit risk. The investor owns the underlying foreign currency investment as well as the forward contract. While it is unlikely to occur, the investor could ask the bank for the proceeds from the maturing deposit and then default on the forward contract. Because of this potential problem, some parties view investment swaps as having the same credit risk as any other forward contract. To eliminate this risk, it is necessary for the deposit to be legally tied to the forward contract. Doing so effectively collateralizes the forward contract, as it guarantees that the maturing proceeds from the investment will be delivered against the forward contract.

Credit Lines

Credit is a resource that needs to be properly managed by all dealing parties. Some general guidelines in its usage should be observed:

1. Forward contract credit-risk lines should be established and monitored for each counterparty dealing forward contracts. The line should establish a dollar limit on the exposure that can be assumed. The line should also specify the maximum term of forward contracts. It may also specify the currencies that are allowed.

2. Few dealers are authorized to deal with a counterparty unless an appropriate credit line has been approved. Assessing credit risk and determining the maximum credit lines to be given to a counterparty are specialized skills, not usually found in dealers. However, the global, 24-hour nature of trading sometimes requires that credit decisions be made when no credit people are immediately available. As a consequence, some senior management in the dealing room may be given authority to make judgments on whether or not to give approval to deals that exceed the formal credit lines currently in place.

   Such delegation of credit responsibility is controlled. A particular individual will be given the authority only up to certain amounts, for certain terms of forward contracts and for certain customers. Senior managers or executives are seldom given unlimited authority to make credit decisions; they are simply given working parameters within which the account management, credit officers, and dealing management are comfortable.

3. Few credit lines for foreign exchange transactions have a fee attached. As there is no apparent direct cost to the credit lines, some companies may not even be aware of their existence. However, it is a credit facility and is part of an overall credit package provided by a bank. All parties should have a limit on the amount of credit that a counterparty is willing to extend to them. Consequently, there may be competition within an organization for credit lines, as use of credit in one area may prevent other credit-driven transactions from being done with that counterparty. For all organizations, but particularly for those that deal in a variety of markets involving credit risk, it is important to have an efficient control system that facilitates effective use of credit.

4. Entities dealing in the foreign exchange markets need to be proactive in setting up their credit-monitoring system. They also need to be proactive in establishing the necessary credit lines that they may require. Credit should not be taken for granted, and delays in getting transactions done because credit was not established on time create unfortunate situations. It must be remembered that individual dealers at banks are usually not authorized to make credit decisions, and while they will want to do the deal, they simply may not have the authority.

Netting of Contracts

Credit risk in the context of global foreign exchange activities is substantial. Attempts to reduce the level of credit risk have been undertaken using a process called *netting*.

Occasionally, a counterparty could have two forward contracts that partially or entirely offset each other. For example, consider Exhibit 15.3 which summarizes Bank A's cashflows from two forward contracts dealt with Company XYZ.

The contracts are equal and offsetting on the USD cashflow. The DEM cashflow difference of 50,000 DEM represents Bank A's loss and Company XYZ's gain on the two contracts dealt with Bank ABC. The two deals may be totally unrelated. They have the same maturity date, but could have been dealt days, weeks, months, or even years apart.

Whether they are related from a trading position or not, the contracts do have a common maturity date. One may think that because the two deals offset each other on a maturity basis, they automatically offset on a credit and settlement basis. If this were the case, the only credit risk remaining would be the 50,000 DEM payable by Bank A to Company XYZ. However, as long as both contracts are still outstanding, they are usually treated separately. Using a 5 percent risk factor, both Company XYZ and Bank A have a 200,000 DEM credit risk (.05 × 4,000,000 DEM) to each other.

In order to net the contracts from a credit standpoint, the two contracts are normally canceled and a new contract is established which consists of the net cashflows between the two contracts. In this case, the new contract would be for Bank A to pay Company XYZ 50,000 DEM and to receive nothing in return. There is no real exchange rate, and Bank A has, from a risk standpoint, a loan of 50,000 DEM from Company XYZ. The credit risk for Company XYZ is 100 percent of the new contract amount, or the full 50,000 DEM. Bank A has no credit risk on the new contract.

Exhibit 15.3. Bank A's Cashflows of Two Offsetting Contracts with Company XYZ

	DEM, in/(out)	USD, in/(out)
Company XYZ sale of DEM at 2.0000	2,000,000	(1,000,000)
Company XYZ purchase of DEM at 2.0500	(2,050,000)	1,000,000
	(50,000)	0

Exhibit 15.4. Cashflows on Netted Forward Exchange Contracts

	DEM, in/(out)	USD, in/(out)
Company XYZ sale of DEM at 2.0000	2,000,000	(1,000,000)
Company XYZ sale of DEM at 1.9000	1,900,000	(1,000,000)
Company XYZ purchase of DEM at 2.1000	(6,300,000)	3,000,000
Company XYZ netted purchase of DEM	(2,400,000)	1,000,000

In this example, the net amount of the contracts is easily discernible. The netted contract is quite unusual in that one currency is to be paid and nothing received in return. If the scenario is changed so that the USD amounts of the contracts do not perfectly offset, we could still achieve a netted contract with an effective exchange rate that is considerably removed from prevailing market rates. Consider Exhibit 15.4.

In Exhibit 15.4, the resulting cashflows show that the netting of contracts would yield a contract for 1 million USD at an effective rate of 2.4000, which indeed bears no resemblance to the rates in any of the three contracts.

Measuring the gain or loss if contracts were liquidated at current market rates is a prudent practice for all market participants to follow. The estimated risk factors may be inadequate and understate the true losses that would materialize should a particular counterparty default. Consequently, additional measures need to be incorporated in control systems that allow for such circumstances. The same is true for netted contracts. In the above example, if the market was at 2.0000 DEM/USD, the loss would be 400,000 DEM, or 16.6 percent of the contract's reported value. The bank's risk factor and lines may be allowing for a smaller amount, perhaps 5 percent.

Netting contracts is clearly beneficial. A summary of the key advantages follows:

1. The reduction of the cashflows at maturity is a way of reducing settlement risk.
2. The use of the forward contract credit line is reduced, allowing additional deals to be made.
3. The credit risk borne by both counterparties is reduced.
4. The reduction in risk may also generate financial savings, if utilization of credit lines with the counterparty in question requires capital to support the line.

Credit Risks of Different Products and Transactions

Forward contracts can be undertaken for several purposes:

1. To hedge foreign currency receivables and payables
2. To hedge foreign currency long-term debt payments
3. To hedge translation exposures
4. To execute investment swaps or fully hedged debt

The credit exposure is basically the same regardless of the reason for the contract. Consequently, a credit facility should be in place and used for all such transactions. One exception does exist on investment swaps. As mentioned before, if the deposit is legally bound to be delivered on the forward contract, no credit risk exists.

Currency options are similar to forward contracts in some respects of credit risk. If Company XYZ bought a currency option from Bank ABC, such as a USD call/GBP put at a 1.8000 USD/GBP strike price, Company XYZ will only exercise the option if the option is in the money (i.e., if the USD is 1.7999 or stronger). If Bank ABC defaults, Company XYZ has a risk similar to that of a forward contract. Consequently, the counterparty buying the currency option faces the same form of credit risk that is found with forward contracts.

If Bank ABC bought this option from Company XYZ, Company XYZ would not have the replacement risk. In order to buy the option, Bank ABC would have paid the premium up front. Company XYZ has no risk should the market move against Bank ABC (and for Company XYZ), as Bank ABC will simply let the option expire unexercised. If the market moves in favor of Bank ABC, i.e., the USD is stronger than 1.8000, the counterparty would want to exercise the option. The replacement credit risk, therefore, lies with Bank ABC and not with Company XYZ. Also, it should be noted that in case of transactions such as the collar transaction, each counterparty both writes and buys an option, and, therefore, each has credit risk.

If Bank ABC bought a currency option and asked for the premium to be paid later, Company XYZ would have a credit risk in the amount of the premium. In such a case, Company XYZ is giving a cash loan. Credit lines would be required for this amount. This style of option, which is covered in Chapter 8, is known as a Boston option. Other option strategies may also involve a deferral of premium, and the resulting credit risk, although not clearly obvious at times, exists and should be handled accordingly.

Related Credit Risks

Payments risk is an associated credit risk that is primarily borne by financial institutions when making payments on behalf of others. If Bank A makes a payment on behalf of Customer B before it receives cleared funds from Customer B, Bank A has a payments risk. Or if a corporation purchases a foreign currency from a bank and wants the currency paid via a wire transfer, it has a payments risk as soon as it pays the bank for the currency. The risk may be limited, but the question remains whether the bank is solvent and will make the wire payment.

Banks use their relationships with other banks to make payments. For instance, a Hong Kong bank paying AUD to a German company may not be able to make the payment directly. Instead, the Hong Kong bank maintains accounts at an Australian bank and uses this Australian bank to make payments. The Hong Kong bank would need to have funds in the account in order to effect payment. If the Australian bank became insolvent, the balances held for the account of the Hong Kong bank could be in jeopardy.

Alternatively, if the payment was made by the Australian bank to another Australian bank where the German company had its account, the second Australian bank might default and not credit the German company. The end loser on the payment may not be easily or quickly determined.

Another risk involves *third-party payments*. Many companies will purchase foreign currency for payment of various goods or services. Consider an Australian company that wants to pay FRF to a French company. The Australian company buys FRF from an Australian bank and asks that bank to wire FRF to a French bank for the account of the French supplier. If it turns out that the payment should not have been made, it would appear at first glance that the Australian company has the problem of trying to get the money back. However, if the Australian bank cannot prove either via a written notice or via taped conversation that it was told to make the payment, it could possibly be held liable for the FRF payment. Consequently, on third-party payments such as this, where the end beneficiary is different from the sender of the payment, banks will often require written authority before they will make the payment.

A third related risk is *country or sovereign risk*. Business in any market is done within a set of rules determined by the government of the country. Should the rules change, a previously favorable dealing environment or transaction could become unfavorable. Outstanding foreign exchange deals, for instance, may not be allowed to be settled. Payments already in process may be beyond recall, and entities may incur settlement risk resulting in a loss of money, either temporarily or permanently. Funds on deposit in a foreign country could be frozen and the bank denied access, again temporarily or permanently. Risk due to changes in the political direction of a country is, of course, critical for all businesses to assess, but foreign exchange transactions form a special category due to the large amount of funds involved. It may be a relatively remote risk, but it is a risk that is always present.

Centralized Clearinghouses

Banks trade extensively with each other and accumulate large credit exposures on forward contracts and options. In addition, major settlement risk is taken each business day. Consider Bank Old, which has $100 million in USD purchases with one bank and $100 million in USD sales contracts with another bank, all of which mature on the same day. If the contracts could be netted between the three banks, there would be a minimum of payments exposure. Moreover, if the contracts could be netted soon after they were dealt, the forward contract credit risk would be minimized as well.

Broader netting can be accomplished if dealing entities form a clearing corporation. Any deals done between members are written up as deals with the clearing corporation, not the dealing counterparty. Consequently, if any deals offset, the central clearing corporation will net them. Automatic netting is a characteristic of futures markets and has served those markets well over the years. To the extent it is used in the interbank market, similar benefits will accrue in terms of minimizing forward contract credit risk, settlement risk, and payments risk between the member banks.

16

Establishing and Managing a Foreign Exchange Hedging Policy

Executive Summary

Chapter 16 addresses the policy issues in foreign exchange exposure management. Proper management of foreign exchange exposures is seldom accomplished by selling or buying currencies on the spot market. Nor is it accomplished by simply shopping for deals with a number of banks or investment dealers. This chapter outlines a framework for the development of an exposure-management policy. It considers active versus passive management of exposures and whether the corporate treasury group should be a profit center. It discusses controls, reports, centralization versus decentralization of exposure management, delegation of responsibilities, and performance measurement systems. Finally, it concludes with a summary of general comments and suggestions on foreign exchange management.

Introduction

Corporate foreign exchange exposure is almost inevitable. The exposure may be obvious, such as a transaction exposure involving a scheduled receipt of a foreign-currency-denominated cashflow six months hence. Or it may be a more subtle, and perhaps more damaging, economic exposure, as in the case of a ski resort catering to an entirely domestic clientele and doing business only in the local currency. One might assume this business would have no foreign exchange exposure. However, if the local currency were to strengthen sharply in real terms, the domestic clientele might take advantage of better ski vacation value abroad, with perhaps disastrous results for the resort.

Some exposures, such as foreign currency receivables, can be easily and completely hedged, for example, if there was an active forward market in the currency in question. Other exposures are more difficult to handle and may require expensive and long-term redeployment of corporate capital and human resources, as is typically the case when dealing with economic exposure. Hedging opportunities for the third major category of corporate exposure, translation exposure, fall somewhere in between. The problem here is to determine whether there is really anything that requires hedging. Since translation exposure affects only reported earnings and not cashflow, it can be argued that there is no problem in the first place.

Because these collective foreign exchange exposures can have a material effect on corporate performance, they deserve the attention of senior management. After all, these exposures probably arose from senior management decisions in the first place. Ignoring foreign exchange exposure is not an absence of policy in the area; it is a particular policy, although one adopted perhaps by default. Many corporations have an effective policy; some do not. This chapter suggests guidelines for establishing and implementing an appropriate policy.

Understanding the Exposures

From a policy formulation point of view, there are three basic questions concerning exchange exposure:

1. What are the exposures?
2. Should the exposures be proactively managed?
3. If so, how should it be done?

To answer these questions it is necessary to understand both the nature and scope of the exposures. For the three types of exposure (transaction, translation, and economic), the assessment can be made on several dimensions, including:

1. *The impact on the company of various degrees or magnitudes of exchange-rate movements.* Simulations using a range of rate movements are useful to explore sensitivity to these adjustments. Incorporating formal probability assessments of the rate movements will produce expected values of gains or losses. While this is most easily done for transaction and translation exposures, it is more difficult for the economic exposures that usually require inclusion of demand-and-supply elasticity assumptions in the data. However, simulation remains a powerful technique for identifying and understanding foreign exchange exposures. In effect, it forecasts the gains or losses that would result from a rate adjustment. The significance of the gains or losses can then be assessed, considering management's tolerance for risk.

2. *A time scale that shows when the exposures created by individual transactions will begin and when they will expire or materialize in the form of cashflow.* This exposure measurement method is most appropriate for transaction exposures and is sometimes called *funds flow mapping.* Determining when an exposure is created can often pose problems. Is it when the budget is finalized, when the price list is established, or when the firm contract is in hand?

3. *The degree to which there are offsetting or built-in hedges, as it is the net position by currency that matters most.* For example:

   a. Receivables and payables are in different foreign currencies. If currency-rate movements are highly correlated, as is the case for the deutsche mark and Dutch guilder, receivables in one currency may offset payables in the other currency from a USD exposure-management standpoint.

   b. Suppliers may exist in many different countries. The ability to switch suppliers may afford exposure-management opportunities to enhance business. At the very least, it will help the company remain competitive.

   c. Local currency balance sheets may be managed to reduce net translation exposure, depending on the translation rule being used.

   d. The profitability of a foreign subsidiary may be enhanced by the same rate movement that reduces the return on exports from the home plant.

   e. Some changes in foreign exchange rates may be passed through to the customer.

   f. A company may have exposure in a currency with interest rates that are strongly driven by the exchange rate. In this situation, if the currency weakens, interest rates will usually rise; and if the currency strengthens, interest rates will tend to fall. If a company in that currency is both a net investor and an importer, the losses caused by a weaker currency and subsequent higher import prices may be partially offset by the higher interest earned on the investment portfolio.

4. *The practice of the industry in regard to whether all competitors hedge or none do.* To the extent that one company differs from the rest, it may gain a competitive advantage or disadvantage. It may be safer to stay with the pack. However, with the globalization of markets, being competitive with other domestic companies may no longer be good enough. Foreign organizations can provide stiff competition, and strategies to meet this challenge must also be considered.

When a thorough review has been completed, the company should have a grasp of its exposure(s) created by movements in foreign exchange rates. Foreign exchange exposure is but one element of the total financial and business risk of the company. The composite nature of the total exposure requires that the exchange exposure be considered in conjunction with all the others; this is particularly important since the foreign exchange exposures arise because of other business pursuits. In addition, many of the exchange exposure-management methods can affect other areas of the company. When all the significant risks and issues are considered as a package, the objectives and strategies for dealing with foreign exchange exposure should be much easier to determine.

Should the Exposures Be Managed?

For any business in which foreign exchange exposure, broadly defined, can have a material impact on performance, this question is a nonissue. It must be managed. Exchange exposure management becomes one more element to consider in the execution of management's mandate to maximize long-run return on a risk-adjusted basis.

The amount of time and effort devoted to management of foreign exchange exposure will vary with the perceived benefit for the firm compared with benefits from alternative use of the resources. It is essentially a judgment call by management, similar to that required for other resource deployments. This decision, however, should be made with good information about what needs to be done and what can be done.

Defining the Policy Objectives

The objectives of a foreign exchange exposure-management policy should be clearly defined in the following aspects:

1. *Is it purely defensive in nature to protect the company from losses? Or is foreign exchange management expected to generate profits?*
The issue of establishing a purely defensive program versus establishing a profit center is important. The program cannot be defensive one day and a profit center the next day. If the program is to be aggressive and designed to generate profits, management's tolerance for risk must be addressed, and the appropriate resources, controls, and structure must be developed.

It should be noted that the foreign exchange markets allow transactions to be easily reversed. Entry and exit costs are minimal in comparison to other business decisions. Moreover, companies can have such significant foreign exchange exposures that effective exposure management requires an aggressive trading group. Aggressive trading can, by disguising the true underlying commercial transactions of the company, be of benefit for major market players. In addition, management may believe that effective management of the corporate exposures can only be done if staff members are committed full-time to trading the markets.

2. *Is cashflow the main concern, or are earnings?*
Changes in the 1980s in the way translation gains and losses are measured and reported have reduced the significance of this issue. Cashflow has clearly become the dominant concern for most organizations. However, the issue should still be addressed.

Financial statements record the past and are conservative by nature. They frequently do not show the current value of many assets such as land and reserves. On the other hand, they also cannot show all the business or financial risks facing the company in the future.

As a result of these and other problems, reported earnings tend to be an imperfect reflection of corporate performance. While the information content of reported earnings may still be important, and in some cases paramount, firms free to focus primary attention on cashflow as a performance criterion do have an apparent advantage.

3. *What is the relevant time frame to consider in developing the exposure-management policy?*
This question focuses attention on the relative importance to the firm of transaction, translation, and economic exposure.

If loss avoidance when reporting historical performance is critical, then translation and transaction exposure management should receive the most attention.

If short-term cashflows are the key focus, then hedging transaction exposure assumes the most importance.

If protecting and enhancing the firm's long-run competitive position is of prime concern, then management should devote time and resources to economic exposure management. However, in almost all cases where it exists, transaction exposure is also worth proper management.

4. *How much risk are organizations willing to take?*

Business and government inherently involve management of risks. Some organizations have a track record of steady growth in both profits and available cashflow. They have a low business or operating risk compared with other companies, which can have exceptional returns one year and very bad results the next year. Low business risk allows the company to take increased financial risks, because of the strong expectation that the resources will be available to handle any financial losses that may occur. Conversely, organizations with high business risk should take fewer financial risks.

Management's willingness to take foreign exchange risk should be supported by the organization's financial ability to support that risk. If risks are knowingly taken, management must know the potential losses associated with those risks and must also have the financial resources available to absorb those losses. Moreover, if significant financial risks are being taken, the company should have proper in-house expertise and resources to manage them properly.

How to Manage the Exposures

From an operational point of view, at least three systems must be put in place for effective exchange exposure management:

1. Currency value forecasting
2. Delegation of responsibility
3. Control and performance measurement systems

Currency Value Forecasting

Management can choose whether to attempt to forecast currency values, and, given the presence or absence of these forecasts, whether to hedge exposures. A policy of never hedging exposures essentially implies a forecast that future rates will be close to or superior to current forward rates. A decision has been made, whether management recognizes it or not, that it is better to wait before placing the hedge. A policy of automatic hedging suggests a high degree of risk aversion, more than the presence or absence of a forecast.

If management is willing to commit resources to the forecasting activity, and if it has the risk tolerance to actively maintain unhedged positions based on those forecasts, then exposure management may logically involve selective hedging. Moreover, the group or area involved could become a legitimate profit center. Chapter 11 discusses in more detail the interaction of forecasting and risk aversion in the formation of transaction exposure-management policy. Chapter 4 describes the forecasting process, while Chapter 10 discusses trading the markets.

The admission by firms of the possibility of being wrong in their forecasts gives true meaning to the term *exposure*. Management's perception of the accuracy and reliability of these forecasts will be a major factor in shaping the eventual exposure-management policy.

Delegation of Responsibility

A system and procedure for delegating responsibility for exchange exposure management form a second key element in policy implementation. This step is often the most difficult of the three. There are two prime considerations:

1. Any delegation of responsibility must be accompanied by the appropriate authority. To do otherwise is to give managers an impossible job.

2. The responsibility has to be lodged with individuals or groups that have the capacity to get the job done. Capacity in this sense goes beyond authority; it includes access to information, skills, knowledge and, in some cases, a willingness to take risks.

In the context of exchange exposure management, the major delegation issues are twofold. First, who should get involved? Second, should the responsibility be centralized in one location, usually the head office, or should it be decentralized in the operating divisions or subsidiaries? The latter issue is of concern only to larger firms, while the first is every organization's problem. Although these issues are interrelated, we will consider them in turn.

Who Should Get Involved?   When establishing a policy, senior executives in finance and treasury will obviously be included. While they may have had previous direct experience in management of foreign exchange, their most valued contribution to the policy development will often be their overall perspective and understanding of the organization from the standpoint of business and financial risk, systems, controls and information flows, and corporate goals, culture, and resources. They should be able to make judgments on what is most appropriate and feasible and what is required to implement the policy.

The treasury manager(s) and market dealer(s) should also be involved in policy development. Their day-to-day involvement gives them expertise and knowledge of the markets, of the policies of other organizations, and of their own organization's exposures, cashflows, problems, and capabilities. This management level often has widespread dealings throughout the company and can, therefore, be the best judge of implementation procedures for certain parts of the policy. Collectively, the treasury and finance staff will be the dominant players in formulating and implementing the policy; however, it is essential that they do not work in isolation. In particular, they must consider the impact of the policy on existing systems and procedures, the most important of which is often the performance assessment and reward system.

The controller's group, if one is defined in the corporate structure, should also be involved in policy development, because it may also become involved in the administration and execution of the deals that follow. The controller's group will have the background in control systems, reporting requirements, and implications for the financial statements. If the controller's department understands the goals and philosophy behind the policy, it will be better able to account for and measure the effectiveness of foreign exchange activities.

For example, as discussed in Chapter 14, accounting records sometimes show foreign exchange gains or losses that do not accurately reflect the true situation. The process of reconciling and explaining the numbers in the foreign exchange gain/loss account is often difficult and time-consuming. If controllers understand the overall picture and the process of determining how to account for the activity, interpreting and explaining the results will be streamlined.

In addition, while the treasury staff will execute the deals, the controller's group is often a good area to be responsible for payments and confirmations on payments and contracts. Such control is especially vital for organizations which proactively trade the markets, and in which the performance of individuals is measured on profits generated through trading.

Finally, the preparation of departmental or corporate budgets and plans may often have foreign exchange as a key variable; therefore, the treasury, control, planning, and operating groups should all work closely together.

Tax considerations may or may not be a factor to consider. If there is any question about tax at all, the taxation manager must be involved. The taxation issue can be complicated and varies from one organization to another. Although it is beyond the scope of this book, this issue may be relevant in the development of hedging policy.

In the development stages, it may also be prudent to solicit the opinions of groups such as sales, manufacturing, purchasing, and corporate planning. Insight can be gained into the origin of the actual exposures, competitive considerations, attitudes toward different approaches to foreign exchange management, potential problems, and logistical issues.

Expertise in foreign exchange varies considerably. Some organizations have tremendous depth and knowledge in the area and can address all aspects of exchange management. Other organizations may be lacking in the area, and outside assistance can be quite valuable. Formal consulting arrangements can be established, but often considerable expertise is available within the banks and investment dealers that service the account. Where a strong relationship exists, it can prove beneficial to have a foreign exchange representative participate in the policy development or review, if only as a resource or a devil's advocate.

When actual transactions do occur, one individual should ultimately have responsibility for hedging decisions. Although decisions by committee offer a form of security blanket to the members in that there is safety in numbers, it is a slow and cumbersome process, usually representing the rubber stamp of the decisions of one or two key individuals in any event. Input from any number of individuals, while valuable, can often lead to inaction. An opinion from a market contact usually carries far less weight than one from a senior executive within the company. Consequently, internal "bits of advice" from senior management can often cause a trader to second-guess his or her own opinion and cause paralysis. Human nature is such that no one wants to hear: "I told you so."

Since exposures can vary considerably within a company, different individuals can have responsibility for different exposures. Small ongoing transactions can be handled by clerical staff, for instance, while economic hedges may require the approval of the chairman. In all cases, it should be made crystal clear who has the authority for the transaction.

Should There Be Centralized or Decentralized Foreign Exchange Management? In multinational firms, this issue needs to be addressed on a global basis, as well as on a country-by-country basis. In addition, some types of exposures may be handled one way, while other types are handled in a different way. Translation exposure, for instance, usually requires a global, centralized approach, while transaction exposure may be best managed on a decentralized, country-by-country basis.

Some of the arguments supporting centralized exposure management include the following:

1. Centralization concentrates the workload in one area. Duplication of effort should be minimized. Staff that are dedicated to looking after foreign exchange and other financial risks on a full-time basis become specialists. One or two people focused strictly on foreign exchange should be more skilled, creative, and knowledgeable than would several people who spend a few minutes here and there on foreign exchange, when and if other priorities permit.

2. Centralizing the resources and expertise facilitates the development of a profit center. By dedicating resources full-time and providing the necessary equipment and tools, it is realistic to expect those resources to generate profits over and above the basic mandate of proper cash management and defensive foreign exchange exposure management.

3. More effective cash management should result from centralization. Foreign exchange exposure management is closely linked to overall cash management; thus, it makes sense to centralize foreign exchange management if cash management is centralized. Management of transfer pricing and taxes may also benefit from having all funds management in one area.

4. Financial markets are very closely related. Gains in both interest rate and foreign exchange management can be achieved if the players work closely together.

5. Many foreign currency positions offset each other. Centralizing of all exposures best facilitates the netting of positions simply because everything is in one place and the net residual exposure that may require hedging is more easily identifiable. This reduces situations where one group is buying at the same time as another group is selling the same currency. "Same time" may be simultaneous or within a day or two.

When offsetting positions are hedged independently, there will sometimes be gains and sometimes losses. While the gains should tend to offset the losses over time, it may not be so. At the very least, the netting process should eliminate the bid-and-offer spread.

6. Centralizing exposures can often mean that a series of small positions can be added together for purposes of hedging in the market. Dealing a market amount, rather than a retail amount, should result in better pricing and reduced administration costs.

7. Centralization also means that the overall exposures of the company and the hedges in place are readily identifiable at any one time. Should a material change in the markets be anticipated, the potential implications are more easily quantified. This, in turn, facilitates faster decisions on what should be done in the markets.

8. The company builds depth of people and expertise in one location. Companies may be better equipped to handle staff movements.

9. The department can serve as a central service department to the rest of the organization. Every other department knows where to go for proper and consistent information. Such a service can be critical to salespeople, for instance, who are regularly making price quotations involving different currencies and different forward dates. For people venturing into new territory, the centralized personnel could help to explain the appropriate way for pricing deals.

If exposure management is centralized, organizations frequently set up their treasury groups as a form of internal bank. Treasury effectively buys and sells the foreign exchange exposure from the operating groups. Treasury then can hedge the resulting net exposures into the market, if and when it sees fit. Actual contracts can be established between treasury and the operating groups, in which each party must live up to its obligations as it would with external counterparties.

Some of the arguments supporting decentralized exposure management are as follows:

1. "Head office" staff that hedge the exposures may not fully appreciate the problems and environment of the operating groups. Some groups may need to hedge, while others may not. Profit margins may vary dramatically depending on the hedging activity; management of those operations may want to control both the operating and financial factors. Foreign exchange management may be the difference between success and failure. Local responsibility for exchange management clearly gives local management the necessary authority in a critical area, if it is to be held responsible for overall profit performance.

2. Communication of all relevant information to one central location may be time-consuming and expensive. If such resources were spent

on people, the expertise on foreign exchange would be more widespread throughout the organization. Moreover, when some staff members are left "on their own," an atmosphere of creativity results which can generate good and profitable ideas. Movement of such people throughout the organization can, in turn, help different parts of the company to work together more effectively.

3. Local banking relationships are enhanced with an active dealing relationship. Moreover, closer access to information, be it political, economic, or otherwise, can enable local decision making to be more effective.

The decision whether to centralize exposure management must depend heavily not only on the nature of the exposures, but also on the corporate culture and on the extent to which other management responsibilities are delegated and decentralized. As a result, two competing and externally similar firms may quite logically organize the exposure-management function in different ways.

Performance Measurement Systems

Objectives. The performance of any hedging program should be measured. The objectives of the measurement system should focus on:

1. The contribution of the chosen strategy
2. The impact of abandoning the strategy to take advantage of specific, perhaps unexpected, market developments
3. The degree to which the staff executed the strategy according to plan

In viewing these elements in more detail, one should recognize that the underlying thrust of such analysis is to provide a context in which to assess the results objectively.

1. Since the strategy undertaken may be one of several alternatives, it is useful to compare and contrast the results with those of different strategies. This kind of analysis should be built into the system at the policy-setting stage because it is important to see the actual results of the other strategies as unforeseen factors arise. If necessary, periodic reviews can also be completed. A strategy that proved to be inappropriate at one point may be the best strategy in subsequent years.

For instance, hindsight may show forward selling of a currency to have been a poor strategy in some years and a good strategy in others.

If one just completed a year when it was a "poor strategy," it may be exactly the wrong time to stop forward hedging. The markets may turn the other way. In addition, it is critical to remember why forward hedging was done. If there were unacceptable risks facing the company, the forward hedging could well have paid for itself in the reduction of financial risk, even though no net financial gain was shown and opportunity losses were incurred.

2. One also needs the ability to determine the outcome if all outstanding exposures were hedged or all existing hedges were liquidated. From a purely business standpoint, it may be prudent to be able to take advantage of unexpected market developments in spite of the stated policy.

3. It is equally important to measure the performance of the staff in executing the strategy. This system should be designed so that it motivates the staff to deal in a manner consistent with the strategy outlined in the hedging policy.

An Example of a Faulty Performance Measurement System. Consider a situation where a company wants all transaction exposures hedged as soon as they are created. However, the performance of the staff administering the program is measured against the spot exchange rate when the foreign exchange contract cashflows are actually delivered. The measurement system creates an incentive for the staff to forget the exchange rates that prevailed when the exposure was created and to worry instead about the future spot rate which could be months down the road. The staff could indeed improve upon that spot rate and show a "profit," but the company could, in fact, have had sizable foreign exchange losses.

Take the case of Company AWOL, which sold some goods for 2,500,000 AUD and expects to be paid in three months. The current forward rate is .8000 USD/AUD, which was also the rate used in pricing the transaction. The company expects to make 50,000 USD on the deal.

	AUD		USD
AUD receivable	2,500,000		
FX rate		.8000	
USD proceeds			2,000,000
USD expenses			1,950,000
Net margin			50,000

The spot rate in three months' time turned out to be .7000. If the treasury group hedged at .7400, it would have made a significant profit according to a measurement system focused on ending rates only.

	Spot rate 3 months hence	Actual hedged rate	Variance
AUD receivable	2,500,000	2,500,000	
FX rate	.70	.74	
USD proceeds	1,750,000	1,850,000	+100,000

The treasury group generated cash proceeds of 1,850,000 USD, or 100,000 USD more than the 1,750,000 USD that a spot sale would have generated. A profit is credited to treasury. However, the company was originally expecting to receive 2,000,000 USD from which it would take a 50,000 profit. If the trader indeed made 100,000 USD for the company, a total company revenue of 2,100,000 USD and profit of 150,000 USD should have been achieved.

Instead, the company received 1,850,000 USD and had a net loss of 100,000 USD as opposed to a net profit of 50,000 USD. Clearly, the results are not what the company wanted. To identify the source of the problem, measuring the hedging rate against the original market forward rate of .8000 USD/AUD would have highlighted the losses incurred by not hedging until the AUD was worth .74 USD.

Measuring hedging results against the spot rate on the delivery date can also lead to poor cash-management practices.

Consider a company that has an option-dated forward contract whereby the company sold JPY and bought USD. Moreover, assume the treasury group has received the JPY on the first day of the option period. The normal reaction is to deliver the JPY on the contract and to take delivery of the USD. In doing so, the company exchanges a low-interest-rate currency for a higher-interest-rate currency. The company will earn the prevailing interest-rate differential for the duration of the option period.

On the other hand, consider a scenario where the measurement system compared the hedged rate with the spot rate on the date of delivery. If the dealer thought the JPY was going to weaken during the life of the option period, he or she might decide to invest the JPY for a short time before delivering on the contract. If correct, the measurement system will show additional gains for the treasury group. Reality, however, is that there is a net interest cost to the company.

Sources of Objective Exchange Rates. In collecting exchange rates for measurement purposes, official spot rates are usually available — from central banks, government agencies, or dealing banks — that can be used as representative market prices. The advantage to using them is that they are reliable and consistent. If a treasury department buys or sells currencies from operating groups and also sets the rates, the department may use a rate that is off-market. If the department hedges the expected exposures immediately, a "profit" for the department may be apparent. However, the profit is artificially created, not earned.

Consider a company that exports goods from Canada to the United States. The sales group has a price list that it sets weekly. Sales average 1 million USD per week. Cash is received approximately 60 days hence. If the current spot rate is 1.2000 CAD/USD, the treasury manager might set a rate at 1.1975, which could well have been the rate earlier that day. The dealer could then immediately sell 1 million USD 60 days forward and receive a rate of 1.2000 plus forward points of, say, .0040 premium. The all-in rate of 1.2040 gives the treasury manager a gain of 65 points.

Current spot rate	1.2000	CAD/USD
60-day forward points	.0040	
Forward rate	1.2040	
Price list rate	1.1975	
Gain	.0065	

However, what is the real contribution of that individual to corporate profit? If the treasury manager had given a rate of 1.2040 CAD/USD to the sales group, which makes it more competitive, and still made 65 points, a real contribution would have been made. Caution must be taken to ascertain whether profits of any dealing group are real or "gimme" profits.

If exposures having future cashflows are measured against the spot rate at the time each individual exposure is created, the treasury manager may start out in either an immediate gain or loss situation, because hedging such exposures will involve the forward points, which can work for or against the treasury manager. In the above case, the treasury manager was in a win position because he could sell the USD receivables forward and pick up the forward points.

If the company was a buyer of USD, the shoe would be on the other foot. One benchmark rate used in Canada is the "noon rate" set by the Bank of Canada around noon, Eastern Time. If the importing company structured its measurement system so that the treasury manager was measured against the average noon rate for the month, the manager could buy USD every day at noon based on the noon rate. An average noon rate could be achieved, and the manager could at least break even against the measurement system.

If, however, the exposures called for payment 60 days into the future, and the USD was more expensive in the forward market, the manager would have to pay the forward points. Assume the forward points averaged 50 points when the USD was bought, and the average noon rate was 1.1800 CAD/USD. In order to break even against the noon rate, the average spot rate when the USD was being bought forward would have had to average 1.1750, or 50 points better than the average noon rate. With a currency that has an average trading range of approximately 35 points per day, the trader is indeed faced with a formidable challenge and must resort to taking bigger risks in order to achieve the measurement yardstick.

In such cases, at least a ballpark adjustment for forward points is needed in order for the real contribution of the manager to be determined. In the above examples, the USD seller should be charged with the relevant forward points, while the USD buyer should be credited with some forward points.

The measurement system for a hedging program is usually done on a shadow accounting basis. Using the formal accounting records of the firm as the source of information can be onerous for several reasons:

1. The pricing of transactions, such as sales of goods in foreign currencies, may be recorded on the company's financial statements based on the current month's average rate. However, the deal may have been priced using the forward rate on the date of the transaction, which could be significantly different from the average rate. Some organizations using this specific forward rate as the basis for recording the sale will not have this discrepancy. However, for others it may be impractical or too difficult to do this. For instance, if a company had a large number of small sales and numerous hedges covering a combination of sales, it would be very difficult for that company to account for each transaction on a specific hedge-rate basis.

2. The FX gain/loss account is often a catchall account for miscellaneous items. Gains and losses recorded there can be quite significant and need to be analyzed to determine what is relevant for the hedging group and what is not. Rolling over forward contracts, for instance, which relate to funding of USD margin for commodity futures hedging, could alter the FX gain/loss account. This gain or loss should really be an interest expense or revenue item, not an ex-

change gain or loss. Accounting for it as an interest item could, however, get complicated and burdensome.

3. Revaluation of forward contracts would be required in order to off-set the translation profit impact of hedged foreign currency cash, receivables, and payables. Revaluing the contracts has merit, but, again, caution must be taken to differentiate contracts for existing assets and liabilities from those for anticipated assets and liabilities. Long-term sales not yet delivered will not show up on financial statements, other than perhaps as a footnote. Any revaluation of related forward contracts should also be excluded from the financial statements, other than again in the footnotes.

4. Foreign exchange transactions may be effective from a cash-management standpoint, but do not really concern the quality of decisions made by the treasury group on hedging exposures. Chapter 9 deals at length with the cash-management swap and the rolling of forward contracts. Such transactions often affect the foreign exchange gain/loss account even though the impact is driven by interest-rate and cashflow considerations. Borrowing and investing using swapped products can also affect the account, although they should not.

Measurement rates that are frequently used include the following:

1. The spot rate on the date that the cashflow materializes
2. The spot rate on the date that the exposure is created
3. The forward rate on the date that the exposure is created
4. The budget rate for the week, month, quarter, or year
5. The best spot rate during the life of the exposure
6. The average spot rate during the life of the exposure

Selecting the measurement rate is dependent on the objectives of the policy and the exposure. No single rate is best for all situations.

In some cases, the company trader may be given two measurement rates, such as the initial spot rate and the spot rate when the cashflow materializes. Once everything has settled, the better of the two rates from the company's perspective is the one that is used for measuring the trader's performance. One effect of this system is that the trader can end up chasing the market and taking more risks than are warranted. Pushing people beyond what is reasonable can cause inaction or excessive action. Neither one may be what the company really wants.

If average or budgeted rates are used, it is prudent to use rates consistent with the planning, budgeting, and reporting cycles, be they monthly, quarterly, or annually. Again, it is critical to look at levels vis-à-vis the current market and develop a measurement system that is fair. Unrealistic targets seldom work.

Executing Transactions

Implementing any hedging policy other than "no hedging at all" will require execution of foreign exchange transactions, a practice which, in turn, requires its own policies or corporate guidelines for efficiency and effectiveness. This is particularly true because the market can only be accessed through the traders and dealers of other organizations, and these people constitute a valuable resource if the relationships are properly managed. The following section is concerned with good business practice in this area.

Shopping the Deal

Foreign exchange deals are often "shopped." In this practice, the company solicits prices from two or more banks or investment dealers and then takes the best price. Certain factors, however, should be borne in mind.

1. If a price is not accepted immediately, the price maker has the right to change the price. Consequently, it is beneficial to have simultaneous calls made and, as the prices are received, to determine immediately the best price and to deal. Some organizations will check prices by calling a bank for a price, hanging up, and then calling other banks. When the call-around is completed, the company then calls the bank with the best price. If the market has moved in favor of the company, the bank will at least give the initial price, and may even improve. Conversely, if the market has moved against the company, the bank may well have changed its price, against the company. The company may accept this revised price or else may call the bank that had the second best price, initially. That bank may also have a changed price, and so the company ends up spending considerable time calling around trying to achieve the last best price. By having two or more phones on the go at the same time, the company could reduce the calling-around problem.

   Clearly, the call-around is not a professional method of dealing in a rapidly changing market like foreign exchange. The call-around method may, however, be appropriate in the money markets, which are usually not as volatile. Here again, however, market conditions on a given day could cause the call-around method to become a chasing activity that could be disadvantageous for the company.

2. If the price is an obvious misquote, the dealer should be asked to double-check the price. Dealers, whether at the bank or the company, live and die by their word. Their word is their bond. However, mistakes do occur, and professional etiquette dictates that a trader be advised of what appears to be a misquote and be allowed to change the price.

    Misunderstandings will occur where one party thinks the deal is on one side of the market, while the other party thinks it is on the other. These mistakes are one of the major reasons why the telephone lines in most dealing rooms are taped. If a problem arises, the tape is pulled and the source of the error is identified and held accountable.

3. If a company has a series of outright forward contracts that it wants to deal, it might find it advantageous to shop the spot-market portion independently of the forward-market position. This facilitates the process for all parties concerned. To do so, one deals the spot portion first. After the winning price has been accepted, the forward portion is shopped via a swap transaction. The near date of the swap and the spot ticket are delivered against each other, leaving the far end of the swap as the only outstanding contract.

4. A company should decide if it wants to be important to a bank or investment dealer. Organizations providing a service such as foreign exchange trading have limited resources and cannot be all things to all people all the time. If their service has no acknowledged value to a client, then this extra service will eventually stop. For instance, if a corporation is required to shop every deal with three banks, and is to award the deal on the basis of the best price, the bank dealers may have little or no incentive to give the extra service such as providing new ideas and strategies. If they do, they run the very high risk that the company will show the resultant deals to other banks. Not only do the other banks see the deal, but they may gain significant information on the strategy when the company asks for the price. Consequently, the company may not be the first priority in terms of being shown the idea. Some entities will aggressively push their banks for better pricing, sometimes for the sole purpose of trying to arbitrage the banks. In other words, a company will ask one bank for its selling price and another bank for its buying price. If the company can buy at a price lower than the price at which it can sell, the company will do both sides and make a bid-and-offer spread. This practice certainly creates additional short-term value for the company, at least as

far as these individual transactions are concerned. Sometimes, pricing by banks is so competitive that no pushing is needed by the company for it to arbitrage the banks. It just happens. That situation is significantly different from the one in which a company pushes banks for prices that are not realistic but that give the company a chance to arbitrage.

The other side of the coin is that companies that demand extremely aggressive pricing may be hurting themselves in other, less obvious, ways. Information flows may be reduced to that company. Ideas that are being circulated in the market may not be presented to the company. Reputations of the company and the individuals can be established which can be counterproductive for them in the long run. Shopping is a common and acceptable practice, but there is a point where companies and/or individuals can overdo their demands for fine pricing. The supplier of services should not be taken for granted nor be expected to lose money to do business. If it does, it is only a matter of time before the service will be dropped.

5. The actual policies under which deals are shopped and executed vary. Some of the common approaches follow:

   a. Call a given number of banks for every deal. The number may vary depending on the size of the deal.

   Small deals below a certain threshold should not be shopped. A bank cannot trade small amounts directly in the market, and it is difficult for a bank to trade them at a profit. Because the bank still has costs to recoup, the only realistic way of doing it is by showing a price that is a few points off the market. Shopping small deals also affects the perceived professionalism of the company and/or the individuals. All players recognize the existence of and the need to do small deals. The issue is to be practical in covering them. Defining what is a small deal depends on the currency, but as a guideline, anything less than 500,000 to even 1,000,000 USD equivalent could be considered small.

   Large deals should also be handled with care. Consider a sale of 50 million USD. If several dealers in the market are shown the deal, one or more dealers may immediately enter the market and sell USD in order to protect themselves in case they win the deal. This hedging activity will often cause the USD to weaken. Thus, the company may "shop" the deal and get what it perceives to be the best price in the market. However, in reality, the result is that the market movement due to the deal being shown around actually caused the market to move against the company, and often considerably more than the perceived one or two points improvement gained by shopping the deal. Defining what constitutes a large deal again depends on the currency and market. A deal for 10 million USD equivalent during the regular day can easily be absorbed in the market. If dealt at the close of business, the bank may have trouble covering it and will thus take protection by showing poorer prices. Consequently, the impact of large deals on exchange rates will vary depending on the situation. As a general guide, deals over 25 million USD equivalent are generally viewed as large deals in most markets.

b. Leave firm orders. This is a common and worthwhile practice. It creates discipline for the company because the deal is executed at the price with which the company was originally happy. If the price reaches this level without an order, there is a tendency to think, "The market is going my way. I think I will just sit back for even better prices." Often those better prices do not materialize, and the original price is no longer there either. Orders not only ensure that a fair price is received, but also give the company the advantage of dealing as soon as the market is at that price.

c. Decide whom on a dealing list to call and in what order. Decisions can be determined in different ways such as:

   (1) Best service.
   (2) Pure rotation basis where each bank quotes and then has to wait its turn. One exception is that the bank that won the last deal is automatically called again the next time.
   (3) The same short list of banks is called every time.

d. In seeking prices, use the following guidelines, especially if you aren't experienced or comfortable with the process:

   (1) Introduce yourself.
   (2) Indicate whether a firm price or an indicative price is required.
   (3) Indicate the currency, the amount that you are selling or buying, and the countercurrency.
   (4) Specify the value date or option period.
   (5) Specify the manner in which you wish to be quoted. This is usually known if an active relationship exists. However, on some transactions, such as currency option deals, it is critical to specify every time how you want the price to be quoted.
   (6) When you are given the price, be sure that the dealer quickly confirms the details of the trade and the related price.

Calling for Prices

Some example formats that a newcomer may want to consider in soliciting prices are set out:

1. Good morning. This is Carolyn from Cardon Management calling. I would like a firm price at which I sell 3 million U.S. dollars against Swiss francs for value July 21 of this year.

2. This is Paul calling from Mysports Inc. Could you please give me a firm price where I buy 5 million deutsche marks against Brazilian cruzeiros for value Wednesday? Please quote in terms of number of cruzeiros per deutsche mark.

3. Nicole calling from Myfashion Inc. Could you please give me an indicative price if I were to sell 5 million Spanish pesetas against Australian dollars value one year forward? Please give me the price in terms of pesetas per dollar. I would also like to see the split between the spot and forward points.

4. This is Suzanne calling from Mymusic Inc. I would like a firm price on a swap, please. I sell 5 million pounds sterling against French francs value spot and buy back the same amount of pounds value one month forward. Please quote in terms of French francs per pound.

5. Kyle from Mybank Corp calling. Could I please get a two-way price on 4 million USD against Mexican pesos value spot?

6. Mary from Smalltown calling. I would like a firm price on options, please. I would like to write a U.S. dollar call, Canadian dollar put, for 10 million U.S. dollars. The deal is American style and expires 60 days hence. Please quote in terms of Canadian dollar points per U.S. dollar as well as the total Canadian dollar premium.

In summary, the dealer must know who, when, what, and how much is to be dealt.

Controls and Reports

One of the major concerns facing any company is ensuring that it has control over its business activities. In the area of foreign exchange, there have been situations where control was lacking and major losses resulted.

Basic control procedures include consideration of the following:

1. Handling of outgoing payments on contracts should be done by an area, such as the controller's group, that is independent of the group actually doing the deals. This clear segregation of duties has a cost, but it helps ensure that the business being conducted is appropriate.

2. All trades should be reported. This is best done by having an independent group receive the confirmations and banking slips direct from the counterparty banks. Forward contracts that were dealt on the wrong side and that turned sour, or that were dealt on the right side but that also turned sour shortly after being dealt, have occasionally been hidden in drawers unknown to anyone but the actual dealer. Having the confirmations going to an independent group prevents information from being hidden.
3. Controls ensuring that all reports be prepared or easily verifiable by another group should be required.
4. Reports should exist on:
    a. Speculative positions held
    b. Comparison of exposures and their hedges
    c. The gain or loss that would exist if existing contracts were liquidated
    d. A performance measurement on both the strategy and the execution by the trader(s)

Management control procedures and reports are vital on all the operations of an organization. Good and timely information on foreign exchange exposure management is no exception.

Summary Comments and Observations

We close the chapter with some general comments and observations on hedging policy.

1. The policy should have the built-in flexibility to change, if necessary or advisable. Consider the following:
    a. If key people leave, a profit center may temporarily turn defensive in nature overnight.
    b. If exposures increase or change significantly, the resources required to manage these exposures may make it logical to establish a (new) profit center. Markets could change so that hedging more or less than initially required may be warranted.
    c. The markets may change suddenly and significantly as a result of a major political or economic development.
    d. New products or strategies may arise that would be prudent to use, but that were not specifically mentioned in the hedging policy. Proper approvals would still be required, but the financial management team should not be constrained by an overly re-

strictive policy from doing what is best for the organization. The policy must outline the spirit and the basic structure, but not be so rigid that it inhibits management from doing what is appropriate.

2. The nature of the exposures will be a significant factor in defining the objectives of the program. For example, if foreign exchange management is a critical variable for corporate success, the objectives of the policy may be more aggressive than if foreign exchange is not significant to the company's business.

3. Situations can be found that support every strategy. The best strategy at any point is the one that best fits subsequent market moves. No one strategy is the best, and no one strategy is the worst. Be careful not to let historical opportunity gains and losses be the only guide for future strategic decisions.

4. Doing nothing represents a decision not to hedge. Not to cover exposures is essentially speculative.

5. Companies that are in the market every day with similar amounts may be relatively indifferent to using forwards versus spot contracts. Over a long period of time, the decision to automatically sell forward all the time can, in fact, generate similar results to those gained by always selling at the (future) spot. Dealing forward, however, does reduce financial risk and identifies in advance what the returns will be.

6. Proactive management, i.e., trading or speculation, will result in some losses from time to time. No one can be right all the time, and management must be prepared to accept losses as well as gains.

7. Many decisions by management are not easily reversed. Financial markets give the flexibility to unwind previous financial-market decisions if desired. This flexibility should not be underestimated. Moreover, if market conditions have changed and it makes sense to unwind an existing contract, doing so does not automatically mean the company is speculating. Rather, it could be argued that the company is proactively managing its risks. In another context, the word *speculation* would usually not be applied to situations where decisions made by the company were reversed. In those situations, one would likely hear comments such as the company took its windfall profit or was cutting its losses. Why should decisions on foreign exchange be viewed any differently?

8. Foreign exchange exposures are usually a by-product of the core business of the company. Forward hedging of most transaction exposures is a defensive maneuver that converts a foreign currency sales price into a local currency sales price. Similarly, a purchase price in a foreign currency is converted into a local currency pur-

chase price. In the case of commodities, the forward contract is designed to convert the purchase and sales price into the inherent currency of the commodity.

There are a number of individuals in both the business and government sector that reject usage of forward contracts because they feel the contracts are speculative or because they got "burned" using forward contracts in the past. Speculation typically occurs when risks are created for the purpose of making money. Certainly, forwards can be used for speculative purposes. If one believes the AUD is going to strengthen against the GBP, one could speculate and buy AUD forward against the GBP. However, if forward contracts are dealt to lock in a specific price on an export sale of widgets, financial risks are reduced, not created. Moreover, the intent is to preserve the returns generated by the export sale, and nothing more. Consequently, the reasons for which the forward contract was placed will determine whether it is speculative or not. In terms of getting "burned," consider the following situation. Both Company A and Company B plan to import some German equipment which can be bought for 500,000 USD, or 1 million DEM. Company A decides to pay in DEM; Company B opts for payment in USD. Company A has a payable for 1 million DEM that is due in six months. The company hedges the exposure by buying DEM forward at a rate of 2.00 DEM/USD. Six months later when payment is due, the DEM has weakened to 2.20 DEM/USD. Company A feels that it got burned by the forward contract because it could have bought the DEM cheaper at the current spot rate.

	Exchange rate	USD, in/(out)	DEM, in/(out)
Purchase DEM forward	2.00	(500,000)	1,000,000
or			
Purchase DEM spot	2.20	(454,545)	1,000,000
Variance favoring spot purchase		45,455	0

The forward contract essentially created a USD purchase price of 500,000 USD for the equipment purchased by Company A. It achieved the same cost as Company B, which had decided to buy in USD. How could Company A justify its belief that it got burned? What has really happened is that Company A got involved in the foreign exchange market and experienced an opportunity loss. If it had not covered its risk, it would have done better. However, if the DEM risk was not covered, this would be identical from a risk standpoint to Company B's buying the equipment in USD and then entering the foreign exchange market and selling DEM forward.

	Exchange rate	USD, in/(out)	DEM, in/(out)
Day 1:			
Sell DEM forward	2.00	500,000	(1,000,000)
Day 180:			
Purchase DEM spot	2.20	(454,545)	1,000,000
Profit on trading DEM		45,455	0

It would be rather uncommon for Company B to do so, and yet the justification to do so is equally valid from a risk standpoint. Merely having a DEM payable does not, in itself, justify taking market risks. Consequently, it is critical for organizations and individuals to remember why forward contracts were done in the first place. If not viewed in the proper context, opportunity costs such as those presented above can taint one's perspective, which could adversely affect future risk-management decisions and activities.

9. Management of foreign exchange can be viewed as supporting the core business of the company. Alternatively, foreign exchange can become another business activity in its own right. If it is a separate business, treat it as such.

10. Dealing exclusively in one's own currency does not mean that there is no foreign exchange exposure. Exposure can result from competition from abroad, domestic manufacturers using offshore supplies, and pricing of items such as commodities whose inherent currency differs from a company's home currency.

11. Markets are often volatile and unpredictable. Management must essentially decide that it can beat the market if any policy other than full and complete hedging is to be adopted.

12. Different strategies may be required for different types of exposures. For example, contingent exposures arising from tendering for contracts or jobs will be handled quite differently if the tendering success ratio is very high versus very low.

   Currency options are a product ideally suited to tender situations. However, options can also be expensive. Companies may, therefore, use one option for a number of tenders. Alternatively, the company may deal options internally in the form of self-insurance similar to what many companies do for property and liability insurance.

13. Accounting records reflect the current value of the exchange rate. They often do not reflect the current value of (offsetting) financial-market assets, and thus reported foreign exchange losses caused by the weakening of a currency may be misleading. It is important to allow economics and cashflows, rather than reported income, to influence, if not dictate, policy.

14. Responsibility for hedging exposures must be clearly defined. Decision making by committee has the benefit of receiving additional ideas and opinions. However, every person in the market has ideas and opinions. Ultimately, someone has to make a decision and deal. In a fast-moving market, quick decisions are required, and the more decision makers that are involved, the slower the process. In fact, group decision making can often lead to paralysis. Consequently, within the established guideline, one person should be charged with the responsibility for deciding on the trades.

    Care must also be taken by senior management not to meddle too much when it comes to dealing. If a senior executive has no responsibility in the area, he or she should not make a habit of giving input on when to enter the market. Staff can often be unduly influenced by senior people, and a difficult market can quickly become more difficult.

15. Information can be gained from dealers and other market participants on a reciprocity basis. In exchange for service, the dealer expects to gain business from which he or she hopes that profits will be generated. Some organizations provide consulting services and charge fees of one kind or another in exchange for market advice and dealing assistance. Either framework can prove to be the best in the short run. In the long haul, the quality of the people involved is the key ingredient. Information paid for via a fee does not mean it is necessarily good or bad.

16. Selling of a strategy internally is sometimes easy, while at other times it is difficult. If the exposures and their significance are understood in the context of the financial and business risk of the company, the basic decision of hedging versus not hedging should be clear most of the time. In determining the degree of hedging, whether to engage in proactive management and pure speculative trading will depend on many variables. One approach that may pay dividends in the long term is to build the program from a basic level to successively more sophisticated levels. This evolution allows the program to grow, to gain credibility, and to build the necessary expertise, control, and reporting systems.

17. Forward contracts, swaps, and buying of currency options all create credit risk with counterparties. Management information systems

should be able to quantify these risks if they are significant. Because credit can become a scarce commodity in tough economic times, management of this resource should not be overlooked.

18. Knowledge is a key part of doing business. Since staff members change jobs, maintaining a degree of this expertise in the form of an updated manual is important to ensuring good continuity in the area.

In summary, a foreign exchange policy can only be determined after an organization has reviewed its foreign exchange exposures in light of a number of issues, including its business and financial risk and its managerial and technical skills and resources. There is no single best answer, but at the very least, a policy should not be chosen by default.

Glossary

NOTE: Many of the terms and definitions in this glossary apply to other markets as well as to foreign exchange markets.

Accounting Exposure: See *Exposure, Translation.*

Adjustable Peg: Exchange-rate structure in which a currency is "pegged" or "fixed" in relation to another currency. The rate can be adjusted from time to time.

After-Hours Trading: Trading that occurs after the official close of a market.

All or None: Market or limited price order that requires that the entire order be filled either at the stated price or not at all.

American Option: A currency option in which the holder of the option can exercise the option on any date during a specified time period. The period is usually from date of dealing to expiry, although shorter periods such as the last two weeks of the option can be arranged. Actual settlement would take place one or two business days after the exercise date, consistent with the settlement of spot contracts for the two currencies involved.

American Terms: See *Quotation Methods.*

Arbitrage: The simultaneous execution of purchase and sale transactions yielding a risk-free profit.

Around: A quotation of forward points in which one side of the quote is a discount and the other is a premium. For example, a market of 5–5 around denotes a bid of 5 discount and an offer of 5 premium. A market of +5–5 denotes a bid of 5 premium and an offer of 5 discount.

Asked: See *Prices.*

At Best: An order that is to be executed immediately at the best possible price. Similar to the term *at market.*

At or Better: An order to execute a trade at a specific level or better.

At the Money (ATM): A currency option whose strike price is equal to the prevailing spot rate (at-the-money spot) or the prevailing rate corresponding to the contract's expiry date (at-the-money forward).

Autonomous Transaction: In balance of payments accounting, a transaction such as an export or an import that occurs because of economic conditions or opportunity. The payment for the export is known as a *compensating transaction*.

Balance of Payments: A financial summary of a country's net transactions with the rest of the world. It includes real goods and services, capital flows, and official payments.

Balance of Trade: A financial summary of a country's net exports and imports of physical goods.

Banker's Acceptance (BA): A negotiable promissory note that is normally issued by a business and subsequently guaranteed by a bank. A BA often originates in an international trade transaction.

Bar Graph: In technical exchange-rate forecasting, a graph that plots time on the horizontal axis against price on the vertical axis. The graph will typically plot the high rate and low rate for each day, which are joined by a vertical line. The closing level is indicated by a dash to the right of the vertical line.

Base Currency: Currency against which other currencies are usually quoted. The USD has been the primary base currency since World War II.

Basis Point: For most currencies, denotes the fourth decimal place in an exchange rate (2.8800 DEM/USD) and represents 1/100 of 1 percent. For currencies such as the Japanese yen (150.25 JPY/USD) and Italian lira (1200.50 ITL/USD), a basis point is the second decimal place when quoted in currency terms or the sixth and seventh decimal places, respectively, when quoted in reciprocal terms.

Bear: A market player who expects the value of a currency to decline. A bear market has declining prices, and the general sentiment is for further price declines to occur.

Best Effort: An order to be executed at the best available prices over a period of time. The decision when to execute the order is up to the dealer handling the order.

Bid: See *Prices*.

Bill of Exchange: A negotiable instrument of exchange used in international trade. It is an unconditional order in writing for the person to whom it is addressed to pay a certain sum to a specific person or to the bearer of the note.

Blocked Currency: A currency that is tightly controlled by the government issuing the currency. Typically, it can be used only for purchases within that country.

Boston Option: A currency option in which the premium is paid at maturity, and not up front, which is the usual practice.

Breakaway Gap: See *Technical Analysis, Gap.*

Breakout: A market move beyond a level where the market had previously stopped.

Bretton Woods: A place in New Hampshire, United States, where, in 1944, an international conference was held to develop a new international monetary framework, designed to promote stability and foster worldwide growth and prosperity.

Broker: An authorized agent or intermediary who matches market bids and offers of market participants. Does not act as a principal to trades, e.g., does not buy or sell for his or her own account.

Bull: A market player who expects the value of a currency to increase. A bull market has increasing prices, and the general sentiment is for further price increases to occur.

Cable: A market term for the pound sterling.

Call Option: A currency option in which the holder has the right to purchase or call a specific currency at a specific price on a specific maturity date or within a specified period of time.

Cash Market: In foreign exchange, refers to deals done for value that day. In other markets, refers to the physical item that is being traded, e.g., a commodity or a financial instrument such as banker's acceptances.

Central Bank: The country's main regulatory bank. Traditionally, its primary responsibility is development and implementation of monetary policy.

Central Bank Intervention: Foreign exchange transactions dealt by the central bank in order to influence exchange rates. The intent may be to slow down or stop a market movement, to reverse the direction, and/or to maintain orderly market conditions.

Chips: An acronym for Clearing House Interbank Payment System. A private-sector, automated clearing operation, it handles USD wire payments between members and participants of the New York Clearing

House Associations. Many of these payments are related to foreign exchange deals.

Collar: A strategy using currency options in which one option is sold and another is purchased. The result is the creation of a range or limit in which both a best price and a worst price are defined. The major benefit is to minimize or eliminate option premium.

Commercial Paper: A promissory note usually issued by a corporation or a government. It can be sold directly to end investors, or it can be sold to market intermediaries for resale to end investors. Maturity is usually less than nine months. It is sold on a money-market yield basis.

Common Gap: See *Technical Analysis, Gap*.

Compensating Transaction: In balance of payments accounting, transactions that occur as a result of autonomous transactions. An export is the autonomous transaction, and the payment for the export is the compensating transaction.

Competitive Devaluation: Devaluation of a currency by a country's government or central bank in order to gain a competitive advantage in international trade.

Continuation Pattern: See *Technical Analysis, Patterns*.

Correspondent Bank: A bank that provides financial services to another bank in an area not served by the latter. In a typical relationship the correspondent bank would provide basic cash-management services for a foreign-based bank. In order to execute payments related to international business, of which foreign exchange transactions are a part, most major banks have one or more correspondent banks in most developed countries. In addition, most relationships are reciprocal. For example, French Bank A will use the services of Australian Bank B in Australia, and Australian Bank B will use the services of French Bank A in France.

Country Risk: Risk (e.g., currency blockage, expropriation, inadequate access to "hard" currencies, etc.) associated with lending or depositing funds, making investments, or doing other financial transactions, including forward contracts, in a particular country or currency.

Covered Interest Arbitrage: A series of transactions in which a currency is borrowed, converted into a second currency, and invested. At the same time, the second currency is sold forward for the first currency. The result is a risk-free arbitraged gain using a combination of the foreign exchange and money markets.

Credit Risk: Risk of loss that may arise on outstanding contracts should a counterparty default on its obligations.

Cross Rate: See *Prices*.

Currency of Determination: See *Inherent Currency of Commodities*.

Currency Terms: See *Quotation Methods*.

Current Account: Part of a country's balance of payments, which includes trade in real goods and services, as well as invisibles such as interest, dividends, and tourism.

Day Order: An order which, if not executed by the end of the day, is canceled.

Daylight Limits: Position limits imposed on traders during a working day. They can be limits on an individual currency as well as aggregate limits for all currencies. Usually larger than the overnight limits.

Deemed Risk: An estimate of the potential cost arising from the replacement of a contract at less favorable exchange rates. It usually is expressed in terms of a percentage of the contract amount.

Delta: In currency option pricing, the change in premium for a small change in the underlying exchange rate. Reflects the probability that the option will expire in the money.

Depth of Market: Refers to the amount of business that can be done without causing a material change in prices. A thin market would see noticeable price changes on a limited amount of transactions.

Devaluation: Decline in a currency's value against other currency.

Direct Quotation: See *Quotation Methods*.

Dirty Float: A floating currency that is subject to intervention, usually by the central bank, and therefore does not float or move freely in response to market pressures.

Discount: See *Prices*.

Economic Exposure: See *Exposure*.

EMS: An acronym for European Monetary System. Initial member countries on its establishment in 1979 included West Germany, France, the Netherlands, Luxembourg, Italy, Belgium, Denmark, and Ireland. Currencies in the EMS move within a specified band, and central banks are all obligated to ensure such bands are maintained for all currencies, not just their own.

Eurocurrency: A currency held (deposited) outside the country that issues the currency. The most widely used Eurocurrency is the U.S. dollar.

European Option: A currency option in which the holder of the option can only exercise the option on the expiry date. Settlement would take place one or two business days after the expiry date consistent with the settlement of spot contracts for the two currencies involved.

European Terms: See *Quotation Methods.*

Exchange Controls: Rules used to preserve or protect the value of a country's currency. Such rules may restrict imports, investments abroad, travel, or other activities requiring the purchase of foreign currency.

Exchange Rate: Number of units of one currency needed to pay for the purchase received from the sale of one unit of another currency. In effect, it is the price of one currency in terms of another.

Exchange Risk: The variability in a firm's value caused by exchange-rate movements.

Exchange-Traded Contract: See *Foreign Exchange Contracts.*

Exercise Price: See *Prices.*

Exhaustion Gap: See *Technical Analysis, Gap.*

Exotic Currencies: Currencies that have limited international dealings.

Expiry Date: Day and time at which an option expires.

Exposure: In foreign exchange, a potential for gain or loss because of movements in the foreign exchange rate. There are three primary types of exposure.

Economic: The change in future earning power and cashflow arising from a change in exchange rates. In effect, it represents a change in the value of a corporation.

Transaction: A potential gain or loss arising from transactions that will definitely occur in the future, are currently in progress, or could have already been completed. A signed but not shipped sales contract, a receivable or a foreign currency payment collected but not converted to local currency would all be examples of transaction exposure.

Translation: The potential for change in reported earnings and/or in the book value of the consolidated corporate equity accounts, as the result of a change in the foreign exchange rates used to translate the foreign currency statements of subsidiaries and affiliates. Also known as *accounting exposure.*

Extrinsic Value: Calculated by subtracting the intrinsic value from the total value of an option. Also known as *time value.*

Fed Funds Rate: The rate at which the fed funds market trades. Federal funds are non-interest-bearing deposits held by member banks with the Federal Reserve. Banks want to minimize any surplus or deficit positions in their balances with the Federal Reserve and thus actively sell funds to reduce unnecessary surplus positions and buy funds to fund deficit positions.

Federal Reserve System: The central banking system in the United States. There are 12 member banks located throughout the continental United States.

Fedwire: The Federal Reserve's electronic system that, among other things, is used for making USD payments between member institutions.

Fixed-Date Forward Contract: See *Foreign Exchange Contracts.*

Flag: See *Technical Analysis, Patterns.*

Floating Currency: Currency that is allowed to fluctuate without any intervention by the government and/or the central bank.

Foreign Currency Reserves: The official foreign exchange reserves of a country, usually maintained by the central bank and used to meet current and other short-term obligations. They are also used in foreign exchange intervention activities.

Foreign Exchange Contracts:
   Exchange-Traded Contract: Contract dealt on a futures exchange. Alternative is to deal on an OTC contract.
   Fixed-Date Contract: Forward contract where delivery must occur on a single day as opposed to an option.
   Forward Contract: Contract calling for settlement beyond the spot date. Can be dealt from a few days to many years into the future.
   Forward Forward: Swap transaction, e.g., simultaneous purchase and sale of one currency for another, where both transactions are forward contracts. For instance, a sale in the three months against a purchase in the six months.
   Option-Delivery Contract: Forward contract that allows one party to deliver in whole or in part on the contract at any point within a period of time. Delivery must be made in full, however, by the last day of the contract. Also known as *buyer's option.*

Outright Contract: A single spot or forward transaction. It is unlike a swap, where there is a simultaneous purchase and sale transaction.

Over the Counter: Contracts made by telephone, telex, or electronic dealing systems as opposed to futures markets. Referred to as *OTC contracts.*

Spot Contract: Contract calling for settlement one or two business days hence. Spot rates essentially represent the market's collective assessment of the value of the contract.

Foreign Exchange Swap: Simultaneous purchase and sale of a currency, but for two different maturity dates.

Forward Book: Positions held by a particular trading institution on the forward market. Generally, spot risk is eliminated wherever possible, and the trader trades the forward market points.

Forward Contract: See *Foreign Exchange Contracts.*

Forward Rate: See *Prices.*

Forward Forward: See *Foreign Exchange Contracts.*

Functional Currency: The working or operating currency of a corporate affiliate, as defined by FASB 52.

Fundamental Analysis: Framework for analyzing the various factors that would affect the supply of and demand for a currency, and hence the valu of a currency. The balance of payments, economic growth, inflation, employment, taxation, and fiscal policy would be some of these factors.

Funds: Term describing the CAD/USD spot exchange rate.

Funds Flow Mapping: A process in which future foreign currency cashflows are identified in terms of currency, amount, and timing.

Fully Hedged Libor: A transaction in which a borrower raises debt, usually USD priced at Libor, in a foreign currency; converts it to the desired currency on a spot basis, and then buys, on a forward basis, the foreign currency principal and interest including any credit spread that may be involved.

Gold Standard: A monetary system in which the value of a currency is pegged to gold. Governments are prepared to exchange gold for the currency at that pegged rate. The gold standard was abandoned in most countries by 1931.

Good until Canceled: Order that remains valid until it is executed or canceled.

Gross National Product (GNP): The total value of goods and services produced within a period of time by a country. It includes government and private spending, fixed capital investment, net inventory changes, and net exports. Real GNP growth reflects the increase in national output after inflation is removed.

Hard Currency: One of the major currencies in the world which is well traded and easily converted into other currencies.

Hedge: Transaction undertaken to reduce or eliminate risk.

Historical Volatility: Mathematical measure of the volatility of actual exchange rates over a period of time. Used to help determine the probability of each outcome, and thus the expected value of a currency option.

Implied Volatility: Calculated from the current pricing of an option in the market. Reflects the market's collective assessment of the future volatility of the underlying currency.

Indicative Rate: See *Prices, Indicative*

Indirect Quotation: See *Quotation Methods.*

Inherent Currency of Commodities: Currency that best reflects the global market's assessment of the commodity's value at a particular time. Value or price of a commodity will not change in its inherent currency due to movements in exchange rates, all other things being equal. Most major commodities are USD-inherent.

In the Money (ITM): A currency option whose strike price would provide the holder of the option with a rate superior to that provided by the current spot rate (in-the-money spot) or the forward rate corresponding to the option's expiry date (in-the-money forward).

Interest-Rate Parity: A situation in which the difference between the interest rates in two currencies is very close to the forward discount/premium in the exchange rate for those currencies.

International Fisher Effect: The idea that the interest differential between two currencies should reflect an unbiased prediction of the future change in the spot rate.

Intrinsic Value: Represents the amount by which an option is in the money. In other words, it represents the amount by which the strike price, from the option holder's standpoint, is better than the current market exchange rate.

Investment Swap: Transaction where an investor converts the investment currency into a foreign currency on a spot basis and then sells, on a forward basis, the foreign currency principal and interest in exchange for the original investment currency.

ISO Code: Three-letter codes for currencies as assigned by the International Organization for Standardization. For example, the Australian dollar is AUD, the U.S. dollar is USD, the pound sterling is GBP, and the Swiss franc is CHF.

J Curve: A particular pattern in the trade balance of a country following a currency devaluation. Initially, the trade balance deteriorates due to the higher cost of imports, but as the volume of exports increases and that of imports decreases, the trade balance improves.

Jobbing: Trading style in which a trader continually buys and sells in an attempt to make many, albeit small, profits.

Kiwi: A term for the New Zealand dollar.

Law of One Price: The theory that the prices of tradable goods and financial assets, adjusted for currency exchange rates and transaction costs, should be the same in all free markets.

Libor: Acronym for London Interbank Offered Rate. Libor is the rate at which banks will lend to each other. The Libor rate, set at 11 a.m. London time, is a key benchmark rate used for many corporate and government loans. As with any market, rates can vary with term and from bank to bank, although such differences between banks are the exception.

Liquid Market: Market in which large amounts of buying or selling can be accomplished without causing any material change in prices.

Long Position: Position where, as a result of one or many transactions, a currency is in a net bought situation. Gains will be realized from increases in prices.

Margin: On futures markets, represents the amount of money or collateral that must be maintained to ensure against losses on open contracts. Initial margin must be placed before trades can be done; variation margin must periodically be added if losses occur.

Mark to Market: Process by which contracts are revalued using current market prices.

Market Amount: Amount that can be easily traded in the interbank market.

Market Maker: Entity that consistently makes two-way prices, that is, provides both a bid and an offer, in a market.

Market Order: Order that is to be executed immediately at the best price currently available.

Money Market: A domestic market in which short-term debt instruments, such as treasury bills, commercial paper, and banker's acceptances, are issued by borrowers and sold to investors.

Official Reserves: Holdings of gold and convertible foreign currencies by central banks.

Naked Position: An unhedged position, either long or short.

Nominal-Exchange-Rate Movement: The total movement in exchange rates. A real exchange rate is the nominal rate, adjusted for inflation differentials.

North American Terms: See *Quotation Methods, American Terms.*

Nostro Account: A bank's account held at another bank, usually in another country.

Odd Date: Forward foreign exchange contract for a nonstandard date. Typical standard dates are one, two, three, six, and twelve months.

Offer: Also known as *Asked.* See *Prices, Asked.*

Open Interest: The total amount of open purchases and sales. Usually associated with transactions in a futures market.

Option Delivery Contract: See *Foreign Exchange Contracts.*

Oscillators: See *Technical Analysis.*

Out of the Money (OTM): A currency option whose strike price would provide the holder of the option with an inferior rate to that provided by the current spot rate (out-of-the-money spot) or the current forward-rate corresponding to the option's expiry date (out-of-the-money forward).

Outright Contract: See *Foreign Exchange Contracts.*

Over the Counter (OTC): See *Foreign Exchange Contracts.*

Overbought Market: Market in which a currency has risen too far too fast, usually in response to extremely strong buying demand. Such movements can also occur in very thinly traded markets. Overbought markets are susceptible to a quick sell-off.

Overnight Limits: Position limits imposed on traders during hours outside the normal, local working day. Can be a limit on an individual currency as well as an aggregate limit for all currencies. Usually smaller than daylight limits.

Oversold Market: Market in which a currency has fallen too far too fast, usually in response to extremely strong selling pressure. Oversold markets are susceptible to quick price increases.

Paper Trading: Trading that is done on a simulation basis. Useful in training exercises or in testing a particular strategy.

Paris: Term describing the French franc.

Pip: One decimal place after a basis point. For most currencies, it denotes the fifth decimal place in an exchange rate (2.88001 DEM/USD) and represents 1/1000 of 1 percent.

Point: See *Basis Point*.

Premium: See *Prices*.

Price Limit: Maximum price increase or decrease in a market during a single trading session. Usually only applies to the futures markets.

Prices:

Asked: Price at which a currency is offered for sale. Opposite to bid price. A well-offered market has more offers than bids at the current market price.

Bid: Price for which a currency will be purchased. Opposite to asked or offer price. A well-bid market has more bids than offers at the current market price.

Cross Rate: Foreign exchange rates between two currencies, neither of which is the USD.

Discount: Discount prices in the forward market imply the forward rate is less than the spot rate. Does not imply weakness, as a forward discount using one quotation method will result in a forward premium on the reciprocal quotation.

Discount in the money market represents the difference between the present value and the face value of the instrument.

Exercise Price: Also known as *strike price*. It is the exchange rate at which settlement will take place if the option is exercised.

Forward Rate: Rate on a forward contract.

Indicative Price: Foreign exchange rate that is provided as an indication of a market rate but that is not to be used for dealing purposes.

Premium: Premium prices. In the forward market, implies the forward rate is greater than the spot rate. Does not imply that strength as a forward premium on a direct quotation is equivalent to a forward discount on an indirect quotation.

Premium in a currency option is the value of the option. It is usually paid up front although it can be paid in arrears as well. The latter is known as a *Boston option*.

Strike Price: See *Exercise Price* above.

Prime Rate: The lowest interest rate charged by banks to their most creditworthy customers.

Profit Taking: Transactions taken to cover a long or short position and lock in trading gains.

Purchasing-Power Parity: The theory that the ratio between the domestic and foreign price levels should equal the equilibrium exchange rate.

Put Option: Currency option in which the holder has the right to put or sell a specific currency at a specific price on a specific maturity date or within a specified period of time.

Quotation Methods:

  American Terms: Quotation that reflects the number of USD per unit of foreign currency. Also known as *North American terms.*

  Currency Options: Premium for currency options quoted in percentages or points. Points are used when the premium is in one currency and the unit of account is in the other currency. If the premium is in DEM and is calculated on the basis of so many DEM per USD, the premium will be expressed in points. If the currency of the premium and the unit of account are the same, e.g., both DEM, the premium is expressed in percentages, such as 2.5 percent per DEM.

  Currency Terms: A quotation method that specifies the currency on which the quote is made. For example, *Australian terms* means the quotation is made in terms of the number of Australian dollars per unit of foreign currency, regardless of the currency.

  Direct Quotation: Quotation that expresses the number of units of local or domestic currency in terms of a single unit of a foreign currency. In Australia, 1.11 AUD = 1 CAD. Often referred to as a *price quotation,* as it shows the price of a foreign currency.

  European Terms: Quotation that reflects the number of units of currency per USD.

  Indirect Quotation: Quotation that expresses the number of units of foreign currency per unit of local or domestic currency. In Australia, .9 CAD = 1 AUD. Often referred to as a *volume quotation.*

  North American Terms: Quotation that reflects the number of USD per unit of foreign currency. Also known as *American terms.*

  Reciprocal Rate: The reciprocal of the customary or standard market quotes. All currencies are traded in international markets on a standard basis. GBP, for instance, is quoted in American terms, e.g., the number of USD per GBP. A quote showing the number of GBP per USD would be a reciprocal quote and is determined by taking the reciprocal of the USD/GBP quote.

Real-Exchange-Rate Movement: The total movement in rates, adjusted for inflation differentials.

Recession: A period of decline in overall economic activity. A recession is typically defined as two consecutive quarterly declines in real GNP.

Reciprocal Rate:: Set *Quotation Methods.*

Relative Strength Index: See *Technical Analysis, Oscillators.*

Reporting Currency: The currency in which the parent firm prepares its financial statements.

Reserve Currency: Currency that is used by central banks to meet their international financial commitments. Such currencies are usually the main currencies used in international transactions.

Resistance Point: See *Technical Analysis.*

Revaluation: An upward adjustment of a currency.

Runaway Gap: See *Technical Analysis, Gap.*

Scale Down/Up: Trading strategy. Scaling down involves buying at regular intervals in a declining market. Scaling up involves selling at regular intervals in a rising market.

Settlement Date: Date on which foreign exchange contracts settle.

Settlement Risk: Settlement risk is incurred when a payment is made to a counterparty on a foreign exchange contract before the countervalue payment has been received. The risk is that the counterparty's payment will never be received.

Short Dates: Trading term relating to foreign exchange and money-market transactions where the term is anywhere from one day to three weeks hence.

Short Position: Position where, as the result of one or many transactions, a currency is in a net sold position. Gains will be realized from future price declines.

Sovereign Risk: The risk of default on a government-guaranteed loan or contract, or the risk that a government will impose regulations on the trading of its currency such that a bank or other trader will suffer losses on its contracts.

Speculator: Entity or individual that creates risks for the sole purpose of making money.

Spot Contract: See *Foreign Exchange Contracts.*

Sterilization: A process followed by central banks to increase or decrease the money supply in order to offset a money-supply change caused by intervention in the foreign exchange markets.

Stop-Loss Order: Order to buy or sell at the best available price when a given price threshold has been reached.

Straddle: Option strategy in which a put and call are either both sold or both purchased. Both contracts have the same strike price.

Strangle: Option strategy in which a put and call are either both sold or both purchased. The contracts have different strike prices.

Support Point: See *Technical Analysis.*

Swap: See *Foreign Exchange Contracts, Foreign Exchange Swap.*

Swap Rate: The difference between the spot and forward exchange rates, expressed in basis points.

Technical Analysis: Analysis of the market using charting and mathematical approaches. The focus is on price, volume, and open interest. It is based on the premise that the price reflects all available information and that historical price patterns will be repeated. Some important definitions follow.

Gap: An area of a chart where a day's trading range is outside the previous day's trading range.

A *breakaway* gap occurs at the end of a consolidation phase, at the end of a key pattern, or after a major support or resistance line has been broken.

A *common* gap is a temporary gap that occurs one day but is subsequently filled in. While it is usually a false signal of a market move, it can be an indication of the direction of the next breakout.

An *exhaustion* gap occurs near the end of a market move. The market jumps forward, but there is little support for the move and the market quickly retraces.

A *runaway* gap arises after a significant move has already occurred. It often signifies the market move has a second wind and will go further.

Oscillators: Mathematical analysis of market movements to identify overbought or oversold markets. The relative strength index is a commonly used oscillator.

Patterns: A *continuation* pattern such as a *flag* or *pennant* reflects a period of consolidation. It is an indication that the market movement will resume its basic trend and that the movement is approximately half complete.

A *reversal* pattern, such as the *head and shoulders, double and triple tops,* and *double and triple bottoms,* signifies the market will reverse direction. Each pattern resembles its description.

Resistance Point: A price level above current market levels which the market may find difficulty moving through.

Support Point: Price level below current market levels which the market may find difficulty in breaking below.

Time Decay: The decline in the extrinsic value of an option because of the passage of time.

Two-Way Price: A price quotation that includes both the buying and the selling price.

Transaction Exposure: See *Exposure.*

Translation Exposure: See *Exposure.*

Value Date: Delivery or maturity date on which a foreign exchange contract is to settle. In an option delivery contract, the value date is the first eligible delivery date. The maturity date is the final eligible delivery date.

Vostro Account: Accounts of another bank, usually from another country, that are held at your bank.

Yard: Term for 1 billion JPY or ITL.

Further Reading

Books

Aliber, R. Z., *The International Money Game*, 3d ed., Basic Books, New York, 1979.

Coninx, R. G. F., *Foreign Exchange Dealer's Handbook*, Pick, New York, 1982.

DeRosa, David F., *Managing Foreign Exchange Risk: Strategies for Global Portfolios*, Probus, New York, 1990.

Eiteman, David K., and Arthur Stonehill, *Multinational Business Finance*, 5th ed., Addison Wesley, New York, 1989.

Folks, William R., Jr., and Raj Aggarwal, *International Dimensions of Financial Management*, PWS-Kent, Boston, 1988.

Gart, Alan, *Handbook of the Money and Capital Markets*, Quorum, New York, 1988.

Howcraft, Barry, and Christopher Storey, *Management and Control of Currency and Interest Rate Risk*, Probus, New York, 1990.

Jones, Eric T., and Donald L. Jones, *Hedging Foreign Exchange: Converting Risk to Profit*, Wiley, New York, 1987.

Kubarych, Roger M., *Foreign Exchange Markets in the United States*, rev. ed., Federal Reserve Bank of New York, New York, 1983.

Lessard, Donald R., ed., *International Financial Management*, 2nd ed., Wiley, New York, 1985.

Livingston, Miles, *Money and Capital Markets*, Prentice-Hall, Englewood Cliffs, N.J., 1990.

Logue, Dennis E., *Handbook of Modern Finance*, Warren, Gorham and Lamont, Boston, 1987.

Madura, Jeff, *International Financial Management*, 2d ed., West, New York, 1989.

Millman, Gregory J., *The Floating Battlefield: Corporate Strategies in the Currency War*, Amacom, New York, 1990.

Murphy, John J., *Technical Analysis of the Futures Markets*, The New York Institute of Finance, New York, 1986.

Reuters Staff, *The Reuters Glossary of International Economic and Financial Terms*, Longman, White Plains, N.Y., 1989.

Riehl, Heinz, and Rita M. Rodriguez, *Foreign Exchange and Money Markets*, McGraw-Hill, New York, 1983.

Rodriguez, Rita M., and E. Eugene Carter, *International Financial Management*, 3d ed., Prentice-Hall, Englewood Cliffs, N.J., 1984.

Sarpkaya, S., *The Money Market in Canada*, CCH Canadian Limited, Don Mills, Ontario, 1989.

Shapiro, Alan C., *International Corporate Finance*, 2d ed., Ballinger, Cambridge, Mass., 1988.

———, *Multinational Financial Management*, 3d ed., Allyn and Bacon, Boston, 1989.

———, *Foundations of Multinational Financial Management*, Allyn and Bacon, Boston, 1991.

Stigum, Marcia, *The Money Market*, 3d ed., Dow Jones-Irwin, Homewood, Ill., 1990.

Stonehill, Arthur I., and David K. Eiteman, *Finance: An International Perspective*, Irwin, Homewood, Ill., 1987.

Swiss Bank Corporation, *Foreign Exchange and Money Market Operations*, Swiss Bank Corporation, Zurich, 1980.

The Canadian Securities Institute, *Canadian Investment Finance — Parts I and II: International Finance and Foreign Exchange*, The Canadian Securities Institute, Toronto, 1990.

The Institute of Chartered Financial Analysts, *Standards of Practice Handbook: The Code of Ethics and the Standards of Professional Conduct*, Irwin, Homewood, Ill., 1986.

Tucker, Alan L., *Financial Futures, Options, and Swaps*, West, St. Paul, Minn., 1991.

Weisweiller, Rudi, *How the Foreign Exchange Market Works*, The New York Institute of Finance, New York, 1990.

Articles

Adler, Michael C., and Bernard Dumas, "Exposure to Currency Risk: Definitions and Measurement," *Financial Management* 13(2): 41–50, 1984.

———, and Bruce Lehmann, "Deviations from Purchasing Power Parity in the Long Run," *Journal of Finance*, 1471–1487, December 1983.

Aliber, R. Z., and C. P. Stickney, "Accounting Measures of Foreign Exchange Exposure: The Long and Short of It," *Accounting Review*, 44–57, January 1975.

Bank for International Settlements, *Recent Innovations in International Banking*, prepared by a Study Group established by the Central Banks of the Group of Ten Countries, April 1986.

Beaver, William, and Mark Wolfson, "Foreign Currency Translation Gains and Losses: What Effect Do They Have and What Do They Mean?" *Financial Analysts Journal*, 28–36, March–April 1984.

Biger, Nahum, and John Hall, "The Valuation of Currency Options," *Financial Management*, 24–28, Spring 1983.

Black, Fisher, and Myron Scholes, "The Pricing of Options and Corporate Liabilities," *Journal of Political Economy*, 637–659, May-June 1973.

Cornell, Bradford, "Inflation, Relative Price Changes, and Exchange Risk," *Financial Management*, 30–34, Autumn 1980.

———, and M. R. Reinganum, "Forward and Future Prices: Evidence from the Foreign Exchange Markets," *Journal of Finance*, 36(5): 1035–1045, 1981.

———, and Alan C. Shapiro, "Managing Foreign Exchange Risks," *Midland Corporate Finance Journal*, 1(2): 16–31, 1983.

Cox, J., and M. Rubinstein, "Option Pricing: A Simplified Approach, *Journal of Financial Economics*, 229–263, September 1979.

Drury, Donald H., and Vihang R. Errunza, *Managing Foreign Exchange Exposure*, a research monograph prepared for the Society of Management Accountants of Canada, 1985.

Dufey, Gunter, and Sam L. Srinivasulu, "The Case for Corporate Management of Foreign Exchange Risk," *Financial Management*, 13(2): 54–62, 1984.

Eaker, Mark R., "Covered Interest Arbitrage: New Measurement and Empirical Results," *Journal of Economics and Business*, 32(3): 249–253, 1980.

Fama, Eugene F., "Short-Term Interest Rates as Predictors of Inflation," *American Economic Review*, 269–282, June 1975.

Finnerty, J. E., J. Owers, and F. J. Creran, "Foreign Exchange Forecasting and Leading Economic Indicators: The U.S.–Canadian Experience," *Management International Review*, 2: 59–70, 1987.

Flood, Eugene, Jr., and Donald R. Lessard, "On the Measurement of Operating Exposure to Exchange Rates: A Conceptual Approach," *Financial Management*, 25–36, Spring 1986.

Friedman, Milton, and Robert V. Roosa, "Free vs. Fixed Exchange Rates: A Debate," *Journal of Portfolio Management*, 68–73, Spring 1977.

Garner, C. Kent, and Alan C. Shapiro, "A Practical Method of Assessing Foreign Exchange Risk," *Midland Corporate Finance Journal*, 2(2): 6–17, 1984.

Giddy, Ian H., "Exchange Risk: Whose View?" *Financial Management*, 6(4): 23–33, 1977.

———, "The Foreign Exchange Option as a Hedging Tool," *Midland Corporate Finance Journal*, 1(2): 32–42, 1975.

———, and Gunter Dufey, "The Random Behavior of Flexible Exchange Rates: Implications for Forecasting," *Journal of International Business Studies*, 1–32, Spring 1975.

Goodman, Laurie S., "How to Trade in Currency Options," *Euromoney*, 73–74, January 1983.

Goodman, Stephen H., "Two Technical Analysts Are Even Better Than One," *Euromoney*, 85–97, August 1982.

Hekman, Christine R., "Measuring Foreign Exposure: A Practical Theory and Its Applications," *Financial Analysts Journal*, 59–65, September–October 1983.

International Monetary Fund, *The Exchange Rate System: Lessons of the Past and Options for the Future*, Occasional Paper 30, July 1984.

———, *Exchange Rate Volatility and World Trade*, Occasional Paper 28, July 1984.

———, *Issues in the Assessment of the Exchange Rates of Industrial Countries*, Occasional Paper 29, July 1984.

———, *Formulation of Exchange Rate Policies in Adjustment Programs*, Occasional Paper 36, August 1985.

Jacque, Laurent L., "Management of Foreign Exchange Risk: A Review Article," *Journal of International Business Studies*, 81–99, Spring–Summer 1981.

Kaufold, Howard, and Michael Smirlock, "Managing Corporate Exchange and Interest Rate Exposure," *Financial Management*, 64–72, Autumn 1986.

Kern, David, "Currency Forecasting: Not a Prophecy But a Guide to Action," *Euromoney*, 137–147, July 1980.

Koveos, Peter, and Bruce Seifert, "Purchasing Power Parity and Black Markets," *Financial Management*, 40–46, Autumn 1985.

Kwok, Chuck, "Hedging Foreign Exchange Exposures: Independent vs. Integrative Approaches," *Journal of International Business Studies*, 33–52, Summer 1987.

Lessard, Donald R., "Finance and Global Competition: Exploiting Global Scope and Coping with Volatile Exchange Rates," *Midland Corporate Finance Journal*, 6–29, Fall 1986.

———, and John B. Lightstone, "Volatile Exchange Rates Can Put Operations at Risk," *Harvard Business Review*, 107–114, July–August 1986.

Levich, Richard M., "Are Forward Exchange Rates Unbiased Predictors of Future Spot Rates?" *Columbia Journal of World Business*, 49–61, Winter 1979.

———, "Analyzing the Accuracy of Foreign Exchange Advisory Services: Theory and Evidence," in Richard Levich and Clas Wihlborg, eds., *Exchange Risk and Exposure*, D. C. Heath, Lexington, Mass., 1980.

Livingston, Miles, "The Delivery Option on Forward Contracts," *Journal of Financial and Quantitative Analysis*, 79–88, March 1987.

Logue, Dennis E., and George S. Oldfield, "Managing Foreign Assets When Exchange Markets Are Efficient," *Financial Management*, 6(2): 16–22, 1977.

Longworth, D., "Testing the Efficiency of the Canadian–U.S. Exchange Market under the Assumption of No Risk Premium," *Journal of Finance*, 36(1): 43–51, 1981.

Madura, Jeff, and E. Theodore Veit, "Use of Currency Options in International Cash Management," *Journal of Cash Management*, 42–48, January–February 1986.

Mishkin, Frederic S., "Are Real Interest Rates Equal Across Countries? An Empirical Investigation of International Parity Conditions," *Journal of Finance*, 1345–1357, December 1984.

Officer, Lawrence H., "The Purchasing Power Parity Theory of Exchange Rates: A Review Article," *IMF Staff Papers*, 1–60, March 1976.

Rodriguez, Rita M., "Management of Foreign Exchange Risk in U.S. MNCs," *Sloan Management Review*, 31–49, September 1978.

———, "Corporate Exchange Risk Management: Theme and Aberrations," *Journal of Finance*, 427–439, May 1981.

Rogalski, Richard, and Joseph D. Vinso, "Price Level Variations as Predictors of Flexible Exchange Rates," *Journal of International Business Studies*, 71–81, Spring–Summer 1977.

Rosenberg, Michael R., "Is Technical Analysis Right for Currency Forecasting?" *Euromoney*, 125–130, July 1981.

Sender, Henny, "The New Case for Currency Options," *Institutional Investor*, 245–247, January 1986.

Shapiro, Alan C., "What Does Purchasing Power Parity Mean?" *Journal of International Money and Finance*, 295–318, December 1983.

———, "Currency Risk and Relative Price Risk," *Journal of Financial and Quantitative Analysis*, 365–373, December 1984.

Solnik, B., "Why Not Diversify Internationally Rather Than Domestically?" *Financial Analysts Journal*, 48–54, July–August 1974.

Srinivasulu, S. L., "Classifying Foreign Exchange Exposure," *Financial Executive*, 36–44, February 1983.

Sweeney, Richard J., "Beating the Foreign Exchange Market," *Journal of Finance*, 163–182, March 1986.

Walmsley, Julian, "The New York Foreign Exchange Market," *Banker's Magazine*, 64–69, January–February 1984.

Wolff, Christian, "Forward Exchange Rates, Expected Spot Rates, and Premia: A Signal-Extraction Approach," *Journal of Finance*, 395–406, June 1987.

Woo, Wing Thye, "Some Evidence of Speculative Bubbles in the Foreign Exchange Market," *Journal of Money, Credit, and Banking*, 499–514, November 1987.

About the Authors

PAUL BISHOP is Associate Professor of Finance, University of Western Ontario. He teaches corporate and international finance in the School of Business Administration, and has provided consulting services and management development programs and seminars in these areas for a wide variety of clients. Offshore assignments have included work in Brazil, Australia, England, and the Peoples' Republic of China. He received his B.S.A. and B.A.Sc. from the University of Toronto, his M.B.A. from the University of Western Ontario, and his D.B.A. from the Harvard Business School.

DON DIXON is Senior Manager, Treasury Group, Bank of Montreal. In this capacity, he is responsible for managing the foreign exchange activities of the bank in western Canada, and for advising bank clients on foreign currency exposure management strategies and policies. Prior to joining the bank, he served as Cash Manager for the Potash Corporation of Saskatchewan, and as a foreign exchange and commodity trader for Cargill Limited. He is an economics graduate of Dartmouth College, and has his M.B.A. from the University of Western Ontario.

Index

Note: An *e.* after a page number refers to an exhibit.